This Little Kiddy Went to Market

The Corporate Capture of Childhood

Sharon Beder

with Wendy Varney and Richard Gosden

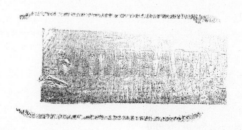

PLUTO PRESS
www.plutobooks.com

First published 2009 by Pluto Press
345 Archway Road, London N6 5AA and
175 Fifth Avenue, New York, NY 10010

www.plutobooks.com

Distributed in the United States of America exclusively by
Palgrave Macmillan, a division of St. Martin's Press LLC,
175 Fifth Avenue, New York, NY 10010

British Library Cataloguing in Publication Data
A catalogue record for this book is available from the British Library

ISBN   978 0 7453 2916 1   Hardback
ISBN   978 0 7453 2915 4   Paperback

Library of Congress Cataloging in Publication Data applied for

This book is printed on paper suitable for recycling and made from fully managed and
sustained forest sources. Logging, pulping and manufacturing processes are expected to
conform to the environmental standards of the country of origin. The paper may contain
up to 70 per cent post-consumer waste.

10 9 8 7 6 5 4 3 2 1

Designed and produced for Pluto Press by
Chase Publishing Services Ltd, Sidmouth, England
Typeset from disk by Stanford DTP Services, Northampton, England
Printed and bound in the European Union by
CPI Antony Rowe, Chippenham and Eastbourne

Contents

List of Figures, Tables and Boxes

FIGURES

TABLES

BOXES

Acknowledgements

I would like to thank Nina Lansbury-Hall for her research assistance with Chapter 11: Teaching Corporate Values. Also thanks to the Campaign for Commercial-Free Education in Ireland for permission to reproduce Table 5.1: Educational versus Commercial Agendas and Professor Geoff Whitty for permission to use a table from his book *Devolution and Choice in Education* in compiling Table 6.1: The New Language of School Reform.

1
Introduction

It is easy to exploit children – any fool can do it. It takes both
strength and intelligence not to do so.

C. Glenn Cupit[1]

Amanda's parents gave her an mp3 player for her thirteenth birthday. She had
been nagging them for an iPod for months but they didn't understand, as her
peers did, the importance of the iPod brand. So they got her another brand that
they thought offered better value for money. Instead of being delighted she was
depressed. It was the same with everything she had. Her mobile was two years old
yet her parents couldn't understand the importance of having the latest model. She
was sure that it was because she had second- or third-rate versions of everything
that she was not popular at school.

Amanda's brother Andrew was in the bathroom vomiting. He had a school
test today and he didn't do well in tests even though his teachers usually gave
him good marks for school projects and essays. He thought too much about the
questions and was able to think of more than one reasonable answer and this
meant he took too long to do the test.

If he failed today's test Andrew would have to do extra classes on Saturday
mornings and might have to give up music classes to make way for more reading
classes. Andrew's parents wouldn't mind too much if this happened because they
had to pay extra fees for those music classes. But music classes were the only
part of school that Andrew liked. Otherwise he hated school. It was so boring!
They never studied anything that he could relate to and it was all so repetitive. It
seemed to be all tests and practice tests and preparing for tests.

Andrew's poor test results were likely to affect his ability to get into a good
secondary school; he might have to go to the dilapidated school across the river
where students have to pass through a metal detector and wear their coats in class
because the heating doesn't work.

Their little sister Angie was having a tantrum in the kitchen because Mummy
wouldn't buy the sugary cereal with Shrek on the packet that she saw on television.
Amanda thought it wouldn't be long before Angie would be taking those little

white pills that so many kids at school took when she was in primary school. In her school some of the older kids traded them along with other drugs to get a high.

Amanda, Andrew and Angie are too young to understand, but much of their discontent and many of their anxieties stem from the corporate capture of childhood, that is, the way modern business corporations shape children's dreams and desires, determine their school experience and influence their behaviour and values.

Modern affluent societies overflow with a cornucopia of goods produced for the entertainment, pleasure, convenience and education of children, yet increasingly there are signs that in some of the most prosperous nations, particularly English-speaking countries, something is amiss. Those same children seem to be less content, more stressed and less healthy than any previous generation.

In 2005 the UK National Consumer Council (NCC) found that British children were 'the least happy generation of the post-war era'.[2] Towards the end of 2006 a group of over a hundred academics, teachers, psychologists and others wrote to the *Daily Telegraph* in the UK to express their deep concern about what was happening to children. They argued that 'the escalating incidence of childhood depression' as well as 'the rise of substance abuse, violence and self-harm amongst our young people', arose from the neglect of children's emotional and social needs. They blamed junk food, screen-based entertainment, 'an overly academic test-driven primary curriculum' and a 'hyper-competitive culture' as contributing factors.[3]

Their concern was backed up by a United Nations Children's Fund (UNICEF) assessment of the well-being of children in 21 affluent nations, published in 2007. It found that children in the US and the UK were worse off than in any of the other nations in the study, particularly with respect to family and peer relationships; behaviours and risks; health and safety in the case of the US; and subjective well-being in the case of the UK. Children aged 11, 13 and 15 were less likely to find their peers 'kind and helpful' in the UK and the US than in any of the other 21 nations apart from the Czech Republic. They ate less fruit and were more overweight. They smoked more cannabis and had more pregnancies. They tended to leave school at an earlier age. In the UK teenagers smoked more cigarettes, had sex, and got drunk more.[4]

In a typical week in Australia, 10 per cent of high school students engage in binge drinking. Almost one in three primary school children is overweight or obese.[5] Many teenagers are in debt.[6] Almost half of children aged ten to 14 do not feel confident about themselves and more than half worry about what others think about them.[7] A significant proportion of Australian children and teenagers are suffering anxiety and depression.[8] One in ten 13- to 19-year-olds reported having mental or behavioural problems. The rates at which 13- to 19-year-olds are hospitalised for self-harm have increased 27 per cent since 1998–99.[9] Suicide rates for males aged 15 to 25 more than tripled between 1960 and 2000 and the rate is now higher than in most other affluent nations.[10]

In the US, suicide is the third highest cause of death for those between ten and 24 years old. Each year 4600 take their own lives and 142,000 are treated in hospital emergency departments for self-inflicted injuries. A nationwide survey of students in grades nine to 12 found that 17 per cent said they had seriously considered suicide, 13 per cent had planned suicide, and 8 per cent had attempted it in the previous year.[11] The numbers of teenagers between 15 and 17 going to prison is increasing twice as fast as the rest of the population.[12]

In the UK children are getting fatter, consuming more alcohol, committing more crime, and are increasingly excluded from schools.[13] The rates of self-harm among young people are higher than anywhere else in Europe and it is estimated that one in 15 young people between eleven and 25 years of age self-harm. Each year 25,000 young people are admitted to hospital emergency departments in England and Wales as a result of deliberate self-inflicted injury. Many more are treated at home and never make it to hospital.[14]

In September 2007 an even larger group of professionals, academics and writers again expressed their concern about the state of Britain's children. This time they blamed a decline in children's play as a major contributing factor in their deteriorating well-being. This in turn was attributed to factors such as 'the ready availability of sedentary, sometimes addictive screen-based entertainment; the aggressive marketing of over-elaborate, commercialised toys (which seem to inhibit rather than stimulate creative play); ... a test-driven school and pre-school curriculum in which formal learning has substantially taken the place of free, unstructured play'.[15]

This book argues that this rapid decline in children's well-being has, in large part, been caused by corporate interference in children's lives and psyches. Chapter 2 covers some of the many ways that corporations are targeting ever younger children with a barrage of advertising and marketing designed to foster discontent in children and turn them into hyper-consumers who define themselves by what they have rather than who they are. Chapter 3 shows how manufacturers and marketers have transformed children's play into a commercial opportunity; Chapter 4 how they have preyed on and taken advantage of childish anxieties and insecurities, reshaping their very identities.

Schools are no longer a haven from these commercial pressures, and Chapter 5 details how funding cuts have made them vulnerable to a massive infusion of corporate messages. Businesses seek to sell their goods to school children, as well as develop brand loyalty now and into the future, through sponsorships, competitions, communication technologies and industry-produced classroom materials.

Chapter 6 will reveal how business coalitions have persuaded governments around the world to turn schools into competing business enterprises where children are treated as inputs to be processed. Widespread reductions in school funding have caused governments to shift the goal of education from quality to efficiency, and the responsibility for school performance to 'devolved' school boards and principals who have to make do with inadequate budgets.

Chapter 7 explains why a widespread emphasis on standardised testing in schools has developed since the 1980s in English-speaking nations and evaluates the consequences. And in case there is any doubt that this push for standardised testing and educational efficiency has come from the corporate sector, Chapter 8 exposes the powerful business coalitions, the many interconnected business-funded advocacy groups, and the campaigns that have been behind it.

Chapters 9 and 10 show that corporations are taking control of more and more aspects of schooling, not only to ensure that schools produce submissive employees with basic skills, but also to prevent the development of critical-thinking faculties in schools. Business interests are driving the renewed emphasis in schools on long hours, discipline, rewards and punishments as well as the narrowing curriculum that emphasises literacy, numeracy, computer skills and a business-friendly view of history and society.

Chapter 11 covers the flood of corporate-sponsored classroom materials that teachers are being offered. These provide a distorted picture of environmental, economic, health and social issues so as to fulfil the public relations needs of industries, particularly those in the health, environment and energy sectors, and also promote a wider ideology of free market economics.

The move towards private provision of educational services that has occurred in many English-speaking countries since the 1980s is covered in Chapter 12. This includes the privatisation of the local educational authorities (LEAs) and the establishment of academies in the UK, and the proliferation of charter schools in the US. The chapter evaluates the outcomes of these privatisations.

The corporate push for schools to compete for students in an educational marketplace, in the name of 'school choice', has manifested as open enrolments in the UK and Australia, and a campaign for school vouchers in the US. Chapter 13 discusses the consequences of this in terms of equity and how the right of every child to receive a high-quality public education has been replaced by the right of parents to choose the school their children will attend. The role of corporations, and the foundations they fund, in promoting privatisation of schooling and competitive education markets, is covered in Chapter 14.

Finally, Chapter 15 reveals how children who are naughty, lively, bored, inattentive or depressed as a result of the assaults described in previous chapters, are identified in schools and disciplined through the use of psychiatric drugs. It analyses the way that the pharmaceutical industry portrays these 'medications' as a way of 'normalising' children's thinking and behaviour in order to expand the child and adolescent market for psychiatric drugs.

The consequence of this corporate capture of childhood has been a generation of children who have been manipulated, shaped and exploited as never before in history. Not only have they lost the opportunity to play and develop at their own pace, their psyches have been damaged and their view of the world distorted. They are trained rather than educated and constantly tested to make sure they have absorbed the 'correct' information. They are supposed to seek happiness in possessions, treat relationships as a means to an end, and incessantly compete with each other. Children have never before been under such pressure to 'succeed, conform and look good'.[16] It is little wonder that so many children grow into youths who are unhappy, stressed, fat, delinquent or self-destructive.

This book will show that nearly all of the problems facing children today are a direct result of the efforts of corporations to make profits from children and to shape and socialise them to suit business interests.

2
Turning Children into Consumers

For the first time in human history, children are born into homes where mass-mediated storytellers reach them on average more than seven hours a day. Most waking hours, and often dreams, are filled with their stories. These stories do not come from families, schools, churches, neighbourhoods, and often not even from the native countries. They come from a small group of distant conglomerates with something to sell.

George Gerbner[1]

Langbourne Rust advises those who are trying to reach toddlers in grocery shopping trolleys, to 'direct information on the cart to the child inside ... The child taking a ride is a captive, and sometimes restless audience, hungry for focus and stimulation.' He recommends that retailers display products at cart height and make sure it is noticeable from 'middle-of-the-aisle distance'. And he counsels advertisers to incorporate the image of children riding in carts in their advertising imagery so the connection can be made by the child between the advertised product and the store.[2]

Rust also suggests advertisers and marketers take advantage of the way toddlers point to things they want by incorporating 'physical gesturing in advertising copy: Why not develop pointing as a routine or ritualistic part of what people do when they see your product?'[3] He suggests that products need to be easily recognisable from long distances so the child can see them coming up the aisle and be prepared to ask for them when they get closer.

Langbourne Rust Research Inc. is one of many consultancies catering to corporations that want to sell their products to children. Its website claims: 'Dozens of companies, including Walt Disney, have used us to teach them about how to reach kids.'[4] 'Kids' is marketing speak for children. The term 'children' evokes notions of vulnerability and adult responsibility to protect them. 'Kids', on the other hand, evokes notions of play and fun.

Children are naive about advertising and can easily be manipulated and exploited by marketers to want and demand their products. Corporate marketers believe that over time they can be shaped into lifelong consumers with brand loyalties that can be profitable for decades to come. What is more, children influence family spending decisions worth hundreds of billions of dollars on household items like furniture, electrical appliances and computers, vacations, and even the family car.

Corporations began targeting their marketing messages directly to children during the 1980s, as affluent adult markets became saturated with consumer goods. Large firms established 'kids' departments and smaller firms specialised in marketing to children. A number of advertising industry publications were created such as *Selling to Kids* and *Marketing to Kids Report*.[5] The academic literature began to feature studies of children as consumers.[6]

In the US the amount corporations spent marketing to children under twelve increased by five times between 1980 and 1990 and ten times more during the 1990s.[7] In 2004 around $15 billion was being spent marketing to children.[8] In Australia the number of advertisements aimed at children tripled between the 1980s and 2002.[9] Conferences on the best ways to market to children are held all over the world. There are also awards for the best advertisements and marketing campaigns, with hundreds of entries.[10]

Much marketing to children now consists of sales promotions such as direct coupons, free gifts and samples, contests and sweepstakes, and public relations exercises such as using celebrities and licensed characters to visit shopping centres and schools. These additional forms of marketing have supplemented rather than replaced advertising as the importance of the children's market has grown.[11] Their aim however is the same as advertising.

The international children's market is increasingly attractive to transnational corporations who seek to make their brands and products popular in different cultural milieus. The food industry was a pioneer in these efforts. In 1997 *Brandweek* magazine noted that McDonald's was the favourite fast food all over the world and Coca-Cola the favourite drink.[12]

COMING TO A SCREEN NEAR YOU

Not only are there many more advertisements aimed at children but they are increasingly infiltrating the private and public spaces where children play and learn. Today's children are confronted with advertisements almost everywhere they go. There are now television stations, radio stations, newspapers and magazines delivering underage audiences to advertisers 24 hours a day. As the amount of money being spent increased, the age that children were targeted decreased. A marketing conference in 2000 in New York was entitled 'Play-Time, Snack-Time, Tot-Time: Targeting Pre-Schoolers and their Parents'.[13] There is even a US cable station, BabyFirstTV, which aims at under-two-year-olds.[14]

Television

Television is an ideal way for advertisers to reach children as it is so omnipresent in homes around the world. In more than a third of the homes of American pre-school children the television is on most of the time, whether or not anyone is watching.[15] By the time they get to first grade American children will have 'spent the equivalent of three school years in the tutelage of the family television set' and by the time they finish high school they will have spent more time watching television than they spent in class for their entire schooling.[16]

Box 2.1   **Extent of Television Watching – Some Figures**

In the US:

- The average child watches more than 21 hours of live television a week and another six hours of pre-recorded television, DVDs and videos.[17]
- Two out of three children over eight years old have a television in their bedroom; as do one in three aged between two and seven and one in four children under two.[18]
- American children see over 40,000 television advertisements each year and more on the internet, in magazines and even in schools.[19]

In Australia:

- The average child watches 17.5 hours of television each week.[20]
- 20 per cent of children watch television for more than 30 hours each week.[21]
- Australian children see up to 30,000 television adverts each year.[22]

In the UK:

- The average child watches around 17 hours of television a week.[23]
- Three out of four children between 5 and 16 have a television in their bedroom.[24]
- UK children view more than 18,000 television adverts each year.[25]

Individual commercials are repeatedly shown for months and 'effectively penetrate' the language and thinking of young children. They repeat advertising jingles and slogans to friends, draw advertising images and logos in their artwork, and discuss advertisements with their friends. Roy Fox, in his book *Harvesting Minds*, pointed out: 'A person's image and language create his or her sense of selfhood. And this selfhood – especially during our formative years – is the most valuable, fragile quality we'll ever embrace.' Yet it is sold as a commodity over and over.[26] Today it is advertising jingles that children sing rather than nursery rhymes.

The internet

The internet, video games and mobile phones have also provided opportunities for 'new, personalized promotions' aimed at children. Children as young as four are being targeted by internet advertisers and often the interaction with the children is unmediated by parents or teachers.[27] UK advertising agency Saatchi & Saatchi noted: 'Interactive technology is at the forefront of kid culture, allowing us to enter into contemporary kid life and communicate with them in an environment they call their own.'[28]

Advertisements appear on banners at the top of websites, on scroll down frames at the side of the windows, and unbidden on pop-up windows. There are even animated product 'spokescharacters' to interact with the children and develop relationships with them so that they can be persuaded to buy something.

Internet advertising is particularly effective at targeting children because they are less able to tell the difference between advertisements and other content. They are more likely, for example, to click on banner ads thinking they are part of the website, offering information or entertainment, and they tend not to take any notice of annotations like 'AD' or 'PAID' that are supposed to indicate advertisements.[29]

The meagre regulations to which television advertising is subject don't apply to the internet. Advertisers and marketers are free to merge content with advertising and exploit children with few if any limits. The ads on internet sites are often integrated with the other content of the internet site – games and competitions, music downloads, video clips, discount coupons, online chat rooms, free email, club membership, gossip, fashion tips or advice – which is designed to keep the children engrossed in play for hours at a time and to keep them coming back. Marketers and advertisers are 'fundamentally reshaping the digital culture, creating new hybrid forms that blend communications, content and commerce'.[30]

For example, the Family Education Network, a division of Pearson Education, runs FunBrain.com and FEkids.com websites for children with 'the hottest collections of games and activities' on the internet. It offers advertisers access to 'over 7.5 million unique kids targeted by age and gender', three quarters of whom are between six and twelve years old.[31]

Three quarters of food manufacturers advertising on the internet have designed websites specifically for children, some for very young children; many others have websites that include a children's section. The address of the website is often given on the product packaging. Most of these websites are plastered with brand logos and advertising claims and include links to other food related sites.[32] On some websites children are encouraged to view television advertisements for the product. On others they are offered branded downloads such as music clips, mobile phone ringtones, desktop wallpaper, screensavers.

Box 2.2   Children and Alcohol

The age at which children begin drinking alcohol is dropping and is now around 13, on average, in the US. Underage drinkers make up a significant proportion – an estimated 20 per cent – of the US market. It is for this reason that alcohol manufacturers spend so much on advertising during television programmes, and with radio stations and magazines favoured by teens, as well as internet sites crammed with games, freebies, contests, downloads and music reviews. Teens see more alcohol advertisements in the magazines they read, and hear more on the radio stations they listen to, than do adults. The most popular television programmes for teenagers feature alcohol advertisements – more than 5000 ads were shown during the 15 most popular of these shows during 2002, at a cost of $52 million.[33]

Studies have found that the more television a child watches in ninth grade, the more likely they will begin drinking in the following year and a half. One study found that exposure in sixth grade to beer advertisements strongly increased the likelihood that the child would drink alcohol in the following year. Yet alcohol is a major cause of death for adolescents, and kids who start drinking before they are 15 are more likely to become alcoholics later in life.[34]

In Australia 75 per cent of teenagers between 14 and 17 consume alcohol at risk levels. Alcohol marketers promote pre-mixed spirit drinks or alcopops: 'bright, sweet drinks that are packaged like soft drinks, and slip down the throat just as easily'. Such products, together with their websites, attract children to alcoholic drinks at an early age and consequently, in the 1990s, became the fastest growing drinks market globally.[35] Recently an alcohol industry insider admitted that the sweet taste of alcopops was an effort to mask the alcohol taste and be appealing to young palates that were more used to sugary drinks. In this way they would not only buy the product but also get used to drinking alcohol.[36]

Most commercial websites elicit personal information from children visiting the site, and require it before they can play games or join a club. Some offer children prizes and free gifts for filling in long surveys that provide marketers with purchasing behaviour and preferences: 'Welcome to Kidzeyes.com, where kids tell us what's on their minds – and get free stuff for doing it! With each survey you complete, you'll earn valuable points that you can turn in for cash and/or prizes.'[37]

Some websites send children an email after they visit, and many send cookies to get unsolicited information from them. Information gathered on websites may be sold on to other marketing companies. In fact, market research is 'in some cases surpassing advertising and sponsorship as the key source of revenue' for websites.[38] This information can also be used to send individualised marketing messages to each child based on their 'unique preferences, behaviours, and psychological profile'.[39]

Such sites take advantage of the way children and teens like to answer questionnaires and surveys about themselves and their families, and their likes, dislikes and concerns, as it gives them a chance to express themselves.[40] Pre-adolescent children, however, often do not understand the problems associated with divulging personal information. Legislation in the US now requires children under 13 to obtain verifiable parental consent before supplying such information. But the regulations do not apply to contest entries, newsletter subscriptions or messages in response to emails from children.[41] Furthermore, it is easy for children under 13 to bypass having to get parental permission by giving a false birth date.

Market researchers are also able to glean much information about children and teens just by monitoring their chat rooms, bulletin boards, discussion groups and other online activities. Many children and teenagers use the internet to socialise and to express themselves. Around half of American children between ten and 17 regularly visit internet chat rooms where they give their opinions.[42] Advertisers have set up chat sites and discussion forums to take advantage of children's natural sociability.

Mobile phones and instant messaging

Marketers are also taking advantage of technologies that children use such as text messaging (SMS) on mobile phones. This enables them to reach children 'in a format and language they relate to'.[43] In the UK, for example, half of all children aged between eight and eleven have a mobile phone and 83 per cent of twelve- to 15-year-olds have them.[44]

In 2005 McDonald's ran a 'mobile marketing' campaign to 'create a compelling way to connect with the younger demographic'.[45] Coca-Cola is using mobile phones as its primary advertising vehicle for Sprite advertisements, and other corporations are expected to do the same.[46] A text-2-win competition by Cadbury promoted on chocolate bar wrappers in 2001, aimed at promoting the brand 'amongst younger audiences', yielded five million messages.[47]

> Wireless technology enables marketers to directly target users based on such information as previous purchase history, actual location and other profiling data ... Increasingly, mobile users will be receiving personally tailored electronic pitches, designed to trigger immediate purchases and timed to reach them when they are near particular stores and restaurants.[48]

Marketers are also infiltrating instant messaging services on the internet such as AOL's Instant Messenger Service (AIM) which has over three million users aged between twelve and 17. The major instant messaging providers 'all promote themselves aggressively to advertisers that want to reach teenagers' and offer them a way to 'engage young people as they communicate with their friends, by surrounding them with branded content and encouraging them to interact with advertising'.[49]

A branded version of MSN Messenger, with integrated advertising, was produced in a deal between McDonald's and Microsoft. Messenger has an estimated 800,000 users under 18. Yahoo offers interactive, branded backgrounds for instant messaging conversations (IMVs – IMVironments) that enable teenagers to 'express themselves' but in the process view an advertising message and send it on to their friends. Kraft and Pepsi are among the companies that have produced IMVs.[50]

> On average, for a specific IMV, we see 1.5 million people download a particular IMV, send over 100 million messages within it, and spend five to 10 minutes per user per day per IMV. This time spent is a particularly impressive statistic when you compare it to how much time in one day that user would spend watching a particular TV commercial for that advertiser.[51]

BYPASSING THE GATEKEEPERS

Marketers study how children nag their parents in order to take advantage of it for their marketing efforts. It has been noted that 'a persistent whine is one of the most powerful forces in the grocery business'.[52] A Harris Poll found that 73 per cent of people working in the youth industry (including advertisers, marketers, media and market researchers) agreed that 'most companies put pressure on children to pester their parents to buy things'.[53]

Children begin to ask for things that they see from the age of two, and at that age they can make connections between television advertising and store contents. Marketers take advantage of this. Westfield shopping centres in Australia have installed screens on their rides that show children's television shows interspersed with advertisements.

When supermarkets found that parents with young children were steering clear of the biscuit and cracker aisle to avoid the pleading and tantrums that would follow they rearranged the store layout so those aisles could not be so easily avoided, for example by placing the cookies on the other side of the aisle from the baby food.[54]

Marketers and advertisers who promote children's nagging knowingly cause stress in families and undermine the values that parents are trying to teach their children – values that are often in conflict with materialism and consumerism but are in the child's interest. Papers are regularly given at industry conferences on fostering pester power. A session at the 2003 Kid Power Conference in Sydney was entitled 'Harnessing Pester Power' and included information on the 'role of the gatekeeper'.[55] Gatekeeper is marketing speak for parents who may want to protect their children from the manipulative effects of advertising.

Marketing consultant, Anne Sutherland, explains: 'I started to see what makes kids tick when I questioned them on how they nagged and cajoled their moms to choose the snacks they wanted and then I had it quantified in persuasion testing. ... The nag factor is a big factor in business today.'[56] In order to take advantage of pester power, advertisements not only have to attract children and get them to want the product, they also have to give them an argument to use on their parents for why they should buy them. 'Child and Parent' studies help marketers to work out whether they are providing sufficient information to children to enable them to make a convincing request to their parents.[57]

Table 2.1   Percentage of Purchases Resulting From Nagging

Toys	46%
Movies	34%
Food	34%
CD-ROMs	33%
Home videos	32%
Theme Parks	20%

Source: A. Sutherland and B. Thompson, *Kidfluence: The Marketer's Guide to Understanding and Reaching Generation Y – Kids, Tweens, and Teens*, New York, McGraw-Hill, 2003, p. 115.

Nagging becomes even more necessary if the products being promoted are not healthy, or are beyond the normal parental budget. The Kid Power 2004 conference ran a workshop on 'The Targeting Dilemma – How to Decide if You Should Choose Moms or Kids' and noted that 'If you are marketer of a pre-sweetened cereal it's pretty easy to figure out who to target.'[58] In other words, if you have an unhealthy product, it is better to get kids to nag for it because parents will not voluntarily buy it.

Exploiting children's lack of cynicism

It is unethical to advertise to children who are unable to distinguish the advertisements from television programmes or internet content, unable to understand the purpose of advertisements, and unable to critically evaluate advertisements and the claims they make.[59]

Between ages two and five most children cannot even differentiate what happens on television from reality. They are very interested in commercials, which they believe without reservation. Marketing consultant, Dan Acuff, notes that until the age of seven children tend to accept television advertising at face value and he advises advertisers how to take advantage of that. For example he tells them that at this age kids are particularly susceptible to give-aways and similar promotions because 'the critical/logical/rational mind is not yet fully developed'.[60]

Studies commissioned by the US Surgeon General have demonstrated the failure of children under eight to understand persuasive intent.[61] Even if they can differentiate advertisements from television programmes (and sometimes the boundaries are blurred so that even adults don't recognise some content as advertising), about half of them still don't understand that the advertisements are trying to sell them something.[62]

A study by Roy Fox, Associate Professor of English Education at the University of Missouri-Columbia, found that children watching athletes in television commercials thought that the athletes had paid to be in the advertisements to promote themselves rather than the products. They believed children in advertisements were real rather than paid actors and they often confused advertisements with news items. Generally they did not understand the commercial intent of the advertisements.[63]

A Swedish Consumer Agency report that contributed to the decision to ban advertising to children under twelve in Sweden noted: 'The results of studies that have attempted to distinguish between different degrees of understanding or levels of awareness, all indicate that it is only *after* the age of 12 that children develop a fuller understanding of the purpose of advertising.'[64]

The problem with not understanding persuasive intent is that children will therefore tend to trust what the advertisement is telling them and recognise neither its bias nor the fact that it may 'exaggerate, manipulate, pontificate, and cajole' in order to get them to buy the product.[65] Psychiatrist Susan Linn notes that even if children say they understand that advertisements can be deceptive, they can still be subject to their influence:

> I recently sat with a group of elementary kids who all told me that commercials do not tell the truth, yet when asked, they all had strong opinions about which was the 'best' brand of sneaker. Their opinions were based not on their own experience but on what they'd seen on TV and in magazine ads. Advertising appeals to the emotions, not to intellect, and it affects children even more profoundly than it does adults.[66]

Moreover, advertisements often set out to deceive children. Forms of deception in advertising to children include the following:

1. The use of celebrities to exploit a child's trust in authority figures.
2. The presentation of products to make them seem bigger than they are to exploit a child's limited perceptive abilities.
3. Focusing on gifts and giveaways rather than the actual product, so that the child is not actually making judgements about the product that is being sold.
4. The use of jargon and complex language to take advantage of a child's limited vocabulary.

5. The excessive use of emotional triggers to exploit a child's insecurities and gullibility.[67]

JUNK FOOD AND OBESITY

Food companies exploit the inability of such young children to understand the purpose of the advertisements and the deception inherent in them. They seek to make food of little nutritional value seem to be exciting, delicious and fun.

Box 2.3   Food Advertising – Some Figures

In the US:

- Food and drink companies spend $12 billion a year advertising their products to children and youths.[68]
- Fast food outlets spend around $3 billion on television advertisements targeting children.[69]
- Saturday morning television has a food advertisement on average every five minutes.[70]
- Around a half of the adverts that are shown during children's television shows are for food, mainly candy, snacks, cereals and fast food.[71]

In Australia:

- Advertisers spend around $200 million a year selling snacks and fizzy drinks to children.[72] In 2003 McDonald's alone spent $50 million on advertising.[73]
- Nearly three quarters of advertisements on television between 3.30pm and 7.30pm are for sweets, snacks, soft drinks, processed food and fast food.[74]
- Australian children are exposed to twelve television food advertisements per hour.[75]

Free gifts are a particularly effective way of attracting child customers. Free toys can double or triple the sales of McDonald's meals to children. One of the most successful was the Teenie Beanie Baby which was thought to have sold 100 million Happy Meals in ten days compared with normal sales of ten million per week.[76]

Fast food and cereal marketers often take advantage of children's natural inclination to collect things by offering gifts in sets as collectors items. For example, when McDonald's gave away toy Hummers with its Happy Meals as part of its 'Hummer of a Summer' promotion there were eight different Hummers to collect.[77] When Frito-Lay offered small collector discs called Tazos free in its Doritos chip packets in 1996 it had to increase production by 40 per cent to keep up with demand.[78]

Food marketers targeting children seek to make their products fun, which means turning food into a form of entertainment or a play thing – this is referred to by the industry as 'eatertainment'.[79] For example Frito-Lay seeks to present 'food for the fun of it'.[80] Woolworths produced sweets that flash when you press a button on the stick holding them.[81] Food packaging is turned into something to play with or it may have games printed on it. Food can be shaped to be played with and toys produced in the shape of particular food brands.

Advertisers not only promote unhealthy foods but also create a culture where food is eaten for pleasure or fun without any need for discretion, limits or care.[82] Often manufacturers use food additives such as colouring solely for the purpose of making it appealing and eye-catching to children. The UK Food Commission found that 75 per cent of food that contains high amounts of added fat, sugar and salt also contains 'cosmetic additives'.[83] These additives, including artificial colour, have been shown to increase hyperactivity in children.[84]

Food marketing undermines the efforts of parents, teachers and doctors to teach children about healthy eating. The onslaught of advertisements for fast foods, sugary foods and salty foods encourage children to favour such foods over more healthy and natural alternatives, such as fruit and vegetables. The US Department of Agriculture claims that children get an appetite for high levels of sugar and salt in their food and drinks before they even go to school.[85]

Effectiveness of food marketing

Many studies have confirmed the connection between advertising, poor dietary choices and weight gain (see Box 2.4). Studies also show that advertisements confuse children about the nutritional value of various types of foods.[86]

In one experiment, children attending summer camp were shown commercials for sugary foods and Kool Aid, or advertisements for orange juice and fruit, or public service announcements about the need to moderate sugar intake, or no advertisements at all during their voluntary television watching. All the children, including those who had seen no advertisements, tended to eat fruit and orange juice rather than Kool Aid and candy except those who had seen the advertisements for these things.[87]

Today's children snack more and get a much higher proportion of their daily food from snacks and sweetened drinks.[88] In Australia toddlers (16 to 24 months) get a quarter of their food from chips, cordial and soft drinks, cakes and biscuits and other nutritionally poor snacks.[89] Older children (eight to 11) get about a third of their daily calories from junk food (defined as food that is high in fat, salt or sugar but has little nutritional value).[90]

Worldwide children are consuming excess calories, sugar, salt and fats and inadequate levels of whole grains, fruit and vegetables, fibre, calcium, iron, potassium and magnesium, which is putting their health at risk.[91] Consequently,

---

***Box 2.4*   Some Studies on the Impact of Advertising on Children's Diet**

- Expert committee of the Institute of Medicine (2006) – advertising associated with increased rates of obesity among children.[92]
- UK Food and Standards Agency (2003) – advertising promotes poor diet and rising obesity.[93]
- World Health Organization (WHO) and Food and Agriculture Organization (FAO) (2002) – marketing a 'probable' cause of weight gain and obesity in children worldwide.[94]
- *International Journal of Obesity* (2006) – New Zealand children's propensity to be overweight correlated with how many hours they spent watching television.[95]
- *Archives of Pediatrics & Adolescent Medicine* (2006) – television viewing hours correlated with increased intake of advertised foods among youth.[96]
- *Journal of Development and Behavioral Pediatrics* (1989) – television viewing hours correlated with increased food intake, food requests and obesity among very young children.[97]
- US Institute of Medicine (2004) – 'television advertising influences the food and beverage preferences of children ages 2–11 years' and is associated with weight gain.[98]
- *Archives of Pediatrics & Adolescent Medicine* (2007) – pre-school children preferred the taste of food and drink if they believed they came from McDonald's, even carrots that McDonald's does not sell.[99]

---

during the 1980s and 1990s children's obesity rates rose dramatically in many nations. The WHO claims that obesity is a global epidemic: 'At least 20 million children under the age of 5 years are overweight globally in 2005.'[100]

Overweight children are more likely to suffer from high blood pressure, clogged arteries, 'hypertension, type 2 diabetes, respiratory ailments, orthopedic problems, trouble sleeping, and depression', as well as heart disease, stroke, circulatory problems, infertility, breast cancer and other problems later in life.[101]

Industry response

The food and beverage industries have denied the link between their products and weight gain in children and funded several studies to support this denial (see Box 2.6). A Yale University survey of 88 studies found that 'Studies funded by the food industry simply did not find the degree of negative health effects from soft drinks that independent scholars discovered.'[102]

In 2002 a draft report of the Joint WHO/FAO Expert Consultation on Diet, Nutrition and the Prevention of Chronic Diseases called for stricter marketing rules and labelling, as well as taxes on sugar-rich food marketed to children. It prompted the American Advertising Federation, the American Association of Advertising Agencies, the Grocery Manufacturers of America, the National

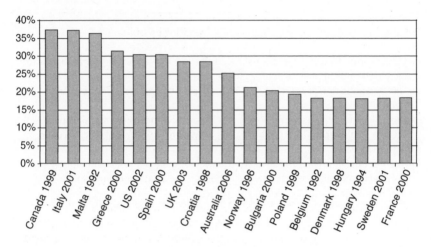

Figure 2.1   Percentage of Overweight Children Around 10 Years Old

Adapted from: 'Obesity in Europe: The Case for Action', London, International Obesity Taskforce and the European Association for the Study of Obesity, 2002, p. 7.

Box 2.5   Changing Diets – Some Figures

In the US:

- The rate of obesity in children between six and ten years old more than tripled in the three decades to 2004 and more than doubled for children aged between two and five years old.[103] Thirty-four per cent of children were overweight in 2004.[104]
- Eighteen per cent of children are now obese compared with less than 5 per cent in the early 1970s.[105]
- Type 2 diabetes – previously known as 'adult-onset' diabetes – has more than doubled in ten years.[106]

In the UK:

- In 2003, 28 per cent of children aged between two and ten were overweight and 14 per cent were obese. The rate has increased by 50 per cent over the past ten years.[107]
- An astounding 45 per cent of girls between eleven and 15 are overweight or obese.[108]

In Australia:

- Obesity rates for children aged seven to 15 more than tripled between 1985 and 1995 from just over 1 per cent to 5.5 per cent for girls and 4.7 per cent for boys.[109]
- Today over 8 per cent of children are obese and around 25 per cent are overweight despite their doing as much exercise as ever.[110]

Box 2.6   Some Denial Studies from the Food Industry

- Coca-Cola was the sole sponsor of an Australian government study into children's exercise habits. The ensuing report in 2004 claimed that it was declining physical activity that was the major cause of rising childhood obesity.[111]
- Cadbury Schweppes donated millions of dollars to the American Diabetes Association, and shortly afterwards the Association's chief medical officer denied the link between sugar and diabetes as well as between sugar and weight gain.[112]
- Coca-Cola donated millions of dollars to the American Academy of Pediatric Dentistry which now prevaricates about the link between soft drink and cavities.[113]
- In Australia McDonald's is paying the National Heart Foundation $330,000 per year in return for the Foundation's tick of approval for nine of its meals. The foundation says the money is to reimburse its costs in testing the meals and auditing McDonald's restaurants.[114]
- A review published in the *American Journal of Clinical Nutrition* in 2007, and paid for by the American Beverage Association, questioned a 2001 study published in the *Lancet* that found that children were 1.6 times as likely to become obese with every can of sweetened drink consumed per day.[115] Two of the authors of the review had links to the soft-drink industry.[116]
- Coca-Cola has established The Beverage Institute for Health and Wellness, to undertake scientific research and educate the public around the world about the role beverages play in nutrition and health.

Soft Drink Association, the Snack Food Association, the National Confectioners Association, the US Chamber of Commerce and several other industry associations to write to the US Secretary of Health and Human Services to 'express our concerns' that the report would harm the US food industry. The industry letter argued the report 'should be substantially modified before being issued by WHO and FAO'.[117]

The following year the Sugar Association 'threatened lobbying to block WHO funding if the report was not changed'. At the behest of industry lobbyists the Bush administration opposed WHO anti-obesity initiatives behind the scenes and objected to the way the WHO identified some foods as 'bad'.[118]

Manufacturers of junk food deny that there are good and bad foods, but instead insist that all foods have their place in a 'balanced' diet. They nevertheless seek to achieve maximum sales of their foods. For example, McDonald's aims for 20 visits per month per customer.[119] In its brochure *Healthy Balance*, it stresses the need for 'a balanced diet and regular exercise' and implies that McDonald's can contribute to that balance: 'A typical McDonald's meal of a Big Mac, French Fries and a Thick Shake contains foods from most of the core food groups, which are sources of riboflavin, calcium, phosphorus, thiamine, niacin, zinc, magnesium, iodine and iron...'.[120] They also add protein and vitamins to the list. However a person would need to walk for around 5.5 hours to burn off the calories of such a meal.[121]

Coca-Cola's Beverage Institute for Health and Wellness emphasises the importance of drinking enough fluids so as not to become dehydrated and argues that any drink suits this purpose, so 'there's no need to stick to plain water if it bores you'.[122]

The food industry also argues that achieving a balanced diet is a parental responsibility and that government regulation of junk-food advertising represents the intrusion of a 'nanny state' into private lives. Advertisers nevertheless seek to market direct to children, bypassing parental gatekeepers where they can, and encouraging pester power to overcome parental resistance. Moreover, the UK Office of Communications (Ofcom) found that mothers 'are at a loss' as to how to make a healthy diet attractive to children in the face of the barrage of marketing making junk food attractive to them.[123]

The food industry also thwarts the exercise of parental responsibility by lobbying against food labelling regulations and other sources of nutrition information being made available to parents. It has successfully lobbied for food disparagement laws in twelve US states, making it difficult for critics to point out the shortcomings of their food.[124] Jeff Richardson, director of the Centre for Health Economics at Monash University in Australia pointed out that 'food marketing was so manipulative that a central free-market principle – that people would act in their own best interests – no longer applied in relation to food consumption'.[125]

Junk-food manufacturers blame lack of exercise, rather than junk-food marketing, for the rising tide of obesity, and have recently been promoting exercise and associating themselves with exercise campaigns as part of their public relations efforts. Several beverage and fast food companies, such as McDonald's, have given out pedometers.[126] Many have sought to associate themselves with exercise and sport including Pepsi, Coca-Cola, Cadbury and Nestlé.[127] However, it is not realistic to believe that regular consumption of junk food can be counteracted with exercise, as we saw with the example of the McDonald's meal.

In 2007, when the food industry was under threat of advertising regulation in the US, a group of major food companies including McDonald's and PepsiCo agreed to voluntarily stop advertising the worst of their foods during children's television programmes. They will not however, stop advertising these same foods during family programmes such as the enormously popular *American Idol*, which most children watch. Similar promises were made by Kraft in 2005 and Kellogg's in 2007.[128]

ADVERTISING REGULATIONS

People concerned with children's health have long called for restrictions on marketing to children – including bans on television advertising to children. A long list of professional societies have also called for restrictions, including:

- the American Psychological Association (APA)
- the American Academy of Pediatrics (AAP)
- the Australian Division of General Practice
- the Australian Consumers' Association
- the Divisions of General Practice (an Australian doctors group)
- the Australian Medical Association (AMA)
- the Public Health Association of Australia
- the Royal Australasian College of General Practitioners
- the WHO.[129]

Australian Consumer Association magazine, *Choice*, found that 82 per cent of Australians favour government regulation of food and drink advertising.[130] However these calls have been ignored in many nations, including Australia, because of the power of the food lobbies.

Box 2.7   **Some Advertising Regulations in Various Nations**

- In Sweden and Norway advertisements aimed at children under twelve are banned.
- In France and Germany television programmes may not be interrupted by advertisements.
- In Finland and Germany cartoon characters and children cannot be used to sell products.
- In Greece toys cannot be advertised between 7 a.m. and 10 p.m.
- In Italy cartoons may not be interrupted by advertisements.
- In Denmark characters that appear in children's programmes cannot be used in advertisements and advertisements are not supposed to encourage children to ask their parents to buy products.
- In the UK children's television characters cannot be used in advertisements before 9 p.m. Junk-food advertisements are not allowed during children's programmes.[131]

Efforts to ban advertising targeting children have been unsuccessful in most countries because of the power of the advertisers, the toy manufacturers, the broadcasters and the programme producers.[132]

In the US attempts to regulate the amount of commercials targeted at children have had a chequered history. Outrage over the issue in the 1970s almost led to a total ban on advertising to children under eight years old in the US.[133] However, as a result of opposition from the National Association of Broadcasters, the Toy Manufacturers of America and the Association of National Advertisers, only a voluntary standard was introduced and even this was abandoned in 1984 by the Reagan administration.[134] The companies which dominate the children's market, such as Philip Morris, AOL Time Warner, Disney and Coca-Cola, are among the top donors to both Republicans and Democrats in the US.[135]

A favourite argument put forward by advertisers for why they should be allowed to advertise to children is that it pays for the programming. However in some countries, such as Australia, broadcasters are required to provide children's programming as a condition of their broadcast licence. The group Compass points out that in the UK,

> Even highly conservative estimates show that the health benefits from a 9 pm watershed for junk food TV adverts would save the nation up to almost a billion pounds a year – at a cost to the whole commercial television industry of £130 million a year. To put this into context, ITV paid out dividends of £300 million to share-holders last year.[136]

In Quebec advertisements directed at children under 13 years of age were banned in 1980 in all forms of media including print. At the time, there were predictions that children's television programming would suffer as a result. However the amount of children's programming has not fallen, mainly because of the efforts of two public broadcasting stations. Also programming increased markedly in 1988 with the introduction of cable channels. In fact, André Caron, Director of the Centre for Youth and Media Studies, University of Montreal, argues that the public stations have provided 'much more choice, in terms of genre and origins' because they don't have to worry about what will attract advertising and have instead concentrated on quality.[137]

Advertisers also like to claim that exposing children to advertising is part of their education and enables them to learn to deal with advertisements and learn critical skills. However, the evidence seems to be that those 'who watch most television tend to be the most easily influenced by a given advertisement' and, in particular, younger children do not become more sceptical of advertisements the more they see. Heavy television watchers tend to ask for the products advertised more often. Critical skills are not gained by watching more advertisements.[138]

3
Turning Play into Business

Wendy Varney and Sharon Beder

> Parents are embattled 'gatekeepers' at best, who year by year
> watch their hold on their children compromised, eroded, out-
> flanked, and eventually wholly loosened by their rivals in the
> marketplace.
>
> Benjamin R. Barber[1]

Among the phrases uttered by the talking doll *Teen Talk Barbie* is 'Let's go shopping!' It sums up the call of today's toys as they move en-masse down the path of cross-promotion and the celebration of rampant consumerism, leaving questions of children's development and meaningful play forgotten in their wake.

Many of today's toys not only entice children to acquire a great many products, they spell out loudly what the products should be. Alongside *Teen Talk Barbie* can be found a range of Barbies and Barbie accessories which promote and are named after fashion houses, cars and other vehicles, soft drinks and fast foods (see Table 3.1 for a selection of these). *Totally Hair Barbie*, the most popular of all Barbies, with over ten million sold,[2] came replete with a tube of Dep hair gel. The Barbie kitchen set has, among its miniature food stocks, Coca-Cola and branded biscuits, butter and apple juice.

Table 3.1 Some Barbie Dolls and Accessories Promoting Brands

Avon Representative Barbie	Kraft Treasures Barbie	Barbie Ford Thunderbird
Calvin Klein Jeans Barbie	Lifesavers/School Cool Barbie	Barbie Porsche
City Shopper Macy Barbie	McDonald's Barbie	Barbie Ferrari
Coca-Cola Picnic Barbie	Barbie Pizza Hut playset	Barbie Mustang
Hard Rock Café Barbie	Harley-Davidson Barbie	Barbie Lamborghini

In many cases, Barbie's clothes, a prominent part of play with these dolls, incorporate the brand name, logos and other symbols of the promoted product. For instance, the *Coca-Cola Barbies* have the Coke logo emblazoned across their dresses or other costumes, as well as Coke accoutrements. Barbie broadcasts where she and the many products she promotes can be purchased.

While Barbie has fittingly been dubbed the 'patron saint of conspicuous consumption', she is not the only toy engaged in such promotionalism.[3] The toy-car range, Hot Wheels, is immensely popular among boys. In 1998 its two billionth car was produced.[4] It has a range of cars, accessories and playsets promoting Ford, Shell, Walt Disney World, McDonald's, Mountain Dew soft drink and Nestlé Crunch among others.

A CHANGING TOY CULTURE

On the advice of marketing psychologists, early twentieth century producers and marketers directed advertising to children as a way of breaking family habits of thrift and resource sustainability.[5] Before long other manufacturers sought to take advantage of parents' new willingness to splurge on their children and to equate toys with child welfare. Food companies produced toys to promote their products. Campbell's Soups were among the pioneers, launching Campbell Kids dolls.[6]

Walt Disney can perhaps be credited with the greatest commercial foresight in the children's arena. Disney, who started his career in advertising, anticipated that toys and licensing would later become the norm for moviemakers. Disney toys expanded from Mickey Mouse dolls and toys in the 1930s to include all sorts of Disney characters and paraphernalia in tie-ins that were forerunners to a marketing trend that took off in the 1970s.[7]

The ambitious Disney 'remarked that every Mickey Mouse product or toy doubled as an advertisement for his cartoons'.[8] He was among the first producers of children's television programming, quickly recognising it as a marketing springboard for his other products, soon to include the theme park Disneyland. Disney also created and managed a consumer craze for merchandise associated with movies.

Disney was astute in recognising – and perhaps helping usher in – a period characterised by 'the rise in America of what can be called the cult of childhood'.[9] This was marked by exhortations to parents to 'enjoy' their children. Disney was both a part of that chorus and a beneficiary of a new relationship characterised by an eagerness of parents to express affection through consumer purchases for their children.

Disney's *Mickey Mouse Club* programme, featuring Disney characters, was unique at the time. Around 550,000 Mickey Mouse hats sold within three months of the programme starting up.[10] Advertisements in *Playthings*, the toy-trade journal, featuring a range of Mickey Mouse and Mousketeer toys, and urged toy retailers to 'Join the Great Mickey Mouse Buying Parade'. In the 1950s clubs boasted over 1 million members, who were all 'potential buyers of Mickey Mouse toys and dolls'.[11]

Another important aspect of advertising directly to children via the *Mickey Mouse Club* was that it enabled Disney to advertise to children every week, thereby creating 'a year-round consumer demand for toys' at a time when they had only been in strong demand around the Christmas season.[12]

Other children's clubs, organised by retailers, producers and media outlets, became popular in the 1980s and 1990s and have proliferated in recent times. For example, *Geoffrey's Fun Club*, run by Toys 'R' Us, features a cartoon giraffe called Geoffrey from Toys 'R' Us advertisements. By 1990, 75,000 children had paid their $2.95 a year to join.[13] *Burger King Kids Club* was established in 1991 and quickly tripled sales.[14]

Clubs offer an opportunity for marketers to develop a more personal relationship with each child; get information about the children for marketing purposes; and regularly promote products to children by age groups and address. Because children do not recognise clubs as a marketing ploy, they accept advice from the club as genuine, rather than just another advertisement. Marketing guru James McNeal observes:

> On a broad scale, clubs give kids *identity* – they belong to something. Thus they receive a degree of individuality as well as affiliation. They are *elevated in stature* by a club. They can refer to their membership just like Dad can his work or Mom hers. They actually possess identifiers – proof of membership and belonging – such as tee-shirts and caps with the club's logo and they get mail (just like Mom and Dad) with the club's letterhead on it. Children can meet their need for *play* as well as their need for *affiliation* through clubs.[15]

Fortune magazine is a bit more pragmatic about it: 'Here's one formula for building brand loyalty amongst kids. Start a fan club and put a cartoon character with lots of personality in charge. Throw in fun premiums [gifts], make it a mite educational – and you're set.'[16]

In the mid 1950s a relative newcomer to the toy industry, Mattel, began advertising directly to children. Ruth Handler, one of Mattel's founders, claimed: 'By advertising on a children's television show, we proved that both a toy and its brand name could be sold directly to the consumer, the child.'[17] This effectively meant that parental approval could be bypassed, especially if children could acquire their own source of money, which increasingly became the case. Questions of whether a toy was good value, beneficial to development, or compatible with the family's values, became largely redundant as filters through which toys passed.

Selling directly to children was part of a new approach to childhood more generally. The notion that children know what is best for them was seized upon by the toy industry. For instance, the giant toy retailer Toys 'R' Us put out a brochure claiming that children are the experts in toys and that others should bow to their knowledge (and desires) in this area.[18] Parents are encouraged to abrogate their own judgement about their children's needs and leave decisions to the children themselves. Given the significant influence advertising and marketing strategies have on children's assessment of their own needs and desires this has meant essentially letting the toy industry and related 'children's industry' decide.

MERCHANDISE LICENSING

Mattel's launch in 1959 of its Barbie fashion doll was an early initiative in merchandise licensing. Since then a vast interlocking of commercial interests has developed with children as their common target audience, including television programming, advertising, movies, toys, licensed products and games. Cartoon characters are launched as movies, followed up with a television series and then merchandised on hundreds of products from t-shirts to toys.[19] The head of Disney explained to *Advertising Age* in 1989 how the Disney Corporation's activities all reinforced each other: 'The Disney Stores promote the consumer products which promote the [theme] parks which promote the television shows. The television shows promote the company.'[20]

Movies

The release of the film *Star Wars* in 1977 was a watershed giving rise to a vast range of licensed toys with multiple marketing strategies in terms of form, price, packaging, collectability and characterisation. Sales by manufacturer Kenner of toys associated with the film reached $100 million in the first year of *Star Wars* toys production.[21]

The ongoing release of films in the *Star Wars* series stimulated frenzied collections and fandom, first among children and later among the adults they became. *Star Wars* action figures and accessories were far more integrated than any toy before them. A child-consumer of such merchandise at the time later reflected on the *Star Wars* range which consisted of

> everything from large-scale vehicles and playsets to smaller accessories, fabulous creatures and a whole host of storage cases ... Kenner had allowed them [kids] to recreate virtually every scene from their favourite movie. Moreover, there was always something new for them to get for the holidays, or for birthday parties, or simply on those occasions when their mothers took them to the local department store and caved in to the constant pleading for a new mini-rig, vehicle or playset – that toy without which that next adventure could not be staged.[22]

From the Lucasfilm/Kenner point of view there is no satisfaction to be had from play sustainability, durability and play satisfaction. In fact the more quickly a child becomes bored and dissatisfied with a toy the better, so they will be more likely to buy the next toy. The success of a toy, and indeed a movie, is measured in terms of its profitability not the pleasure it gives a child.

When the animated movie *Land Before Time* was launched in 1988 with co-ordinated in-store promotion at more than 1,400 Penney department stores and 5,800 Pizza Huts, the multi-pronged tie-in was described as 'perhaps the most extensive in Hollywood history'. Penney executives claimed retail was becoming 'an extended form of entertainment' with children expecting 'to be able to extend the fantasy of a film and take the characters home with them, either in the form of a book, a tee-shirt or whatever'.[23] The industry term for this was 'entertainment alliances'.

Often the licensed products and sales of toys make more money for a movie producer than the movie itself. For example the movie Aladdin cost $20 million to make but $25 million was spent promoting it to ensure the predicted sales of licensed products worth some $250 million, videos worth $200 million and video games worth another $200 million.[24] The first two *Star Wars* movies grossed about $600 million but the merchandise tied into the movies was worth some $2 billion by 1985.[25]

Movie studios naturally favour movies that are shopping-mall friendly. The general manager of Columbia Pictures Merchandising stated that 'There is no question people look at scripts for their licensing potential', and do market studies of this potential. The tendency towards sequels in movies is partly driven by the need to keep the characters emblazoned on the products current and fashionable.[26]

Toys

Toy makers followed the lead of movie makers, turning their toys into licensing juggernauts. Today movies are based on already existing toys such as those based on Bratz dolls and on Hasbro's Transformers in 2007.[27] Re-enactment now features as a central form of play, more commercially lucrative than simply associating the toys with a film or its characters.

Shortly after its venture into *Star Wars* toys, Kenner collaborated with American Greeting Cards to develop a female character that would lend itself to toy form and extensive licensing. The result was Strawberry Shortcake, as well as a mass of associated merchandise, a film and a breakfast cereal by General Mills, Kenner's corporate parent.[28] The doll appeared on every imaginable item from children's furnishings to toiletries and was given prolific publicity including a hot-air balloon advertising her in Britain.[29] The doll grossed $100 million in sales in the US alone during its first year and licensing reaped another $500 million the following year.[30]

Kenner immediately followed up with another similar concept for young children, Care Bears, licensed and publicised along similar lines to the Strawberry

Shortcake dolls. The release of Care Bears followed exhaustive research by General Mills and American Greeting Cards to establish what designs, symbols and characteristics would best lend themselves to a range of licensing opportunities. To ensure journalistic enthusiasm, an extravagant expedition was organised, in which journalists were flown to Amsterdam, wined, dined, entertained, accommodated and the following morning taken by coach to an idyllic castle where the complete range of bears and merchandise was presented. After being feted, the journalist from *Toys International and the Retailer* suggested the toys and other goodies 'are bound to appeal to both children and adults'.[31] In 1993 over nine million Care Bears were sold.[32]

Food manufacturers got on the bandwagon, using toys to promote their brands, including McDonald's and Burger King. Confectionery manufacturers followed suit, with Hershey's, M&Ms, Reece's Pieces and Cadbury's all involved in toys promoting their products.[33] Soon even the multinational corporation Lever Brothers was promoting its Snuggles nappies through dolls, bears and puppets. By 1985 there had been a drastic change in toys, such that what was being marketed was not a toy but a 'concept' around which all manner of merchandise and a string of entertainments could be sold.[34]

Television programming

In 1969 Mattel sponsored a television cartoon series called *Hot Wheels*, based on its toy cars of the same name, but following complaints to the Federal Communications Commission (FCC) about the nature of the show, the series was discontinued.[35] By 1983, however, there was a completely different regulatory climate in the US and the FCC let it be known that it would no longer look unfavourably upon what were essentially 'program-length commercials' or PLCs.[36]

This prompted Mattel to produce a television programme for the US market based on its toy line *He-Man and Masters of the Universe*. In 1984, $500 million worth of He-Man gear was sold.[37] He-Man marked a watershed and there was soon a frenzied fray of toy companies seeking to take advantage of the relaxed regulatory climate. By 1984 there were eight Saturday morning network programmes in the US based on toys and other merchandise, including Strawberry Shortcake and Care Bears.[38]

Toy manufacturers sought to promote their toys by having them at the core of children's television programmes. This not only gave publicity to the toys but suggested exactly how play should be enacted around them, in much the same way as *Star Wars* had done. It was most profitable for television shows to feature several characters needing various accessories so as to maximise the product lines that could be sold.[39] The well thought-out marketing driven programme involves a team of toy heroes, their enemies, costumes, weapons, vehicles and other accessories.[40]

Toy manufacturers have become key players in the development and promotion of children's television programmes.[41] They often subsidise the production of programmes that will promote their products, and some even go so far as to offer the programmes for free to the media, in return for a share in the advertising time the programme has allocated to it.[42] This makes it much more difficult for educational and non-commercial programmes to compete. Consequently, television programming is determined by toy manufacturers' interests rather than children's interests.[43] Programmes are developed specifically to sell toys.

Cartoons and characters

The use of cartoon and licensed characters is a highly successful marketing strategy when it comes to children, particularly the youngest, who can 'form powerful bonds' with television, movie, radio and story-book characters. Jennifer Blows of Kid Industries noted that babies as young as seven months old request products on the basis of characters on their packages: 'The colours, form, shape and sounds all connect in some way to make meaning for the child and that meaning is, at this very early age, happiness and contentment. They feel secure. If your brand is able to offer that then you're doing something very right indeed.'[44]

What is more, small children often look up to fictional characters and tend to do what they ask of them. *CMO Magazine* noted: 'Marketers have found that putting a cartoon character on just about anything can increase its sales. That's why a growing number of consumer electronics companies are producing kid-branded items, from Barbie cell phones to Hello Kitty radios to TVs and DVD players branded with SpongeBob and other characters.'[45]

Advertising consultancies seek to 'build emotional connections with kids' by using characters they hope will 'draw kids in and engage them in the brand'.[46] A workshop after the 2003 Kid Power Conference in Sydney focused on the use of characters in marketing to help brands 'become a child's "best friend" ... Characters should capture the hearts and minds of children'.[47]

Chris McKee, from the Geppetto Group, denies that marketers use characters to sell brands to kids but admits that what he loves about characters is the way 'two- and three-year-olds develop such a strong affinity for them. You see the way they bond with these characters.'[48] What marketers aim for is to have children, who may not even be able to speak yet, point to and demand products when they recognise a character or brand logo, and in this way get their mother to buy them.[49]

Advertisers feature cartoon or other characters in order to imply that those characters endorse their products. This is known as 'host selling'. Around the world, junk food is promoted with the use of popular characters such as Scooby Doo, Bob the Builder and Nemo.[50] A 1996 study of fifth-grade boys found that 86 per cent of them recognised alcohol seller Budweiser's cartoon frog, a recognition rate similar to that of Bugs Bunny. A later survey found that Budweiser was the favourite television advertisement for children.[51]

Youth Media Australia (YMA) found in a survey in 2005/6 that 87 per cent of parents said their pre-school children requested food that had TV or movie characters depicted on the packaging.[52] Children often believe the things a favourite character says. For example a survey showed that more than half of Australian eight- and nine-year-olds questioned believed Ronald McDonald knew best what children should eat.[53]

Advertisements are even placed in the breaks of the television programmes about such characters, thus blurring the distinction between programming and advertising and taking advantage of the affection children feel for the characters.[54] Host selling is now banned in some places. Yet it is highly effective. In 1999 Burger King doubled its UK sales to 50 million over six weeks by giving away Teletubbies beanbag toys with its meals.[55] (Teletubbies is a BBC-produced television programme aimed at toddlers.)

Box 3.1   Cartoon Characters and Cigarettes

Around 2000 children start smoking each day in the US and around one third of them will die as a result of it.[56] After the cartoon character Old Joe Camel was introduced by Camel cigarettes, illegal sales to children skyrocketed from an estimated $6 million in 1988 to $476 million per year in 1991.[57] One study found that a third of children who bought cigarettes despite being underage, bought Camel brand.[58]

In a study of children aged three to six years old, more than half were able to match the Joe Camel character to cigarettes. Other cigarette logos were matched by 18 per cent of children in one case and 33 per cent in another. The older children (aged six) recognised Joe Camel 91 per cent of the time, a rate similar to that of Mickey Mouse for the Disney Channel. Considering tobacco advertising is not shown on television (apart from incidentally on sports broadcasts), their exposure to the Joe Camel character must come from movies, billboards, video arcade games, and licensed products such as t-shirts.[59]

Tobacco companies recognise children as a significant market, if not a current market then a potential market. Internal documents from Philip Morris stated 'Today's teenager is tomorrow's potential regular customer ... the smoking patterns of teenagers are particularly important to Philip Morris.' Documents from R.J. Reynolds showed that they viewed 14- to 18-year-olds as an increasing market in which they needed to position themselves through the establishment of a new brand.[60]

PRODUCT PLACEMENT

Product placement in children's movies and television shows, where the producer is paid to insert one or more branded products into scenes, is becoming more common. Most movies now contain more than ten product placements.[61] For example, 'Pepsi has a whole department dedicated to product placement', which has paid to have its products appear in many movies including *Teenage Mutant Ninja Turtles, Flashdance, Fantastic Four, Spider-Man 2* and *Back to the Future II.*[62] Almost 11 per cent of minutes on American network television included a branded reference in 2006 and there was a 13 per cent increase in product placements in prime-time network television during 2007 – almost 26,000 instances in the top ten programmes.[63]

Product placement helps to make a product seem familiar and gives it status when it is used by a child's heroes. It is particularly hard for children, who use the media as a way of learning what is cool, to discern the advertisements concealed in the content of the media. Even college students, who admit they take notice of products used in movies and television, seldom realise that companies pay for their products to appear.[64] Product placement enables advertisers to bypass the cynicism that older children may have towards standard advertisements because they are not obviously advertisements and the association between the film stars and the product is more subconscious.

Box 3.2   Alcohol and Tobacco

Product placement has been a favourite strategy of alcohol and tobacco companies which are prevented from advertising directly to children. Eight alcohol companies placed their products in some 233 motion pictures in 1997–98 and in 181 television series.[65] Cigarette smoking in movies has been increasing in recent years with three out of four films showing onscreen smoking in 2006.

Studies have shown that children between ten and 14 are almost three times more likely to begin smoking if they have been exposed to a great deal of smoking in movies, particularly if they come from a non-smoking home, presumably because smoking seems more glamorous to them.[66] The *American Academy of Pediatrics* noted in 1999 that:

Increasingly, media messages and images are normalizing and glamorizing the use of tobacco, alcohol, and illicit drugs. Tobacco manufacturers spend $6 billion per year, and alcohol manufacturers $2 billion per year, to entice youngsters into 'just saying yes.' Popular movies are often showing the lead character or likeable characters using and enjoying tobacco and alcohol products.[67]

At its extreme product placement becomes the total rationale for a movie or television show. In other words the movie concept begins with a product and is designed around the product. The $50 million animated movie *Foodfight!*, released in 2002, was basically a movie length advertisement for multiple products aimed at children. It was set in a supermarket and portrayed 'adventures of hundreds of internationally branded characters from the familiar packages of products including Mr. Clean, Twinkie the Kid, Charlie the Tuna, Mrs Butterworth ... as they battle the evil Brand X for control of the store.' *Foodfight!* allowed the producers to showcase products and brand characters representing 'all of the biggest consumer companies in the world'. For each country the movie was released in, the products showcased were digitally changed and customised to suit the local market.[68]

Product placement is not confined to movies and television programmes. In 2005 McDonald's offered to pay rap artists who included Big Macs in their songs.[69] The company Maven Strategies specialises in getting paid product placements into rap songs, which some major brands see as a way to reach a younger audience and be seen as cool.[70]

Product placement is already occurring in comic books.[71] Similarly children's books can include product placements and also product integration, where the product becomes part of the storyline. Books based on licensed characters from movies, television shows and consumer products are now commissioned by marketers and churned out by publishing houses. These books have no literary merit but can have the effect of diverting children from more character-building reading.[72]

Teen magazines merge editorial content with marketing and the articles promote a consumer-oriented lifestyle, with a heavy emphasis on fashion and material concerns. Magazines aimed at children also include articles, advice columns, games, cartoons and quizzes that often seek to sell products without the young reader being aware of it. This is referred to as advertainment and is used by companies such as Hershey's, Colgate and Foot Locker.[73]

Video games and advergames

Product placement and integration is also an increasing part of video games. In the US 84 per cent of children play video games – on the internet, on game consoles or on mobile phones – many spending hours each week at it.[74] In 2006 advertisers paid $150 million to advertise on game sites and in the games themselves, more than double the amount in 2002.[75] Games can be used 'to introduce new cartoon characters and even warm up audiences for a major film's release'.[76]

Advertisements often appear on billboards in background scenery of the games. For example Activision's game, *Street Hoops*, includes billboards and buses with Sprite advertisements on them. Some games have rooms built into the game that give players the opportunity to interact with brands so that the game fosters 'deeper engagement with users'.[77] Product placements are more effective, however, if the game characters and players actually use the products. Activision's game, *Pro Surfer*, has its characters using Nokia mobile phones. Electronic Arts received millions of dollars to design *Sims Online* so that players communicate using Intel computers and eat McDonald's hamburgers and chips for nourishment.[78]

Some games enable advertisers to secretly monitor players and the choices they make during the game so they can tailor the advertisements to the player. Increasingly games developers use 'dynamic product placement' 'to incorporate their brands into the game's storyline but also to respond to a player's actions in real time, changing, adding, or updating advertising messages to tailor their appeal to that particular individual'.[79]

Massive, which is now owned by Microsoft, advertises itself as 'Your channel to the gaming audience' and boasts that its video-game network 'enables marketers to reach and engage the millions of young adult males playing games every day ... wherever they are ... in the world'. It has clients in the US, Canada and Europe including Coca-Cola, Ford, General Mills, General Motors, Reebok, Subway, Wendy's, Universal Pictures and many others. It claims that its 'truly unique, ultra-immersive entertainment experiences' achieve a 64 per cent increase in brand familiarity (100 per cent in the case of automobile brands).[80]

Massive's games are examples of advergames, games that are specifically created by marketers as advertising vehicles. Individual manufacturers also produce advergames. Three quarters of children's websites created by food manufacturers include advergames. On the kids.icecream.com website kids play branded games, for example, where they 'bop' Nestlé Push-up Frozen Treats, which pop up on the screen.[81] On Sony's Everquest II video game, teenagers can order an actual pizza from within the game by clicking on a link to Pizza Hut's online order website.[82]

By placing their brand in video games, marketers get millions of 'quality brand impressions' which 'means that teens playing the game over and over make deep positive associations between the brands and the game'. Brands are associated with an 'ambiance' created by the game.[83] McDonald's advertising agency notes that this is a good way to 'reach a difficult-to-reach audience', which is otherwise sick of advertisements: 'Any time you can reach them in a way that is contextually relevant to their lives is very important.'[84]

Industry studies show that product placements in games are far more effective than advertisements in achieving product recall some time afterwards.[85] Moreover they fill the gap created by self-regulation of junk-food ads on children's television. Many parents are unaware of the advertisements in video games so advertisers can bypass the 'gatekeepers'. In most countries, advertising codes aimed at protecting children from advertising do not cover video or web-based games. Video games are being pitched to ever younger children with games being designed for pre-schoolers.[86]

Doll web sites are also growing rapidly and attract millions of visits. On these sites young girls dress up virtual dolls, and such sites are often supported by advertising. Others are established by corporations such as Mattel which has introduced BabieGirls.com which allows children to dress-up Barbie dolls and chat with each other.[87]

RAMIFICATIONS FOR PLAY

The consumerist message in some form is seldom absent from today's toys, games and children's entertainment. Toys have taken a highly commodified form which has lent itself to product and brand promotion as well as the promotion of consumerism in general. In today's marketing-driven global playground merchandise substitutes for open space and exploration. Children's toys and other areas of children's play are seen as 'cash cows', there for milking. Marketers emphasise children's 'need' for toys rather than their need for play, and they imply that children should amass as many toys as possible.

Play is becoming less physical, more computerised and, most significantly, more isolated. According to Philippe Ariès, games and amusements once 'formed one of the principal means employed by a society to draw its collective bonds closer, to feel united'.[88] The contrast with modern times is evident. Whereas historically play was a socialising activity, the focus of contemporary toys and games is on materialism and individualism.

The idea of children playing alone with their toys, 'inconceivable' several centuries ago, is now the basis for much toy marketing.[89] However, children today, who have seen advertisements for toys, tend to prefer to play with the toy than with a friend and they tend to prefer to play with a child they don't like if the child has a coveted toy than with a child they like.[90]

Further emphasising the shift from communal to individual play, the design of many contemporary toys suggests that playmates are somewhat superfluous. A toy is represented not only as a plaything but as the embodiment of a friend, and sometimes a needy one. The box of the *Baby Chris Gift Set*, for instance, claims the doll 'needs your love and care', while advertisements for *Pink and Pretty Barbie* sentimentalise the doll's feigned needs: 'Pink and Pretty Barbie has everything but the one thing she wants most. A true friend. Will you be Barbie's friend?'[91] Friendship is reduced to simply another commodity available for purchase at toy supermarkets.

Co-operation should be one of the important social learning areas of children's game play, with chances for rules to be renegotiated, re-interpreted or improved.[92] If children are isolated and generally play alone with their toys, they are largely deprived of this benefit.

From creativity to scripted play

Probably the most commonly expressed concern is that play is becoming much less creative because toys offer less open-ended play opportunities. Whereas toys were once props around which children could use their imaginations and devise any number of play scenarios and play these out, the scenarios, characters and the frameworks for play in modern toys are already spelt out in the movie and television scripts they derive from. This tends to close off other options and provide less scope for the use of imagination.[93] Moreover, if the play is tightly scripted, there will be less room for spontaneous experimentation.

That is not to say that some children won't still devise their own play, but that this is not encouraged by the toys and will be the exception rather than the rule. Carlsson-Paige and Levin found, in their study of play, that when play is shaped by commercially driven and formulaic television programmes toys tend to be over-defined and play is impoverished.[94] Such toys are poles apart from those that could be thought of as flexible props and that lead to the sort of play that gives children a sense of belonging and ownership of their play.[95]

The paucity of play opportunities is often seen in relation to the most blatantly promotional toys. A toy McDonald's restaurant can be little else, and does not encourage children to think of it as anything else when they have seen it so heavily advertised with child actors playing in very specified ways informed by the 'McDonald's experience.' This is 'brand-name' play rather than developmental play.

The same is true of video games which provide little room for children to define their own play. One might argue that children get some practice in hand–eye co-ordination and in cause-and-effect from these games, but a multitude of other items could fulfil that role just as well or even better, while also providing much richer play experiences.

Learning consumer culture

It suits marketers to have play so well defined because sharply focused characters are an effective marketing ploy and scripted play scenarios help to promote individual products as well as consumer culture. The real learning experiences gained from such toys are about consumption, self-gratification and the extent of the dazzling array of commodities on offer. Despite the rhetoric of individuality and opportunity that toy makers employ, the major identity offered by their toys is that of conspicuous consumer. Play has effectively been turned into a business and consumed within notions of consumption.

Marketing aimed at children is ubiquitous and every avenue of children's play and entertainment is branded. There seem to be no limits to where advertisers and markets are willing to go. Children are exposed to advertisements every waking moment; the mission of corporations is to make sure their products and brands are always in the minds of children.[96] According to a senior vice president of Grey Advertising: 'It isn't enough to just advertise on television ... You've got to reach kids throughout their day ... You've got to become part of the fabric of their lives.'[97] Moreover, the distinction between advertising and content, between marketing and entertainment, is becoming more and more blurred so that children don't even know they are being marketed to.

The time children spend listening to and watching marketing messages far outweighs the time they spend listening to parents. Even children themselves are disturbed by the amount of marketing they are subject to. An Australian survey found that 88 per cent of children felt companies were trying to sell them things they didn't want.[98]

The consumer world that children are immersed in is also addictive and self-replicating. Children come to crave the sugar, fat and salt-laden foods that are marketed to them. They are introduced to addictive substances such as alcohol and cigarettes at an early age. The video games, television programmes and virtual worlds are addictive. Indeed, games are deliberately designed to be 'addictive'. Some even include a 'viral component', that is, a way for players to contact friends to invite them to play the game.[99]

Most addictive and self-replicating, however, is the culture of consumerism and shopping. Children are persuaded that they will not be happy unless they have the toys and clothes that other children think are cool, and this is encouraged with viral marketing (see the next chapter). This can be expected to have repercussions for areas of children's social development, with their well-being subordinated to corporate goals of profit and growth. This may in turn lead to a complex and largely un-investigated range of psychological and social damage.

4
Branding Childish Identities

The fresh neurons of young brains are valuable mental real estate
to admen. By seeding their products early, the marketers can
do more than just develop brand recognition; they can literally
cultivate a demographic's sensibilities as they are formed.

Douglas Rushkoff [1]

The Girls Intelligence Agency (GIA) claims to have 40,000 'secret agents' aged
from eight years old. Their mission is to spy on their girlfriends on behalf of
corporations such as Disney, Hasbro, Mattel, Nestlé, Lego, Sony and Warner
Bros. GIA takes its clients 'behind enemy lines' to 'see what is inside her bedroom,
closets, drawers, backpacks and bathroom'. GIA monitors instant messaging (IM)
between girls who are 'sharing secrets and advice among their peers' and it uses
spy cams to 'watch the girls interact' with its clients' products. [2]

GIA is best known for its slumber parties that are held in the homes of their
secret agents, attended by ten to twelve friends. The agents receive a 'Slumber
Party in a Box' with branded games and activities and free samples. GIA tells
clients that this Box 'gets you into the guarded fortress – the girls' bedroom' and
'prompts a very intimate focus group' with 'unedited feedback' on their product.
GIA claims that each of these girls will talk to ten or so other girls about the party
and they in turn will talk to ten more so that '1000 parties connect you to nearly
1MM [million] girl friends'. [3] GIA's website offers 'Espionage you can trust'. [4]

The Agency's 'secret agents' are not paid but manipulated into collecting
marketing intelligence for the Agency with free samples, games and music previews.
The website where the girls apply to be agents, which is a different website to the
one where it boasts of its ability to access private information about the girls, has
all the appearance of being an exclusive club for specially selected girls. On this
website for girls it refers to its marketing function as follows:

GIA: Ruthless spies saving the world from making more lame stuff for girls.
You talk, IM, email, (ahem, totally CONFIDENTIAL)
we listen and decode and translate ... to help companies go from LAME to
SWEET! [5]

Secret agents are asked to take note of their friends' reactions to products for the Agency: 'be slick and find out some sly scoop on your friends'. The Agency recruits girls 'by playing to their need to be recognized as special when in fact the girls are being used and deceived' and encouraged to do the same to their friends.[6] Such schemes have been criticised for commercialising human relations and encouraging teenagers to treat their friends as advertising pawns.[7] Welcome to the cold new world of viral marketing.

BRAND LOYALTY

James McNeal, in his book *Kids as Customers*, points out that retailers and manufacturers have two sources of new customers: those who they can persuade to change from their competitors, and those who have not yet entered the market. Those who switch are likely to switch again but those who are nurtured from childhood are likely to be more steadfast. This is why it makes sense to aim for brand loyalty from children.[8]

Advertisers recognise that brand loyalties and consumer habits formed when children are young and vulnerable will be carried through to adulthood. The CEO of Prism Communications noted: 'they aren't children so much as what I like to call "evolving consumers".'[9] Toys 'R' Us president, Mike Searles, says 'If you own this child at an early age ... you can own this child for years to come.'[10]

In addition to forming lifelong loyalties whilst young, marketers recognise that children can form attachments to products well before they are ready to buy them. A Ford executive noted: 'Car branding indirectly happens at every stage of life ... Ford's goal is to be there at every stage of the consumer's life. The earlier, the better.'[11] Media buyer, Irwin Gotlieb, concurred: 'If the first time you saw an ad for a Mercedes was when you could finally afford it, then it is too late. You have to create aspiration in the male by the age of 12 or they won't be buying one at 35.'[12]

Increasingly corporations differentiate their products on the basis of brand because there is so little difference between products of the same type.

Brand awareness

McNeal advises those wanting to generate brand loyalty amongst children to firstly create awareness by taking advantage of the child's curiosity and eagerness to learn: 'Therefore, frequent presentations of the firm's logo, slogans, and brand names within the child's environment will produce awareness of a firm.' He cites Coca-Cola as a good example of this, with its advertising and logos maintaining a 'major presence in practically everyone's environment', including children's.[13]

In an effort to reach the very youngest potential consumers, well before they can actually buy their products, 'companies such as Ralph Lauren and Harley

Davidson are now targeting infants and toddlers by putting out items like tiny T-shirts and sweatshirts with their logos on them'. Other companies sell 'nursery linens, mobiles, and crib toys decorated with brand logos or images or licensed characters' so as to teach babies their brand logo before they can even say them.[14] For example, Pepsi logos can be found on nipple-topped baby bottles.[15] 'The more frequently an infant sees an image, the more familiar it becomes, bringing comfort and, eventually, emotional attachment.'[16]

Modern children who watch television can recognise brands by the age of two, before they can even read.[17] Four out of five children recognise the McDonald's brand by the time they are three years old (even before some of them know their own surnames), and they know that McDonald's sells hamburgers.[18]

Whilst targeting marketing at toddlers is thought to be unacceptable by most people, marketers often get away with it by giving it an educational facade, for example, by featuring brand logos and characters on 'educational' posters, videos and books.[19]

Brand associations

The second step is to interest the child in the company symbols as 'need satisfiers'. This may involve pairing a product with a child's interests, for example, collectable cards, or toys in packets, or clubs for children such as the Kraft Cheese & Macaroni Club.[20]

Brand bonding can be helped along by associating the brand with pleasant experiences. This is done by sponsoring events such as concerts, sporting fixtures, festivals, sports leagues and entertainment outlets. For example, Denny's restaurants sponsor Major League Baseball, and McDonald's sponsors Fox Kids Network and the National Basketball Association (NBA). According to McDonald's internal papers, its association with the NBA is intended to encourage those watching its ads to associate its french fries with 'the excitement and fanaticism people feel about the NBA'.[21]

Brands today are presented not only as a set of products manufactured by a particular corporation, but as representing a set of experiences or values, as a lifestyle.[22] Advertisers seek to associate their brands 'with culturally valued images, feelings and sensibilities'.[23] It is for this reason that companies like to associate their brands with television shows and movies. When Coca-Cola bought global marketing rights for Harry Potter for $150 million, its press release claimed that it was 'reinforcing the core values and attributes shared by Harry Potter and Coca-Cola'.[24]

Celebrity endorsements are also used to associate brands with the feelings of loyalty and admiration that those celebrities inspire amongst young people. Companies such as Coca-Cola, Pepsi and Nike spend millions on signing up pop stars or sports stars for this purpose.[25]

Brand bonding

McNeal's third step in achieving brand loyalty is getting children to believe in the firm and its products as providers of satisfaction in themselves. For products that are not used by children this may mean that the products or the brand need to be aligned with values such as environmental protection, patriotism, or good health.[26] The objective is to create an emotional connection between children and brands. Successful brands 'generate recognition, familiarity and even affection amongst children'.[27]

Companies go out of their way to turn brands into friends. Cheryl Berman, a founder of KidLeo, a consulting arm of advertising agency Leo Burnett, advised marketers to 'connect with kids as an enduring, responsible friend'.[28] McDonald's seeks 'to make customers believe that McDonald's is their "Trusted Friend".'[29] The Geppetto Group worked with psychologists to study the character of different children's relationships so as 'to mirror the best of those relational feelings in building product relationship messages' and therefore develop 'effective brand imaging' imbued with 'kid-familiar personality characteristics'.[30] Its clients include Coca-Cola, Kraft, Frito-Lay and McDonald's.[31]

Advertisers D'Arcy Masius Benton & Bowles explain how it is desirable to create a personality for products being advertised to small children in order to promote loyalty: 'Identify and individualize some characteristic of the brand and endow it with "magic power" which may not be believed at the rational level but can create an aura about the brand. Brand names should receive special emphasis and repetition.'[32]

The latest research into brand bonding uses the term 'engagement'. According to the chief research officer of the Advertising Research Foundation (ARF), Joe Plummer: 'The heart of engagement is "turning on" a mind. ... This is a subtle, subconscious process in which consumers begin to combine the ad's messages with their own associations, symbols and metaphors to make the brand more personally relevant.' Modern advertisements do not seek to outline the advantages of a product so much as to 'seduce the consumer into beginning that subconscious processing of the brand'.[33]

Box 4.1   Children's Brand Recognition – Some Study Findings

- Children have a set of around 100 preferred brands by the time they start school and this increases to some 300–400 by the time they are ten years old.[34]
- 52 per cent of three-year-olds, 73 per cent of four-year-olds and 92 per cent of eight- to 14-year-olds ask for particular brands.[35]
- A third of eight- to twelve-year-olds around the world are 'bonded to a fashion brand' and 40 per cent are bonded to a car brand.[36] Their brand information is mainly gleaned from television.[37]

COOL MARKETING

Marketers expend much effort in spotting trends and often utilise children and teenagers who are identified as trendsetters in an effort to make their products and brands 'cool'. Marketers often rely on child trendsetters to do market research for them in return for a few freebies and the flattery of having their opinions taken seriously, as we saw in the case of GIA. Children test and give feedback on products, complete surveys, take part in focus groups, email suggestions about what is 'in' and give extended interviews.[38]

In the UK, children can become 'Dubit Informers' by filling out online surveys for which they are paid a small amount (50p to £2), or enter a prize draw. Dubit makes an effort to make them feel special: 'As a member of Informer you will be part of an exclusive group of teenagers that is given access to new ideas, new ad campaigns and new technologies – all before anyone else!!'[39]

Increasingly however, it is the companies who are defining what is cool by marketing their products to the coolest kids. Suzie McInerney, Marketing Manager of Funtastic, gave a conference paper to Kid Power 2003 in Sydney on 'Staying ahead of the trends and defining what's cool' which promised to help the audience build 'on the fad momentum' and dictate 'what's cool'.[40]

Marketers create the impression that their product is cool by giving stock to those identified by their peers as being cool, in the hope that when they wear or use it, then everyone will want it – this is variously referred to as 'seeding' or 'real life product placement'.[41] Children identified as trendsetters may even be paid to wear and be seen in a particular line of clothing.[42] Cheerleaders have become a popular means of spreading advertising messages because they tend to be envied by other girls in high schools.[43]

Toy manufacturer Hasbro sought out the boys who were known amongst the children's community to be the coolest amongst eight- to 13-year-olds in Chicago and offered them free samples of its new portable game console to keep and distribute to ten friends.[44] In this way they made sure their product was perceived as cool and therefore in demand.

Also people revered by children and teens as cool – rappers, artists, actors and athletes – are given free clothing and shoes to wear in order for the products to get their imprimatur as cool.[45] A related method is to identify a sub-community of young people, such as surfers, who might adopt a brand and give it an identity others might want to adopt.

Status and identity

Children are not as concerned with price and rational comparisons between products as adults[46] and are more likely to prefer brands that are in demand by their peers. From as early as six, children are aware of what is cool and what is not and wearing cool clothes – particularly those with high-status labels and logos – may be necessary not to experience social exclusion, as a study of English children between six and eleven found.[47]

Because of the efforts of marketers since the 1980s children are more brand conscious than any previous generation, 'particularly so when it comes to names, labels and brand symbols on the clothing they wear. Clothing has become more important to kids at an earlier age, and stature is conferred when the right brand name is on display'.[48]

This is particularly so for tweens, a developmental stage identified by marketers as being between childhood and being a teenager, somewhere between eight and 14 years old: 'They are in a transitional stage whereby peer acceptance is paramount but parental influence is still present. They are too old for toys but too young for teenage/adult entertainment.'[49] Sutherland and Thompson say this age is 'prime brand imprinting territory' because from age eight they 'look outside the family for information, socialising and context' and they are particularly susceptible to peer pressure and want to fit in: 'Brands are badges that help people belong, and kids want and need to belong.'[50]

Marketing consultant, Martin Lindstrom, notes of children between eight and 14, that 'to have the best is much the same as being the best' and that for nearly half the world's children of that age, 'the clothes and brands they wear describe who they are and define their social status'. He says that brands 'have become an integral part of the way tweens define' and express themselves, in school, at home and with their friends.[51] They are 'passionate' about brands.[52]

Brands are also integrated into teenage culture and identity, and teens indicate which group they identify with through their choice of brands.[53] 'Once kids bought an article of branded clothing at a department store; now they buy an entire identity, a whole set of clothes by one manufacturer at that brand's ersatz boutique. Kids become Prada girls or Old Navy chicks or Pacific Sun, a.k.a. PacSun boys.'[54]

Children also seem to be increasingly brand conscious in other products such as toys, video games and records/cassettes.[55] By definition cool is socially exclusive, and this is often because it is expensive.[56]

Viral marketing

Since cool is transmitted primarily between children, marketers seek to generate a 'buzz' about their products that is spread by word of mouth between children. This 'word-of-mouth marketing' is also referred to as 'viral marketing'. Viral marketing has the advantage that the product endorsement gains credibility because it comes from friends and personal contacts rather than from anonymous company spokespeople or advertisements. A survey of marketers found that half intended to use viral marketing in 2006 and thought it was the most important way to market to youth.[57]

Viral marketing is cheap and very effective because much of the marketing is done by the children themselves at no cost to the advertiser. These days it is not limited to face-to-face contact. Internet chat rooms, mobile phones, and email not only enable such communications to be fast but also to reach beyond immediate neighbourhoods to other states and other countries.

Marketers produce 'internet-based video clips, interactive online games, images or jokes' as well as animated icons (for example Kellogg's) and e-cards (McDonald's) for children to email to their friends.[58] Burger King, for instance, won an award for 'Most infectious viral campaign' for a website that featured a man dressed up as a chicken who was programmed to obey orders typed in by children on their keyboards.[59] The site was visited 46 million times in the first week as a result of its URL being passed around various internet networks.[60]

YouTube is increasingly used by marketers for viral marketing.[61] Wendy's posted several videos on the YouTube website designed to appeal to a young person's sense of humour. The videos had their commercial intent disguised and did not openly mention Wendy's but those who viewed them were directed to a Wendy's website.[62]

Three quarters of websites designed for children by food companies cultivate email-based viral marketing. Emails may include news and entertainment and brand characters and links to games or other incentives on the website. Children are often given incentives such as free gifts if they tell their friends about the site.[63]

In 2000 Procter and Gamble founded Tremor, a consultancy that uses teenagers to spread the word about its own products and those of around 50 other clients in the entertainment, consumer goods and other retail industries. It claims to have a team of 250,000 boys and girls aged between 13 and 19 it calls 'connectors' who have 'wide and deep social networks and a propensity to share product news'. These teens do not get paid but are attracted by expectations of being amongst the first to sample new products, listen to unreleased music and new movies, help design video games, and receive backstage concert passes, discount coupons and invites to parties.[64] Tremor connectors do not have to disclose to their friends that they are working for Tremor when they promote products.

UK children can become 'Dubit Insiders' and promote brands on the street, by talking to their friends about them, wearing and using the products, putting up flyers, and just telling everyone about it. For this service they get 'free stuff, prizes and cash'. Products such as Fanta and BiC use Dubit Insiders.[65]

Underground marketing

Viral marketing is part of a new suite of marketing techniques that seek to disguise themselves so that people do not realise they are being advertised to. These techniques are particularly successful with children and often go undetected by the gatekeepers: parents, teachers and community leaders.[66]

Underground marketing may involve sending people into schools, dressed as school girls, to give out energy drinks.[67] Nintendo Gameboy sends people dressed up in space suits to find birthday parties and playgrounds where they offer children the chance to try out its games. US marketing specialist Jonathan Ressler says: 'Maybe only 15 kids are hit [by the Nintendo squad] at a birthday party but kids talk, a lot – at school, with SMS, by phone.' He estimates that 15 kids can spread the word-of-mouth message to thousands more kids.[68]

Undercover marketing, sometimes referred to as buzz marketing, uses paid actors to pretend to be ordinary people in public places who just happen to be enamoured of a product. John Ressler, founder of Big Fat Promotions, which specialises in undercover marketing, says: 'If people ever know they're being marketed to, we're not doing our job properly.'[69]

The setting for undercover marketing may be a chat room or internet bulletin board where children come together. Marketing firms hire young gamers who are already active in these forums and so have established their credibility. They are given gift certificates and free games in return for posting messages that are enthusiastic about a particular video game.[70]

Marketing agents monitor children's chat rooms for long periods of times to immerse themselves in the culture and language, they then take part in the chat room and give out web addresses to 'drive traffic' to fake websites that have been created for marketing purposes. This is also termed 'infiltration marketing'.[71] According to Lindstrom there are several thousand 'product placement' or 'false' websites purporting to be put together by individuals.[72]

> They construct their site so it looks as if it's been created by a tween. It's essentially an ad, but it masquerades as a tween talking personally about life, friends and hobbies. As part of the conversation, brands are mentioned, specific links are targeted and there are even images that are designed to look unprofessional.[73]

Social networking websites such as Facebook and MySpace, which is very popular with teenagers all over the world, have also been utilised by marketers. Teenagers post profiles of themselves, including personal information, photos, blogs, videos and music. According to a report by the Berkeley Media Studies Group, 'The ability to capture data about millions of youth is a key reason why Rupert Murdoch's News Corp. (Fox TV) paid nearly $600 million to acquire MySpace.'[74]

Such sites have become attractive to advertisers who can create a profile for a brand, pay for banner ads, sponsor online interest groups, and pay members 'to talk up their brands'.[75] Advertisers spent around $350 million on networking sites in 2006 and this figure is expected to reach $1.8 billion by 2010.[76] Social networking sites provide great opportunities for viral marketing. Teenagers compile lists of 'friends' on these sites and in this way create networks with whom they can communicate all at once, for example through shared message boards and instant messaging. This gives advertisers the opportunity to create a character profile for their brand that can make friends and build networks. Some brands are even creating their own social networking sites for this purpose.[77]

MySpace offers advertisers 'a range of digital marketing opportunities for "Viral Networking" and "Digital Word of Mouth," including sophisticated software that can track the number of users viewing a branded ad' and 'custom promotional packages to help drive traffic to the branded profile'. For example, Wendy's fast food chain has almost a hundred thousand 'friends' in its MySpace network. It 'has been highly successful, generating "exponential" exposure for Wendy's every day.'[78]

Virtual worlds

Virtual worlds offer children an opportunity to create identities for themselves but increasingly they are being hijacked by commercial interests. For example, Habbo Hotel is a website with a three-dimensional chat environment and 2.9 million registered members. It targets ten- to 18-year-olds. Players adopt the identity of an animated character – an avatar – and interact with each other in a virtual world. Marketers are able to put brands on virtual products in this environment so that players not only see them but interact with them.[79]

Habbo Hotel is one of several internet sites designed by Alloy Media & Marketing. Others include alloy.com and delias.com, both fashion websites targeting twelve- to 24-year-old females, and ccs.com, an action-sports website for twelve- to 17-year-old males. Alloy claims to have '1500 clients including half of the Fortune 200' and that its youth network reaches 8.2 million young people.[80]

Virtual worlds are proliferating on the internet. Some virtual worlds are specifically designed to promote particular products, such as Kellogg's Go-Tart's site and MyCoke.com.[81] In others marketers create their own avatars to spread marketing messages. 'Chatbots' have been developed that utilise software to enable marketers to infiltrate and spread spam and advertising to chat sites and provide speech for marketer's avatars in virtual worlds by responding to cue words used by those participating. Coca-Cola and Burger King are reported to be using chatbots.[82]

Whyville.net is one of the several virtual worlds that have been specifically designed for children. It claims to have 1.7 million members and purports to offer education as well as entertainment, but it also sells marketers the opportunity for product placement.[83] Whyville has a newspaper, a beach, a museum, a town square, a City hall, games and activities, and an economy with its own currency.

Webkinz is a virtual world aimed at little girls, where they can purchase a virtual pet and care for it, as well as virtual dolls for which they buy a range of products like lip gloss and body spritzes and thereby learn about adult products that they will buy for themselves when they grow up. Websites like Webkinz that run virtual economies teach children to be consumers and portray the world as one where being a good citizen involves buying 'the right stuff'.[84]

Nickelodeon also launched a virtual world for children (six to 14) in 2007 called Nicktropolis where they can create a three-dimensional video version of themselves and design and fill virtual bedrooms with consumer items. They can go shopping in the virtual world as well as play games at a virtual amusement park. A Nickelodeon executive said: 'We are working with our partners to figure out the most appropriate way to insert advertising into the site that will not take away from the user experience yet still provide marketers the most value.'[85]

Such sites enable children and teenagers to create a fantasy identity with invented physical features, immerse themselves in a branded world, and interact with branded products including dressing their avatar in branded clothes. This enables them to experiment with possible identities at a time when they are forming their own identity. The danger is that their personal identity is likely to become associated with and shaped by brands.

EXPLOITING CHILDISH VULNERABILITIES

In Chapter 2 we discussed the way advertisers exploit children's lack of cynicism. Advertisers and marketers argue that today's children are more sophisticated than previous generations and, because they have grown up with ever-present selling messages, they understand them better. Such assertions are not backed up with empirical evidence. Children today may be more media savvy and cynical about advertisements but marketers are becoming more adept at hiding their intent. The boundaries between advertising and educational or entertainment content are disappearing.

Advertisers and marketers are also becoming far more knowledgeable about how to target children emotionally and get past their defences. Their research and marketing tactics are far more sophisticated than they ever were. They mine the academic literature and employ psychologists, anthropologists and market researchers to observe, survey, interview and study children, hold focus groups and even analyse children's drawings.

Marketing consultants want to know the ambitions and fantasies, desires, fears and concerns, behaviour and relationships of children so as to 'exploit their developmental vulnerabilities' and turn them into customers, now and in the future. Innovation Focus explains to its clients that its 'program has been designed to explore the hopes, wishes and dreams of children and to apply those discoveries to the growth of your business'.[86]

Marketers describe their efforts to bypass parental gatekeepers as 'kid empowerment'. They claim they are encouraging children's 'freedom' and 'autonomy' when really they are trying to 'justify making the young more vulnerable to the seductions of commercial predators'.[87] In 1999 a group of psychologists and related professionals wrote to the American Psychological Association about their concerns that psychologists were selling their expertise to companies, to provide them with insights into children's needs and relationships, so that they can better manipulate and exploit them. In the letter they stated:

> Advertising and marketing firms have long used the insights and research methods of psychology in order to sell products, of course. But today these practices are reaching epidemic levels, and with a complicity on the part of the psychological profession that exceeds that of the past. The result is an enormous advertising and marketing onslaught that comprises, arguably, the largest single psychological project ever undertaken.[88]

Anxieties and insecurities

Children, who may have begun to realise that advertisements are trying to persuade them to buy the product, are nevertheless easy prey to the manipulations of advertisers because of the pressure they feel 'to conform to group standards

---

Box 4.2   Marketing Conferences – Some Quotes

- *Kid Power Market Research 2002*, London[89]
  'Understand the basis of children's emotional loyalty and use these emotions effectively for marketing.'
  'Neuropsychology has proven that whenever rational thinking conflicts with emotion, emotion will win – if harnessed this can be a very powerful tool for marketing.'
  'Demonstration of cutting edge physiological recording techniques; eye tracking and Event Related Potential (ERP's) show the parts of the brain which become activated by different products and adverts.'

- *Teen Insight 2002*, London[90]
  'How do you identify teen need states and respond effectively to stay ahead?'
  'Semiometrie is a qualitative research tool that can effectively access the subconscious desires of respondents.'
  'Diary studies enable you to immerse yourself within teen culture where you can tap into their thoughts and feelings.'
  'Capture teens unarticulated motivates creating a more nuanced understanding of their unmet needs and expectations.'

- *Kid Power 2004*, Las Vegas[91]
  'How to use innovative research techniques to get under the skin of Gen X and Gen Y … specific examples of how to break into young people's heads and enlist them as participants in your brand experience.'

and mores' in order to belong.[92] Advertising manipulates them through their insecurities, seeking to define normality for them and shaping the identity they are beginning to form:[93] 'marketers have closely studied the adolescent process of identity formation, tailoring their strategies to the key emotional and behavioral experiences that are part of these important explorations of self'.[94]

Marketers promote identities based on branded 'lifestyles'. They hijack real emotions and attach them to trivial products thereby trivialising those emotions and encouraging children to form emotional attachments with products rather than people.[95] Marketers set out to make being cool the sole determinant of social success among young people. Advertisements promise that by purchasing their products children will be popular, successful and/or attractive. Consultant Nancy Shalek stated:

> Advertising at its best is making people feel that without their products, you're a loser. Kids are very sensitive to that. If you tell them to buy something, they are resistant. But if you tell them they'll be a dork if they don't, you've got their attention. You open up emotional vulnerabilities, and it's easy to do with kids because they're the most vulnerable.[96]

The emphasis of advertising on creating anxieties and insecurities has resulted in a generation that is insecure, lonely, frustrated and depressed. 'Bombarded with images of how they should look and what they should own, children struggle to keep up, suffering from stress; anxiety; increasingly lower satisfaction with themselves and their lives.'[97] For example, advertisers prefer to use long-legged, thin yet buxom, clear-complexioned, beautiful female models and this produces 'feelings of inadequacy and discomfort' amongst girls. The National Consumer Council (NCC) revealed that for adolescent girls in the UK their dissatisfaction with their body shape was correlated with how much they read fashion magazines and other studies correlate it to viewing television advertisements.[98]

In the world promoted by advertisers where every dissatisfaction can be fixed through a purchase, it is no surprise that the instances of teenagers accessing plastic surgery are rapidly increasing, particularly given the bombardment of pro-plastic surgery stories in magazines and on television shows.[99] Boys are not immune either. Many teenage boys are now buying powdered drinks, nutritional supplements and even steroids to achieve the muscular bodies featured on toy action figures, cartoon characters, and in advertisements.[100]

INCREASING MATERIALISM

Advertisements actively encourage children to seek happiness and esteem through consumption. Their interaction with marketing-based websites, games and other venues ensures that the 'languages and values of commerce' gradually become 'accepted as the standard filter' through which they 'read, interpret, understand and behave in the world'.[101]

The pervasive message that the endless barrage of advertising and marketing sends is that all problems can be solved and discontent banished by buying things, that it is cool to be wealthy, and that those who live modestly or shop at discount stores are 'losers'.[102] 'The process is so insidious that by the time a child gains the language and capacity to grasp what is occurring, his or her attention patterns, preferences, memories and aspirations cannot be neatly separated from the images and poetics of corporate strategy.'[103]

By promoting consumerism to children, marketers and advertisers are seeking to breed a new generation of hyper-consumers, and studies suggest (see Box 4.3) that they may be well on their way. Annual surveys of students starting university in the US have found that the percentage who say that developing 'a meaningful philosophy of life' is very important has been declining – reaching its lowest point (39 per cent) in 2003. This compares with 86 per cent in 1967. In contrast the percentage who say it is important to succeed financially hit a 13 year high of 74 per cent in 2003 compared with 59 per cent in 1977.[104]

Box 4.3   Materialism in Young People – Some Study Findings

In the US:

- What sixth-grade boys want most is money.[105]
- More than one in three nine- to 14-year-olds prefer buying things to most other things they do. Almost two thirds are only interested in jobs that pay lots of money.[106]
- Ninety per cent of parents believe that media-based marketing 'contributes to their children becoming too materialistic'.[107]
- Almost two thirds of parents believe that 'their children define their self-worth in terms of what they own' and more than two thirds think commercialism has an undesirable impact on their children's values and worldviews.[108]

In the UK:

- Young people aged ten to 19 'are now avid shoppers' but 'they are the least happy generation of the post-war era'.[109]

In Australia:

- Children between eight and twelve, particularly boys, are 'obsessed' with money and entrepreneurship.[110]

Allen Kanner, a child psychologist, has observed that children are becoming increasingly consumerist, with a growing desire for material goods and to be rich when they grow up, rather than becoming famous or a top athlete or very clever: 'The most stark example is when I ask them what they want to do when they grow up. They all say they want to make money. When they talk about their friends, they talk about the clothes they wear, the designer labels they wear, not the person's human qualities.'[111]

The US-based Motherhood Project claimed that the values promoted in advertising – 'that life is about selfishness, instant gratification, and materialism' – were in conflict with the values that parents try to teach their children: 'that children should care about others, that they should be able to govern themselves, and that there is more to life than material things'.[112] It claimed that small children were being targeted with 'sophisticated advertisements designed to cultivate as early as possible a restless and insatiable appetite for wanting and buying things' and taught a value system that 'promotes self-indulgence, assaults the idea of restraint' and 'promotes the notion that our identity is determined by what we buy'.[113]

The deception and manipulation involved in advertisements aimed at children is likely to undermine the ability of children to trust others.[114] It also teaches young people how to manipulate others.[115] This is exacerbated by the use of children in viral marketing campaigns. Kanner notes that as children 'come to identify with brands, logos, and ultimately with corporations themselves ... their ability to critically evaluate the corporate structure and to decide if it is truly delivering on its utopian promises' is likely to be undermined.[116]

Advertisements encourage children to be impulsive and hedonistic.[117] The 'preoccupation with individual consumption', which is encouraged by marketing, is damaging to individual well-being and detrimental to society.[118] The more time people spend thinking about consuming material goods, working to attain them, and shopping to get them, 'the less time is devoted to activities that satisfy non-material needs – family and friends, creative and artistic endeavours, spiritual practices, etc.'[119]

A number of studies have demonstrated that people in various countries who are strongly materialist tend to be more stressed and anxious, have less satisfying relationships, poorer self-esteem, and be less concerned about others and the environment.[120] Psychologist, Tim Kassell, claims that a materialist orientation leads people to be less content with their lives, and to be more likely to take drugs and over-indulge in alcohol.[121] Juliet Schor's research has also found that 'Involvement in consumer culture causes dysfunction in the forms of depression, anxiety, low self-esteem, and psychosomatic complaints.'[122]

5
Teaching Consumer Values

The '3 Rs' have now become the '4 Rs,' with the fourth R being 'retail'.[1]

Young Minds Inspired (YMI) produces corporate materials for schools that masquerade as 'educational' but are in reality a 'targeted, effective, and cost-efficient marketing vehicle'.[2] Its website sells the following service to corporate advertisers: 'Each YMI program transforms your brand, service and/or product into the central focus of engaging, motivational and educational materials that are used over a period of weeks or months to generate high student interest, interaction and learning.'[3] YMI claims to be able to reach over eight million pre-school students, 28 million elementary school students, 23 million secondary school students and 15 million college students: 'We reach all these audiences in the uncluttered environment where students spend the better part of their day and where lasting attitudes are formed – in the classroom.'[4]

Established as Youth Marketing International in 1995, YMI expanded 'the concept of in-school marketing' from the US to Western Europe, Mexico, Latin America, Asia and the Pacific Rim.[5] YMI's clients include Toys 'R' Us, Kraft, Pfizer, Lego, McDonald's, Hasbro, and several entertainment conglomerates and television networks. One of its many projects included designing a middle/junior high school programme for Clearasil, to promote its skin care products, that 'wove product information into a comprehensive program addressing basic hygiene, skin care, and self-esteem issues commonly associated with puberty'. YMI helped to introduce Care Bears to a pre-school audience through a kit that supposedly taught children the importance of caring as well as counting and colour recognition skills.[6] YMI claims its programs will:

- Integrate your brand into lessons and activities that students will spend hours interacting with in a positive and meaningful way.
- Give your message special credibility and importance to young people as well as their parents, by having teachers they admire and respect present these materials in the classroom.
- Extend your message beyond the classroom via take-home activities.
- Deliver the message that your company values learning and cares about families.[7]

In the UK, MBA is a business communications agency that offers corporate clients 'a highly effective means ... to build their brands and extend their market' with classroom materials that can reach 4.4 million school children. Its clients include AstraZeneca, Cadbury Schweppes, IBM, Kellogg's, McDonald's, Nestlé, and Procter & Gamble.[8]

Corporate produced educational materials are not new. Schools have been used by corporations to promote consumerism since the 1920s. However today there is a corporate stampede to get commercial messages into schools through 'educational' resources while potential customers are very young. US schools receive around $2.5 billion each year from commercial relationships with corporations,[9] money that the schools desperately need because of a deficit in government funding. 'Corporations eager to enhance their public image, increase product visibility and establish consumer lifestyles are responding to America's education crisis en mass.'[10]

Public relations firms and advertisers have targeted school education in a big way since the 1990s throughout the English speaking world. In the UK the National Union of Teachers (NUT) notes the 'unprecedented increase in the use of commercial materials in schools, with UK brands spending an estimated £300m a year on targeting the classroom to increase sales'.[11] Businesses seek to sell their goods to children, develop brand loyalty now and into the future, and improve their image. A brochure for a Kid Power Market Research conference in London offered to help companies 'Assess how kids understand the marketing process and how to use it to advantage or circumvent it within the school environment.'[12]

Schools are an attractive environment for advertisers because they are relatively 'uncluttered' – there are not thousands of other advertisements so the few advertisements stand out more and will attract more attention. What is more, because children have to attend school and pay attention when they are there, they are a 'captive' audience – they can't change channels or stations and are not distracted by other things going on. Parents are not present to act as gatekeepers. Advertisers also gain from the positive association with education and the implied endorsement and tacit approval of educational authorities and teachers for their messages.

DE-FUNDING SCHOOLS

Under-funded schools are especially vulnerable to the intrusion of commercialism. They are offered cash, books, computers and equipment in return for the minds and market potential of their students. In the UK the NUT has expressed its concern that the school funding crisis 'is placing pressure on some schools to be involved in corporate promotions because of their budget difficulties'.[13] In Canada, the Ontario Secondary School Teachers' Federation claims that budget cuts by provincial governments in the 1990s have made the school system a major target for business interests who seek to fill the resource gap.[14] In Australia state departments of education have encouraged corporate sponsorship of school activities, a situation which the Federation of Parents and Citizens Association of NSW views as 'a Government abrogating its responsibility to provide a free, secular education'.[15]

School funding cuts began in the 1980s in many English-speaking nations as part of broader government policies of reducing government deficits and tax burdens on business. In New Zealand teaching workloads have increased and class sizes are large in many schools.[16] Some schools are forced to defer maintenance.[17] In Britain, the Thatcher government reduced school funding in real terms by 10 per cent between 1979 and 1986.[18] Some 50,000 teachers were removed, against the trend in most other developed nations, so that class sizes began to increase, despite declining pupil numbers. Music and French classes, sport and library facilities, were cut. Schools sold off more than 5000 playing fields between 1981 and 1999 to make up for funding inadequacies.[19]

In Australia, payments from the federal government to the states fell and state tax revenues declined in the early 1990s. As a result, state governments cut educational expenditure causing class sizes to rise.[20] Hundreds of public schools were closed[21] and 'over 8000 teaching position were designated in excess of need'.[22] Public spending on school education declined from 5.9 per cent of GDP in the mid 1970s to 2.7 per cent of GDP at the turn of the century, despite the desire of a vast majority of voters that more be spent on schools.[23] Australia's school spending ranking fell to 15th out of 17 OECD countries.[24] Consequently many schools around the country became dilapidated.

In NSW, for example, whilst the government was spending $1.6 billion on the Olympic Games, school maintenance programmes were suspended, leaving schools with blocked toilets, termite infestations, leaking roofs and other problems.[25] NSW schools depend on fundraising to pay for the most basic educational provision as well as gas and electricity bills, school buildings and teacher salaries.[26]

In Canada, total government spending on public education declined from the late 1990s. This was in response to government budget deficits created by large tax cuts that had been given to wealthy individuals and corporations.[27] In Alberta school funding was cut by 12 per cent over three years.[28] In Québec, the education budget was cut in terms of percentage of GDP by some $2.5 billion between 1992/3 and 2002/3.[29] In Ontario school funding was cut by more than a billion dollars during the mid 1990s, causing a decline in educational quality that saw many parents moving their children to private schools.[30]

The funding shortfalls mean that Canadian teachers are often forced to use their own money for essential teaching tools, professional development and humanitarian purposes such as lunches for hungry students. Teachers spend an average of $1000 a year on teaching aids and courses, according to an estimate by the Canadian Teachers Federation.[31] The same is true in poor American schools where individual teachers spend their own money on basic stationery items for their classes such as paper, pencils and paper clips and sometimes even soap and toilet paper for school bathrooms. (It is estimated that in aggregate this cost is around $1 billion per year.[32])

By 2006 all but five state governments in the US had been sued for failing to provide adequate funding for a sound basic education, a right guaranteed by most state constitutions.[33] Between 1989 and 2006, 20 states lost education funding adequacy lawsuits and seven states won them. Lawsuits were pending in twelve states.[34] Adequate funding was defined in a New York lawsuit as funding that would provide for 'sufficient numbers of qualified teachers, appropriate class sizes, adequate buildings, up-to-date books, libraries, technology and laboratories and an expanded curriculum for at-risk students'.[35]

Despite the lawsuits, 17 states cut school funding in 2002 and at least twelve made cuts in 2003 because of dwindling state revenues and an unwillingness to increase taxes.[36] These cuts were made even though the public tends to view public education as a top priority, according to the polls, and is opposed to school funding cuts.[37]

In 2003 the New York Court of Appeals ruled that the state was not fulfilling its responsibility to provide a minimal standard of high school education to all students because of deficient funding by the state to schools in New York City. One in five of these schools, which are mainly attended by poor black and Latino students, don't have gymnasiums, while more than half don't have playgrounds. After 13 years of litigation the New York Court of Appeals ruled in 2006 that the state must spend at least $1.93 billion extra on public schools in New York City each year.[38]

School fundraising

In order to raise money for essential educational resources such as computers, software, building extensions, libraries and curriculum materials, schools have to raise extra funds. They do this with food drives, raffles, dances, fetes and fun runs, as well as hiring out facilities. Parents in NSW 'are also putting in thousands of hours of voluntary labour to clean toilets, maintain gardens and repair playground equipment'.[39] Schools also increasingly raise money through sponsorship deals and marketing arrangements such as the leasing or selling of school land and sale of advertising space.[40]

In Australia fundraising provides approximately one-third of the average public school's operating expenses not counting government-funded salaries and capital costs.[41] Victorian schools raise funds to pay for 'up to 60 per cent of school discretionary budgets for computers, staff, libraries, and capital works'.[42] In New

Zealand, most schools cannot meet their commitments, including staffing for additional learning support for subjects such as English as a Second Language and for children with special needs, without fundraising efforts.[43] Canadian schools are also forced to undertake their own fundraising activities.[44]

It is as if under-funding of schools is part of a corporate strategy to enable advertisers better access. At the very least corporate 'sponsorship' of school activities and donation of school resources enables the under-funding of schools by governments to continue.[45]

PRODUCT SALES

Junk food

In the 1990s soft drink and fast food companies began offering schools various deals for selling their products within school boundaries to the exclusion of other brands. In the case of beverages such contracts are called 'pouring rights'. In return companies like Coca-Cola and Pepsi offer schools that install their vending machines a percentage of sales and sometimes extras such as signing bonuses, equipment, scholarships and internships.[46]

Often schools are given a financial incentive to sell as much soft drink as they can so that the schools actively promote soft drink consumption. In one well-

---

Box 5.1 **Junk Food in Schools – Some Examples**

In the US:

- Seventy-five per cent of high schools had exclusive agreements with beverage companies for vending machines.[47]
- Some schools have replaced their federally subsidised school lunch programme with privatised food services from fast food giants Taco Bell, McDonald's, Pizza Hut and Subway.[48]
- Taco Bell is in 3000 school cafeterias and Pizza Hut in 4500.[49]

In Canada:

- 56 per cent of high schools have an exclusive agreement with soft drink manufacturers.[50]
- Some high schools in British Columbia also offer McDonald's, Kentucky Fried Chicken (KFC) and Subway food outlets for school lunches.[51]

In the UK:

- Vending machines selling soft drinks, crisps and sweets can earn English schools the equivalent of two teachers' salaries.[52]
- Branded vending machines have been banned in Scotland and Wales.[53]

publicised example, in 1998 a Colorado school district official sent a letter to schools instructing principals to let students have free access to Coca-Cola vending machines all day, and even to let students drink Coca-Cola in class, in order for the district to receive a bonus payment for the sale of 70,000 cases of Coke in a year.[54] In another school district the contract required the school to sell the equivalent of 1.6 cans of Coke per pupil every day for ten years.[55]

In 1999 it was noted in *Beverage Industry* magazine that it was important to get elementary school children drinking soft drinks because at that age they 'are still establishing their tastes and habits'. By 2001 soft drinks, or soda, had 'become a staple food for American children' with teenage males drinking more than two 20 oz cans per day.[56]

This increased consumption of soft drinks not only raised the incidence of obesity but, because it often replaced milk, increased the incidence of osteoporosis and bone fractures as a result of low levels of calcium; increased the incidence of dental cavities because of the acidity of the drinks; and increased classroom behavioural problems because of the caffeine in cola drinks. The money gained by schools for these contracts is therefore at the expense of the long-term health of the school children.[57]

Legislation to stop in-school marketing of junk foods has been resisted in the US for several years now. Coca-Cola hired Holland & Knight to lobby against the federal Better Nutrition for School Children Act of 2001 which would have prevented soft drinks from being sold or provided as part of school lunches.[58] As opposition to pouring rights contracts grew in the US in 2003, Coca-Cola became a sponsor of the National Parent Teacher Association (PTA).[59]

Efforts to legislate against junk food in schools were defeated by vested interests in Maryland in 2001, and in Connecticut, Arizona, New Mexico and Oregon in 2005.[60] By 2006 38 states were trying to bring in legislation to regulate food in schools, and particularly vending machines, and 14 states had passed such laws. Beverage companies were also under threat of legal action by the Center for Science in the Public Interest (CSPI) for promoting and selling unhealthy products in schools.[61]

Consequently, in 2006 Coca-Cola, PepsiCo and Cadbury Schweppes, which 'control more than 90 percent of school sales' announced that they would phase out sweetened drinks from elementary schools.[62] Similar voluntary agreements were made in Canada and NSW, Australia in 2004 in the wake of government efforts to ban them, although in these cases, soft drinks would still be sold in high schools.[63]

Such agreements allow the companies to continue promoting their brand through sales of bottled water, low-fat milk and pure fruit juice. Winning brand loyalty from a new generation is more important to soft drink companies than actual school sales, which make up less than one per cent of total sales in North

America.[64] Moreover, schools trying to get out of existing contracts with these soft drink companies are finding it too expensive because of contract penalty clauses rendering the voluntary industry agreement ineffective for the term of their contracts, which can be up to ten years.[65]

Fundraising schemes

Schools around the world raise funds by selling commercial products such as chocolate, sweets, drinks, sweet baked goods, magazines and other items, often door-to-door or at fundraising events. They also engage in coupon redemption programmes. These are schemes whereby marketers increase their sales by offering schools computer equipment or other 'free' gifts in return for a certain number of cash register dockets from the participating store, collected by pupils, parents and teachers. For example Apple Computers has operated a number of such schemes in conjunction with supermarket chains in the US and Australia and WHSmith and Boots introduced promotions involving donations of school equipment in return for shopping purchase vouchers in the UK.[66]

Other retailers offer a percentage of sales receipts to schools when parents sign up. These include Target and Office Depot.[67] McDonald's, KFC and Domino's Pizzas have also given schools a portion of profits from fast food sales, thereby encouraging students to coerce parents and others to buy pizzas or hamburgers in order to raise money for their schools.[68] McDonald's McTeacher nights involve teachers, principals and school administrators serving as McDonald's behind-the-counter employees for a night in return for 20–25 per cent of takings going to their school.[69] In Canada schools get free gym equipment for allowing Ronald McDonald to visit their school to talk to children about healthy living.[70]

Companies taking part in fundraising schemes not only encourage sales of their products, but gain favourable publicity and community goodwill for their

---

Box 5.2   Some Coupon Redemption Schemes

Campbell's Labels for Education
Seventy-five thousand schools and organizations, covering 42 million students, participated in the US and Canada.[71]

General Mills' BoxTops4Education
More than 71,000 schools participated in 2002.[72]

Nestlé's Box Tops for Books
Thousands of schools in the UK participate.[73]

Walkers' Books for Schools
By 2004, 36,000 schools and nursery schools in the UK (85 per cent of them) had taken part.[74]

'philanthropy', which comes at a very small cost. For example, Tesco's corporate objectives in running its *Computers for Schools* scheme in the UK and Ireland include enhanced corporate profile in the community, improved customer loyalty, recognition as an innovative retailer and increased sales.[75]

The children associate the brand with getting 'free' equipment for their school and both parents and children become promoters for the company in their efforts to collect dockets or vouchers and eat fatty, sugary or salty food for the sake of the school. In the meantime, there is less pressure on governments to fund schools adequately so they can afford to buy the computing and sports equipment they need.

However, the returns to schools are very small. For example, in the UK, teachers and librarians involved in collecting and submitting coupons for Walkers' *Books for Schools* scheme generally found that the time and effort was not worth it for the disappointing assortment of books they received. They claimed that the choice of books was limited and included 'old titles and unsuitable texts'.[76]

Similarly Australian families spent $82 million in 2001 at Westfield Shopping Centres in return for $1 million worth of Packard Bell computers. Winning schools later complained that the computers were defective and many broke down after their warranties expired.[77] UK families spent £110,000 at Tesco supermarkets in return for a single computer.[78]

DIRECT ADVERTISING

Increasingly schools are selling themselves as sites for advertising, which is appearing on sporting scoreboards, in hallways, on gymnasium floors, on bulletin boards, on school stationery and equipment, and even on rooftops. School lunch menus have advertisements on them for movies and toys.[79] Some schools sell businesses the right to public-address announcements at sports events.[80] Schools also receive free product samples and discount coupons.[81] Schools in the US, Canada, the UK and NZ have sold the right to name parts of the school, most commonly sports facilities such as the Shop Rite gymnasium in a New Jersey School, as well as for the whole school such as the Bairds Mainfreight Primary School in NZ.[82]

A European Commission report from the 1990s found that advertising exists in schools throughout Europe, regardless of whether it has been banned – as in Belgium, France and Germany – or is unregulated – as in the UK, the Netherlands and Ireland. The report claimed that schools benefited from 'the penetration of marketing into schools' because it provided resources and even some educational value in that it exposes school children to the world of business and advertising techniques.[83]

JazzyMedia produces JazzyBooks which are free exercise books for UK school children that contain pages of games along with advertisements. JazzyMedia also distributes advertising-oriented displays, activities and samples.[84] Its products are used in 10,000 schools in the UK and by hundreds of thousands of Australian students.[85] Its clients include Cartoon Network, Disney, EMI, GlaxoSmithKline, Hasbro, Masterfoods and Pepsi.

Schools in the US receive cartons of unsolicited book covers prominently featuring advertisements for a variety of products including clothes, snacks, television shows and toiletries.[86] Cover Concepts provides free book covers to schools that feature advertisements from companies such as Kellogg's, McDonald's, Nike and Calvin Klein. It also distributes other sponsored material including comics, teachers' guides, bookmarks, locker posters, calendars, colouring sheets, growth charts, and health and beauty samples. It claims to reach 30 million school students in 43,000 public schools, as well as 1.2 million children in day-care centres and five million in libraries.[87]

Broadcasting

In the late 1980s Chris Whittle realised that teenagers were 'the new pipeline into American households'.[88] To take advantage of this pipeline, Whittle Communications founded Channel One. From 1990 Channel One loaned schools VCRs, televisions and a satellite dish 'in exchange for students' minds for 12 minutes each day'.[89] By 2007 Channel One was being shown to seven million students across the nation – 30 per cent of middle and high school students in the US.[90]

Box 5.3   Alloy Media and Marketing

Alloy Media and Marketing took over Channel One in 2007. The company is already oriented towards advertising and marketing to children. It runs various virtual worlds for children, including Habbo Hotel (see Chapter 4), and claims to be the industry's largest in-school advertising network of media boards, covering 8 million US students. Alloy tells its clients: 'We have the power to connect you to students ... our print and web products reach them at home, school, and online to meet your specific marketing goals.'[91]

Channel One's contract with schools requires 90 per cent of the students at a school to watch the twelve-minute program 90 per cent of the time, from beginning to end and without interruption.[92] That twelve minutes includes two minutes of paid advertising, although Alloy has stopped the advertising for sweets, soft drinks and snacks that once dominated these ad breaks. Channel One marketers can promise their advertisers an environment without 'the usual distractions of telephones, stereos, remote controls, etc.'.[93] It is also an opportunity to reach children who don't watch television much at home.

> Students in schools with *Channel One* are required to attend to the television screen in a fashion unprecedented in the history of the medium, they watch ads in a structured environment with an authority figure demanding their attention. They watch in an environment of peer influence.[94]

The deal is quite coercive for schools that sign up for a three-year contract. If they break the contract, for example if teachers interrupt or turn off the broadcast whilst it is being aired, then schools are 'financially liable for the cost of cabling school buildings and for the removal of video equipment'.[95] Channel One facilities are found mainly in poorer neighbourhoods. Schools that can afford their own video equipment tend to reject the deal and sign up with a commercial-free news programme.[96]

In a study investigating the effects of Channel One advertising, researchers at Michigan State University found that children exposed to it 'expressed more consumer-oriented attitudes than nonviewers' and had more materialistic attitudes. Whilst children often watch ads on television at home it has been found that discussing the ads with parents negates the effect of the ads to some extent and reduces the subsequent materialism in children whereas Channel One precludes that. The researchers concluded that 'advertising to school students is harmful to their value system'.[97]

Another study by a researcher at the University of Missouri-Columbia, found that most teenagers were quite naive about the advertisements they saw on Channel One. They were not always able to distinguish between advertisements and news items. One Pepsi advertisement, which less than half the students identified as a real advertisement, even confused the student teacher.[98] A study of 3000 Channel One viewing students in North Carolina found that most of them thought the products advertised would be good for them because they were being shown the advertisements at school.[99] A recent study found that students watching Channel One had purchased an average of 2.5 out of eleven items advertised on Channel One in the previous three months. And 27 per cent believed the commercials had been approved by their teachers.[100]

Channel One is not the only outfit broadcasting advertisements into schools. In Canada, Youth News Network offered schools a very similar service of news programmes interspersed with advertisements but ended up being banned in six provinces and went out of business.[101] BusRadio is a national radio programme broadcast exclusively to US school buses and offers advertisers 'a unique and effective way to reach the highly sought after teen and tween market'. It reaches 1.5 million school students on 14,000 buses. There are a maximum of eight minutes of straight advertising in every hour of broadcast plus two minutes for contests. Most of the rest is music and news.[102]

Field trips and theatre

In the US, the National Theatre for Children is a for-profit company that puts on short plays in schools that contain corporate messages. Its brochure offers corporations a way to incorporate their brands 'into a fun, educational setting'. However schools often assume that the National Theatre for Children is a non-profit organisation with no commercial agenda.[103]

Field Trip Factory Inc. began operating in Chicago in 1998 and organises thousands of business-sponsored field trips for school children to places like Dominos' Pizzas and Toys 'R' Us stores in 43 states. The trips are free for the children but the businesses visited pay Field Trip Factory to organise the field trip, train company personnel and create a curriculum to give the trips an educational feel.[104]

Individual companies also run field trips. Nike offers poor schools a partnership that includes four free field trips and payment to the schools for each hour the students spend at the Nike Campus, where they are given a tour, shown pre-release Nike commercials and given a bag full of free gifts 'all emblazoned, of course, with the Nike swoosh'.[105] In the UK school children can visit Tesco stores where they are shown healthy foods, how an electronic till operates, and how to buy flowers for Mother's Day. They are given a chance to ice a biscuit and some freebies to take home.[106]

CORPORATE PROMOTION

Corporate promotion does not necessarily aim to sell goods directly, but to foster brand loyalty in children over time, through familiarity gained from exposure to corporate brands and their positive association with school activities, as well as implicit messages about branded products. In Australia, Nestlé, Telecom, Pepsi, Coca-Cola, Hungry Jack's, North Forest Products and BHP have all sponsored school activities.[107]

Many firms sponsor and fund scholarships and contests as a way of associating their brands with educational endeavours. (Contests and competitions often have the additional aim of promoting direct sales of a product, through visits to the store or website.) For example, the American Automobile Association runs a national competition, the AAA Travel High School Challenge, which promotes the idea of travel and at the same time advertises a number of airlines, hotels and other sponsors.[108] Paul Kurnit, president and founder of Kidshop, a marketing consultancy, points out that contests are much cheaper than television advertisements but still give children 'the brand experience'.[109]

Box 5.4   **Some Examples of Contests and Scholarships**

In the US:

- Forty-five per cent of Californian schools participated in scholarship programmes run by food and beverage companies.[110]
- Nestlé gives a $10,000 prize and five $5000 prizes for creative art that features their product SweeTarts. In 2003, 5200 schools took part in the contest.[111]
- Oscar Mayer gives $10,000 prizes for singing its advertising jingles for its weiners and bologna.[112]

In Canada:

- Toyota funds fifteen $5000 scholarships for students who have excelled in environmental community service. This not only advertises the Toyota brand but associates it with environmental protection at a time when car manufacturers are being criticised for their contribution to air pollution.[113]

In Europe:

- Kellogg's has organised competitions on nutrition.[114]
- Bayer has organised science competitions.[115]

In Ireland:

- Real Event Solutions in Ireland specialises in 'Creating unique and exciting schools-based events and competitions in the Republic of Ireland and Northern Ireland' that achieve national media coverage and 'branding opportunities'. Its clients have included Coca-Cola, Hewlett Packard (HP), Wella and Pot Noodle.[116]

Motivational and incentive schemes are also effective at associating brand names with school success – a first step in creating loyal customers. Dunkin' Donuts, Krispy Kreme doughnuts, Papa John's Pizza's and McDonald's all provide free products to students for good grades or good behaviour.[117] Pizza Hut's *Book It* programme awards free pizzas as learning incentives for students in various countries to achieve reading goals. According to Pizza Hut, *Book It* involves 22 million school students in 900,000 classrooms.[118] The programme has even expanded to pre-schoolers – who have the books read to them.

McDonald's also offers incentives for good spelling and reading.[119] In an internal 'Operations Manual' for local store managers in the 1990s, McDonald's noted: 'Schools offer excellent opportunities. Not only are they a high traffic [sales] generator, but students are some of the best customers you could have.'[120] The judge in the McLibel case subsequently ruled that McDonald's 'exploits children' with its marketing.[121] However, as McDonald's argued at the time, its marketing is not very different from other food companies.

Motivational schemes which offer meals not only give the child 'an opportunity to increase restaurant visits by potential customers'[122] but usually involve the whole family accompanying the child when they go to collect their prize and buying additional meals for other family members. Moreover, instead of teaching children the joy of reading, motivational schemes bribe children to read and there is the danger that they will read shorter, easier books to reach their goal of free fast food earlier: 'Instead of an interest in reading the activity promotes an interest in pizza.'[123]

Sponsorship is another way that marketers achieve brand awareness and the association of the company symbols with 'need satisfiers', for example the association of children's sporting events or arts events with particular brands and logos. Nike and Levi's also sponsor end-of-year parties for schools.[124] Sponsorship is 'a cheap and effective way for corporations to gain goodwill in the community' whilst getting an 'enormous amount of exposure' for corporate brands.[125]

Thirty per cent of Canadian schools have some sort of sponsorship arrangements with business to provide services such as tutoring, technology courses, extracurricular activities, staff and even academic courses.[126] In North Vancouver, Home Depot donated money to build a playground and at its opening school children had to wear Home Depot shirts and sing 'Who are we! Home Depot! What do we do? Build playgrounds!'[127]

SPONSORED EDUCATIONAL MATERIALS

Teachers today are being overwhelmed with free and unsolicited curriculum material from public relations firms, corporations and industry associations.[128] The great advantage of commercial messages in sponsored learning materials over more direct advertising materials is that any residual scepticism with which conventional advertisements might be treated disappears altogether when it comes to advertisements and public relations material secreted within school lessons. As one writer pointed out: 'Imagine – your target market not only reads your ads – they get tested on them.'[129]

In the UK the Department for Education and Skills (DfES) encourages the production and use of corporate materials in schools. It states on one of its websites that the benefits to corporations include the opportunity to 'gain new and more loyal customers'.[130] The DfES, the Consumers' Union and the ISBA (the association for British advertisers) have put together a 'Best Practice Principles' for commercial activities in schools that say commercial activities can be of benefit to schools but: 'Explicit sales messages should be avoided where possible, but may be unavoidable in the context of collector schemes. ... The level of branding should be appropriate to the activity.'[131]

Product placement in class

In the 1990s some corporate-sponsored educational materials were blatant in their advertising. Software for teaching children to read required them to read sentences such as 'I like eating at McDonald's' or 'I like drinking Pepsi'.[132] Campbell's early lesson-plan posters, distributed to 12,000 teachers, showed children how to do science with an experiment to show how its spaghetti sauce is thicker than its competitors'.[133] A science course put together by Pepsi and others involved the students doing taste tests on cola drinks, analysing them and taking a video tour of a Pepsi factory as well as actually visiting one.[134]

In 1998 a literacy kit, 'Brand Knew', was launched in Perth, Australia. It purported to teach reading and word skills to children from four years old with games and stories incorporating brand names and corporate logos. The rationale was that children recognised brand names before most other words and the aim was to sell a place in the kit to corporations for $10,000 each, in return for 'brand recognition and awareness'.[135] A similar rationale was used in an instructional reading software program for the same age group entitled 'Read-A-Logo' which was used by schools in Texas.[136]

McGraw-Hill's textbook *Mathematics: Applications and Connections*, published in second edition in 1999, used brand names, photos of products and corporate logos to teach how mathematics applies in the real world. Students work out problems like how long it would take to be able to buy a pair of Nike shoes, given a particular weekly allowance.[137] They are asked to 'express the diameter of an Oreo cookie as a fraction' but as part of the background information for the exercise are told that 'The best-selling packaged cookie in the world is the Oreo

---

Box 5.5   **More Examples of Product Placements in Class Activities**

- *Reese's Pieces: Count by Fives; Hershey's Milk Chocolate Bar Fractions Book; Skittles Math Riddles;* and *The Cheerios Play Book,* of which 1.2 million copies had been sold by the end of 2000, all teach young children to do maths using branded products.[138]
- Nabisco's math curriculum asks children to estimate the number of chocolate chips in a bag of its Chips-A-Hoy.[139]
- Revlon's school materials teach children about 'good and bad hair days'.[140]
- Disney's *Comics in the Classroom* uses comics to teach third-grade children to read and write.[141]
- Procter & Gamble produces an educational package entitled *Always Changing: About You: Puberty and Stuff* that includes a video and reading materials, which advise students about using antiperspirant, and product samples such as an Old Spice stick for boys.[142]
- The makers of Clearasil distribute an 'educational' package on skin care complete with product samples and a brochure directing students to a website with games and sweepstakes.[143]

cookie.' The book was used by schools in 15 states in the US and was originally offered free in California.[144]

McGraw-Hill's website has included maths lessons that featured Crayola and Hershey products: 'One exercise has students selecting items from Hershey's online catalogue and then calculating the shipping charges and taxes.'[145] Breakthrough to Literacy, a McGraw-Hill company, produces *Take-Me-Home* books as a classroom resource. Its current website suggests one activity might be to 'place marshmallows or M&M's on words matching those read by the teacher'.[146]

These days the corporate message tends to be more subtle. The materials can be hard for teachers to resist, particularly those from poorly resourced schools,[147] because they are professionally produced with lots of colour and games, prepared homework assignments and even computers that automatically grade the students work, and are generally offered free of charge.[148]

COMMERCIALISM IN EDUCATION

The shortage of funding, prompted in no small part by the unwillingness of corporations to pay their taxes, is encouraging schools to allow those same corporations to turn schools into yet another advertising and marketing venue. In the process, the health, well-being and critical-thinking skills of school children are being undermined in the name of education.

The corporate infiltration of the school buildings and curriculum is training students to be consumers and corporate supporters rather than citizens with a capacity for critical thought. In a limited curriculum, the more business/consumer oriented material there is, the less alternative material there will be. Moreover,

Table 5.1   Educational versus Commercial Agendas

Educational Agenda	Commercial Agenda
Learning is student-centred	Learning is product/brand focused
Student as citizen	Student as consumer
Democratic and egalitarian in outlook	Discriminates according to purchasing power
Learning as a questioning, critical process	Closed, pre-determined learning outcomes – just swallow the message
Active, discovery-learning	Passive, receptive experience
Coherent, thematically-based spiral curriculum	Fragmented, isolated lessons depending on the sponsor
Led by educational research and local tradition	Led by commercial interest, subject to the highest bidder

Source: 'Opposing Commercialism in Schools: Distorting Education', Campaign for Commercial-Free Education, Ireland, http://www.commercialfreeeducation.com/opposing-distortingeducation.html

the more dependent a school is on corporate funds, the less likely they will be to teach students 'to question the means and motivations of business'.[149]

George Gerbner notes that with advertising and commercialism infiltrating every aspect of life, education has been – until now – 'the only large-scale institutional corrective capable of reordering priorities and cultivating within students some sense of detached, analytical skill'. But this is being undermined by the increasing infiltration of schools by corporations. True education stimulates 'a skeptical and critical view' whereas corporations promote their products.[150]

Similarly Michael J. Sandle argues in *The New Republic*:

> Advertising encourages people to want things and to satisfy their desires: education encourages people to reflect on their desires, to restrain or to elevate them. The purpose of advertising is to recruit consumers; the purpose of public schools is to cultivate citizens ... Rather than raise the public funds we need to pay the full cost of educating our schoolchildren, we choose instead to sell their time and rent their minds to Burger King and Mountain Dew.[151]

The irony is that whilst advertising and public relations material is taking up more and more of the school day, advertisers are starting to fear that this may affect literacy and the ability of consumers to read their advertisements. An article in *Brandweek* was subtitled: 'Lower academic standards affect ability of marketers to reach consumers.'[152]

6
Turning Schools into Businesses

> Allan White is the general manager of a $4.5 million business with 1000 teenage clients all wanting to buy a bright future. In short he runs a high school ... [It] boasts a management team, which includes the executive officer (principal), and line managers (two assistant principals and a pivotal business manager).[1]

In New York City, Joel Klein was hired to run the schools in 2002. He had almost no experience as an educator and his previous job was as CEO of the transnational media company Bertelsmann. Klein believes schools should be run like businesses. He hired private consultants to advise him and 'installed a cabinet of mostly noneducators making six-figure salaries'.[2] On occasion he would refer to 'children as cars in a shop, a collection of malfunctions to be adjusted. Teachers need to "look under the hood," he says, to figure out the origins of the pings.'[3]

Klein worked with the Bill & Melinda Gates Foundation, which donated $125 million to the reform of New York schools so as to bring 'a CEO mentality to education'.[4] He put Jack Welch, retired head of General Electric, on the board of his New York City Leadership Academy, which trains school managers – previously called principals.[5]

UBS, a major transnational financial services company, which is one of many corporations that contributed $75 million to the Academy, paid for Klein to visit Australia in November 2008 to promote his business-oriented school reforms. Australian federal education minister, Julia Gillard, who was impressed by Klein's school 'reforms' on a visit to the US, is seeking to apply some of them to Australian schools.[6]

Business coalitions have pushed for a more business-like approach in schools that, according to the UK National Association of Head Teachers, reduces children 'to widgets on a production line'.[7] Chris Whittle, who founded Edison charter schools (see Chapter 12), said the 'biggest contribution business can make to education is to make education a business'.[8] However businesspeople have no deep understanding of educational processes, how they are fundamentally different from production processes, and why they cannot be judged by the same criteria.

Writing in the business magazine *Fortune*, financial journalist, Peter Brimelow, cheerfully put aside issues of quality to compare learning to factory production:

> Leaving quality questions aside, public school productivity, measured by the number of employees required to process a given number of students, seems to have declined by 46% between 1957 and 1979. Even the poor old steel industry managed to increase its output per worker-hour 36% during that same period. Overall business sector productivity rose 65%.[9]

Efforts to instil corporate culture into US schools initially took the form of vision statements, 'slogan buttons', 'in-service day programs filled with overhead presentations', and 'team-building' exercises.[10] However, some schools went much further. When the Kellman Corporate Community Elementary School, named after a Chicago businessman closely involved in its formation, was founded in 1990 it was hailed by the *Wall Street Journal* as the new model of school education:

> Schoolhouse and board room have merged at the Corporate/Community School. Dismayed by the faulty products being turned out by Chicago's troubled schools, some 60 of the city's giant corporations have taken over the production line themselves ... For the corporate school's founders are after something rarely seen in urban schools today: productivity. And they vow to solve the central dilemma of school reform: how to vastly improve education quality for all children without a vast increase in costs ... The key, the school's founders believe, is in the corporate management model.[11]

The application of the business model to schools has not been confined to the US. The language and practice of school reform around the world borrows heavily from business management literature (see Table 6.1). For example the minister for education in Ontario, John Snobelen, described 'his vision' for Ontario's schools in 1995 in terms of 'clients', 'customers' and 'front-line service providers' (teachers) who would be 'customer and client-focused'.[12]

Successive UK governments developed various ways to get businesses involved in school management so as to inculcate schools with business culture and management styles.[13] The National College for School Leadership (NCSL) was established to train school principals to be more like business managers:

> The function of the NCSL is the ideological re-engineering of the culture of school management in order to secure not just the compliance of teachers with the government's agenda but their commitment to it. The vehicle is a model of 'transformation leadership' imported from the world of business management.[14]

Books aimed at head teachers had titles such as Total Quality Management and the School, Human Resource Management in Education, The Income Generation

Table 6.1   The New Language of School Reform

Bureaucratic professionalism	New managerialism
Public-service ethos	Customer-oriented ethos
Driven by commitment to professional standards and values such as equity	Driven by efficiency, cost-effectiveness and competitive advantage
Cooperation	Competition
Managers with educational backgrounds	Managers trained in economics, business management
Focus on inputs, control of processes, teacher qualifications, qualitative outcomes	Focus on goals, measurable results Consequences for poor results – accountability

Schools	Educational Enterprises
Parents	Consumers/customers/clients
Learning	Production/product
Students	Products/clients
Teachers	Workers/producers/classroom managers/service providers
Principals	Managers/leaders/entrepreneurs

Source: adapted from G. Whitty, S. Power, and D. Halpin, *Devolution and Choice in Education: The School, the State and the Market*, Melbourne, Australian Council for Educational Research, 1998, p. 54.

Handbook and Managing Educational Property. 'In these texts, head teachers are being encouraged to develop business plans and promotion strategies and apply business consultancy approaches. They are being taught how to use management techniques borrowed from commerce.'[15]

Education departments are also expected to be more business-like. In Australia, 'bureaucrats with no experience in education, were hired as senior administrators by the education bureaucracy for their business credentials'.[16] They had replaced educators as education department heads throughout Australia by 1992.[17] The idea that education policy should be made by those with experience in education was replaced by the idea that policy should be set by politicians and implemented by managers appointed for their business skills and ability 'to operate efficiently to achieve goals'.[18]

At state level, old-style bureaucracy was jettisoned in favour of corporate management techniques transported from industry. Bureaucracies were stripped back into flatter, leaner and meaner organizations, where education workers are responsible for achieving goals set by their 'line managers', who are in turn striving to attain the outcomes determined by the line managers above them.[19]

The new business-oriented managers in the education departments brought with them a new culture and the motivation for radical change. They viewed educational institutes and schools as 'stand-alone corporations in a market, with their own products, clients, shareholders, revenues, shadow profits...'.[20]

However there are good reasons to believe that a business model, with its focus on cost-effectively producing outputs, is inappropriate to education. Business-people have no deep understanding of how educational processes differ from production processes and why they cannot be judged by the same criteria. Learning should be about discovery, exploration and curiosity, not just performance and achievement, which is all the business model is concerned with.[21] Learning is not work and teaching is not production. Graduates are not manufactured. Lewis Finch, a Colorado school superintendent, pointed out:

> Corporations want us to operate public schools like they operate their businesses. They can carefully select their raw materials to produce, say, the best Oreo cookies in the world. But out behind the plant is a pile of refuse made up of those that don't qualify. Is that the kind of school system we want for America? I think not.[22]

DRIVE FOR EFFICIENCY

The introduction of business models into school management has been impelled by education funding cuts along with corporate rhetoric about the superiority of business practices. During the last two decades schools in English-speaking nations have been restructured and 'reformed' in the name of efficiency and accountability. There has been a marked shift in government attitudes towards school education. The ideal of education as a social/public good whose equitable provision is a collective responsibility has been almost totally replaced by corporate ideologies of efficiency, individual achievement, competition and consumer choice (see Chapter 13).[23]

For a greater part of the twentieth century investment in education had been seen as 'nation-building',[24] an investment in future citizens, and a way of giving students from a variety of ethnic and racial backgrounds a common educational experience, integrating them and building a democratic, equalitarian, national culture, thereby preparing children to be respectable citizens. During the 1960s increasing investment in education was based on the theory that the more money invested in education the better the outcomes in terms of national prosperity.[25]

However, during the 1970s governments began to reverse the trend and cut school budgets. Instead of investing as much as possible in education, the new emphasis was to educate as many as possible for the least cost. Education came to be 'viewed as a cost rather than an investment'.[26] It wasn't that there was not enough money for education, it was just that it was no longer seen as a high priority.[27]

It was a time when many businessmen argued that the cost of government-supplied services was too high because of bureaucratic inefficiencies and because of government efforts to meet social objectives such as equity.[28] Think tanks, flourishing with the inflow of corporate money, advocated less government spending, lower budget deficits and reduced collective provision of public services. Their 'experts' depicted the public provision of education and other public services as 'unproductive and wasteful, a "tax burden" on society'.[29] They produced theories to dispute the connection between educational investment and student outcomes.

Throughout the English-speaking world, as part of a broader push by neoliberals to reform public services, education departments were subject to various forms of corporatisation, variously termed the 'new public management', 'new managerialism', 'entrepreneurial governance' and 'corporate managerialism'.[30] Education departments, like other government departments, were expected to be primarily concerned with efficiency, accountability and rates of return on investment rather than with serving the public interest.

Federal and state taxes

The decline in school funding was fuelled by an unwillingness on the part of businesses, property owners and the wealthy to pay taxes. Corporate taxes have declined in many nations. The share of general tax revenue paid by Canadian corporations declined from 20 per cent in the 1960s to 8 per cent in the 1990s.[31] In the UK one out of three businesses pay no corporate tax. The average tax rate for the largest corporations in the OECD has declined from 34 per cent in 2000 to less than 29 per cent in 2005. 'Half of all world trade passes through tax havens so that corporations can avoid paying tax.'[32]

In the US the corporate contribution to federal revenue has declined both in terms of its share of federal revenue and proportion of GDP (see Figure 6.1) as a result of lowered tax rates, increasing tax breaks and the use of tax shelters.[33] Corporate taxes in the US have also been declining over time as a percentage of their profits. 'Nearly 95 percent of corporations now pay less than 5 percent of their income in taxes. This is despite a tax rate that officially stands at 35 percent.'[34] In fact some end up getting more money from the government than they pay in taxes giving them a negative tax rate.[35] Corporate federal taxes fell from $207 billion to $132 billion during the first three years of the Bush administration (2000–03).[36]

The situation is similar at the state level. Between 1978 and 2005 the corporate contribution to state and local taxes declined from 0.47 per cent of GDP to 0.29 per cent.[37] An analysis by the groups Citizens for Tax Justice and the Institute on Taxation and Economic Policy found that '252 of America's largest and most profitable corporations' – all *Fortune 500* companies – paid an average of 2.3

per cent tax on their profits compared to a statutory state corporate tax rate of 6.8 per cent. Between 2001 and 2003 these companies avoided $41.7 billion in state taxes.[38]

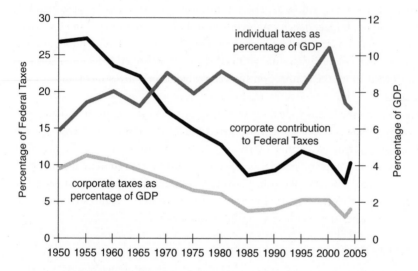

Figure 6.1   Declining Corporate Income Taxes 1950–2004

Source: 'Historical Tables: Budget of the United States Government Fiscal Year 2006', Washington, 2005, http://www.whitehouse.gov/omb/budget/fy2006/pdf/hist.pdf

Property taxes in the US

US schools traditionally get their funding from a combination of local property taxes, sales taxes and income taxes. However, during the 1970s and 1980s there were a series of tax revolts that caused local property taxes – the major source of school funding – to be dramatically cut. It all began in California in the early 1970s when the Californian Supreme Court found that the system of school funding was unconstitutional because it violated the right of all children to a good education.[39] The court ruled that property tax distribution should be done in a more equitable way with a transfer of property taxes from wealthy areas to poorer districts.[40] However people in wealthy districts objected to their taxes being used to pay for schools in other districts, rather than being used to give their own children an advantage. In addition, massive increases in house prices caused homeowners all over the state to suffer property tax increases as the market value of their homes escalated.[41]

Proposition 13, passed in 1978, reduced property taxes by an average of 57 per cent and capped them at 1 per cent of property values. Also property taxes would be based on the last price the property was sold for rather than its market value.[42] At the time of Proposition 13, the Californian state government had a large surplus of billions of dollars and people who voted for it were not voting to have school funding reduced but, rather, for the state government to pay a higher share of school funding and other public service expenses.[43] The state government at first made up the shortfall in revenue for schools and local government resulting from Proposition 13, but over time school funding declined.[44]

Government funding of schools in California has gone from being one of the highest in the nation to one of the lowest.[45] Average class sizes became the largest in the nation, teachers less qualified, 'the ratio of counsellors, nurses, librarians among the nation's worst; the condition of the schools among the shabbiest'.[46] In wealthy areas parents were able to supplement school funding with their own fundraising efforts, supplementing school budgets by hundreds of thousands of dollars.[47] Not so in poorer areas.

The children at Luther Burbank Middle School in California have to share outdated textbooks that they are unable to take home. Their classrooms are infested with vermin and roaches, and they do not have computers. There is no librarian. The library is out of date and seldom open. The toilets often lack toilet paper, soap and towels. More than a third of the 35 teachers are not certified and half have been teaching at the school less than a year. Children have to wear coats, hats and gloves in class during the winter to keep warm.[48]

The biggest winners of the property tax cuts have been large corporations because they are less likely than homeowners to buy and sell their property. Many are today paying taxes on the price they paid for property acquired decades ago.[49] Consequently a company such as Disney pays as little as a nickel per square foot in property taxes for its Disneyland site.[50] An effort to change the legislation in 1991 to have corporate property periodically reassessed was defeated by corporate lobbying and influence and the California Chamber of Commerce continues to oppose any changes to the law.[51]

Between 1979 and 1984 there were over 58 similar ballot measures across the US.[52] Consequently schools all over the nation now receive less funding from local property taxes and state governments have generally not made up the shortfall.[53] Corporations were the major beneficiaries. By 1990, the share of property taxes contributed by corporations nationwide in the US had declined from 45 per cent in 1957 to 16 per cent in 1995.[54]

In addition cities used tax breaks to attract corporations which deprived schools of even more money and diverted hundreds of millions of dollars from schools to corporations.[55] For example, the Louisiana state government gave companies a ten-year exemption from property taxes for new manufacturing plants and extensions to existing plants, reducing school funding by almost $1 billion during the 1980s. By the 1990s Louisiana was 'ranked last among the fifty states in its number of high school graduates, forty-ninth in its poverty rate, forty-seventh in its rate of adult illiteracy'.[56]

Corporations that want to minimise the tax they pay towards public schools pay lip service to supporting public education whilst lobbying against the raising of taxes that could be used for that purpose. Corporate executives and managers are able to give their own children educational advantages by sending them to private schools or living in affluent suburban neighbourhoods where there is a high local tax base, but are unwilling to fund adequate education for other children. For example, 'executives of General Motors, ... who have been among the loudest to proclaim the need for better schools, have been among the most relentless pursuers of local tax abatements'.[57]

As corporations pay less and less taxes towards public schooling they invest token amounts in sponsorships, grants and scholarships to earn the reputation of being school benefactors. They ensure that schools are dependent on their advertising and public relations-based educational materials, as well as their largesse, which they can bestow discriminately to those who run schools the way they want. Schools no longer have the secure long-term funding that once came from taxes.

DISCONNECTING FUNDING FROM OUTCOMES

As a result of school funding cuts during the 1980s and 1990s in English-speaking nations fewer teachers were employed and those remaining had to work longer hours. Class sizes increased. School facilities deteriorated. Teachers and students were demoralised.[58] School managements focused on ways of managing scarce resources and 'doing more with less', rather than on providing a better education for students.[59]

Governments which cut school funding were naturally subject to criticism that they were harming the quality of education. Consequently they needed research to show that funding was not an important factor in achieving a quality education. They funded their own research on this and corporate-funded think tanks augmented their efforts.[60]

In the US Eric Hanushek, an economist and fellow at the Hoover Institution in the US, published various studies purporting to show that there was no relationship between levels of educational expenditure and measures of student achievement. His findings were cited in policy papers and newspaper editorials around the world. Others who demonstrated that Hanushek's data could be interpreted to show that levels of expenditure actually did make a significant difference were largely ignored by the mainstream media and policy makers.[61] The Heritage Foundation declared in 1989 that 'Virtually all studies of school performance, in fact, reveal that spending has little bearing on student achievement.'[62]

Australian think tanks such as the Centre for Policy Studies used Hanushek's data to argue that student–staff ratios were not important to educational outcomes.

Their findings were then promoted in the newspapers by conservative columnists such as Paddy McGuinness who argued that 'pupil–teacher ratios, expenditures per pupil, the age and quality of physical facilities, the number of books in libraries – none of this has any relationship to outcomes'.[63]

Another research aim was to shift the blame for declining educational quality from funding cuts to the inadequacies of particular schools and teachers. A 1990 book by John Chubb and Terry Moe, *Politics, Markets and America's Schools*, published by the Brookings Institution, was one of the most widely cited on education policy in the English-speaking world during the 1990s. It argued that it was good leadership and teaching as well as high academic standards and goals and strong parental support that made for effective schools, not being well-resourced or located in areas of high socio-economic background. Therefore the responsibility for effective schools lay with head teachers, teachers and parents, not with governments. The way to promote good practice in schools, they claimed, was through market competition.[64] Both authors, formerly with the Brookings Institution, are now fellows of the Hoover Institution.

Similarly the Business Roundtable (BRT) argued that 'reform cannot be premised on increased public spending'.[65] Corporations demanded that schools achieve better student performance without resort to the traditional remedy for educational shortfalls – increased school funding; smaller classes; more qualified, better paid teachers – which are measures likely to raise taxes. They helped shift the focus from inputs and processes to outputs.[66]

This view that what matters is outcomes and that these do not depend on the resources available came to dominate government policy circles in all English-speaking nations. In Australia the Quality Education Review Committee (QERC) was established by the federal government to reorient education policy away from demands for more resources to an emphasis on school performance and efficiency.[67]

Instead of increasing school resources and interpreting accountability in terms of how funds were spent and what practices were adopted, the emphasis shifted to evaluating student performance without reference to funding inputs (see next chapter).[68] Business-funded think tanks around the world still argue that funding is not a key element of school success. For example, Chester Finn, president of the Thomas B. Fordham Foundation, and a widely cited commentator on school education issues, claims 'there is no direct relationship between the amount of resources a school receives and its level of academic performance'.[69]

Yet it is obvious that smaller classes, better qualified teachers, access to up-to-date good quality textbooks, and the quality of resources such as science labs and computers, have an important impact on student learning. Lack of funding in US schools has led to a dramatic increase in uncertified teachers. There are 47,000 uncertified teachers in California alone, mainly in schools catering to working-class and minority students. In Baltimore, more than one in three teachers is uncertified.[70]

In Californian schools hundreds of thousands of children are 'trying to learn in overcrowded, out-of-date [and] unsafe classrooms' or 'in temporary trailers' on the school playgrounds. Almost one thousand schools have classes scheduled all year so students can attend school in staggered shifts. Court documents have detailed schools where there were no chemicals for chemistry labs, no books for literature classes, and no computers for computer classes – where the teacher explained what they would be doing if they had computers – and classrooms without enough seats for all the children attending.[71]

In Kansas school funding shortages have caused teachers and school librarians to be retrenched, classrooms to be closed, guidance counsellors, art teachers and Spanish teachers to be ditched, and intramural basketball games cancelled. Some schools claim they can no longer afford textbooks or air conditioning, others have reduced the school week to four days to save money. A district court judge found in 2004 that Kansas public schools were under-funded by at least $1 billion.[72]

In Oregon 84 school districts out of 198 were forced to close schools up to three weeks before the scheduled end of the year in 2003 as they had run out of money to operate because of state education budget cuts.[73] State government legislation passed in August 2003 to raise taxes to cover the budget shortfall had been repealed by a ballot measure launched by corporate front group, Citizens for a Sound Economy (CSE), whose funders include General Electric, ExxonMobil, General Motors, Eli Lilly and Shell.[74]

Outside of Oregon the length of the school year is often specified by law so that schools have had to use other measures to cut costs to cope with an estimated $50–80 billion public education budget shortfall nationwide.[75] They have cut costs by increasing class sizes, cutting teachers, having four-day school weeks, cancelling summer and after-school programmes, closing libraries, increasing the cost of non-educational services such as school lunches, reducing non-teaching employees such as janitors and cafeteria workers.[76] Families are being asked to supply basic stationery – paper and pencils – and even soap.[77]

Independent studies show that minor increases in funding, when allocated appropriately, can dramatically increase student achievement.[78] A 2003 National Center for Schools and Communities study of New York City's 1100 public schools found that students performed better, regardless of race or socio-economic background, in schools that were better resourced and had more experienced teachers. Also, schools 'with fully functioning libraries and modern computers' had better student attendance rates, lower suspension rates and less crime.[79]

It is also evident to corporate executives that funding matters. Many willingly spend $20,000 to $30,000 a year on each of their own children's private education to ensure they have an educational advantage whilst arguing that public schools need far less to achieve academic excellence.

DEVOLUTION

The need to shift responsibility for performance outcomes from government funding to school management and teaching staff led to the restructuring of the school system, in English-speaking nations, along business lines. In the new structure, each school is like a company subsidiary, responsible for its own budget and personnel but reporting to company headquarters, which makes all the major policy decisions. This is called devolution.

In most cases devolution has been presented as shifting responsibility to local units and therefore being more decentralised, democratic and responsive to local communities. However centralised bureaucracies retained firm control of what should be taught. They establish the goals of education, methods of performance evaluation, core curricula, and resource allocation. The crucial decisions about goals and objectives are made by unelected technocrats in government departments with little experience in education, who are far removed from local school communities. For example, in Australia:

> By the end of the 1980s, state education systems were awash with corporate plans, performance indicators. These served to reshape the labour process of teachers, whose room for autonomous action was now far more tightly constrained than it had been for two decades. In addition, teachers, along with parents, academics and non-corporatised groups, were invariably excluded from participation in policy-making groups.[80]

The real goal of school devolution is not local control and school autonomy, but to enable governments to abdicate responsibility for funding shortfalls. Individual schools are now responsible for turning out highly skilled students despite declining resources. More budgetary control does not mean more resources. Yet failure to meet centrally determined quality objectives is blamed on poor school management and poor quality teaching rather than a lack of resources and funding.

Principals have to make the hard decisions about whether to cut teaching positions to fund educational programmes or whether to sell school land to finance building maintenance.[81] Instead of providing educational leadership to teachers, principals have had to become employers – 'entrepreneurs, whose job it is to manage the school as a business and to maximise the school's "market advantage"' – and 'line managers', ensuring that education department objectives are carried out and performance targets met.[82] They have had to turn their attention away from educational matters to focus on strategic plans, budgets, personnel issues and fund-raising.[83] And instead of being able to collaborate with other principals and learn from each other they are now expected to compete with them.

Box 6.2   **School Devolution Around the World**

Local management of schools in England
  During the 1980s the power of local educational authorities (LEAs) was greatly reduced with policy making and curriculum decisions being centralised in government. Administrative, staffing and fiscal responsibility was shifted to individual school governing bodies that were to have 50 per cent of their membership coming from business, industry, the professions or other relevant fields of employment. These changes were retained by the subsequent Labour government.[84]

Site-based/school-based management (SBM) in the US
  By 1990 a third of US school districts had adopted some form of school-based management and since then various states have introduced legislation to ensure all schools do so.[85] Most recently the New Commission on the Skills of the American Workforce has called for each school to 'have complete discretion over the way its funds are spent, the staffing schedule, the organization and management of the school, the school's schedule and its program, as long as it provided the curriculum and met the testing and other accountability requirements imposed by the state'.[86] Similarly devolution is on the agenda of various city mayors.

The 'self-managing school' in Australia
  Following lobbying by the Business Council of Australia, schools in most states have been given responsibility for school budgets. Principals have been refashioned as corporate managers and school councils have taken on management responsibilities.[87]

Tomorrow's Schools in New Zealand
  A highly centralised school system was restructured following the recommendations of an educational taskforce – headed by Brian Picot, 'a prominent supermarket magnate' – which stressed the need for devolution, efficiency and better management practices. Regional educational boards were abolished and school administration transferred to decentralised boards of trustees for 'stand-alone' schools, which managed centrally allocated budgets and personnel hiring.[88]

Such pressures have led to high turnover rates in principals in Australia, New Zealand and the UK.[89] In 2007, a study by PricewaterhouseCoopers, commissioned following a decline in the numbers of teachers seeking head teachers' positions in the UK, suggested that schools could be headed by non-teachers who were experts in finance, human resources and project management.[90]

MAKING PARENTS PAY

As devolved public schools have scrambled to deal with reduced budgets they have increasingly begun to charge parents fees and levies. This situation makes a mockery of the Universal Declaration of Human Rights that states 'Everyone has a right to education. Education shall be free, at least in the elementary and fundamental stages', and the International Covenant on Economic, Social and Cultural Rights that calls for 'the progressive introduction of free education' at the secondary level.

In Australia during the 1990s increasing numbers of public schools began charging fees and levies to fund teaching positions or building works. It overturned the former Australian ideal of 'free, compulsory and secular education'. Schools also began charging for various costs that had not been charged for before, including course materials, textbooks, computer and library access and sporting equipment. Fees were even charged in some cases for doing elective subjects such as computer science, technical drawing and languages, so that children from poorer families were excluded from these subjects.[91] In 2005 parents in NSW contributed over $400 million to public schools in fees and donations.[92]

Whereas once parental donations to schools were for the extras – special projects, landscaping, additional sports equipment – these voluntary donations are not only increasingly necessary to the basic running of schools but there is more coercion to pay them. This coercion can include the withholding of reports, textbooks, school diaries and educational materials, and preventing students from accessing libraries and attending graduation ceremonies and other school functions.[93]

The ability of schools to charge fees and raise funds differs dramatically depending on the affluence of the parents of their students (see Box 6.3). The more reliant schools are on parental spending the more wealthy parents are able to give their children an advantage over other children.[94] In the past governments concerned with educational equity tried to make up for that difference with extra funds to disadvantaged schools.[95] That is no longer the case.

In the US, while parents in poor districts struggle to raise a few thousand dollars for their schools, parents in wealthier districts raise tens of thousands and sometimes hundreds of thousands of dollars for their schools.[96] Wealthy parents can raise money for 'everything from extra-teacher salaries to field trips, to make sure the differential between their kids' schools and other schools is maintained'.[97] They fund libraries, art and music lessons.

Governments once sought to provide the same comprehensive education to all students, whatever their socio-economic background. This usually meant there was a system of fairly uniform public schools, run by centralised government bureaucracies, that all students in a school neighbourhood were able to attend for little or no cost. There was a widespread public belief that people from all walks of life and backgrounds should have equal opportunity in education and that education was 'an important means to achieve social equality'.[98]

The overriding goal of economic efficiency in education, forced by the funding cuts, has led to the introduction of business management methods into education.

Box 6.3   Funding Inequities – Some Figures

In the US:

- In New Jersey, government funding of schools can vary from $7400 to $33,800 per student.[99]
- In Santa Monica and Malibu school districts funds raised by parent–teacher associations vary between schools from $25,000 to $750,000 per year.[100]
- Teachers in the wealthier schools can be paid over $40,000 more per year.[101]
- In suburban schools a typical class size is around 18 children whereas it is more like 30 in overcrowded urban schools.[102]

In Australia:

- Funds raised by parents and citizens (P&C) groups in NSW vary between schools from $500 to $100,000 per year.[103]
- In the 1990s poor Australian families were finding it difficult to afford textbooks, school camps and excursions, fees and levies, and even the cost of computer disks. Some were missing meals to be able to pay for school costs.[104]

In the UK:

- Twenty per cent of public primary schools and 5 per cent of public secondary schools could not even raise £1000 per year whereas 1 per cent of primary schools could raise more than £25,000 and 3 per cent of secondary schools could raise more than £250,000 in a year.
- More than one third of private schools were able to raise £250,000 in a year, and 22 per cent could raise over half a million pounds.[105]

The aim is to achieve better educational outcomes for less financial inputs. Batteries of student tests have been introduced so that school productivity, cost-effectiveness and performance can be measured (see next chapter). Schools are now economic enterprises with economic goals. Social goals, such as promoting a vibrant democracy of educated citizens, and individual goals, such as student self-actualisation and fulfilment, have been neglected.[106]

Education is now viewed, in policy circles around the world, as a 'private consumption item', a commodity that is most efficiently produced by business enterprises and that is purchased by parents to give their child a competitive advantage in the career market.[107] Children are no longer viewed as future citizens whose potential should be nurtured and developed but rather as consumers of the educational product, human resources for the economic growth machine, and 'the problem that schools have to solve'.[108]

7

Making Schools Accountable

> The danger with high-stakes testing, of course, is that schools become test-taking factories in which the only thing taught or learned is how to take high-stakes tests.
>
> Robert B. Reich[1]

The constant testing of children in schools has resulted in record numbers of children being depressed. Children get so stressed over the tests that some are vomiting on the morning of their tests. Parental opposition to high-stakes testing is growing.[2] In 2008 the annual US report, *The State of Our Nation's Youth*, found that 79 per cent of high school students said that pressure to get good grades caused them problems compared to 62 per cent in 2001.[3]

The increased intensity of academic schooling, pushed by business coalitions in many nations, is making school an unpleasant place for children. 'The present emphasis on testing and test scores is sucking the soul out of the primary school experience for both teachers and children.'[4] Schools which are striving to improve test results are reducing or even cutting recesses so as to spend more time preparing for the tests so children get no opportunity to stretch or play or develop social skills (see Chapter 9).[5] In some cases nap time is being eliminated in kindergarten to make way for test preparation.[6]

William McKeith, principal of a Sydney school, notes that the culture of testing in NSW is causing children to lose the time they need to play, relax and 'construct their own activities ... Some of us can remember after school hours, fun times, filled with bicycle riding, dress-ups and cricket in the backyard with friends. ... Many of our children are now either too tired or too busy for such innocent activities. It isn't surprising that increasingly we are hearing doctors and psychologists report concerns with childhood stress, anxiety, poor sleep and obesity.'[7]

In the UK, according to the Association of Teachers and Lecturers, children as young as five are not able to play because they are under so much pressure from regular testing in preparation for national tests at age seven. They become bored with the constant assessment and dislike school from their first year.[8] Rising truancy rates and increasing numbers of children leaving school early have been blamed on high-stakes testing which, according to the National Association of Head Teachers, is causing children to feel stressed and disenfranchised and reducing schools to 'exam factories'.[9] The *Times Educational Supplement* found that 'more than a third of seven-year-olds suffer stress over national tests and one in 10 loses sleep because they are so worried about them. ... By the age of 11, two thirds of children show symptoms of stress as they revise for national tests.'[10]

In the US, children as young as third grade cannot proceed to fourth grade without passing standardised tests.[11] Consequently children who develop later get an inferiority complex early in life. Pre-school and kindergarten children are especially likely to be distressed by tests and labelled as poor performers before they even begin school.[12] Yet there are standardised tests in kindergarten in some states. In Alabama, kindergarten children are subjected to tests three times in a year.[13] In some states children are even tested in pre-school programmes for literacy and math, when they are only four years old.[14]

Standardised testing for reading readiness has been introduced for four-year-olds in pre-school Head Start programs. States with pre-school programmes that demonstrate they can teach literacy skills get bonuses from the federal government.[15] In tests toddlers are asked to count and name letters, geometric shapes, animals, body parts and various other objects. Early childhood experts say testing on such young children is not only invalid, but is likely to traumatise them.[16]

Standardised testing and accountability

The takeover of schools by testing regimes has been driven by business lobbies, as we will see in the next chapter. Business groups like to focus 'on bottom line gains in student achievement' because this is the way they run businesses.[17] In the US, business leader Edward Rust pointed out that in business it is necessary to 'constantly monitor progress against projected results and actual returns'.[18] Craig Barrett, CEO of the US-based Intel Corporation, claimed: 'We need to provide our public schools with what business brings to the table: our emphasis on setting goals, measuring results, and getting things done.'[19]

The Business Roundtable (BRT) ran a campaign that changed the way educational progress was measured, from 'traditional indicators such as per-pupil spending and student–teacher ratios' to 'bottom-line gains in student achievement'.[20] Because businesses depend on quantitative measures they insist schools rely on them also. And in a devolved school system, measurable outcomes are necessary to maintain control of what is happening out in the branches. In this way, test results have become the main way of making schools accountable.

This form of accountability has meant that education department bureaucrats around the world do not have to judge teaching methods, which would require educational professionals in senior positions, but instead judge outcomes in terms of aggregated scores in tests, sometimes supplemented by other measures such as absentee data and retention data. Test results allow schools to be compared if you ignore the fact that test results more often reflect the resources the school receives, and the socio-economic background of their students, rather than the educational qualities of a school.

For test results to be used as a way of comparing schools, children have to sit the same tests, which means they must have a shared curriculum on which to be tested. A key element of accountability is therefore central control of a standardised curriculum to enable standardised testing. A standard curriculum also allows business to more easily influence what is taught in schools (see Chapter 10). In several countries today children are tested from an early age, and frequently (see Box 7.1).

Standardised testing achieves many objectives for business including those that are publicly stated:

- measuring whether schools are performing – accountability
- providing a basis for parental choice of schools (see Chapter 13)

and those that are unstated and will be elaborated further in the coming chapters:

- ensuring teachers and school principals focus on centrally determined curricula
- screening and sorting students for employers (see Chapter 9)
- facilitating discontent with public schools (see Chapter 14)
- shifting the blame for economic and social problems to schools (see Chapter 8)
- enabling a few corporations to profit from test preparation materials, tutoring and running and evaluating tests (see Chapter 8)
- fostering a corporate ideology of competition, evaluation, obedience to authority, reward and punishment (see Chapter 9)[21]

Teachers have always used tests of various kinds to assess how well students are learning and which students are falling behind. However, standardised tests are aimed at assessing teachers and schools rather than for educational purposes. In New York, for example, tests don't provide any useful feedback for teachers as they often don't get the scores back till the students have moved on to the next grade.[22]

The Basic Skills Test in NSW introduced in 1989 was not able to be used for diagnostic purposes and the results were provided to teachers too late to be used to pinpoint individual weaknesses and help to improve them. Instead students 'were compared with each other and plotted against a State average'. Also, because it tested a narrow range of basic skills such as spelling, punctuation, numbers and

Box 7.1   **Accountability and Testing in Various Nations**

In the UK:

Accountability was one of the 'five great themes' of the Conservative government in the UK during the 1980s.[23] The 1988 Education Reform Bill established 'a national curriculum with specified core and foundation subjects' for all students attending government schools.[24]

The Blair Labour government in the UK increased the emphasis on standard national curricula, testing and accountability.[25] Children were given standardised tests at ages five (entry to primary school), seven, eleven and 14 as well as sitting school leaving exams and pre-university exams. By the time they left school at 16, students had sat 70 public tests and exams. The 'external testing regime imposed on English schools' was said to be 'the most extensive, and many would say, oppressive, in the world'.[26] Criticisms of the tests and problems in marking them forced the government to abolish tests for 14-year-olds in 2008 (standardised tests for five-year-olds were stopped earlier).[27] Scotland does not have standardised testing and Wales has discontinued it.

In Australia:

By the 1990s standardised testing had been introduced in all Australian states, generally starting in year three in primary school, and supplemented by national tests in years three, five, and seven for literacy and numeracy. Subject standards are set at the state level. These tend to be outcome-based, that is, prescribing levels of performance and knowledge to be acquired at each grade. Results are reported to ensure accountability.[28]

National curricula are currently being developed for all levels of schooling starting with English, mathematics, sciences and history.

In Canada:

Alberta led the way with 'an extensive program' of standardised testing that was expanded during the 1980s.[29] In Ontario, the New Democratic Party (NDP) government formed an Educational Quality and Accountability Office (EQAO) in 1995 and the Progressive Conservative government introduced a system of standardised testing with the Education Improvement Act in 1996 which today involves testing of children in grades three and six for reading, writing and mathematics, nine for mathematics and ten for reading and writing literacy.[30]

In the US:

Curricula standards are set at the state level and 'children are tested to an extent that is unprecedented in our history'.[31] In New York, for example, students are tested five times a year in elementary schools, four times a year in high schools. In 2001 the No Child Left Behind (NCLB) Act required states to set standards for mathematics, reading and science. Students have to be tested every year in grades three to eight and schools have to show improvement in student test scores over time.[32]

measurement it provided inadequate feedback to parents who were concerned with their child's ability to gain a broader understanding of the world as well as attain basic skills.[33]

In many countries teachers and their unions have opposed testing and other assessments that rank and compare students because it turns education into a competition between students, with some students branded as failures. They argue that assessment should be used to help the individual student develop and improve.[34] The UK National Union of Teachers (NUT) found that most teachers do not believe that standardised tests are a reliable measure of student performance.[35] A survey of US teachers found that only 7 per cent thought standardised testing provided an effective measure of the quality of schools and less than 10 per cent thought they were particularly useful, accurate, beneficial, worthwhile or valid. In contrast 42 per cent said that standardised testing was completely unhelpful to their teaching.[36]

Standardised tests are sometimes the sole basis for judging the quality of teaching and schools even though testing measures little more than the ability of children to take tests. The publication of league tables of schools based on student test results turns accountability into a shaming exercise for the worst performing schools as media outlets have a field day with their headlines: 'Halls of Shame ... the worst of the worst ... the dirty dozen'.[37] Blame is shifted to the poorly performing school and factors such as neighbourhood demographics and lack of funding are ignored.

The concept of high-stakes testing assumes that schools alone are responsible for differing levels of student performance and by implication that all students begin at the same point in terms of knowledge, skills, parental support and resources. This enables governments and parents to judge schools in terms of student outcomes and to find many public schools to be deficient.[38] Testing makes schools accountable for student performance but the government – the senior bureaucrats and the politicians – are not held accountable for the lack of resources to provide for an adequate education in those schools.[39]

HIGH-STAKES TESTING

To ensure that the standardised tests are taken seriously, even though they have little educational value, educational authorities have attached various rewards and punishments to performance in them. Attaching these 'high stakes' to test results is also a way to ensure that schools teach to the curriculum.

In the UK 'failing' schools – those whose students are under-performing on standardised tests and exams – are threatened with closure. Teachers' promotion and progression up the pay scale is dependent on their progress in the classroom as measured by student performance in tests.[40] Also, the idea of the 'failing teacher' was introduced in the early 1990s by the Office for Standards in Education (Ofsted), which claimed there were some 15,000 of these failing teachers in the UK.[41]

In 'high-stakes' testing in the US, teachers, principals and schools are all evaluated according to student tests, and those that do well are rewarded: teachers and schools get bonuses (like sales bonuses in the world of business) and the best-performing students get prizes, scholarships and even exemptions from other exams.[42] Some state funding is also dependent on test scores. In California, $700 million was allocated on the basis of average school scores in a single standardised test in 2002.[43]

Schools that are funded at $5000 per student are compared with schools that get $15,000 per student, as if the difference in funding is of no account.[44] This makes accountability programmes into 'little more than ceremonies for awarding prizes, honors, and extra finances' to wealthy schools attended by the children of affluent families.[45]

The idea of helping low-performing schools to improve by granting them additional resources is seen as rewarding poor performance.[46] This ignores the fact that in poor neighbourhoods classes are much larger; students may come from families where parents speak English as a second language; parents are often unable to coach their children or pay for tutors; and many students don't have time for homework because they have to work. Moreover, rewarding teachers whose students do well has provided a disincentive for teachers to work in these schools. High-stakes testing therefore tends to exacerbate the disadvantages of schools in poor neighbourhoods.

Students who do badly on standardised tests can be held back a grade, have enrolment rejected at a school or be denied a high school diploma. Some states are even requiring schools to retain elementary students if they do not pass a standardised reading test, despite evidence that children learn to read at different rates and start at different levels when they begin school.[47] The high stakes attached to standardised testing has resulted in a push for students to begin academic studies at an earlier age as schools compete to outdo each other in the tests.

Surveys show that whilst the public is in favour of the idea of rigorous academic standards and testing to help schools and parents evaluate student performance and parents to evaluate schools, they have many reservations about testing and prefer grading and evaluation by teachers to decide if children should go ahead a grade or graduate. According to a BRT survey, they thought tests were a bad idea because:

- some students perform poorly even though they know the material (86 per cent)
- they can't measure many important skills (71 per cent)

- teachers begin teaching to the test and drop other important ideas and curriculum components (64 per cent)
- teachers and students spend too much time preparing for tests (53 per cent)
- they put too much pressure on elementary school children (50 per cent)[48]

By 2000 one in three states in the US that had instituted high-stakes testing 'slowed or scaled back their original efforts' and softened the stakes, giving children many second chances and allowing some to avoid the tests.[49] This was seen by business as a repudiation of their 'reform' programme. The No Child Left Behind (NCLB) legislation introduced in 2002 doesn't allow such recalcitrance by the states. It requires that schools which fail to meet performance improvement goals, as measured by standardised tests, are punished with escalating sanctions for each year of failure including:

- second and subsequent years – students must be given the option to transfer to another public school in the district; schools are required to work with parents, teachers and outside experts to improve test scores
- third and subsequent years – the school is required to offer supplementary educational services, including outside tutoring
- fourth year – the school is required to replace poorly performing teachers, introduce new curricula, extend the school day or the school year, restructure the school, or make similar fundamental changes
- fifth year – the school is required to develop an 'alternate governance' plan that involves converting the school to a charter school; replacing most teachers; contracting with a private company to run the school; allowing the state to take over the school; or other equally fundamental changes
- sixth year – the alternate governance plan must be implemented.[50]

School districts have to set aside 20 per cent of their funding for low-income students for transport and tutoring expenses required by the Act. In addition individual schools have the extra burden of negotiating contracts and supervising the private companies that provide the supplementary educational services.[51] This means that poorly funded schools in poor districts are further punished when they don't do well in these tests because of their lack of resources.

THE TOLL ON TEACHERS AND CHILDREN

Teachers all over the world are under much more pressure to get their students to perform well on tests in an environment of reduced resources and larger classes. At the same time they are having to fulfil extra managerial, entrepreneurial and administrative tasks, familiarise themselves with new reporting technologies and requirements, and even foster business partnerships. In such a situation they have little time for professional development and there are 'rising rates of teacher stress, burn-out, cynicism and resignation'.

In Australia this has 'been the impetus behind the numerous government and academic inquiries into the teaching force'.[52] In NSW, Australia, teachers accounted for almost half the stress payments in 2003 for all government employees. Nearly 40 per cent of newly graduated teachers leave the profession within three years.[53] In New Zealand, the changes in teaching role and the increased administrative workload have led to declining job satisfaction and increased teacher turnover.[54]

In the US a study by the National Commission on Teaching and America's Future estimated that the cost of escalating teacher turnover was $7 billion in the 2003–04 school year.[55] Around 500,000 teachers leave the profession each year and teachers have to be recruited and trained to replace them.[56] Well over 90 per cent of teachers surveyed in the US believed the NCLB Act with its various requirements was contributing to 'teacher burnout'.[57]

In the UK teachers have also been deserting the profession in droves. The number of teachers retiring early from the profession increased dramatically in the five years to 2006.[58] In 2005 only 60 per cent of qualified teachers remained in the profession three years after graduating.[59] The NUT claims that one in three teachers have suffered mental health problems because of the stress of the job.[60]

High-stakes testing assumes that teachers and principals will not do their best unless they are bribed or threatened and that students won't study unless they are offered rewards and punishments. A 1999 business summit on education issued an action statement that said: 'To date, our education system has operated with few incentives for success and even fewer consequences for failure. The job security and compensation of teachers and administrators have, in large measure, been disconnected from teachers' success in improving student achievement.'[61]

However teaching is not just a matter of hard work and long hours and those who think it is have no understanding of the teaching profession. Teachers tend to be more motivated by the satisfactions of a job well done, and being able to help children to develop, than by extra margins of pay that depend on the performance of their students in standardised tests. 'Introducing crude monetary incentives', and at the same time depriving teachers of basic resources to enable them to do their jobs properly, can distort the whole process of teaching, encouraging 'staff to compete rather than cooperate with each other' and to focus on preparing students for tests rather than inspiring children to learn and encouraging creativity and curiosity.[62]

Impact of standardised tests on teaching

Standardised testing encourages poor teaching practices. A UK Select Committee found that high-stakes testing 'has led schools and teachers to deploy inappropriate methods to maximise achievement' by students in tests.[63] A national survey of teachers in the US found that two thirds of teachers claimed that standardised testing encouraged them to 'use rote drill in my teaching' and 'to emphasize the teaching of factual recall knowledge'. Only 17 per cent agreed that the testing 'has changed my instructional practices for the better'.[64] One study of upstate New York teachers, whose students were required to pass standards tests, found that 'Essentially, they turned into drill sergeants, removing any opportunity for the students to play an active role in their own learning.'[65]

In the US as much as a quarter of the school year can be devoted to test preparation and test taking. Some schools stop teaching for weeks before an important test and just drill their students and give them practice tests.[66] Others give trial tests every six weeks to give the children practice and make sure they are able to do them.[67]

'Teaching to the test', that is, drilling students on material likely to be in the test, has become very common wherever standardised teaching is introduced. A survey of US teachers found that 84 per cent of them believed the NCLB Act was encouraging teachers to 'teach to the test', 85 per cent admitted to spending a lot of time teaching 'content that I know will be on the state/district test' and 78 per cent admitted spending 'a lot of time teaching my students test-taking skills'.[68] A federal Early Childhood Longitudinal Study found that teaching to the test was particularly damaging to bright students in poor schools where teachers focus on lower performing children to make sure they will pass the tests. Those who can easily pass the tests are neglected so they don't fulfil their full potential.[69]

In the UK, too, 'Testing dominates the curriculum, and teaching to the test has become the norm. Schools strive to reach their set pupil attainment targets with a battery of preparatory tests and "booster" classes for those just below the threshold.' Also there is a 'disproportionate focus of resources on pupils on the borderline of targets'.[70]

The business emphasis on accountability and measurement in schools means that activities with short-term benefits that can be quantified have become paramount. The focus is on achievement rather than learning. Performance-based assessments that involve doing projects, essays, science experiments and reports have become undervalued, even though they are far more important to learning. Instead of aiding their students to develop their potential, teachers help them to remember the authorised knowledge modules for long enough to pass the test. The emphasis on this shopping list of knowledge leads to the teaching of grammar and spelling as technical skills to be mastered, rather than a means of self-expression and understanding of others.[71]

Students, too, tend to internalise the implicit message that material that is not tested is not important. They are not encouraged to be intellectually curious and creative. Cultural, sporting, social or other attainments are downplayed or even discouraged.[72]

Leaving children behind

The idea of making students repeat a year when they get poor test results, or making them do extra classes outside of school time, is largely based on the idea that such punishment will provide an incentive for students to work hard. Yet, as Brent Staples notes in a *New York Times* editorial, 'the notion that young children fail academically because they are lazy passed out of fashion with platform shoes' and what actually happens is 'that children held back in early grades do worse academically – and are more likely to drop out – than children with similar test scores who get extra help' after going into the next grade.[73]

Moreover standardised tests are designed so that a significant proportion of the children will fail.[74] In the US those who compile standardised tests for schools have found that students tend to get better scores each year – as teachers and students become accustomed to the tests – so that the tests have to be recalibrated every seven years to ensure that an average student will score around 50 per cent. This ensures that no matter how good the schools are, a certain number of students will fail.[75] Being labelled as a failure does not help anyone.

High-stakes testing has caused higher rates of suspensions, exclusions and dropouts in the US. This is partly because schools are making children repeat grades to ensure the school's test scores improve in important state tests.[76] Studies show that grades one to three are getting larger whilst the fourth grade, when the state test that ranks schools is taken, is much smaller.[77] Also, the number of students in ninth grade in 2000 was 13 per cent larger than the number of students in the eighth grade the year before, indicating that the extra students had been held back from grade ten, another important test year.[78]

Texas, cited as the model for the NCLB Act because of its ability to boost test scores, did so by removing poorly performing students from doing the tests through retention in lower grades and a high number of drop-outs, hidden from public view through manipulated records.[79] In New York and Chicago school drop-out figures also seem to have been manipulated.[80] In New York the *Times* reported that the number of students pushed out of school to make the school's performance look better is increasing, with students pushed out at ever younger ages.[81]

The steadily closing achievement gap between black and white children that had been occurring since the Second World War was reversed during the 1990s as a consequence of the school funding cuts and 'reforms' that have occurred since the 1980s. Not only are fewer black students graduating but 'the enrollment of minority students at a number of our most prestigious public universities has dropped alarmingly'.[82]

Another method of boosting student test scores is through cheating, which is much more of a temptation if teacher pay and school funding depends on it. Hundreds of Texas schools are suspected of cheating on standardised tests.[83] In California dozens of schools admitted to cheating. For example, teachers helped students with answers or allowed students to consult reference materials or to use calculators. Some even changed the answers on test papers after the test.[84] Cheating has also been uncovered in Massachusetts, New Jersey, New York and in other states.[85] In the UK an ethical code was introduced in 2008 to 'discourage teachers and markers from giving in to pressure to help test cheats'.[86]

KNOWLEDGE VERSUS UNDERSTANDING

Standardised tests are very good for testing the sort of knowledge that can be drilled into students, rather than real learning. Because testing is most efficient and cost-effective when it requires short answers or multiple choice questions that are easily scored, the sort of knowledge it tests tends to be memory-based, or a contrived exercise in logic, rather than 'more meaningful forms of assessment that require human beings to evaluate the quality of students' accomplishments'.[87] The tests 'merely sample the curriculum and do not assess depth of understanding, meaningful application of knowledge, or original thinking'.[88]

President of the US National Academy of Science, Bruce Alberts, notes that 'it's easier to test for facts than understanding' and an emphasis on tests tends to reduce primary school science to memorising facts such as the 30 different kinds of whales rather than understanding how the world works.[89] Tests may be okay for finding out how much information a student has absorbed but education also involves making connections, finding patterns and imagining possibilities, none of which standardised tests deal with.[90] Similarly, the Australian Council of Education Deans notes that standardised tests rely on memory at a time when information is readily accessible and they only 'measure certain limited kinds of intelligence ... Tests are an excellent measure of a person's ability to do tests, and not much else.'[91]

Because tests are timed, students are being tested for speed over and above thoughtfulness or thoroughness. Critical thinking does not help get higher marks. Students have to find quick answers rather than reflect and critically analyse their subject. Students who are 'actively' engaged in their learning, seeking to connect it to other things they know and questioning what they are learning tend to do more poorly in such tests, though not always, than students who just focus on memorising what they have to, skipping things that are too difficult, and guessing answers.[92]

For the questions to have right and wrong answers, either the answers are biased and reflect a particular point of view, or the material they are testing tends to be superficial so that there is no disagreement about the answers: 'For example, it's easier to get agreement on whether a semi-colon has been used correctly than on whether an essay represents clear thinking.'[93]

What matters in testing is getting the right answers, not the process used to get those answers. It is possible to get the right answer without understanding the underlying concepts and to get the wrong answer although one understands the concepts. In maths tests, students are able to get high scores by memorising steps and procedures rather than understanding why they are carrying them out. Less than 5 per cent of questions in such tests require 'high level thinking skills such as problem solving and reasoning'. In other tests, skills such as the ability to formulate a logical argument are not tested.[94] 'Standardized tests can't measure initiative, creativity, imagination, conceptual thinking, curiosity, effort, irony, judgement, commitment, nuance, good will, ethical reflection, or a host of other valuable dispositions and attributes.'[95]

What students are likely to learn from these tests, and from the emphasis their schools put on preparing for them, is that education is all about memorising facts and methods and that intelligence is about how much you know and how fast you can regurgitate it. Worse still, they may come to believe that there is a right and wrong answer for everything, including life's problems, and that someone in authority has that answer.[96] Therefore there is no point in questioning facts, critically assessing reports, or applying one's own intellect to coming up with an individual interpretation of a problem.

According to the Australian Council of Deans of Education, the focus on learning 'narrow, decontextualised, abstract and fragmented' information that is encouraged by standardised testing is likely to produce 'compliant learners, people who would accept what was presented to them as correct, and who passively learnt off by heart knowledge which could not easily be applied in different and new contexts'.[97] This seems to be what business leaders want.

Learning outcomes

For the first few years of any testing regime, as students get used to sitting standardised tests, as teachers learn how to teach to the tests and coach students in test-sitting techniques, and as schools narrow school curricula, test scores tend to improve, as happened in UK primary schools.[98] This enables governments to claim that students are learning more, but whether the quality of their learning is improving is questionable. As scores level off, as they usually do, more lenient exams and lowered pass marks are necessary for governments to continue to claim their policies are leading to improved student performance.[99]

There is little evidence that higher test scores are correlated with success in later life, let alone with better college or job performance.[100] Students who are able to remember facts in the short term and master test-taking techniques may be able to get good test scores but they do not necessarily understand the underlying concepts well enough to master more advanced material in later grades nor 'to apply their knowledge independently to new contexts'. This may explain the 'apparent decline' in UK students' performance when they go to secondary school.[101]

Similarly in the US, students at poor urban elementary schools who made the 'dramatic gains ... cannot set down their ideas in sentences expected of most fourth and fifth grade students in the suburbs' when they get to secondary schools, despite having had longer school days, longer school years, no recess and 'cancelling or cutting back on all the so-called frills (art, music, even social sciences...)'.[102]

The *Washington Post* reported how Washington students who have been schooled with constant testing are finding the college environment a shock because it requires a different mode of learning where memory skills do not have much of a role. John Bader, the associate dean for academic programmes at Johns Hopkins University, points out that students who are 'tested within an inch of their lives so regularly and so intensely' at school have to quickly adapt to an environment where, for many courses, 'there is no clear answer. There is no right or wrong.'[103]

Similarly in the US, university professors have noted that students are poorly prepared for university study because they lack deep understanding of subjects, are 'unable to solve problems in real-world situations', and lack the ability to think critically and independently. Instead they tend to want to know the right answers and are 'very assessment-oriented'.[104]

Critical-thinking skills are particularly important in an internet age when so much information is available. Without such skills, students cannot discriminate between fraudulent information and accurate information, useful information and trivial information, poor quality information and high quality information. Yet an emphasis on tests trains students to accept all information provided rather than be able to assess its worth and credibility.

Nor is there much evidence that a focus on testing and accountability has helped children to attain a better education. In states in the US that have the severest penalties for failure in standardised tests, students get below average results in the National Assessment of Educational Progress (NAEP), an exam that predates the current wave of standardised testing and covers a broader range of learning.[105] Overall high school students are getting worse results on NAEP reading tests than they did in 1992.[106]

Despite the negative impacts of standardised testing on education and the poor learning outcomes it promotes, standardised testing has been strongly advocated by business leaders who seem more concerned with restructuring schools as businesses, and having a set of numbers available with which to hold schools to account for how they spend taxpayer funds.

8
Business Campaigns

> Soon, it seemed no area of school life was beyond corporate scrutiny or without business involvement. Corporations helped train teachers and administrators, offered scholarships to deserving students, provided instructional materials, subsidized school programs, and cosponsored the activities of professional organizations. Businesspeople toiled as tutors, served as mentors, and offered their organizational knowledge to schools willing to learn the lessons of the corporate management 'revolution'.
>
> Alex Molnar[1]

Edward B. Rust, Jr., is at the centre of a vast network of business interests determined to have US public schools adopt standards and testing as a way to make them accountable to employers, who depend on schools to provide them with compliant, work-ready employees.

Rust is the CEO and chair of State Farm Insurance Companies, as was his father before him and his father's father before him. The Rust clan have run State Farm for more than 50 years. You might imagine this is a family firm but it is in fact a mutual automobile insurance company for rural drivers that is owned by its policy holders.[2]

Rust, who has worked at State Farm since 1975 when he graduated, plays a key leadership role in a number of business coalitions and think tanks as well as educational advocacy groups, government advisory groups and commissions (see Figure 8.1). His continuing refrain in each of these positions is a call for standards, testing and accountability in schools. For Rust, accountability in schools is important because 'large organizations like schools "don't change because they see the light; they change because they feel the heat"'.[3] It is therefore surprising to find that the organisation he heads is far from being a paragon of high standards and accountability.

In 1999 a jury asked State Farm to pay $456 million and $730 million punitive damages because it had misled policy holders about the quality of the replacement parts it used. The judge found that State Farm had 'violated' the trust of policy holders.[4] In 1998 the firm paid $200 million 'to settle a class action charging

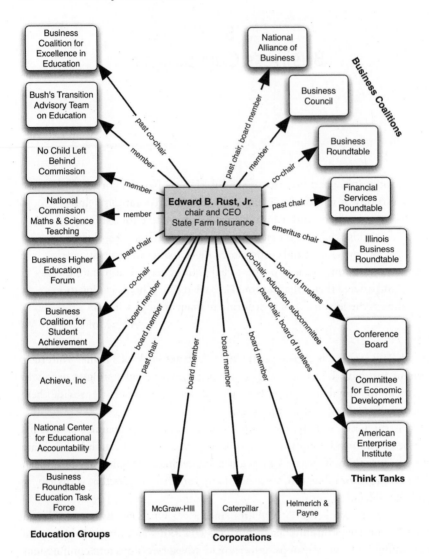

Figure 8.1   Edward Rust's Connections

Source: State Farm Insurance, 'Edward B. Rust, Jr., Chairman and CEO', http://www.statefarm.com/media/
edrustjr.htm

that agents engaged in a variety of misleading sales practices'. That same year
State Farm was forced to pay millions in various cases, including $25 million for
'systematic destruction of documents' and 'systematic manipulation of individual
claim files to conceal claim mishandling'.[5]

Business Week noted: 'If there's a common theme in State Farm's big court
losses, it's that judges and juries think the company has taken cost-cutting too far.'[6]

In 2001 a Utah Supreme Court went further, referring to State Farm's 'decades-long policy of fraudulent and dishonest practices'.[7] Nevertheless, Rust unselfconsciously led the business campaign for more accountability in public schools throughout the 1990s.

Rust is not the only businessman to make a project out of school 'reform'. In 1989 the business magazine *Fortune* argued: 'Business needs to do a better job of telling our schools what it wants and expects from graduates' including 'more emphasis on the basics – reading, writing and arithmetic' and better vocational training.[8]

At *Fortune*'s second annual education conference in 1989 business leaders decided to use their muscle to force change in schools. John Sculley, chair of Apple, pointed out: 'Chief executives of global enterprises are becoming as powerful as many heads of state.' Those attending agreed that 'Top managers might also play lead roles in supporting reform-minded politicians and maverick educators or in lobbying local taxpayers to join the crusade.'[9] A couple of years later Robert Kennedy, CEO of Union Carbide, exhorted business executives to make more use of their bully pulpits: 'we can begin by communicating the urgency of the problem to our own employees and getting them involved'.[10]

David Kearns, CEO and chair of Xerox, was one of those business leaders who took up the call to arms and conducted, in the words of *Business Week*, a 'crusade' in which his 'mantra' was 'quality, standards, choice, competition'. He co-wrote a book with Dennis Doyle (see Chapter 14) subtitled 'A Bold Plan to Make Our Schools Competitive'. Kearns is credited with bringing Xerox back from the brink with massive workforce downsizing, and he believes that similar restructuring is necessary for schools.[11] According to Kearns: 'Business is having to do the school's product-recall work for them. Frankly, I resent it.'[12]

After retiring from his CEO position Kearns became deputy to Secretary of Education, Lamar Alexander, during the first Bush administration. Kearns was also a member of various think tanks and business coalitions including the Council on Foreign Relations and the Trilateral Commission. He founded New American Schools (NAS) in 1991 to promote the improvement and innovation of American schools by demonstrating model curricula and funding educational entrepreneurs who design them. With his high level corporate and political contacts, Kearns was able to raise $140 million for NAS. By 1999 around a thousand schools had adopted NAS curricula designs.[13] In 2005 the Bill & Melinda Gates Foundation granted NAS in conjunction with San Diego City Schools $11 million to transform three large high schools.[14]

Another educational crusader, Louis Gerstner, contributed a million dollars of start up money and some office space to NAS. Gerstner has been CEO of RJR Nabisco, CEO and chair of IBM, and chair of the Carlyle Group. Like Kearns at Xerox, he is credited with turning IBM around through draconian restructuring.[15]

Well connected in the corporate world, Gerstner has been on the board of directors of the *New York Times*, American Express, AT&T, Caterpillar, Bristol-Myers Squibb and various other corporations, as well as a member of the advisory boards of DaimlerChrysler and Sony Corporation, a member of the board of the Council on Foreign Relations, and a member of the Business Council.[16]

Gerstner founded and chaired the Teaching Commission, 'comprising 18 leaders in government, business, philanthropy, and education' – including Barbara Bush but only one teacher – to advise government on how to improve teaching quality in schools. It promotes merit-based pay for teachers based on their students' test performance.[17] Gerstner also co-wrote a book with Denis Doyle: *Reinventing Education: Entrepreneurship in America's Public Schools*. In it students were referred to as 'human capital' and schools were urged to compare themselves with each other in the way that 'Xerox compares itself to L.L.Bean for inventory control'.[18]

'Reinventing Education' was also the title Gerstner gave to an IBM project in which school districts in 21 states use IBM 'technology and technical assistance to eliminate key barriers to school reform'. Reinventing Education has been introduced to other countries. For example it runs in Victoria, Australia, in partnership with the Department of Education and Training. Gerstner received a British knighthood in 2001 for his services to education.[19]

BUSINESS COALITIONS

Businesses believe that the poor basic skills of school graduates is costing them money. UK employers believe that millions of workers cost their companies money because of literacy and numeracy mistakes.[20] In the US, the Business Coalition for Student Achievement claims that businesses lose $2.3 billion a year because a lack of maths and reading skills are reducing their productivity.[21]

Businesses have driven school 'reform' in many nations,[22] but nowhere have business efforts been so well co-ordinated and documented as in the US. In 1989 the US Business Roundtable (BRT) began a major ten-year campaign 'to reform the entire system of public education'. It argued that 'too many students were leaving school unprepared for productive work and effective citizenship'.[23] It claimed that school graduates 'arrive at our doors unable to write a proper paragraph, fill out simple forms, read instruction manuals, do essential mathematical calculations, understand basic scientific concepts or work as a team'.[24]

What business leaders wanted were standards 'that spell out what students should learn in school and how well they should learn it'; tests that ensure that teachers and schools stick to the material spelled out in the standards; and consequences for those that don't – standards, assessment and accountability; as well as devolution of schools.[25] The BRT pointed out that standards were required to be met in other realms of life, particularly business, so why not schools?

What BRT actually did was to conflate the idea of a high standard education with the idea of standard content in curricula. It constantly referred to standards as 'high academic standards' whereas what it really wanted was for the content of school education to be more standardised across the nation so it would cover a narrow range of knowledge and skills that business leaders thought was necessary for employees, and for that standardised content to be reinforced with tests.

Roundtable members enrolled state governors and business leaders in each state to promote the corporate agenda.[26] This was facilitated by a series of national education summits beginning in 1989 and attended by corporate CEOs and state governors, but not by school principals, teachers or students. Each summit, held at IBM headquarters and co-organised by IBM, emphasised curriculum standards, testing and accountability. The 'Goals 2000: Educate America Act' that was passed by the federal government in 1994 was based on a paper – co-authored by Kearns – that came out of the first summit, which President Bush attended. It established a National Education Standards and Improvement Council to promote national curriculum standards for core school subjects.[27]

BRT not only lobbied to get curriculum standards and testing into schools, but actually sought to influence those standards and therefore determine what was being taught. It urged businesspeople to 'participate on committees that determine the types of tests (or test questions) used and the standards of proficiency (how good is good enough)' to make sure that tests 'are both rigorous and relevant'. 'Setting standards, we believe, is business leaders' most important opportunity to act on their dissatisfaction with the nation's education system.' BRT pointed out in *A Business Leader's Guide to Setting Academic Standards* that businesspeople should at least 'Make sure the standards are measurable and organized so they emphasize the skills and knowledge you believe are most essential.'[28]

Yet despite all this business involvement, the funding of schools remained inadequate. Corporations preferred to give small amounts of money through gifts and sponsorships, and be seen as benefactors, than to pay the taxes required to fully fund the schools. Alex Molnar, author of *Giving Kids the Bu$iness*, estimates that the total amount donated by corporations to US schools would run those schools for less than two hours a year.[29] US Senator, Howard Mertzenbaum, noted:

> The supposed largesse of corporations is further reduced by the fact that these donations are generally tax deductible. In speech after speech, it is our corporate CEOs who state that an educated, literate work force is the key to American competitiveness. They pontificate on the importance of education. They point out their magnanimous corporate contributions to education in one breath, and then they pull the tax base out from under local schools in the next.[30]

In 1998 the BRT launched its 'Keep the Promise' Public Awareness Campaign. This national advertising campaign placed $250 million worth of 'public service' advertisements in the media to get the public to support the business campaign for curriculum standards and testing in public schools. BRT aimed to 'dramatize the urgency of the need to raise standards in America's public schools'.[31]

The BRT has also campaigned to extend standardised testing to pre-schools. It argues that providing appropriate pre-school programmes for disadvantaged children, which ensure they are ready to learn when they arrive at school, 'can significantly reduce teen pregnancy, poor school performance, dropping out, criminal activity, and other negative and expensive behaviours in later years'.[32]

The BRT joined with Corporate Voices for Working Families (CVWF), another corporate coalition, in a campaign that argued for children in pre-school to be taught English language literacy and numeracy and for state pre-school curriculum standards aligned to standards in the early grades of schools. The toddlers should have their learning progress measured to ensure that pre-schools are accountable and there should be 'incentives for meeting or exceeding objectives as well as consequences for persistent failure to achieve intended outcomes for children'.[33]

State-based campaigns

The BRT put out a guide to businesspeople in 1998 about how to build public support for 'tests that count', that is, tests aligned to state-based curriculum standards. It explained that first they had to persuade state policy makers to adopt standardised tests. This might involve surveying candidate commitment to this goal during election years; testifying at hearings; and regularly meeting with legislators to reinforce the business community agenda.[34]

As part of their campaign, BRT members divided up the states between them in order to work with state governors and chief state school officers to reform schools. So, for example, Boeing's CEO took on Washington, whilst the CEOs of Lockheed Martin, Potomac Electric Power Company and Citigroup took on Maryland by forming the Maryland Business Roundtable for Education (MBRT).[35]

The BRT was joined by the National Alliance of Business (NAB), and together they played a key role in 'developing and expanding' state and local business coalitions. They formed the Business Coalition for Education Reform (BCER), which co-ordinated 'a network of more than 500 state and local business-led' education coalitions around the nation in the campaign for standardised testing, school-to-career initiatives and business-style management of schools.[36]

The NAB had been formed by Henry Ford II in 1968 with the help of President Lyndon B. Johnson. Its membership included 5000 businesses, and by the 1980s its focus was on school 'reforms'.[37] It managed the state and local business coalitions and convened the BCER and the Business Coalition for Excellence in Education (BCEE).[38] Rust, who was active in both the BRT and the NAB, wrote:

By mixing agitation with collaboration and patience with urgency, these groups are accomplishing more than any single company alone could have ... Roundtable companies are at the forefront of a national effort by businesses to stimulate academic progress by aligning their hiring, philanthropic and site location practices with our education reform agenda.[39]

NAB also led a nationwide campaign by business groups, 'Making Academics Count', aimed at ensuring that employers, large and small, use student test records when they hire workers. This was another way to make sure performance in standardised tests had a consequence for students.[40]

State-based public relations campaigns were also run. For example, the Maryland Business Roundtable 'recruited, organized and trained a 45-member Speakers Bureau' to enable them to spread the message about the value of standards and testing with the help of a video and brochure. In Washington State, McDonald's put sample test questions on place mats designed to promote standardised testing. Companies also targeted their own employees with 'brown bag lunches' and talks.[41]

In Washington State, the Partnership for Learning (formed in 1995) underwrote a video and handbook and other materials aimed at persuading, firstly, 'opinion leaders, community movers and shakers, editorial writers, and chambers of commerce', and then parents, of the value of standardised testing. Funding came from Washington-based businesses such as Boeing, Microsoft, Washington Mutual and Weyerhaeuser. The Partnership also ran public relations workshops for businessmen, PTA leaders and school district PR managers on how best to express the message when dealing with media, community groups and other audiences.[42]

The BRT claimed that the state-based campaign taught them that if business speaks with one voice it has more influence; that it is important to forge alliances with state political leaders; that business expertise can be used strategically to change schools; that public opinion research can be used strategically to stimulate reform; and that as 'major employers and community leaders, CEOs are forceful, credible advocates of reform positions and can influence candidates and elected/ appointed officials' views on key education issues'.[43]

No child left behind

The greatest victory of business reformers was the No Child Left Behind (NCLB) Act. The BRT claims that the BCEE, whose members included 69 national business organisations and individual corporations, had 'a tremendous impact on the legislation with most of its key recommendations incorporated into the new law. Some reforms that business sought would have turned out weaker or been dropped altogether without the advocacy of the Business Coalition.'[44] The coalition particularly focused on the law's testing requirements.[45]

Having succeeded in having the NCLB passed into legislation, the BRT ran a series of advertisements in 2003 promoting it and its goals. It also campaigned for the business community to ensure that NCLB was fully implemented in each state. To this end it produced a tool kit for business leaders, *Using the 'No Child Left Behind Act' to Improve the Schools in your State*, which urged businesspeople 'to use business resources – the bully pulpit, financial and in-kind investments, and influence'; to convene taskforces and working groups; to testify, lobby, visit key state officials, educate and involve employees; and to 'identify the leverage points in the implementation process where influence can be applied', all to ensure that 'the strongest outcomes envisioned in the law' were implemented in each state.[46]

In the lead up to the reauthorisation of the NCLB Act in 2007, the BRT and the US Chamber of Commerce formed a coalition with some 80 corporations and business groups, including Intel, Ernst & Young and Microsoft, named the Business Coalition for Student Achievement, to push for the reauthorisation of the NCLB legislation and its expansion to cover high schools and include science testing.[47] The new coalition is chaired by the ubiquitous Edward Rust of State Farm, Craig Barrett, chair of Intel, and Arthur Ryan, chair & CEO of Prudential Financial.[48] Business leaders see business as the 'largest consumer of American education' and they 'are now more prominent and more focused on specific details than ever before'.[49]

In addition, the Bill & Melinda Gates Foundation and the Broad Foundation teamed up in 2007 for a $60 million 'Strong American Schools' campaign to ensure that education is a strong election issue and to promote strong curriculum standards, standardised testing and merit-based pay for teachers, that is, pay based on the test scores of their students.[50] The US Chamber of Commerce also produced a report, *Leaders and Laggards*, giving each state a grade based on how well it conformed to the business formula for schools. Considerations included how much control principals in the state had over budgets and the hiring of teachers (progress towards devolution); the extent to which student test performance data was used; the ability to improve student test results; and the extent to which teacher pay was affected by student test results.[51]

Business networks

Many of the seemingly independent groups campaigning for standardised testing in schools are run and funded by business coalitions, individual corporations and foundations based on corporate fortunes (see Box 8.1 and Figure 8.2).

INTERNATIONAL COMPETITIVENESS

Businesses portray education as a key to a nation's international competitiveness. By linking falling education standards with declining economic productivity

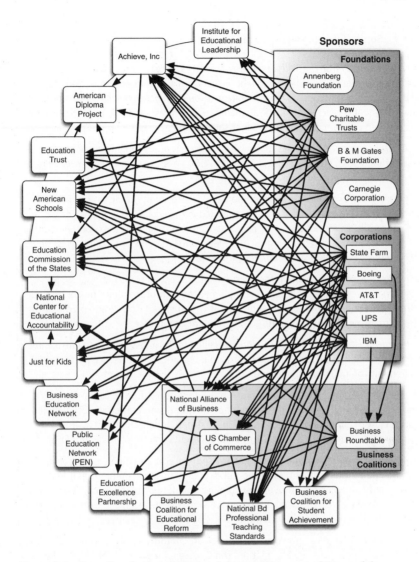

Figure 8.2   Some Standards and Testing Advocacy Groups and Some of the
Organisations that Fund Them

business leaders have an excuse to shape educational policy agenda and determine
educational directions. They argue that, because teaching methods affect business,
they have a right to influence them. The irony is that the failure of corporations
to pay their fair share of taxes has been a major factor in depriving schools of
the necessary resources to provide a high-quality education.

Many government and business reports have emphasised that 'the realities of
the new global marketplace necessitate the subordination of all school functions

---

Box 8.1   Some More Business Advocacy Groups

The New Commission on the Skills of the American Workforce features a panel of business executives, former US education and labour secretaries, retired governors and mayors and education superintendents.[52] Its 2006 report *Tough Choices or Tough Times* proposed that better-quality teachers could be attracted to the profession if pension entitlements were reduced to pay high starting teacher salaries and a system of merit pay.[53]

The Conference Board bills itself as 'the world's leading business membership organization, with a global network of nearly 2000 enterprises in 61 countries'.[54] It is co-author of the report *Are they Really Ready to Work?*

The Committee for Economic Development (CED) is mainly made up of corporate managers with a few university presidents added in to give it credibility. It receives its funding from large foundations.[55] It has produced a number of reports on education that promote standardised testing such as *Measuring What Matters: Using Assessment and Accountability to Improve Student Learning* (2001).

The National Association of Manufacturers (NAM) has called for 'a national system of skills standards designed by industry' complemented by more testing. The Conference Board, the CED and NAM are all sponsors of the Business Coalition for Education Reform, mentioned above, as is the US Chamber of Commerce.

The Business Task Force on Student Standards called for business leaders to participate in setting standards and for those standards to integrate the 'workplace performance requirements of industry and commerce'.[56]

Achieve was founded at the 1996 National Education Summit to campaign for standardised testing. Its sponsors include the Annenberg Foundation, AT&T, the Bill & Melinda Gates Foundation, Boeing, Citicorp, Eastman Kodak, DuPont, GE, IBM, Intel, Pew Charitable Trusts, P&G, State Farm Insurance, UPS and the Xerox Foundation.[57]

The American Diploma Foundation is in turn sponsored by Achieve, the Thomas B. Fordham Foundation, the NAB and the Bill & Melinda Gates Foundation. It was set up 'to spearhead a national movement to align standards, assessments, curriculum and accountability with the demands of postsecondary education and work'[58] and has developed benchmark standards in maths and English.[59]

The Education Trust also sponsors the American Diploma Foundation. It is itself sponsored by Annie E. Casey Foundation, the Carnegie Corporation of NY, the Bill & Melinda Gates Foundation, and State Farm Companies Foundation.[60]

---

to the productivity needs of capital'.[61] Schools have been blamed for failing to provide an adequately skilled workforce, so therefore the way to improve competitiveness is to 'reform' schools.

In 1983 the US National Commission on Excellence in Education (NCEE) published a report, 'A Nation at Risk', which raised concern that the US education system was not serving the economic interests of the nation: 'Our Nation is at risk. Our once unchallenged preeminence in commerce, industry, science, and technological innovation is being overtaken by competitors throughout the world.'[62] The NCEE was comprised of educators, businesspeople and politicians. It was formed on the premise that the education system was the cause of the declining competitiveness of US corporations.[63]

This report 'provided the underlying justification' for subsequent 'corporate involvement in the reform of America's public schools'.[64] It blamed the decline in US industrial competitiveness on a lack of productivity due to the 'mediocre performances in school and on the job, by students, teachers and workers ... School was complicit because of easy grading, easy admission to college, too little homework, watery textbooks, too little writing and reading, poor teaching and weak incentives for excellence among teachers.'[65]

There was, however, no evidence of any decline in worker productivity in the US, which was amongst the highest in the world.[66] Nevertheless, the idea that schools were producing inadequate workers was taken up by the media.

> Numerous glowing reports on Japanese schools appeared, connecting disciplined classrooms with productive workplaces. The education–economy link was made also in *Time*'s cover-story on the 1983 crisis ... *Fortune* also ran a cover story on the new school debacle, suggesting that 'schools were the main cause of the decline in America's industrial might.'[67]

Several business-generated reports took up the rallying cry of competitiveness. That same year *Action for Excellence: A Comprehensive Plan to Improve Our Nation's Schools* was produced by business executives on the Education Commission of the States' Taskforce on Education for Economic Growth.[68] The BRT asserted: 'More and more, we see that competition in the international marketplace is in reality a "battle of the classrooms".'[69]

More recently, business leaders have claimed that their interest in the No Child Left Behind (NCLB) law and other education policy 'can be summed up in one word: competitiveness'.[70] A survey by the Conference Board of 430 business leaders found that they were concerned that the US was 'losing its competitive edge to economies such as India and China' because school graduates lack basic English skills.[71] The Conference Board of Canada claimed the 'skills of the Canadian workforce are not keeping pace with the demands of a more competitive world economy' and it needed to be better educated and job-ready.[72]

The US Chamber of Commerce has formed an Institute for a Competitive Workforce to enable business leaders to liaise with education policy makers to ensure future graduates contribute to making businesses economically competitive.[73] The 2006 report by the New Commission on the Skills of the American Workforce stated: 'If we continue on our current course, and the number of nations outpacing us in the education race continues to grow at its current rate, the American standard of living will steadily fall relative to those nations, rich and poor, that are doing a better job.'[74]

Many governments accepted the business argument that the economic competitiveness of workforces is being damaged by deficiencies in schooling. In New Zealand, the National party produced an education manifesto for the 1987 election entitled 'A Nation at Risk', which made similar arguments to those in the US report it was named after. It argued that NZ was less economically competitive because school students were often illiterate and performed badly in comparison with students of other nations.[75]

Fears about a loss of international competitiveness also prompted educational reform in Australia during the 1980s.[76]

> From the late eighties onwards, the purpose of education was no longer primarily to do with nation building and the public good. It became instead an integral part of the state's armory, used to fight the economic war and stave off economic ruin, with its primary role being the development of human capital.[77]

The European Commission also produced a number of white papers during the 1990s on the role of education policy in international competitiveness.[78] And more recently – in 2006 – Gordon Brown, then UK Chancellor, stated that Britain must focus on improving education if it is to compete globally.[79] Similarly the 2006 Leitch report, an audit of UK skills, estimated that improving the education of the workforce would benefit the economy by £80 billion over 30 years through improving productivity. Lord Leitch argued that the UK was 'on track to achieve undistinguished mediocrity', and that unless work-related education was improved the economy would shrink and the British standard of living decline.[80]

Diversion

During the 1980s unemployment and poverty were also blamed on faults in the school system, enabling corporations to divert attention from their own role in lowering wages, downsizing and casualising the workforce, and the global sourcing of workers. It was argued that school graduates were unable to get jobs because they lacked literacy, numeracy, a good work ethic and work skills (see next chapter).[81] An Australian government report, the Williams Report, published in 1979, blamed youth unemployment on an inadequate education system.[82] In the US, the UK and NZ, too, the education crisis provided an explanation for high levels of unemployment.[83]

Literacy also served 'as a sort of proxy for cooperativeness, trainability and employee loyalty' in the minds of many businesspeople. Just as nineteenth-century writers associated illiteracy with 'alcoholism, criminal behavior and indolence', modern business executives often associated it with teenage pregnancies, drug-use and violence.[84]

A 1989 Ford Foundation report associated school drop-outs with teenage pregnancy, crime and welfare dependence. It suggested that the inability of those who had jobs to support a family on low wages was a consequence of their low education, rather than of the poor wages being offered by employers. It stated that the problem of unemployment was 'not so much a lack of jobs, but rather a growing mismatch between the skill requirements of jobs and the skills that many young people bring to the labor market'.[85]

This scapegoating continues today.

PROFIT SEEKERS

The push for high-stakes standardised testing has created many business opportunities, as government funding is channelled into tests and texts rather than teacher training and reducing class sizes. This has fed a massive industry in test-related materials that reached $592 million in sales in 2003, and over $8 billion in textbook and related educational materials in the US alone in 2006.[86]

The profits to be made from the testing industry ensure that, as well as the general business support for testing, there is a dedicated band of business lobbyists who have their own vested interests in pushing standardised testing. 'At every hearing, every discussion, the big test publishers are always present with at least one lobbyist, sometimes more.'[87]

Private companies are paid not only to produce the test and supply materials for test preparation but also to grade the tests. The NCLB has provided such a windfall for business that it has been dubbed the Testing Company Welfare Act. There are now some 17 tests required by NCLB for each school district each year as well as state tests and practice tests. Money previously earmarked for helping low-income students has been diverted to be spent on NCLB initiatives 'including $3.7 billion expected to go to businesses developing supplemental curriculum,

---

Box 8.2   Money to be Made from Testing – Some Figures

- It costs a state in the US around $10 million to have school performance evaluated – mainly on the basis of standardised tests – and published.[88]
- The market for school assessment, tutoring, test-preparation services and supplemental content supplies is worth $25 billion in the US.[89]
- Educational Testing Service (ETS) earned $75 million from designing tests for California, New Jersey and Puerto Rico in 2003.[90]
- McGraw-Hill's contract to supply tests to Kentucky in 2002 was worth $30 million.[91]
- Kaplan's revenue had doubled by 2003 following introduction of NCLB. Kaplan offers a $3,000 half-day course to help teachers understand testing.[92]

$3.5 billion to professional development services, and $1 billion to tutoring and test preparation companies'.[93]

Private test companies receive little government oversight: 'In fact, there is more public oversight of the pet industry and the food we feed our dogs than there is for the quality of tests we make our kids take.'[94] In the UK, markers walked out in protest at mismanagement by the American-based company ETS Europe, which meant test results would not be available to schools before the end of the school term[95]

The money spent on commercial test-preparation materials diverts funds from very needy schools without any proven results. For example, Professor Linda McNeil, co-director of the Rice Center for Education, describes a primarily Mexican-American school in Houston 'that had no library, almost no lab equipment and a shortage of textbooks. Instead of addressing these basic educational needs, the administration spent $20,000 for commercial test-preparation books. Scores at the school failed to improve.'[96]

The companies supplying the testing juggernaut in the US are also increasingly supplying other nations with materials and services as the testing phenomenon spreads internationally.[97] An example is the transnational corporation McGraw-Hill.

McGraw-Hill

McGraw-Hill has 290 offices in 38 countries and had sales in 2005 of $6 billion. Its subsidiaries publish textbooks, instructional materials, software and school programs tailored to standardised curricula and standardised tests. They also evaluate schools, largely on the basis of standardised test results, provide assessment reports for individual schools and teachers, and offer various tools to help teachers and students improve standardised test results.[98]

McGraw-Hill dominates the test market and in 2005 its company CTB had contracts in 23 states.[99] It is influential in US politics through the close connections between the Bush family and the McGraw family that go back three generations. It enjoyed a 'cozy relationship' with the Bush administration[100] and its board members and CEO are active in key business coalitions (see Figure 8.3).

Companies such as McGraw-Hill lobby for standardised testing, for their own standardised tests to be used, and for curriculum standards that fit with the textbooks they produce.[101]

For example, McGraw-Hill lobbyists used the statewide results on their own California Achievement tests to convince the state legislature that California schools needed the McGraw-Hill Open Court and Reading Mastery program to improve students' reading performance. According to Richard Beach, professor of literacy studies at University of Minnesota, 'The testing arm of the company serves the textbook arm' and promotes a standardized educational package that has very little to do with real learning.[102]

McGraw-Hill claims that the standardised tests they set are not driven by the content of their textbooks or instructional programs but by state standards. However, McGraw-Hill is also able to influence state standards. In Texas, McGraw-Hill 'experts' advised governor George W. Bush on a suitable reading curriculum that was then adopted in Texas schools. 'Not surprisingly, McGraw-Hill products matched the specifications and gained a dominant share in the Texas textbook market.'[103]

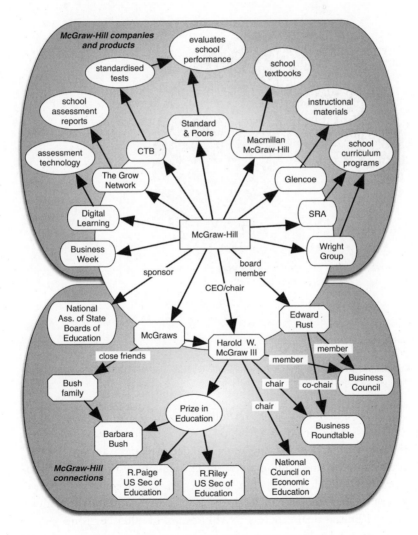

Figure 8.3 McGraw-Hill Companies, Products and Connections

Other publishing companies

McGraw-Hill is not the only company with its finger in various related pies. In fact four companies dominate the school instructional materials and testing market: McGraw-Hill, Pearson, Houghton Mifflin and Harcourt (see Figure 8.4). Harcourt marketed its textbooks in states where it designs the standardised tests by sending out a flyer to school districts saying: 'Why choose Harcourt Brace for your math program? ... [It is the] only program to have texts written by the same company that helps to write the TAAS tests...'.[104] It was later persuaded that this kind of promotion was not wise.

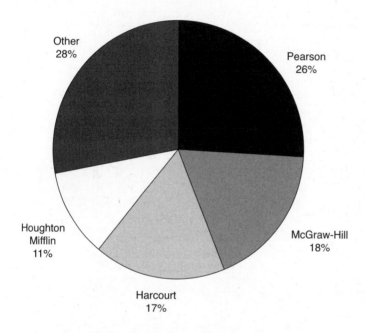

Figure 8.4   Publishers Share of K–12 Market

Source: K.K. Manzo, 'Reading Law Fails to Bring Innovations', *Education Week*, 13 December 2006, http://www.edweek.org/ew/articles/2006/12/13/15read.h26.html

Pearson is a London-based corporation, which also owns Penguin and the *Financial Times*, and turns over $7 billion a year. It includes various textbook and learning programme brands including Prentice Hall and Addison Wesley.[105] Pearson claims to be 'the leading pre K–12 curriculum, testing, and software company in the US, reaching every student and teacher in that country with one or more of our products and services'. It also marks the SAT exam and the National Assessment of Educational Progress (NAEP) exam. In 2005 Pearson's sales of school products worldwide increased from the previous year by 16 per cent (to over $2 billion), and its profits from these increased by 29 per cent with the help of the NCLB legislation, which boosted Pearson's school testing sales by more than 20 per cent.[106]

Even the Bush family is profiting from the NCLB Act. At least 13 school districts used NCLB funds to purchase learning materials from Neil Bush's company, Ignite! Learning. The company investors include his parents George and Barbara, the head of a Kuwaiti company, as well as 'fugitive business tycoon', Boris A. Berezovsky, and his partner. 'Most of Ignite's business has been obtained through sole-source contracts without competitive bidding. Neil Bush has been directly involved in marketing the product.' Barbara Bush gave a donation to a Hurricane Katrina relief foundation on the condition that the money be used to buy Ignite's materials for local schools.[107]

Tutoring

Commercial companies play up parental anxieties about their children's test performance so as to gain business in test-preparation materials and tutoring. There are test-preparation materials that are tailored to suit almost every test in every state at every level. Since test scores can determine whether students will progress to the next grade or be allowed into academic tracks, parents who can afford them and want to give their child the best educational advantage are buying them.[108]

Tutoring is now a $2.2 billion industry in the US and almost 2 million children are being tutored outside of school classes.[109] In Washington alone parents spent $149 million on tutoring and educational support services in 2004 compared with $44 million in 1994.[110] Online tutoring for standardised tests is also part of this burgeoning industry.[111]

Under NCLB, US schools that are performing badly can be forced to divert some of their funding to private tutoring firms. Consequently the latter's profits have risen dramatically in recent years.[112] The 'initiative has set off a stampede, with 1,000 companies rushing to recruit armies of tutors'.[113]

9
Made to Order

No need to hope
For a good-paying job
With our first-grade skills
You'll do nothing but rob
You got to read, baby, read!
You got to read, baby read!
KIPP classroom chant[1]

The children are strangely quiet in the corridors of KIPP schools where 'motivational' signs read 'Excuses are for losers!' and 'There are no shortcuts!'. The children wear bright yellow shirts emblazoned with similar motivational messages. KIPP stands for the Knowledge is Power Program. There is no exuberant shouting, and no sign of the baseball caps, baggy pants, makeup, jewellery or cell phones that might be found in other publicly funded schools. 'Between classes, the students are required to stand in neat rows, backs ramrod straight and mouths closed, and march along the black lines that bisect the corridors.'[2]

In class they sit unnaturally straight and their eyes follow the teacher's every move. When a pair of eyes wander the teacher stops the lesson until they again focus on the teacher.[3] In the front of the class a student sits on a low bench, ostracised and shamed in front of her classmates because she forgot to get her mother to sign her homework. This is the 'porch' – 'a symbolic jail where they are required to wear their shirts inside-out and forbidden from talking to classmates'. She also has to 'write letters of apology to her "teammates" (what the students call each other) for behaving irresponsibly'.[4]

Remnant childhood exuberance is channelled into the disciplined chants that are used to drill knowledge into the students and motivate them, in much the way cheerleaders motivate a football team.

'Ten, ten, ten, ten, ten, ten, tenths, then hundredths, thousandths,' the students sing, to the tune of War's 'Low Rider' song.[5]

Banging on desks and stomping their feet, the students chant daily – not just multiplication tables and state capitals but big thoughts, too: 'Knowledge is power, power is freedom, and I want it.'[6]

Ten-year-olds arrive at school by 7.30 a.m. and don't leave till 5 p.m. or later. They come to school on alternate Saturday mornings and spend another three or four weeks at school during the summer break. They attend school for over 60 per cent more time than other students in public schools.[7] They do two or three hours homework (called 'life work' in KIPP schools) each evening as well. Some children have to leave for school at around 6.15 a.m., getting home around 6.15 p.m. and working on homework till 10 p.m.[8]

Welcome to the brave new world of schooling.

TURNING LEARNING INTO WORK

KIPP schools have become the darlings of the business world because they promote the very values that many business leaders want to see in schools. Crucial elements of the KIPP formula are the back-to-basics teaching methods, the extra time the students work, and a strict system of discipline 'that a drill sergeant could admire'.[9] It is a formula which promotes the value of hard work and obedience.

Survey after survey in Europe, Britain, Australia and the US has shown that what employers want most from school graduates – apart from basic literacy and numeracy skills – is a good attitude, a strong work ethic, honesty, loyalty, dependability, trustworthiness and, of course, compliance.[10] Business leaders want schools to condition children to accept authority and the exercise of power over them, to teach children that 'the acceptance of leadership – the contented submission to the will of others – is a normal and commendable thing'.[11] The importance of schools in ensuring that future workers have these qualities is evident to employers:

> Certain basic components of the work personality appear to be laid down in the early school years – the ability to concentrate on a task for extended periods of time, the development of emotional response patterns to supervisory authority, the limits of cooperation and competition with peers, the meanings and values associated with work, the rewards and sanctions for achievement and non achievement, the effects (both positive and negative) which become associated with being productive.[12]

In the US a swag of government reports such as *What Work Requires of Schools* and *Learning a Living* and corporate reports such as *The Fourth R: Workforce Readiness, Labor Force 2000*, and *Business Leadership: The Third Wave of Education Reform*, all emphasise the role of schools in preparing students for the workforce.[13] The Business Roundtable (BRT) 'emphasises the important values of personal responsibility and hard work. To prepare students for a demanding future, schools must exemplify these values.'[14] Similarly the Australian Chamber of Commerce and Industry has called for a national school certificate focused on 'employability skills'.[15]

In Australia various national committees were appointed, chaired by prominent businesspeople, to advise secondary schools on how to develop workplace skills and competencies.[16] In 2007 the Council of Australian Governments (COAG) again reiterated that education was 'central to human capital reform' and 'positively linked to increased labour force participation rates; ... higher levels of employment and lower levels of unemployment; lower levels of welfare dependency; and higher levels of productivity'.[17]

Business leaders believe that academic rigour will teach students to work hard and that this is necessary to raise the productivity of the workforce. The New Commission on the Skills of the American Workforce claimed in 2006 that 'we have failed to motivate most of our students to take tough courses and work hard, thus missing one of the most important drivers of success in the best-performing nations'.[18]

The renewed emphasis on testing and discipline means that schools replicate the 'conditions of the office or factory' in that students have no control over their education, often have little interest in their school work, and are motivated by external rewards.[19] This has long been the case but it is even more so under the school 'reforms' sweeping the world. Children today are encouraged to view their learning at school as work and to work hard and long.

However there are important differences between what goes on in a business and what goes on in a school, or there should be. In business the end product is what is important. In schools there are end products such as essays and reports but the process of producing these is more important than the end product. If children see their learning as work, then the process becomes just a means to the end product, something that has to be done, rather than something that can be enjoyed and explored for its own sake.

Long hours

Writing in the Canadian magazine *Maclean's*, Ross Laver argued that Japanese and German schools do a much better job of instilling the work ethic. He described the long hours of classes, homework and private tutoring schools that many Japanese children endure. This demanding schedule, Laver argues, is a major reason why Japanese children are better at maths and science than Canadian children and why Canadian children do not learn the value of hard work.[20]

Employers and their allies believe that school hours are too short. They view the hours outside school as non-productive and therefore wasted and some even believe that the free time encourages anti-social activities in older children. The CEO of Union Carbide criticised the short time children spend at school as an anachronism from the past.[21] Chester Finn, of the think tank, the Thomas B.

Fordham Foundation, suggests that long school days are a good idea because children would otherwise spend the time watching television, or partaking in juvenile crime and sexual activity leading to teenage pregnancy.[22]

Many political leaders have subsequently embraced the idea of longer school hours.[23] The UK government has proposed that schools be opened on Saturdays to allow slower children to catch up on their lessons and more academically-gifted children to do extra subjects that no longer fit in the normal curriculum, like arts, music and dance.[24]

In the US many schools utilise summer breaks for extra teaching. Many schools make students who do poorly on standardised tests do extra schooling during the summer to prepare for a retest: 'These are summer institutes of sweat and drill and tension and anxiety, sited in the same unpleasant buildings where the children spent the other ten months of the year, which would not be needed for most of these children if their schools were not so flagrantly deficient [in resources] in the first place.'[25]

Homework ensures that school work extends beyond normal school hours. The load of homework has been steadily increasing in many schools over recent decades. So much so that some school authorities are putting limits on how much schools can set. In Australia 'over the past 20 years, setting significant amounts of homework for children in early years of primary school has become common for the first time in a century'. In the US the time spent by children between the ages of six and nine on homework had almost tripled since 1981 to more than two hours each night.[26]

The evidence about whether homework improves academic performance is mixed. Professor Harris Cooper at Duke University surveyed the research and found that whilst homework does improve student results in school, too much homework can be counterproductive: 'Even for high school students, overloading them with homework is not associated with higher grades.' Cooper notes that homework is used in early grades to teach students time management and study skills rather than to help them learn more.[27] In other words, it is more about developing work skills than education.

Too much homework can also be disruptive of family life and detract from time the family has for shared activities. Homework also disadvantages children that don't have a quiet place to themselves in the home to do their homework; who don't have computers and internet access for assignments; or whose parents are unable to help them with the homework.

Work versus play

Long hours at school work reduce the hours available for play and other non-school work pursuits that are necessary to ensure the overall balanced development of a child. Children lose the little carefree time they have when they can play and relax. They are often tired after a long intense school day and not performing at their best. The view that schools should transform childish playfulness into the material of 'a stable quiescent labor force' prevails in schools, however.[28]

Childhood experts are fairly unanimous about the value of play for a child's development. It is how children explore the world and experiment with relationships and learn about themselves. If it is unstructured it fosters independent thinking. According to paediatrician Berry Brazleton from Harvard Medical School: 'If we don't pay attention to this, we're going to create obsessive-compulsive people.'[29] However, the idea that recess may be 'enjoyable and healthy' is not a good enough argument for those intent on 'maximising productivity'. In Atlanta, the school superintendent said in 1998 that you can't improve academic performance when children are 'hanging on the monkey bars'.[30]

Box 9.1   Eliminating Recess – Some Figures

- In 1999 some 40 per cent of surveyed school districts around the US were considering reducing or eliminating recess or had already done so.
- By 2006 only three US states required schools to have recess.
- Recess has been eliminated in 80 per cent of Chicago schools.
- Elimination of recess has become so common that some schools are even being built without playgrounds.[31]
- A new 'super school' in the UK will have no outdoor space for students to play so that learning can be maximised.[32]

Children learn better in an environment that emphasises 'self-expression, independence, and spontaneity'. Learning is more likely if it happens naturally, for example in games, songs, stories or as a result of a child's curiosity. Such ideas have little influence in today's schools. Kindergartens, where this sort of play was once encouraged, are now criticised as undisciplined and providing inadequate preparation for school.[33] There is now a push for kindergartens to give children basic reading skills, at the expense of social and developmental skills that come from being allowed to play with other children. 'Once focused heavily on a child's social and emotional development, kindergarten is now a largely academic experience – sometimes with math drills and daily homework and worksheets. In many schools, time for music, art, recess and games has withered.'[34]

Play is being replaced by 'scripted teaching', desk work and computer-based learning. This has created more work for occupational therapists because it delays the development of coordination and motor skills in children.[35]

Discipline

Increasingly schools are emphasising discipline. In Edison schools (see Chapter 12) students are required to walk quietly about the corridors in single file with arms folded across their chests. Students who talk out of turn in class tend to be subject to disciplinary hearings. Those who are well behaved get merit points that count towards entry into school extracurricula activities like Friday night dances.[36]

Discipline in KIPP schools is based on traditional punishments – detention, suspension and expulsion – and shaming punishments – such as having to wear t-shirts inside-out and not being allowed to speak to other students – as well as peer pressure: 'When one student misbehaves in class, all the students must stand, leave the room, and reenter in silence. If one student talks on the stairwell, the whole class has to walk back down the four flights and up again.'[37] In other schools discipline involves silent lunches and silent recesses on days when the children have misbehaved. The children may be kept indoors on such days and forced to sit in rows on the floor.[38]

Some US public schools have installed surveillance cameras, similar to those used to catch shoplifters in Wal-Marts, not only in corridors but in the classroom, as a way of improving discipline. Of 950 new public schools that opened in 2002, three out of four included a system of surveillance cameras. Critics argue that this teaches students to behave because they are being watched rather than 'because it's the right thing to do'.[39]

In Chicago, the public school system includes 16 middle and 43 secondary school military programmes. According to the head of Chicago public schools, Paul G. Vallas, 'a former senior instructor at the Illinois National Guard's Officer Candidate School', the military programmes provide 'children with the kind of character-building, discipline, and leadership opportunities in a structured environment that they can't get elsewhere'.[40]

The congressman for the district, Frank C. Bacon, claims: 'They've got to learn discipline. It teaches them how to learn to take orders without being personally offended by them, because it's for the good of the team.' He claims that parade-ground drilling is important for academic success: 'If you can follow direction by command and do what you're told without thinking about it, you're ready to receive instruction.'[41]

The corporate appreciation of such schools is manifest in their funding donations. For example telecommunications company, Ameritech, a subsidiary of AT&T, donated $1.2 million to the establishment of the Bronzeville Academy, a military school in Chicago. According to the superintendent and commanding officer of Bronzeville Academy, leadership in the school context is 'getting someone to do what they ordinarily wouldn't do and be happy about it'.[42]

Rewards and punishment

Discipline can be achieved through a system of rewards as well as punishments. In the UK, the City Academy, an inner city secondary school in Bristol, gives quite substantial financial rewards to students who do as well as or better than expected on exam results. In 2005 the school awarded £37,000 to 165 students who sat their final exams.[43]

In some US schools, students receive payments for good attendance records or school work, which they receive on graduation. 'Others are doling out gift certificates, coupons, and checks if students earn straight A's or land on the honor roll.'[44] In some primary schools the whole learning process is being turned into a business transaction in which children learn to sign contracts to finish their lessons and to negotiate with other children for a book or toy or crayon. And whilst teachers have always rewarded children with stars and stamps, the introduction of classroom banks, simulated or even real money, pay packets and charts of earnings for learning, takes these rewards into the realm of the workplace.[45]

Although rewards and punishments may be appropriate in a factory setting where people doing boring repetitive tasks need external incentives, there is no reason why such methods should be used in schools where students and teachers can be motivated by the task at hand. In such a context, rewards and punishments can kill that intrinsic task motivation and demoralise those who do not come out on top of the competition.[46] Students who compete with their peers for rewards and punishments decided by school authorities do not tend to learn 'to be critical thinkers, lifelong intellectual explorers, active participants in a democratic society'. But, apparently, they do learn to be good corporate employees.[47]

Those who promote rewards and punishments in school tend to view learning as unpleasant work that has to be coerced, and increasingly it is. When learning is converted into work, then a system of rewards and punishments is necessary to replicate the incentives that are available in the workplace to ensure work is done. 'A sour "take your medicine" traditionalism goes hand in hand with drill-and-skill lessons (some of which are aptly named "worksheets") and a reliance on incentives to induce students to do what they understandably have no interest in doing. Such is the legacy of seeing school as work.'[48]

What is rewarded in schools such as KIPP is not initiative, creativity or emotionally oriented behaviour but hard work, 'docility, passivity and obedience', and those attributes most valued in future workers.[49] Financial rewards are registered on mock weekly pay cheques and can earn t-shirts, books, and most sought after of all, attendance at the end-of-year field trip to places like Disney World.[50]

THE WORK EXPERIENCE IN SCHOOL

The vocational content of schools has been beefed up in recent years in the name of preparing children for transition to the workforce. This goes beyond inculcating a work ethic in schools and is often little short of job training.

Today there is a variety of methods used for introducing work-related activities into schools. Apart from actual work experience, which involves spending time in the workplace, work situations can be set up at school. Students may become involved in taking on the running of the school restaurant, shop, crèche or some other mini-enterprise. In the US, banks even operate full service branches at some schools, staffed by students doing a class on banking and finance.[51]

Alternatively business experiences can be simulated using games and artificial projects. Also students can be involved in studying work situations by shadowing real workers in the workplace.[52] Some schools seek to create the work experience at schools by emulating workplaces, for at least some of the time:

> While the school uses the 'paycheck' system to teach youths to earn rewards and manage their money, it also serves as an introduction to the working world. Every Friday, even the ten-year-olds dress like corporate executives, in suits and ties or full-length skirts, their long cornrows often tucked under their blazer collars, their braids pulled into buns.[53]

At some schools children are assigned, or in some cases have to apply and interview for, tasks that are given work-like names – coat-room manager, door manager, pencil sharpener manager, paper-collecting manager and the like. In some schools there is even a time manager to keep the teacher on schedule.[54]

In some countries a separate system of vocational schools exists, whilst others incorporate vocational elements into general schools so that all students graduate from school 'work ready'. There is an increasing push by business groups for vocational material to be included in every school curriculum to ensure that school leavers are prepared for employment.[55] The advantage to employers in terms of savings in job training is obvious. Training can be a huge cost to firms.

In the US the School to Work Opportunities Act provides hundreds of millions of dollars to schools to incorporate work-related skills into the classroom, training teachers about the workplace and providing workplace experiences to school students.[56] In Britain, the 'understanding of and preparation for the so-called world of work' became 'an important educational aim' in the 1980s, with bipartisan political support.[57] Academic qualifications such as A-levels now include vocational subjects.[58] In a 2004 paper, the Department for Education and Skills (DfES) stated:

From autumn this year, work-related learning will become a statutory requirement for all pupils. Schools will be encouraged to use the full range of opportunities inside and outside the formal curriculum to bring out the relevance of what students are learning to the world of work, and to develop the skills needed for employment and enterprise.[59]

To facilitate this the system of comprehensive secondary schools is being replaced with specialist schools that offer a common basic curriculum in literacy and numeracy but with specialisms in subject areas such as technology, science, business and enterprise. In early 2007, 84 per cent (2695) of UK secondary schools were already specialist and all were expected to become so.[60]

Specialist schools incorporate work experience at local businesses and the specialisms are often primarily designed by employers. Microsoft sponsors more than 100 specialist schools.[61] Academies, which are privately managed public schools (see Chapter 12), also specialise in vocational courses. The Academy at Peckham, south London, has vocational courses in motor engineering, hospitality and catering in its sixth form and most students take them.[62]

The Australian government has also announced its intention to create specialist senior high schools that would specialise in a trade relevant to business activity in the region where the schools are sited. The schools would be governed by a council with local business people on it and 'chaired by a local business or industry representative'.[63] In NSW specialist senior high schools are being established along the lines of the UK specialist high schools: 'Business values will strongly inform college culture, with each governing body "chaired by a local business or industry representative with other members from the local business community".'[64]

Australian education ministers decided in 1999 as part of *The Adelaide Declaration on National Goals for Schooling in the Twenty-First Century* that every school student should have 'participated in programs of vocational learning during the compulsory years and have had access to vocational education and training programs as part of their senior secondary studies'.[65]

On-the-job schooling

In the Australian state of Victoria school students are able to incorporate part-time work at McDonald's restaurants as part of their studies towards their high school graduation certificate and assessment of this work contributes towards their university entrance marks. The 'Certificate II in Food Retail (McDonald's)' consists of 300 hours of on-the-job training at McDonald's and 294 hours study on topics like interacting with customers, balancing a cash register and performing routine housekeeping duties. McDonald's is responsible for selection, training and assessment even though the subject counts towards a state educational certificate. These matters are not open to public scrutiny so as to protect McDonald's 'commercial secrets' and 'competitive advantage'.[66]

This initiative is part of the Victorian VET (Vocational Education and Training) in Schools programme introduced in 1993, which seeks to prepare students for work whilst in school, through enabling them 'to develop skills and approaches to work most valued by employers'. According to the Victorian Board of Studies, VET in Schools is beneficial to employers because it 'enables industry to influence educational programs in schools'; 'enables employers to use the program for selection purposes'; and provides training not only for future employees but also supervision experience for their own employees.[67]

NSW students can work ten hours each week on the cash register at Big W as part of a school retail operations course.[68] Students can also train in automotive trade skills with Toyota's T3 programme, as part of their higher school certificate, spending one day of their school week in a Toyota dealership.[69] In South Australia, students can work at Mitsubishi Motors, or one of Mitsubishi's dealers or suppliers, as part of their school certificate of education.[70]

In NSW seven new vocational subjects were added to the Higher School Certificate (HSC) curriculum in 2001 and they can count towards a university entrance mark. For example some 2000 students enrolled in Business Services–Office Administration and learned office skills such as filing, word-processing, answering the phone politely and sending an invoice. At Mackellar Girls' High School, 'students spend two of every six periods working at their vitamins business Vitamacs, a virtual firm, created to generate paperwork'. In addition students have to spend 70 hours working at a real business.[71]

By 2007 one in three HSC students were taking vocational courses in NSW, and the most popular was hospitality, much more popular than economics or geography.[72] In Victoria '44 percent of all students enrolled in a senior secondary certificate were enrolled in VET in Schools'. Tourism and hospitality, business and clerical, and computing made up half the programmes offered.[73] The take up is much lower in private schools with only 16 per cent of senior students in non-Catholic private schools doing VET subjects, and 33 per cent in Catholic schools.[74]

Workplace learning is also being promoted at the national level in Australia. The government report, A Working Solution, stated that workplace education had a place in schools because it helped young people 'to align' their attitudes 'with those of employers'. It strongly recommended extending workplace training, such as that offered by McDonald's, into the early years of high school:[75]

McDonald's training is so successful in developing positive work related attitudes in young people that its employees are universally valued by other employers. McDonald's employs thousands of inexperienced young people, teaches them skills, builds their self-confidence and instils self-discipline as it motivates them to become the world's most productive hamburger vendors.[76]

In the UK McDonald's has been approved as a school exam board enabling students working there to gain A-level equivalents by doing staff training in a 'basic shift manager' course. Two other companies, Network Rail and airline Flybe, can also award national qualifications and others are expected to follow.[77]

Enterprise education

Enterprise education has been proliferating in schools around the world.[78] It aims to give students an understanding of economics and business, as well as to encourage them to be 'enterprising' and to view business enterprise as 'positive and worthwhile'. In many cases enterprise education involves the students running a very small business, often a virtual business but sometimes a real one.[79] Enterprise education is aimed at producing employees with the skills and characteristics that many employers are now looking for.[80] These are spelled out in various educational policy documents and include being task-oriented, materialistic and personally ambitious.

Enterprise-minded students are expected to seek self-advancement, make the most of opportunities, solve business problems creatively, take risks, adapt to – rather than fight – changed circumstances, and use others to achieve their goals. Such characteristics contrast with those expected of citizenship (see Table 9.1) which tend to be more community-oriented. Citizen education promotes critical thinking, a willingness to cooperate to achieve a better future for all, and an ability to politically oppose things that undermine citizen rights.

In the UK, over 200 specialist schools have a business and enterprise specialism and as a result are expected to 'Develop strong curriculum business links and teaching strengths in business education, financial capability, work-related learning and enterprise-related vocational programmes.' It is expected that these schools will teach students about enterprise culture and enhance their understanding and appreciation of business.[81] The government allocated £60 million per year for three years from 2005 to provide enterprise education in English schools. The aim was to provide enterprise learning for all 14- to 16-year-olds as part of the mandatory work-related learning in schools that was introduced in 2004.[82]

Enterprise education in the UK, as elsewhere, has been driven by business (see Box 9.2). In a paper on 'Creating an Enterprise Culture', Enterprise Insight and the Small Business Service argue that it is good for the business environment if school graduates have an 'entrepreneurial mindset' and 'positive attitudes towards enterprise'. Although surveys showed that people admired those who ran their own business, most corporate executives felt that people in the UK didn't regard entrepreneurs and entrepreneurial behaviour as highly as people in other nations and a significant percentage associated business success with low morals or ethics.[83]

Scotland has a school programme, *Determined to Succeed* (DtS), which aims to bring enterprise education to all Scottish schools. The aim is to change young

Table 9.1   Enterprise versus Citizen Education

Enterprise Education	Citizen Education
• Understanding business	• Understanding the world
• Contract-based	• Ethics-based
• Self-motivation	• Self-motivation
• Acquisitiveness, materialism	• Concern with social justice
• Taking responsibility for one's own actions and future	• Socially responsible
• Creative, innovative	• Critical thinking
• Flexible, adaptable	• Challenging the status quo
• Ability to take advantage of opportunities	• Ability to see what the problem is
• Willingness to take risks	• Analytical and creative skills
	• Avoiding unnecessary risks
• Task-oriented, outcomes focused	• Community-oriented
• 'can-do' attitude	• Politically active
• Pro-active, taking initiative	
• Skills in negotiating	• Skills in cooperating and collaborating
• Ability to manage and use a network	

***Box 9.2*   Organisations Fostering Enterprise Education in the UK**

- Enterprise Insight, founded and run by British Chambers of Commerce (BCC), the Confederation of British Industry (CBI), the Institute of Directors and the Federation of Small Businesses, organises a national Enterprise Week each year with over 1000 events around the country.[84]
- Academy of Enterprise aims 'to assist schools and higher education institutions develop an enterprise culture'.
- Businessdynamics is 'a business education and enterprise charity that aims to bring business to life for young people'.
- The National Federation of Enterprise Agencies.
- Business in the Community aims to 'support business in continually improving its positive impact on society'.
- The National Education Business Partnership Network.
- Shell LiveWire.[85]
- Personal Development Curriculum (PDC) has classroom materials on 'how real entrepreneurs became successful'.[86]
- YoungBiz runs courses and workshops for students in the UK, the US, South Korea and Hong Kong, publishes classroom curricula, and trains teachers.[87]
- Rolls-Royce has developed Profitable Pursuit, a business simulation tool 'adapted to suit the school curriculum in order to provide students with realistic business challenges across a full range of functions'.
- National Foundation for Teaching Entrepreneurship (see Table 9.2).

Table 9.2   Some International Enterprise Programmes

Organisation	Reach	Funding	Activities
Junior Achievement (JA)[88]	6 million students each year in over 100 countries on six continents, 4 million in the US alone	Hundreds of corporations including Best Buy, Deloitte, AIG, Mastercard International, 3M, PricewaterhouseCoopers and Morgan Stanley	Courses, textbooks, study guides, games, from kindergarten up
Young Achievement Australia (YAA)[89]	170,000 students each year	BHP Billiton, Westpac, IBM Australia and hundreds of other corporations ($2.5 million)	Business mentors, economics programmes from primary school up
Young Enterprise, UK[90]	320,000 each year	3000 businesses, including HSBC Bank, Cadbury Schweppes, Hewlett Packard, Nestlé UK, Procter & Gamble and TNT Express	Primary school modules teach children how to be good workers and consumers; *Project Business* for secondary students
Young Enterprise Scheme (YES), NZ[91]	35,000 each year including 40% of secondary schools	Enterprise New Zealand Trust (ENZT)	Students run a business and earn credits towards school qualifications
National Foundation for Teaching Entrepreneurship (NFTE)[92]	100,000 students in 14 countries	Goldman Sachs foundation (over $2 million), Microsoft Corporation (over $1 million), Merrill Lynch, Scaife Family Foundation, Morgan Stanley Foundation, and many others	online curriculum – BizTech; a textbook; various school and after school programmes; and business camps

people's attitudes and produce young people with positive attitudes towards business who understand entrepreneurship. It is supported by funds from businesses and £2 million from the Hunter Foundation.[93]

The Australian Commonwealth Government actively promotes enterprise education. It initiated an Enterprise in Schools programme in 1995 aimed at 'the inculcation of enterprising cultures, mindsets and qualities in young people', and allocated $3.2 million for the 1997–99 triennium.[94] In 1999 the Ministerial Council on Education, Employment, Training and Youth Affairs (MCEETYA) included enterprise education as 'a priority area within the National Goals for Schooling in the Twenty-First Century'.[95] The education department also allocated $10 million to the Enterprise Learning for the 21st Century Initiative between 2004 and 2007.[96]

The state education departments also embraced enterprise education during the 1990s. Victoria incorporated enterprise education at various stages and subjects from kindergarten to year ten. A dedicated subject, Industry and Enterprise Studies, was introduced for senior students. Enterprise education has also been integrated throughout the curriculum in South Australia and a programme called 'Ready Set Go' was implemented there at a cost of $9 million over three years from 1997.[97]

EDUCATION VERSUS TRAINING

The history of school education reflects a struggle between a utilitarian approach that attempts to shape school education to equip children to be workers and the view that school education should develop the human potential of individual children without reference to what might be expected of them as workers in the future.[98] Business has always argued for the utilitarian approach and it is clearly winning the battle with more and more school time devoted to vocational training.

Whilst vocational training in schools has obvious benefits for employers, the benefits for the students themselves and for society are more ambiguous. A major difference between training and education is that training is aimed at fitting a person towards a specific end, whereas education is aimed at giving people choices in life. Ideally education avoids behavioural objectives since it seeks to equip people to make their own decisions.[99] Many educators have argued that such narrow and specific goals deprive future generations of other qualities that could otherwise be more fully developed, such as creative and critical faculties.

The business-driven emphasis on standardised testing is also contributing to the task of preparing children to be workers. As are 'the short segmented tasks stressing speed and neatness that predominate in most schools, the emphasis on rules from the important to the trivial, and the obsession with bells, schedules, and time clocks'.[100] Literacy is seen by employers as a skill that is necessary in the workplace rather than a means of self-expression, self-understanding or social understanding. This shapes the way literacy is taught (see next chapter).[101]

Whilst there is inevitably some overlap between training and education, training is about giving a person the skills and knowledge to carry out a particular occupation or type of occupation; education is more about helping people to attain an understanding of the world they live in and their relationship with it.[102] Education is supposed to foster independent learning and critical thinking which are often inimical to the needs of employers. It is highly improbable that vocational training gives children the opportunity to critically analyse the role of work in society or even to know and exercise their rights as workers.

Education is about understanding 'the reasons behind things', something training not only fails to provide but is likely to deliberately 'obscure'.[103] The propensity to question and show initiative, which a good education breeds, may be quite unsuitable for some jobs, particularly those at the bottom end of the occupational hierarchy where intellect just gets in the way of operating a machine or obeying orders.[104] In contrast to education, for vocational training:

> The test of the relevance of any subject, its place in the hierarchy of classroom knowledge, depends not on the insight it gives into the fundamental workings of nature or culture, nor the extent to which it develops particular creative or critical sensibilities, but how far it contributes to the formation of general dispositions for manual or mental labour in capitalist or bureaucratic organizations.[105]

The more employers influence and shape education the more it will tend towards worker training and away from citizen education.

10
Dumbing Down Future Citizens

> In factory-like schools, you will often hear words like
> 'performance' and 'achievement,' but rarely words like 'discovery'
> or 'exploration' or 'curiosity.'
>
> Alfie Kohn[1]

In country after country, beginning in the mid 1970s in the US, education was declared to be in crisis. This did not reflect the real state of education. Rather, businesspeople and their allies manufactured the perception of crisis for the purpose of discrediting the public school system and making their change agenda more widely acceptable.[2] In 1975 a cover story of *Newsweek* declared:

> Willy-nilly, the US educational system is spawning a generation of semi-literates. Nationwide the statistics on literacy grow more appalling each year ... The cries of dismay sound even louder in the halls of commerce, industry and the professions, where writing is the basis for almost all formal business communication.[3]

The theme was taken up by other media and the idea of educational crisis spread. Ira Shor, in his book *Culture Wars*, wrote: 'You did not count in education unless you could wring your hands over student illiteracy, tabulate an impressive amount of failure, denounce the levellers who brought us to the brink of savagery, and impose martial plans to remedy the problem.'[4]

During the late 1970s, schools in England also came under an orchestrated media attack for low standards, 'rising disorder', and a failure to prepare students adequately for work.[5] Media attention focused on the failings of state schools in the UK, particularly those in inner city areas that were said to be controlled by left-leaning local education authorities (LEAs), because they focused on equity issues. The Thatcher government sought to undermine LEA control[6] after it came to power in 1979, following an election campaign that 'Educashun isn't working' and claims that reading and writing standards were falling.[7]

The perception of crisis in public schools in the US and elsewhere was helped along by funding cuts that created real difficulties for schools in poor areas. It was reinforced by a shift by those who could afford it to more affluent suburban public schools and private schools. This exodus from poorer public schools enabled those who wanted change in schools to argue that this was also what the public wanted.

Actually, the surveys showed that those who had least experience of schools were most dissatisfied with them. People who had only the media accounts to go by were far more likely to rate schools as poorly performing than were those with children attending public schools. Also people tended to rate their local schools, those they knew most about, much more highly than schools in general.[8]

Moreover the statistical basis for claims of falling literacy and numeracy standards was faulty. In the US the claims were largely based on average scores in the Scholastic Aptitude Tests (SATs), a voluntary test, mainly taken by students wanting to go on to higher education. The minor decline in SAT scores between 1963 to 1980 coincided with an increase in the proportion of students going on to higher education. Whereas before only the top performing students went on to higher education, now a wider range of students of differing academic abilities were taking the test.[9]

When the SAT scores were analysed it was found that the scores for the top-ranking high school students had not declined, nor had they for other groups of students. Other tests such as the National Assessment of Educational Progress (NAEP), which attempts to assess reasoning ability, showed no decline during the 1970s or 1980s, but rather a slight improvement in writing ability, reading comprehension and inferential skills.[10]

School critics also claimed that American students didn't score very well on international tests compared with other nations. Again this was partly a result of more students staying on in high school. Other nations often had 'much more selective education systems' that 'weeded out' less academic students at an earlier age and sent them on a vocational track earlier. They therefore had a more elite group taking the tests that provided the basis for national comparisons. Also other countries did not always have fully representative student samples.[11]

Average scores also mask a great variability in US schools, which include some of the best in the world and some of the worst in the world. This is because of the variability in funding that occurs in US schools (see Chapter 6) – more than in most other affluent nations – and the large variability in incomes in the population as a whole.[12]

Every decade the crisis message has been renewed. The 1983 'A Nation at Risk' report (see Chapter 8) created a second crisis for education. It claimed there were high levels of illiteracy in 17-year-olds, particularly amongst minorities, and falling achievement levels at a time when the need for skilled workers was increasing rapidly. It recommended that schools 'adopt more rigorous and measurable standards and standardized tests'.[13]

The report cited no studies to support its claims of crisis in America's schools but this did not stop newspapers, radio and television stations around the US covering the report uncritically and spreading its message of crisis.[14] 'The media brought the bad news into every living room and put the school crisis on the front-pages.'[15]

In 1991 President Bush again sounded the alarm: 'Every day brings new evidence of crisis.'[16] *Time* magazine declared 'the nation's schools are mired in mediocrity'.[17] In 1992 a government report entitled 'Adult Literacy in America' suggested that almost half the population was illiterate, however a later report, based on the same data, that found it was actually less than 5 per cent went unreported. Ten years later, the statisticians admitted that they had misread the data for the original report. In the *Chronicle of Higher Education*, Dennis Baron, noted that this admission would 'not be able to dispel the deeply rooted conviction that there is a literacy problem in the Unites States, and that only school reform and increased testing can turn it around'.[18]

That deeply rooted conviction was not helped by the 'lopsided' reporting of educational progress by the media. The corporate-owned media highlighted every test score decline in public schools. Good news was not reported, such as a Rand study showing how government funding (Title 1) targeting low-income students had 'resulted in dramatic improvements by black and Latino students' between the 1960s and 1990s.[19]

The business-fed perception of crisis in schools has continued to the present day in the US and the UK. The media still periodically publishes alarmist headlines about the state of literacy and numeracy in the population. Various literacy crises have also been staged in Australia, beginning in the 1970s. The aim of the manufactured crises has been 'to undermine the legitimacy of public belief in state schooling' and to enable governments to implement reforms including curriculum benchmarks and standardised tests.[20] One such crisis occurred in 1996–97 when media reports and politicians discussed literacy in terms of 'crisis', 'deficit', 'national disgrace', 'shame', 'deception' and other derogatory and emotional terms. The Minister for Schools, Vocational Education and Training, David Kemp, released the results of a National English Literacy Survey on the television program *60 Minutes* on which he described the 'scandalous' state of literacy in schools that was being hidden from parents.[21]

In reality literacy in Australia, as in many other nations, is linked to issues such as cultural diversity and poverty and problems tend to be most pronounced amongst recent migrants of non-English-speaking backgrounds. Anthony Welch in his 1997 book on Australian education noted that there was little evidence of a literacy crisis and in fact most academic surveys of literacy showed either improvement over time or no significant change, which was an impressive achievement given the increasing numbers of non-English speakers in the population.[22] The most recent effort to characterise schools as delivering falling literacy and numeracy standards came in 2006 when the federal government pushed for a national curriculum. This was despite the fact that Australian students had scored near the top of international tests in science, maths and reading.[23]

In New Zealand a 'crisis was "manufactured" by treasury officials, the conservative National Party in opposition, the media and the business roundtable'.[24] An educational crisis was declared in Ontario in the late 1980s when the media reported that children performed badly on international standardised tests. The reports continued into the early 1990s and in 1993 when a Royal Commission on Learning was set up. That year reading and writing tests were introduced into schools at grade nine.[25]

NARROWING THE CURRICULUM

The manufactured literacy and numeracy crises enabled business to pressure schools to narrow and standardise the school curricula in English-speaking nations to emphasise literacy, numeracy, computer skills and a business-friendly view of history and economics. This narrowing has been firstly a means of minimising costs by cutting away extraneous subjects and learning so that schools will concentrate their efforts on teaching the 'basics'.

Various US reports published during the 1980s by business-funded groups (including reports from the Carnegie Foundation, The Twentieth Century Fund, and The Governor's Commission on the States[26]) agreed that what schools needed included reduced student choice of subjects, fewer electives, less time spent on extracurricular activities and more focus and time on reading and writing, math and science. As we saw in the previous chapter, business leaders tend to see education as a process of acquiring the information and skills necessary to be a productive worker.[27]

Milton Goldberg, vice president of the National Alliance of Business in the US, told a Senate Committee that schools did not spend enough time on core academic instruction because they were so busy teaching non-core subjects like consumer affairs, conservation and energy, and dealing with non-academic activities such as counselling, gym, homeroom and lunch. He argued for the need to 'reclaim the school day for academic instruction'.[28] The vice president of MacMillan-Bloedel argued that the Canadian high school curriculum should consist of just six subjects: English, maths, physics, chemistry, showing up for work and how to get along with others.[29]

However the narrowing curriculum has also been a means of ideological control, a way of undermining alternative views of society and avoiding subjects that develop critical tendencies in future employees. 'What business wants is an easily quantifiable set of skills that does not allow a young intellect to stray from a straight and narrow "three R's" training.'[30]

The promotion of academic rigour and a narrow, back-to-basics curriculum is partly a reaction to the broadening of the curriculum that occurred during the 1960s and 1970s. During this time many young people subscribed to a counter-culture movement that questioned central aspects of mainstream materialist culture, including its inegalitarian structure, business values and impacts on community and the environment. The movement influenced schools and brought a new emphasis on equity and critical thought that affected not only the content of classroom discussions but the methods used to teach. Teachers encouraged debate about social institutions and current news topics.

Educational curricula in many nations began to include sex education, peace studies and feminist studies, and to be inclusive of the concerns of indigenous people, immigrants, people of differing ethnic backgrounds, and the poor.[31] Subjects such as 'film-making, peace education, drama, sociology or personal development' were introduced. These were considered irrelevant by business groups but also undesirable as they promoted a 'personal development and a liberal outlook' that were at odds with what employers required.[32]

The changing school curricula stirred fears of rebellion, lawlessness and social disorder amongst some businesspeople and their allies. Business leaders and conservatives disliked the growing activism of school students which seemed to arise from the broadened school curricula.[33] Teachers were accused of being left-wing and 'espousing an anti-business, or anti-industry stance'.[34] From the point of view of business leaders: 'Too many people were studying foreign policy, hiring practices, job injuries, pollution and product-safety ... Knowledge was out of control ... The protest period had brought together too many people who had learned they had a right to criticize the whole system.'[35]

Kevin Donnelly, who writes on education policy for the Australian corporate-funded think tank, the Institute of Public Affairs (IPA), argued that political correctness, education fads and left-wing ideas had skewed education in Australia so that teachers spent their time advocating homosexuality, multiculturalism and Aboriginal concerns rather than teaching the three R's.[36]

In 2007 Australian state education ministers promised to eliminate the subject 'Studies of Society and Environment', which had been a key learning area, and replace it with 'the traditional disciplines of history, geography and economics'.[37] Former prime minister, John Howard, labelled school curricula as 'politically correct' and claimed that traditional subjects such as English, history and geography had been displaced by 'incomprehensible sludge'.[38]

The role of standardised testing

The desire of employers to reduce the curriculum down to basic skills with more focus on the so-called three R's of reading, writing and arithmetic has been aided by the new emphasis on standardised tests. Standards and high-stakes testing not only dictate what should be in the curriculum but also, by taking up most of the time, what should not be in it.

Frederick Hess of the American Enterprise Institute argues that 'coercive measures – incentives and sanctions – to ensure that educators teach and students master specific content' are necessary 'to compel students and teachers to cooperate'. According to Hess, high-stakes testing forces teachers and administrators to make painful changes, such as cutting electives so students spend more time learning the basics. He points out that proponents of coercive accountability reject the idea that poor student performance 'is caused largely by factors outside the control of teachers or administrators'.[39]

A major consequence of high-stakes testing is that activities and subjects have been dropped if they offer no competitive advantage with other schools and are not included in academic league tables. Casualties include health education, environmental education, social sciences (history and geography), civics, art, music, creative writing, drama and physical education.[40]

The Center on Education Policy found in its survey of the impact of the No Child Left Behind (NCLB) legislation that 71 per cent of school districts reduced the time spent on at least one other subject so as to spend more time on preparing children for maths and reading tests.[41] An American Federation of Teachers survey found that 87 per cent of members claimed that important subjects and activities were being forced out of the school curriculum.[42] 'Elementary teachers report that they devote more than a month to test preparation for the English Language Arts exam by eliminating all subjects other than language arts.'[43]

In many states poorly performing students are being required to do double the normal number of classes in English and mathematics and therefore have to drop electives such as art, music, social studies and languages. They 'are being deprived of a well-rounded education and the opportunity to explore new subjects'.[44]

In England and Wales the introduction of a national subject-centred curriculum, with a core that is subject to testing, has meant that students are much less likely to get the 'benefit of a rich, well-designed and broad curriculum'. Boyle and Bragg have shown that between 1997 and 2004 more class time has been spent on English, Maths and information technology and less on all other subjects including science, history, geography, art, music and physical education.[45] Other educational elements such as social sciences, humanities, foreign languages, or the arts are considered 'needlessly inefficient and expensive'.[46]

A UK Select Committee has found that the curriculum taught in schools has been narrowed as a result of high-stakes standardised teaching, and this has been 'at the expense of a more rounded education for pupils'. Ninety per cent of primary and 79 per cent of secondary schools have claimed that 'national testing has led to pupils being offered a narrower curriculum'. Moreover, within each subject the teaching has become narrower – only material likely to be tested is covered – and more shallow – facts and information likely to be in the test are taught rather than deeper understanding of concepts.[47]

TRADITIONAL VERSUS PROGRESSIVE EDUCATION

Business publications derided the progressive teaching methods that flourished in the 1960s and early 1970s and aimed to develop students to be 'questioners, caring and cooperative people who value democratic participation and social justice'.[48] Writing in a right-wing conservative magazine, *The Public Interest*, Heather MacDonald attacked the progressive trends in education: 'Rather than studying possessive pronouns, students are learning how language silences women and blacks.'[49]

In Australia 'support for more rigorous examinations was coupled with demands for a more traditional academic curriculum and demands for an end to undiscipline, moral license and progressivist experiments'.[50] Donnelly criticised the progressive paradigm for being based on 'a belief that education was essentially a political process where students had to be "socially critical" and "empowered" so as to enable them to "challenge the status quo"'.[51]

Business leaders called for a return to the traditional paradigm of education whereby education is supposed to develop character and virtue in the child, through discipline and the transmission of a common cultural heritage.[52] During the nineteenth century, educators sought to educate children 'by two disciplines – that of the will in correct habits, and by that of the intellect in the correct view of the world'.[53] The purpose of rigour in school subjects was to provide mental training and discipline.[54]

In contrast, the progressive paradigm of education which arose early in the twentieth century and gained dominance in the 1950s stressed the development of individual intellectual potential, creative self-expression, analytical thought, and the development of responsible citizens, and reflective and critical thinkers. It placed the development of the child at the centre of education with interdisciplinary topic work, an integrated school day, curriculum content relevant to situation and student backgrounds, a co-operative work environment, and teachers as facilitators rather than disciplinarians or authority figures (see Table 10.1).[55]

Table 10.1   Educational Paradigms

Progressive	Traditional
Integrated subject matter	Separate subject matter
Teacher as guide to educational experiences	Teacher as distributor of knowledge
Active pupil role	Passive pupil role
Pupil participation in curriculum planning	Pupils have no say in curriculum planning
Learning predominantly by discovery techniques	Accent on memory, practice and rote
External rewards and punishments not necessary	External rewards and punishments used
Not too concerned with conventional academic standards	Concerned with academic standards
Little testing	Regular testing
Accent on co-operation and group work	Accent on competition
Teaching not confined to classroom	Teaching largely confined to classroom
Emphasis on team teaching	Emphasis on individual teaching
Open plan layout	Closed classroom layout
Accent on creative expression	Little emphasis on creative expression

Source: Neville Bennett, quoted in D. Hill, '"Education, Education, Education", or "Business, Business, Business"?', paper presented at the European Educational Research Association Annual Conference, Lahti, Finland, 22–25 September 1999, p. 17.

For those who believe in the progressive paradigm of education, education is not simply a matter of acquiring a body of knowledge but rather about giving people the types of 'dispositions and orientations' that will enable them to solve problems, learn autonomously in new situations, deal wisely with change and diversity, and be 'flexible and creative'.[56] The traditional paradigm sought to fit the child to the existing social order, whereas the progressive paradigm sought to give students the capacity to transform it.

In 1986 the US Department of Education published a booklet on *What Works* in schools that championed a return to the traditional paradigm as demanded by business groups. Its prescription for schools included enforcement of discipline, memorisation (of spelling, literary passages and historical dates), moral awareness, academic rigour, good character, continuous assessment and positive work attitudes.[57] It advised:

Teachers can encourage students to develop memory skills by teaching highly structured and carefully sequenced lessons, with frequent reinforcement for correct answers. Young students, slow students, and students who lack background knowledge can benefit from such instruction. In addition, teachers can teach 'mnemonics,' that is devices and techniques for improving memory.[58]

What Works was part of the push for 'back-to-basics' schooling, promoted by business interests under the rubric 'educational excellence'. Excellence was a euphemism for discipline, business-determined standards, a narrow academic approach and traditional values. The call for 'excellence for all' was a way of displacing concerns about equity.

Some of the key characteristics of back-to-basics methods are:

1. Most of the school day will be devoted to reading, writing and arithmetic. Phonics is the method to teach reading rather than whole-word or phrase methods.
2. In high school, the basic subjects are English, science, math and history. Textbooks should not display non-traditional values in sex, religion or politics, nor promote criticism of the nation or the family.
3. Pedagogy is teacher-centered with stern discipline.
4. Frequent drills, homework every day, testing, and class recitation on required material.
5. Traditional letter or number-grading, issued often.
6. Corporal punishment permitted. Dress codes should be enforced, including student hair styles.
7. Academic criteria for promotion; no social promotion.
8. No 'frills' such as 'clay modeling' and 'sex education'.
9. Fewer electives, increase required courses.[59]

This list serves equally well as a list of business demands for school 'reform' and most of its elements are being introduced into schools in English-speaking nations. The more recent demands by business coalitions for rigorous academic standards for all students and regimes of testing are in fact a call for a return to the traditional paradigm of education. Business lobbyists argue that students should cover specific content and achieve certain learning outcomes, such as basic

---

Box 10.1   'Back to Basics' in Mathematics Teaching

Traditional mathematics emphasised drills and memorisation of methods and caused many people in earlier generations to hate mathematics. Progressive methods of teaching mathematics aim to get children to understand how mathematics works and to relate it to their lives. For example, Chicago teacher Eric Gutstein uses the conflict between tomato pickers and growers to get students to perform mathematical calculations to work out the merits of each side's argument; how long pickers have to work to get the amount growers claim they earn, whether they earn more or less than the minimum wage, etc.[60]

Progressive methods encourage students to find their own ways to solve maths problems. Now it is claimed that US students are falling behind students in other nations in their ability to do international maths tests and there has been a call for a return to basic drills and memorisation.[61]

proficiency in reading, writing and maths. High-stakes testing in fact encourages a return to the traditional paradigm of teaching in its tendency to promote teaching to the test.[62]

The Australian Council of Deans of Education describes back-to-basics methods:

> The process was learning by rote and knowing the 'correct answers'. 'Discipline' was demonstrated in tests as the successful acquisition of received facts and the regurgitation of rigidly defined truths ... Actually, the very idea of the basics indicated something about the nature of knowledge: it was a kind of shopping list of things-to-be-known – through drilling the 'times tables', memorising spelling lists, learning the parts of speech and correct grammar.[63]

REDUCED TEACHER AUTONOMY

In England during the 1960s and 1970s teachers had a great deal of autonomy with respect to the curriculum, methods of teaching and evaluation of students, and primary schools, in particular, were 'once celebrated world wide for [their] creative child-centred approach'.[64] However the school reforms of the 1980s changed all that. Now the central government specifies not only the syllabus for English and maths but the methods for teaching them in primary schools, 'down to the level of sections of each hour-long daily lesson'.[65]

A recent survey of teachers in England found that almost 90 per cent of them wanted more freedom to tailor the school curriculum to student needs. For example, they cannot adapt it to suit a more ethnically diverse group of students. Teachers believe that if they were able to focus on teaching skills using knowledge that was of interest to the students they would be much more motivated to learn.[66] The UK Association for Science Education, for example, argues that testing 'results in a culture that limits innovation and enjoyment of learning' and the Select Committee has recognised that teachers 'find it more difficult to explore the curriculum in an interesting and motivational way'.[67]

In the US, the imperatives of high-stakes testing and the push for traditional educational paradigms are leading to increased use of learning drills and scripted lessons that involve direct teacher command and controlled student responses which punish student spontaneity, eliminate humour, laughter and fun, and formalise student interactions.[68]

> Teachers across the map complain that the joy is being drained from teaching as their work is reduced to passing out worksheets and drilling children as if they were in dog obedience school. Elementary 'test prep' classroom methods involve teachers snapping their fingers at children to get responses, following scripted lessons where they simply recite prompts for students...[69]

In poor urban schools in the US, commercially produced scripted teaching programmes are used as a way of making the curriculum teacher-proof – that is, avoiding opportunities for teachers to insert their own opinions, teaching skills, or curriculum broadening tendencies. They are also a way of ensuring a uniform product, both in terms of the learning experience and the student. Instead of textbooks, students are given workbooks with names like *Test Best* and *Bridging the Test Gap*, and teachers are given manuals to ensure that on any 'given day everyone is at the same place in the sequence'.[70] In some cases students learn to read, not from literature, but from disconnected sentences on which they are then quizzed.[71]

Box 10.2   Open Court by McGraw-Hill

Open Court, produced by McGraw-Hill, is a scripted teaching programme that has been mandated by some school districts. The programme requires teachers to teach lessons in an undifferentiated way to all students at the same time, with minimal interaction between students and teacher.

Teacher Elizabeth Jaeger describes how these materials prevented her and other teachers from teaching in an active, holistic and co-operative manner: 'In kindergarten and 1st grade, teachers now taught the least meaningful aspects of literacy – letters and sounds – and postponed emphasis on meaning for nearly two years.' According to Jaeger, children were bored and frustrated since their ability to actively participate was limited. McGraw-Hill trainers would come into the classroom whenever they liked and even interrupt classes to reprimand teachers who were not following the script.[72]

In the reading curriculum in use within the school, for instance, teachers told me they had been forewarned to steer away from verbal deviations or impromptu bits of conversation, since each passage of instruction needed to be timed ... and any digressions from the printed plans could cause them problems if a school official or curriculum director happened to be in the building at the time.[73]

Chanting answers in unison, as happens in KIPP schools, may encourage the production of the 'team players' that employers want, but it discourages 'mavericks, critics and dissenters' and those who can ask the penetrating questions; people who are so necessary for social development and wisdom.[74]

CORE KNOWLEDGE

Rather than tailor the curriculum to the interests and talents of the children, an aim of business-driven reforms is to define core knowledge and coerce schools to teach it.[75] During the 1980s, business leaders seeking to influence the choice of core knowledge promoted a book by E.D. Hirsch entitled *Cultural Literacy*. Hirsch, who is now a visiting fellow at the conservative think tank, the Hoover

Institute, argued that schools paid too much attention to students' emotional and psychological well-being and not enough to teaching them basic knowledge.[76]

Hirsch claimed that the idea of teaching children how to learn rather than teaching them particular content was creating children who were ignorant of essential cultural knowledge, which he referred to as 'core knowledge'. This was knowledge of world history, geography and literature (great books).[77] In other words, core knowledge is that knowledge deemed by the political and business elite to be essential.

In the UK, where the curriculum authority has a heavy business representation (see Box 10.3), the National Curriculum emphasises 'British history, British geography and "classic" English literature'.[78]

Box 10.3   Membership of the UK Qualifications and Curriculum Authority (QCA)

- The 13-member board is made up of six business people (two from Unilever), two education bureaucrats, four head teachers and a former school inspector.[79]
- The chair is Sir Anthony Greener, formerly chair of Diageo Plc, the largest multinational alcoholic beverages company in the world. He has also held positions with the Confederation of British Industry (CBI) and the Chartered Institute of Marketing. His knighthood was awarded for services to the drinks industry.
- The deputy chair was chair of Unilever.

The idea of a 'core curriculum' is a way of avoiding 'the ideology diversity of the protest era' and imposing an official, 'cleansed' view of history and a standard view of English. The aim is to support the status quo and transmit 'an official value system disguised as universal knowledge' instead of empowering students or encouraging diverse and pluralistic curricula.[80]

In Australia, the Australian Council for Educational Standards (ACES) – founded by Ray Evans, a former business executive with Western Mining Corporation and co-founder of various business-financed right-wing activist groups – campaigned for schooling to reinforce mainstream Australian moral, political and economic values rather than question them.[81]

Anthony Welch, in his book on *Class, Culture and the State in Australian Education*, claimed that the concern with literacy 'standards' signified 'a desire to return to an ideal society, embodying traditional discipline, traditional moral codes, and more monolithic cultural, racial, religious and gender regimes'. Hence the emphasis on literature from the elitist English traditions.[82]

In 2006 the Australian minister for education, Julie Bishop, argued that a 'back-to-basics uniform national curriculum' was necessary because left-wing 'ideologues' had 'hijacked' the curriculum and school students were subjected to 'trendy educational fads'.[83] Prime minister at the time, John Howard, noted:

'Until recent times, it had become almost *de rigueur* in intellectual circles to regard Australian history as little more than a litany of sexism, racism and class warfare.'[84]

Box 10.4 Standard English

In 1974 the National Council of Teachers of English (NCTE) in the US agreed to a policy called 'Students' Rights to their own Language' which recognised that the language of Standard English was the language of teachers, literature and the elite but that most people spoke a different form of English.[85] Teachers wanted to widen the English curriculum to accept 'white colloquial, black bi-dialectical, Hispanic bilingual' language.

Conservatives and business people sought to reinforce Standard English (which is used in business) and ensure that colloquial English and the 'language of the left' were declared illegitimate.[86] *Newsweek* blamed the changes in educational philosophy that allowed students to use 'colloquial, slangy, even illiterate' speech, and neglected written language and the study of 'syntax, structure and style', for a decline in student literacy.[87]

The NSW education minister, Carmel Tebbutt, argued against the attempt to 'limit history to one "approved" version' claiming it did students a disservice because it was important for them to understand the historical context of events, in particular that they are subject to interpretation from a variety of viewpoints, as well as to recognise that some viewpoints and voices have been excluded.[88]

Nevertheless the four-person committee appointed to draft a national history curriculum included Gerard Henderson, head of a right-wing think tank, and Geoffrey Blainey, a controversial historian associated with a number of right-wing causes and critical of what he calls the 'black armband view of history'.[89] This is a term used to describe a critical view of history which supposedly induces shame for the way Aborigines, immigrants and women were treated in the past.

Business leaders and politicians in the US have promoted history standards that portray the US as a land of willing immigrants with a 'White Anglo-Saxon' culture, where hard work produced prosperity and progress; 'a history that emphasized U.S. accomplishments and provided students with uplifting ideals' rather than one that covered negative aspects of history such as the Ku Klux Klan and McCarthyism. Their preferred version of history ignored the experience of many ethnic groups in the US, including African Americans, Native Americans and Mexican Americans.[90] Writing in *Rethinking Schools*, Barbara Miner, says:

One of the most interesting yet untold stories of the history of standards is how the governors and corporate leaders, aided by conservative think tanks, took over the standards movement and transformed it into a top-down process that establishes an official version of knowledge and sets back efforts to forge a multicultural vision, in the process valuing discrete facts, memorization, and 'basics' over critical thinking and in-depth understanding.[91]

For corporations, the important thing is to teach a set of political and social values that support business values and do not question the contribution of business to social well-being. 'More than anything, these vested interests fear a schooling which encourages critical thinking.'[92] They have therefore sought to reduce education to modules of knowledge that it is desirable for employees to have.

Box 10.5   Excerpt of Fifth-Grade Citizen Education Content Standard[93]

The Business Roundtable published this excerpt of a fifth-grade content standard for citizenship education that it approved of. It requires students to be able to:

- Identify three branches of government in the United States and describe their legislative, executive and judicial function.
- Describe the three levels of government in the United States and list examples of authority of each (local, state and federal).
- Compare how governments in the United States, Canada and Latin America select leaders, establish laws and receive their authority.
- Explain specific changes that have taken place in government over time.
- Identify and state the significance of symbols, people and events to the development of the United States, Canada and Latin America.

In this way citizenship education is reduced to a core of 'facts' that students should know rather than an analytical and critical approach to democracy.

ECONOMIC EDUCATION STANDARDS

The promotion of curriculum standards for economics by business interests provides a good example of how corporations and their allies seek to promote particular views as standard core knowledge.

The National Voluntary Content Standards for Pre-College Economics Education were established in the US in 1997. They consisted of 20 standards specifying knowledge to be obtained and benchmarks for what students should understand and be able to do at various stages of their schooling.[94]

Like NCEE, the Canadian Foundation for Economic Education (CFEE) runs a programme, supported by the Royal Bank of Canada and the Canadian government, entitled EconomicsCanada, which has produced a proposed consensus Canadian 'guideline for economic literacy' that outlines target economic concepts that students need 'to understand in order to understand economic events and realities' such as comparative advantage, economic efficiency and economic freedom.[95]

Box 10.6   **Organisations Behind the National Voluntary Content Standards**

National Council on Economic Education (NCEE)
   The NCEE operates both in the US and internationally. Its funders include State
   Farm, International Paper, UPS, Procter & Gamble, American Express, the Ford Motor
   Company Fund, the International Paper Company, the Exxon Educational Foundation,
   Unilever, Georgia-Pacific, Chrysler, AT&T, 3M, Olin, the Business Roundtable and
   the US Department of Education.[96]

Foundation for Teaching Economics (FTE)
   The FTE was formed in the US in 1975 'in response to a concern that too many
   young people lack an understanding of the basic concepts of market economics'. It
   has close associations with a number of conservative think tanks and is funded by
   corporate and right-wing foundations including the Citigroup Foundation, the GE
   Fund and the Sarah Scaife Foundation.[97]

National Association of Economic Educators

American Economic Association's Committee on Economic Education

---

The US voluntary standards provide a business oriented view of the world. For example Content Standard 13 states: 'Income for most people is determined by the market value of the productive resources they sell. What workers earn depends, primarily, on the market value of what they produce and how productive they are.' This promotes the view that the market sets wages automatically and anonymously according to supply and demand (as opposed to wage setting being the result of a power struggle between employers and workers) and that everybody gets what they deserve on the basis of their talents, education and effort (as opposed to poverty being the result of injustice, discrimination, lack of opportunities, bad luck, or a lack of adequately paid jobs being available).

The economic education standards also expect students to learn that price controls 'reduce the quantity of goods and services consumed, thus depriving consumers of some goods and services'. They learn that whilst increased government spending may increase employment and output in the short run, in the long run it will lead to increased interest rates that will reduce private sector investment, offsetting 'partially, if not entirely' those gains in employment and output.[98]

In an article on the standards in the *Journal of Economic Education*, two of the authors of the standards admitted that the standards reflected a neoclassical model of economic behaviour but defended this by stating that in order to produce 'a single, coherent set of standards to guide the teaching of economics' it was necessary to use a majority paradigm. They argued that including 'strongly held minority views' would be too confusing for teachers and their students.[99] They agreed that in the area of macroeconomics they were struggling to find a 'consensus paradigm' and that some economists would criticise their standards in this area.

Similarly they omitted many of the assumptions on which the economic principles were based: 'Almost all economics principles are conditioned on assumptions. To report all of those assumptions each time would detract from the effectiveness of the standards.'[100]

By 2002 the number of US states with economics standards was 48, many of them utilising the National Voluntary Content Standards. Three quarters of these states required the standards to be implemented and 27 states required students to be tested for economic knowledge.[101] By 2007 a third of the states required an economics course for school graduation.[102]

The National Voluntary Content Standards have facilitated the introduction of national economics testing for students, which began in 2006.[103] Questions reflected the neoclassical model of economics and the answers were by no means uncontroversial.

11
Teaching Corporate Values

> In-school commercialism is at its worst, we believe, when it masquerades as educational materials or programs and offers half-truths or misstatements that favor the sponsor of the materials. It may be difficult if not impossible for most teachers to correctly judge the objectivity and accuracy of such materials. ... Unfortunately, a teacher's use of a sponsor's materials or products implies an endorsement, and any benefits of such use may come at the cost of teaching children to scrutinize marketing messages objectively.
>
> US Consumers Union[1]

In 1992, following the Exxon Valdez oil spill, Exxon distributed a video to schools entitled *Scientists and the Alaska Oil Spill: The Wildlife, The Cleanup, The Outlook*. Michael Fry, a research physiologist at the Center for Avian Biology, who specialises in studying the effects of pollutants like petroleum on birds, described the video:

> By selecting topics carefully, and by using a carefully phrased script, Exxon conveys the impression that the spill was not severe and that it did minimal damage to wildlife and to shorelines. All the people who appear in the video seem unanimous in their opinions and actions, helping to promote Exxon's version of what happened ... Exxon's visual material consists largely of footage showing laboratory workers, clean shorelines, pristine vistas and healthy wildlife. The video almost entirely avoids showing the oil spill itself or its effects.[2]

Fry details the many ways in which the video distorted the truth for public relations purposes. For example, the video says that after the spill only 15 of the 113 eagles trapped by Exxon's teams were in such poor condition that they had to be rehabilitated. It does not say that the trapping was done between two and four months after the spill and that immediately after the spill 140 oiled eagles were found dead, nor that federal scientists believed that hundreds more died but had not been found, nor that those which survived were less able to reproduce than unaffected eagles in nearby areas.[3]

Industry-sponsored materials have been used in US schools since the mid twentieth century. By the 1970s '64% of Fortune's 500, 90% of the trade associations, and 90% of the utilities' were sending 'informational' material to schools. The four main subject areas these materials covered were nutrition, energy, the environment and economics, and that is still the case today.[4]

Industry-sponsored school materials are now common in all English-speaking nations. They take various forms, including classroom games, comic books, videos, CD-ROMs, books, brochures, posters, lesson plans and guides for teachers, virtual and real tours for students and teachers, and websites. They are advertised in teachers publications, distributed by district boards and given away free at teacher conferences. Materials provided directly to teachers bypass official curriculum review committees, so that they are not subject to any scrutiny apart from individual teachers who may not be able to discern the accuracy or bias in the materials.[5]

Industry-sponsored school materials tend to give students a misleading picture of environmental, health and social issues. They portray an industry or company as environmentally or socially responsible and beneficial to the community and defend the industry from its critics. They usually do not include blatant mistruths or inaccuracies but often distort an issue through omission of relevant information, reliance on biased industry studies, and a deceptive emphasis on particular aspects of an issue.

In a 1995 report entitled *Captive Kids*, the US Consumers Union analysed 111 different sets of school materials sponsored by commercial enterprises, trade organisations and corporate-backed non-profit organisations. It found that nearly 80 per cent of them contained 'biased, self-serving and promotional information' and this posed a 'significant and growing threat to the integrity of education in America'.[6]

Some companies use consultants or teachers to design, or at least endorse, the materials so as to ensure their credibility and acceptability in the schools and give the impression that the materials, although sponsored, are neutral and independent. Sometimes the corporate or trade association name does not appear on the materials at all, only the name of the company that produced the materials, so that teachers are not alerted to the likelihood that it is biased.[7]

Teachers usually do not have the resources or knowledge to balance the material with differing viewpoints. And there is little competition from non-corporate views because community and environmental groups and others seldom have the funding to develop professionally produced materials and distribute them widely. The industry materials sometimes come with multiple class sets or are made easily photocopiable. They are designed for specific grades and they often purport to teach the skills required for particular reading, math and/or science standards. Sometimes teachers are trained to use industry-sponsored materials.

Each year hundreds of thousands of teachers in the US attend workshops run by corporations in conjunction with their school materials.[8]

Business groups also do their best to influence school curricula to reflect the corporate view. In Australia, the NSW Employers' Education Consortium recommended that the 'social goals' section of the school business studies syllabus be deleted, as it had 'no part in a business studies course', and that the section covering environmental impact statements focus on the cost and time they take to prepare rather than the environmental goals they seek to achieve. The consortium wrote to the minister saying the entire course should be rewritten 'from a business viewpoint'.[9]

Similarly the Employer's Education Consortium of Victoria – a coalition of nine of Victoria's largest companies – had a major input into the state's high school curriculum with the introduction of a compulsory Australian studies unit on the 'World of Work'.[10]

Consultants

Lifetime Learning Systems was one of the first companies to compile educational materials on behalf of corporations and trade associations, beginning in 1978. It created some 2000 educational programs, and serviced more than 350 corporations in the US alone, including American Express, AT&T, Coca-Cola, General Mills, GM, Hershey, McDonald's, Microsoft, Nabisco, Pepsi and Walt Disney, as well as associations such as the American Nuclear Society, and claimed to reach almost 100 per cent of US schools – 63 million young people every year.[11]

In 1999 Lifetime Learning became part of WRC Media, 'the largest publisher and distributor of student periodicals and educational materials in the world'. WRC claims its materials are used in over 90 per cent of US school districts. Its *Weekly Reader* is a magazine designed for grades Pre-K-6 and is sent to 7 million children at 50,000 elementary schools.[12] After *Weekly Reader* was taken over in 1991 by K-III – which is owned by Kohlberg Kravis Roberts, the owner of cigarette manufacturer RJR Nabisco – the proportion of articles on smoking in which there was 'a clear and consistent no-use message' fell dramatically from 62 per cent to 24 per cent.[13]

According to its advertising material, WRC's other school magazines, including *Read*, *Writing*, *Current Science* (all grades six to ten) and *Current Health 2* (grades seven to twelve), 'reach more than 2.2 million teens who are looking for *anything* to take their minds off school work! <u>Your</u> message gets <u>their</u> attention'.[14] (WRC Media merged with the Reader's Digest Association in 2006 and is now called RD School and Education Services.)

Video Placement Worldwide distributes company-sponsored videos, CD-ROMs, teacher guides, posters and worksheets to 90 per cent of US public schools. It claims that it can 'successfully create demand for and deliver sponsored messages (print, video or CD-ROM) into the classroom' where they are used over and over, exposing each new class to the messages. It offers companies the opportunity to 'help develop loyalties about your industry'. The materials it distributes include a Mastercard video on managing personal credit and a Jelly Belly Candy Co. video on manufacturing candy.[15]

EdComs is a UK-based educational consultancy that seeks to 'communicate our clients' images and values' to school children from pre-school up, through classroom resources, theatre in education, teacher training, videos, CD-ROMs, websites, award programmes and ceremonies for schools. Its clients include BP, BT, Weetabix, Nestlé, Wrigley's Gum and BSkyB. EdComs developed the 'Energy for Everyone' pack for Weetabix in an effort to 'reach pupils and parents through a fun activity that would reinforce the brand's core value as a source of energy'. The pack came with the bonus of free sports equipment and was requested by 48 per cent of British primary schools, as well as gaining 'extensive coverage in the media'.[16]

There are many other companies that produce material for corporate clients in various parts of the world. Naturally, these companies compete for business on the basis of how well they can help corporations achieve their goals rather than on the basis of the educational merit of their materials.[17] Even traditional suppliers of school materials, such as Scholastic, put together school materials for corporations such as AT&T, Coca-Cola Foods, M&M/Mars, Procter & Gamble, Campbell Soup and Warner Bros. Scholastic InSchool Marketing specialises 'in the development and distribution of branded in-school and consumer marketing programs'.[18] Scholastic also produces sponsored magazines, videos, contests, posters, teacher guides, software and books for corporate clients.[19] Scholastic's '6 and Under Custom Marketing' targets pre-schools, childcare centres and kindergartens. Programmes include Ronald McDonald Reading Corners that have 'reached over a million children' and Ford's 'Clue into Classroom Safety' that has reached 'over 3.3 million children and their parents'.[20]

In 1988 Scholastic senior vice president, Mark Evens, wrote in *Advertising Age* that

> The education system can provide a unique opportunity for companies to support vital social needs while achieving basic marketing and public relations goals ... More and more companies see education marketing as the most compelling, memorable and cost-effective way to build share of mind and market into the 21st century.[21]

NUTRITION AND HEALTH EDUCATION

Food companies have been keen to associate their products with healthy eating and have put together sponsored classroom kits on nutrition and health that downplay or don't mention the unhealthy aspects of their food products. In the process they distort the concept of healthy and nutritious eating.

The Sugar Association has put together lessons on dental health which tell students it's okay to eat sugary foods as long as they clean their teeth afterwards.[22] NutraSweet's 'Total Health' school lessons teach students how NutraSweet can stop them gaining weight.[23] Kraft foods has created a teaching unit that promotes processed cheese as 'economical, wholesome, and versatile'. Oscar Mayer's 'Making Food Safe' lessons claim 'all food is made of chemicals' and limit the discussion of fat to its essential role in the diet.[24]

Kellogg's education kits on nutrition promote Pop Tarts and Fruit Loops.[25] They focus on the need to reduce the fat content of breakfasts rather than reduce sugar or salt content.[26] Kellogg's Australian lesson ideas include one on occasional snacks:

> Snacks can be described as 'foods which are eaten outside of usual meal times'. Snacks play an important role in the diet of both children and adults and can provide important nutrients to the diet. Children have smaller stomachs than adults meaning that it can be difficult for them to get all their nutrient needs in three meals a day.
>
> Everyday snacks that are high in carbohydrate are important for children as they help provide them with the energy they need to be active, as well as the energy they 'burn' while being active.[27]

No mention is made of the health problems associated with eating too many sugary or salty snacks.

Similarly, material distributed to 25,000 primary schools in the UK in 2003 by the Food and Drink Federation, an industry association, explained how snacks and drinks can be part of a healthy diet.[28] KFC's UK website includes lesson materials on healthy eating which state: 'you should always try to choose lower fat options such as pure chicken breast meat (as served at your nearest KFC!)'. However, as the UK Food Commission points out, by the time KFC has finished with it, that chicken meat has four times as much fat as when it started.[29]

Nestlé offers nutritional education in many countries around the world including glossy school materials for the Asian market that promote its sweets and chocolates.[30] It sponsors a Good Nutrition Program for Russian schools with 'educational' materials that reach 250,000 children a year in 5000 schools.[31] In Jamaica it visits primary schools as part of its Good Nutrition Program and gives away samples of Nestlé products.[32] In Australia it has teamed up with the Australian Institute of Sport to produce an education programme for schools that includes teachers' units on health, food and nutrition.[33] A Nestlé subsidiary, Juicy Juice, and Scholastic produced a free nutrition curriculum distributed to almost 200,000 teachers in the US.[34]

ENVIRONMENTAL AND ENERGY EDUCATION

During the 1970s and 1980s, as the modern environmental movement grew and people became more aware of environmental degradation, many companies and trade associations, particularly those involved in the mining, oil, forestry and chemical industries, turned to school materials to get their message into schools.

For example, the American Nuclear Society produced a kit which told children about the beneficial uses of nuclear technology and attempted to describe the problem of waste disposal in harmless terms: 'Anything we produce results in some "leftovers" that are either recycled or disposed of – whether we're making electricity from coal or nuclear, or making scrambled eggs!'[35] In the UK all the major energy companies produce classroom materials including British Nuclear Fuels.[36]

Industry-sponsored school materials on environmental issues seek to:

- promote the benefits of their products
- downplay or omit mention of their environmental impacts
- stress how environmentally responsible an industry or company is
- point to new technologies that are being developed and implemented to avoid, minimise or rectify any environmental impacts
- present pollutants and chemical inputs as natural
- omit discussion of, or dismiss, alternatives to an industry's products
- stress what individual students and their families can do to help the environment rather than what industry should do

Forestry industry

In many countries the forestry industry produces classroom materials. Generally they boast the prevalence of wood products and their recyclability. They portray forests as a renewable resource where wood is not logged but 'harvested' and replanted. In these materials, logging companies do not cut down forests but 'manage' them; forestry is a sustainable activity; and the industry does everything possible to protect the environment including protecting species habitat from harm.

International Paper's classroom materials exclaim over the great variety of modern products made from trees: '*Whew!* What would we do without the use of a renewable resource like trees?'[37] US forest industry materials present forestry as a type of agricultural endeavour – 'tree farming'[38] – where the rate of replanting exceeds the rate of 'harvesting' with no damage to the environment or loss of species habitat.[39] Weyerhaeuser school materials claim: 'Unlike materials such as steel, cement or plastic, wood is renewable. This means forests can be grown over and over again.'[40]

However, forests are not renewed. Instead they are replaced by plantations that require heavy use of agrichemicals, including fertilisers, chemical weeding and herbicides that pollute waterways. Plantations reduce soil fertility, increase erosion and compaction of the soil, and increase the risk of fire. In addition they may lead to a loss of biodiversity because they are monocultures and because their densely packed uniform rows do not provide the variations of form and structure found in a forest.[41]

Many forestry companies fund Project Learning Tree (PLT), 'a project of the American Forest Foundation' and 'one of the most widely used environmental education programs'. It boasts more than 15,000 products, books and classroom kits. 'To date, more than 500,000 educators are trained in using PLT materials, reaching approximately 26 million students in the United States and abroad.'[42]

Like other forestry industry materials, PLT gives a rather incomplete picture of forestry, omitting 'meaningful discussion' of environmental impacts or the role of its funders in resisting legislation to protect forests.[43] This is no surprise given that its Education Operating Committee includes representatives of Weyerhaeuser, International Paper, the World Forestry Centre and Plum Creek Timber Company amongst its 13 members.[44]

The Canadian Forestry Association teaching kit includes activities in which students study species conservation but the role of forestry in species extinction is downplayed, and the range of conservation measures it suggests teachers cover does *not* include a reduction in forestry or changes in forestry practices.[45] Habitat loss is blamed on urban development rather than forestry.[46]

The National Association of Forest Industries (NAFI) in Australia has produced 'Timber Trek', a resource that also attributes habitat loss to non-forestry activities: 'The process of clearing forests for these purposes and not growing them back is called deforestation. This should not be confused with forestry, which is careful harvesting and regrowing of trees.'[47] No mention is made of the use of poison 1080 to stop wallabies and possums eating the new seedlings, which results in the killing of hundreds of thousands of native animals each year.[48]

Forestry companies portray clearfelling as something they do for the benefit of the forest, rather than admitting that it is an efficiency measure that provides easy access to the desired trees and afterwards enables forests to be replaced by plantations which can be more easily 'managed'. International Paper's classroom materials make the highly contentious claim that 'Clearcutting is the ecologically preferred method for regenerating many forests that mimics natural disturbance processes like storms and fires. It removes all the overstory trees in a stand for the purpose of developing a new stand in a shade-free environment.'[49] Weyerhaeuser says 'clearcut harvesting ... allows sunlight to reach the ground so newly planted seedlings quickly take root and regenerate the forest'.[50] Similarly, NAFI in Australia argues that clearcutting is necessary 'to expose seedlings to sunlight and reduce competition for water and nutrients'.[51]

Clearfelling, far from being accepted as environmentally sound, is highly controversial. Scientific studies have shown that in Australia clearfelling is detrimental to species such as the greater glider that tend to die when they lose their habitat rather than move to a new area.[52] The Wilderness Society (TWS) points out that clearfelling has various adverse environmental impacts, such as removing the old trees with holes and hollows that provide habitat to owls, bats, pygmy possums, sugar gliders, cockatoos and other birds and animals.[53]

NAFI's school resources give a similarly rosy and one-sided view of woodchipping, suggesting that it is only used for 'poorer quality trees, which may be diseased or have badly bent trunks',[54] whereas environmentalists argue that eucalypt trees that are hundreds of years old and provide habitat to many native birds and animals are being woodchipped. In some cases up to 96 per cent of a forest, that would otherwise not be economical to clearcut, may be woodchipped. [55]

Fossil-fuel industry

In 1998 a poll commissioned by the American Petroleum Institute (API) revealed that the public had a low opinion of the environmental performance of the oil and gas industry. The polling organisation, Wirthlin Worldwide, recommended that the industry promote the ways that 'petroleum improves the quality of life' and 'inoculate against opposition messages'. At the annual Independent Petroleum Association of America conference, Kathryn Ratte of the Political Economy Research Centre (PERC) recommended that this situation be addressed with specially designed school materials and teacher workshops 'in resorts or campuses in pleasant surroundings'.[56] She pointed out the advantages of teaming up with an organisation such as her own. 'If it has a corporate logo on it, it is propaganda ... You need a foot in the door where somebody else is pushing the door open for you. The people best able to push open the door are non-profit education organizations that teachers already think of as being credible.'[57]

The API subsequently teamed up with the American Association for the Advancement of Science to produce classroom materials on energy. They describe how students and society 'depend on oil' and how miserable life would be without it.[58] Shell Oil's materials talked about how you need petrol and cars to get to nature.[59] Similarly, the classroom materials of the Australian Institute of Petroleum (AIP) emphasise 'the importance of oil and gas in our lives'.[60] The AIP and the Australian Petroleum Exploration Association provide project materials, classroom speakers and site visits, amongst other activities, for Australian schools.[61] The petroleum industry has been active in schools in both Australia and NZ since the 1990s.[62]

Fossil-fuel industry education materials generally say little about the contribution of the industry to global warming, and until recently have emphasised the uncertainty surrounding the issue and not taken responsibility as an industry for its contributions. For example, the American Coal Foundation claimed in its 'Power from Coal Activity Book' that some scientists believe that additional carbon dioxide from coal and fossil fuels will warm the climate but 'other scientists do not believe this is likely ... Still others' research indicates the earth could benefit ... More time is needed for researchers to gather information on these questions.'[63]

The Foundation's current materials, found on its teachcoal.org website, tend to omit the question of global warming altogether. For example, its 'educational' article on 'Coal and the Environment' says 'coal has some environmental challenges to overcome' but that the 'industry is working hard to ensure that the mining and use of coal does not permanently damage land or pollute air'. It cites the various technologies that are available to reduce emissions from coal burning such as sulphur, nitrogen and dust particles. There is no discussion about the extent to which such technologies are actually used in practice.[64]

Industries that are criticised for their pollution produce materials stressing the environmental measures their companies are taking to minimise that pollution. Often these are measures required by law, but they are presented as an act of corporate responsibility. One of the Australian industries' books for primary students, *The Big Book of Oil and Gas*, claims:

> The air we breath is healthier because scientists have developed petrol which makes less harmful gases when used to fuel engines. That's why car engines are now designed to run on unleaded petrol ... The oil and gas industries care about the environment and are always looking for new ways to protect the world we live in.[65]

The book does not mention that the AIP lobbied against the introduction of unleaded petrol and published a booklet 'Why keep lead in petrol?' that argued against unleaded petrol.[66] The American Petroleum Institute similarly boasts of improvements undertaken by the oil industry, even though they were required by laws that the industry had fought against.[67]

The fossil-fuel industry likes to emphasise individual responsibility for energy use. Electricity companies such as Commonwealth Edison produced materials stressing the role of the individual in using energy wisely rather than the role of corporations in deciding how the electricity will be produced.[68] ExxonMobil's *Energy Chest* website states 'We all need to live more sustainable lifestyles to slow down the rate of global warming and conserve our precious resources.'[69]

Project Learning Tree classroom materials on energy also stress the role of students in reducing their personal energy use rather than considering industrial energy use or who makes the decisions to choose fossil fuels as a source of energy. Its Energy and Society programme 'was made possible with a generous grant from the American Petroleum Institute (API)' and the advisory committee includes representatives of the API, the Alliance of Automobile Manufacturers, the American Coal Foundation, and Pacific Gas and Electric Company (PG&E).[70]

Plastics industry

The plastics industry promotes the use of plastics as being superior to alternatives and better for the environment without mentioning the problems of toxic chemicals used and emitted in plastics manufacture, nor the problems associated with the disposal of plastics. Rather, students are encouraged to recycle and reuse some plastic items and no mention is made of those items that cannot easily be reused or recycled.

The American Chemistry Council (ACC) produces a series of classroom materials entitled 'Hands on Plastics' that includes games and activities 'designed to teach elementary school students about the positive impact plastics have on our everyday lives'.[71] The Plastics and Chemicals Industry Association of Australia (PACIA) education materials claim that 'Chemicals Saved the Whale' by producing soap, leather, linoleum, pharmaceuticals and cosmetics synthetically rather than with whale oil. They also claim that 'Plastics Saved the Elephant' by replacing ivory.[72]

The ACC gives students the impression that the more plastic they use, the better off the environment will be. On its Plastics 101 website the ACC stresses the benefits of plastics – that without plastics, packaging would be heavier and need more energy to manufacture; that foam polystyrene containers take less energy to make than paperboard containers; that many more trucks would be needed to deliver paper grocery bags than plastic grocery bags.[73] The issue of disposal is not addressed nor the fact that plastic bags clog drains and waterways and kill many birds, whales, seals and turtles that ingest discarded plastic bags.[74]

PACIA claims that 'plastics help save resources, fossil fuels and energy. Plastics products also save water and preserve food'.[75] No mention is made of the pollution and waste products from plastic manufacture or the disposal problem the end products create. The plastics industry contributed 14 per cent of the toxic releases into the air in the US during the 1990s and seven of the top ten manufacturers ranked by total releases were plastics factories: 'Producing a 16 oz. PET bottle generates more than 100 times the toxic emissions to air and water than making the same size bottle out of glass.' There is also the problem that additives in plastics can be toxic or carcinogenic and migrate into the air or food, and also out of toys, during use.[76]

When environmentalists were pushing for the use of PVC to be banned in the Sydney Olympic Games village because of the many environmental problems associated with it, ICI Australia put out a pamphlet on PVC for schools. It argued that all environmental problems associated with PVC had been solved, and that since 65 per cent of PVC products were designed to last for between 15 and 100 years, PVC, on the whole, 'is not designed to be wasted'. It concluded '[s]o you can see, you're wasting more if you don't use plastic'.[77] The UK Chemical Industry Education Centre (CIEC) describes PVC as being made from salt and natural gas or oil, making it sound perfectly harmless.[78]

The plastics industry deals with the problems associated with plastics disposal by focusing on the fact that they are lightweight: 'plastics constitute a mere 9.4% by weight of all waste generated in the United States'.[79] However the real problem with plastics in landfills is not their weight but the fact that they take up a lot of space and they do not easily decompose.

The US Society of the Plastics Industry (SPI) produces a teaching resource for grades two to five entitled 'Don't Let a Good Thing Go To Waste' that is used in over 10,000 classrooms. Plastic, rather than being presented as a disposal problem, is presented as a material that can be reused and recycled. Plastic bags are claimed to be perfect for putting trash in because they 'are strong, waterproof and easy to carry and hold a lot of trash'.[80]

The ACC even touts the benefits of burning plastics with other municipal solid waste as a way of generating electricity, without mentioning the toxic gases that are generated by such incineration except to claim that 'Modern air pollution control devices are used to control and reduce potentially harmful particulates and gases from incinerator emissions' and 'most plastics, when properly combusted, produce energy, waste and carbon dioxide as the principal products of combustion'.[81]

PACIA is one of the industry sponsors of *Ollie's World* which has released classroom materials in the UK, US and Australia. *Ollie Saves the Planet* comes on CD and via the internet. It focuses on what individuals can do to help the environment and neglects the role of industry in environmental issues. For example the module on waste focuses on household waste and litter and doesn't even mention industrial waste and the problems associated with its toxicity and how it is disposed of.[82] 'Students are told that as long as they change their individual lifestyles – for example, by recycling – the planet will be saved. Not surprisingly, the prospect of joining with others to confront corporate interests is never presented as an option.'[83]

ECONOMIC EDUCATION

Businesses have been very active in promoting business values in schools since the 1940s in the US, and since the 1970s in the UK, Canada, Australia and NZ.[84] Corporate-sponsored economic education, business studies and enterprise education (see Chapters 9 and 10) are aimed at persuading young people to view the world through the eyes of employers and to accept that what is good for employers is good for them. This is insidious because most children and young people will become employees and their interests will often conflict with those of employers and corporate executives. Their self-interest may well be served by joining unions and fighting management to protect their pay and work conditions, particularly as labour markets around the world are increasingly deregulated.

The National Council on Economic Education (NCEE – see Chapter 10) is at the forefront of the business push for economic and business education to be mandatory in schools. To this end it sets economics curriculum standards for schools and publishes teaching materials including internet-based programs. It runs EconomicsAmerica which teaches 120,000 teachers how to teach economics to eight million students, through 'a vast network of state councils and university-based centers'. NCEE is also working on distance learning and internet technologies to reach thousands more teachers in the US.[85]

The NCEE's international program, EconomicsInternational, reaches millions of students in 21 countries. It trains teachers, translates and adapts American instructional materials, and advises on the development of standards, curricula and assessment. It is mainly aimed at the formerly communist countries in Europe, 'helping our international partners reform their educational systems and educate their citizens for the transition to a market economy'.[86]

The Foundation for Teaching Economics (FTE – see Chapter 10) runs workshops for teachers covering topics such as market solutions to environmental problems. Its purpose is to introduce selected high school students 'to an economic way of thinking about national and international issues'.[87] FTE lessons on economic forces in American history teach that the push for regulation of big business in the late nineteenth century came from small businesses, and their success 'in securing protection against competition from big business imposed significant costs on consumers'.[88] Similarly its lesson on the Great Depression diverges quite markedly from a more scholarly interpretation of history in order to defend unregulated markets:

> The Depression itself resulted from disruptions to international trade and faulty government economic policies before and after the downturn came. Curiously, even though government policies had much to do with bringing on the Depression and making it more severe, the economic crisis of the early 1930s became grounds for greatly expanding the role of government in American life ... Unfortunately, New Deal programs did not fulfil expectations and, indeed, may have delayed recovery as they further disabled market operations.[89]

In 2003 the John Templeton Foundation gave FTE $550,000 to produce a set of classroom materials, entitled 'Is Capitalism Good for the Poor?', to help teachers explain the 'innate fairness of capitalism' to students.[90] With corporate and foundation funding the FTE is able to offer its programmes free to teachers and cover their accommodation costs for out-of-town workshops and conferences as well.

The Canadian Foundation for Economic Education (CFEE), set up in 1974, produces educational resources including teaching kits and student materials – in print, on video and CD-ROM – on the economy, economics and entrepreneurship. It also holds seminars, workshops and teachers conferences, and develops curricula. CFEE claims that its resource materials reach some 300,000 Canadian students each year and that 'it works in collaboration with provincial Ministries and Departments of Education' as well as private organisations such as Finance Canada, the Canadian Banker Association, and Investors Group. It is also supported by a number of corporations including Imperial Oil, Shell Canada and Suncor.[91]

In Australia the Centre for Economic Education (CEE), a 'Melbourne-based, national education centre ... dedicated to promoting economic literacy within the community and, in particular, supporting economics education in Australian schools', operated until 2004. It provided teaching and learning resources to teachers, travel awards to the annual US Economics America Conference and student essay competitions.[92] CEE's publications included materials on the benefits of international trade, foreign investment and lower tariffs.[93]

Shareholders

School materials on share ownership and the stock market are a form of enterprise education (see Chapter 9). In English-speaking nations, school children can play stock-market games where they are allocated a notional sum of money to invest and the value of their shares depends on real share-market movements. The games usually come with lesson plans, worksheets and teacher guides as well as prizes for teams of students that 'win'.

One of the best-known US stock-market games for schools is *The Stock Market Game*. It is distributed with curriculum activities, lesson plans and teachers newsletters and workshops developed by the NCEE.[94] It is designed to be used in several subjects, including social studies, mathematics, business, and language arts, as well as for economics.[95] 'Every year more than a million U.S. primary, middle, and high school students play the stock market at school.'[96] In Australia more than 80,000 students in years seven to twelve take part in the ASX Schools Sharemarket Games sponsored by Citigroup and Bond University.[97]

In the UK, share-market games and school resource materials are provided by Proshare. In 2002, 3500 school teams entered its ProShare Portfolio Challenge, the winning team receiving a trip to New York as part of their prize.[98] There is a dedicated website and enough material to provide for 'an entire term's work' or, alternatively, teachers can use the material for individual lessons in subjects like economics and maths.[99] The Business Academy, Bexley, devotes a whole day to business studies and 'has its own mini stock exchange and trading floor'.[100]

All these games and curricula materials suggest that winning on the stock market is a matter of intelligence and ingenuity and willingness to take risks and therefore, by extension, wealth in the wider society is deserved by those who acquire it. The fact that many people don't have enough money to invest in the stock market to start with is not discussed, nor is the reality that most shares are owned by very few people (10 per cent of shareholders own 90 per cent of stock and 1 per cent own more than half).[101]

The 'stock market is portrayed as a wise judge, rewarding those who make the right choices' and providing companies with much needed capital at the same time. The fact that the stock market actually provides only a very small percentage of business capital is not examined, nor are problems caused by stock-market speculation. Instead students are taught to regard gambling in shares as company ownership, despite the lack of influence individual shareholders have.[102]

Most importantly, students learn to interpret world events and government policy from the point of view of an investor. One stock-market game producer boasts:

> Students find that economic concepts such as supply and demand, inflation and recession, and competition come alive for them as they manage their hypothetical investments. They gain understanding of the benefits and tradeoffs of different financial instruments and strategies. They start to see the impact of world events on their investments.[103]

SUPPORT FROM GOVERNMENT AND TEACHERS ASSOCIATIONS

Many education authorities around the world support corporate sponsorship of educational materials. As noted in Chapter 5, the UK the Department for Education and Skills (DfES) encourages the production and use of corporate materials in schools. In Australia, state government education departments have worked together with business groups in Australia to produce materials. In Western Australia the Ministry of Education has prepared curriculum materials sponsored by Woodside Petroleum, BHP, BP, Shell, Mitsui, Mitsubishi and Cal Asiatic for all secondary schools in the state.[104]

The NSW Department of Education and Training recently had a webpage of online resources with links to industry-sponsored curriculum resources that included a link to the Australian Institute of Petroleum education website and endorsed its fact sheets, curriculum kits and resource books as 'highly recommended' and 'drawn from respected scientific sources',[105] even though the resources were written by public relations people and mainly cited industry sources.[106]

Far from acting as gatekeepers against the incursion of corporate materials into schools, many teachers associations around the world encourage it. They have their professional conferences sponsored and underwritten by corporations and have corporate displays and booths at those conferences. Some have links to suppliers of corporate school materials on their home pages.

For example the UK Association of Science Education (ASE) includes industry-sponsored school science materials on its webpages, including ExxonMobil's *Energy Chest* website, electricity company, E.On's *Energy Nation* website, and Bayer's *Making Science Make Sense* website. It also partners with Unilever, Pfizer, GlaxoSmithKline, The British Aerosol Manufacturers' Association, the Association of the British Pharmaceutical Industry and others to provide resources to science teachers.[107]

Similarly the US National Science Teachers Association (NSTA) partners with and receives contributions from a variety of companies including Alcoa, the American Chemistry Council, the API, the American Plastics Council, Dow Chemical, Lockheed Martin, Shell Oil and many others. It co-sponsors contests and grants with Toyota, Toshiba, Lysol and others.[108] The Association also runs annual summer workshops with Dow Chemical. The NSTA has partnered with oil company ConocoPhillips and with the American Petroleum Institute to produce teaching materials on oil,[109] and the API funded NSTA's webpages on energy. The 10,000 to 14,000 teachers attending the NSTA's annual convention are able to pick up 'armloads of free corporate lesson plans' from the hundreds of corporate and trade association displays.[110] It is said that when attending an NSTA conference 'Bring two suitcases: one for your clothes and one for all the freebies!'[111]

In their turn corporations, such as ExxonMobil's foundation, give millions 'to key organizations that influence the way children learn about science'.[112] According to ExxonMobil's president, Edward Ahnert, 'NSTA is such a natural partner for us. No other organization has the ability to reach thousands of teachers.'[113] ExxonMobil even has a representative on the NSTA's corporate advisory board. When the producers of Al Gore's film, *An Inconvenient Truth*, offered 50,000 DVDs of it to teachers, the NSTA rejected the offer saying it would place 'unnecessary risk upon the [NSTA] capital campaign, especially targeted supporters'.[114]

12
Privatising Schools

In the early 1990s media entrepreneur Chris Whittle became the darling of the free-market, antigovernment right by promising that private, for-profit businesses could manage schools better than public boards of education. His Edison Schools, he claimed, would grow into a corporate giant by educating children better and more cheaply than public schools.

David Moberg[1]

Chris Whittle's dream of creating hundreds of private, for-profit schools attracted the support of republican governors such as George W. Bush, when he was governor of Texas.[2] Whittle, a magazine publisher who had introduced Channel One into schools (see Chapter 3), established the Edison project in 1992. Investors such as J.P. Morgan and Paul Allen, co-founder of Microsoft, invested tens of millions.[3]

Venture capitalists and investors became enchanted with the idea, too, lured by presentations from Merrill Lynch, an early Whittle backer, that spoke of an inefficient secondary-education industry that spent $1 billion a day, only half – half! – of which was spent directly on education. The rest, it was implied, was pork and featherbedding easily trimmed by sharp-eyed, reform-minded businesspeople.[4]

Initially Edison managed public schools under contract to school districts, but in 1997 it began establishing charter schools. Charter schools are privately run schools that are government funded. They represent a milestone towards the dream of a privatised school system that is the goal of some business leaders.

Whittle believed that, because school bureaucracies were wasteful and inefficient, Edison could run schools for less money than school districts, even with a profit margin, and do a better job of it. Investors believed him. After Edison went public in 1999, the value of its shares doubled in two years. As it turned out, Edison was unable to make a profit from running schools and in many cases its schools offered an inferior education at a higher cost.

In order to win charter and school management contracts Edison produced glossy handouts, canvassed door-to-door, and promised parents free computers for their children. It presented school districts with 'a high-pressure, slick sales pitch'.[5] It 'established a marketing, media and government relations operation that is far more sophisticated and aggressive than those of many corporations, let alone most school systems'.[6] In San Francisco, where its schools were the worst performing in the city, Edison hired Digital Campaigns, a public relations company, to boost parental support for its schools.[7]

When Philadelphia faced a crisis because poor and highly inequitable funding of schools inevitably led to poor student performance, it paid Edison $2.7 million to recommend changes. A previous report by Judge Doris Smith, which recommended increased school funding, fairer distribution of funding, and smaller class sizes, had been shelved and ignored. Not surprisingly Edison recommended that 60 poorly performing schools be taken over by private companies, 45 of them by Edison. Consequently Philadelphia 'embarked on the nation's largest experiment in private management of public schools' in 2002. However, because of political opposition fewer were privatised than Edison recommended and only 20 were awarded to Edison.[8]

To save money in its Philadelphia schools – where it received $750 more per student than the school district provided other public schools – Edison closed school libraries and installed computerised test-taking drills. Despite this exclusive focus on test scores, the scores in fact fell in many Edison schools.[9]

Although the media and business leaders hailed Edison as an example of how the market can provide quality schools for children in poor neighbourhoods for less funds, Edison relied on corporate and foundation philanthropy and often received higher per-student funding than other public schools.[10] In the Chester Upland District of Pennsylvania, where Edison had taken over all nine schools, Edison demanded that the district almost double its fee after test performance dropped in each school during 2002. Edison threatened to pull out of the schools unless it was paid $4.4 million a year, claiming that if the district wanted 'better schools, they must pay for them'.[11]

In 2002, Edison stock fell from $37 to 14c as a result of various scandals. It was facing several class actions by investors who claimed the company had misreported its revenues. Despite philanthropic donations and above average funding at many of its schools, Edison was in debt to the tune of over $330 million. Edison had lost $354 million in twelve years and one in four of its contracts had been terminated because they were too costly for school districts, unprofitable for Edison, or because of poor student test performance.[12]

Several of its schools had discipline problems, poor test performance, and declining student numbers. Some schools were accused of cheating on test results. The *Wichita Eagle* interviewed seven former Edison teachers and reported that four of them claimed that Edison had required them 'to do whatever it took to make sure students succeeded on standardised tests, including ignoring time limits, reading questions from a comprehension test aloud and in some cases correcting answers during a test'.[13]

Under pressure to show they could be profitable, Whittle proposed that Edison schools could save money by using students to do some of the school administrative work, 'commenting that 600 pupils working one hour a day was the equivalent of 75 full-time adult staff'. Not surprisingly, parents were outraged, pointing out that this was 'the equivalent of child labor', particularly since most Edison's students were elementary-aged.[14]

Edison was saved from bankruptcy by a buyout in 2002 leaving Whittle $21 million better off. In 2003, Edison was the largest company to be managing schools, with 136 public schools in 23 states covering over 130,000 students. During the first half of 2005 it lost seven of its 41 school management contracts, making a total of 25 contracts lost out of 59 over its 13-year history.[15]

By 2006 Edison was managing 97 schools in 19 states and the District of Columbia, and around 60,000 students. Less than half these schools were charter schools. The rest were management contracts with school districts.[16] Most were in poor neighbourhoods with mainly African-American or Latino students. Middle-class school districts are generally happy with their schools and didn't want to turn them over to a for-profit company. It was only the desperate, badly resourced schools in poor urban areas who were willing to give Edison a go.[17]

Despite its downturn in business, Edison is still today one of the largest Education Management Organisations (EMOs) in the US.[18] Edison's involvement in schools includes alliances, partnerships and charter schools. In some cases Edison manages schools in partnership with school districts under a performance contract. In others, the school district manages the schools but Edison provides a customised programme and onsite support. Such arrangements are encouraged by NCLB requirements for schools to show that they are putting in place strategies to raise student performance.[19] Edison also runs summer and after-school programmes and offers consultation services for schools on how to improve student achievement.

Edison has expanded into the UK market with its consultation services and customised programme.[20] It has partnered with 50 government-funded schools in the UK to provide training and consultancy services and recently won a £900,000 contract to provide the senior management for a government school in North London, including the head teacher.[21]

CHARTER SCHOOLS IN THE US

The first charter school in the US was established in 1992 in St Paul, Minnesota. The number of charter schools grew steadily with the introduction of supporting legislation in various states that was often written with the help of EMOs. More recently, charter schools have been facilitated by the NCLB legislation, which can require failing schools to convert to charter schools or to have their management taken over by EMOs. By 2007 there were 4100 charter schools in 40 states and the District of Columbia, covering 1.2 million students (an 8 per cent increase on the year before). Most are in California, Michigan and Texas.[22]

Rather than having to comply with the government regulations that are applied to normal public schools, charter schools are bound by a charter, which is a contract that includes the 'school's mission, academic goals and accountability procedures'.[23] The freedom from regulation and bureaucracy is supposed to enable the charter schools to innovate; to introduce different curricula and teaching methods – including online classes – so as to offer choice in the type of school available to parents.

Charter schools, like KIPP and Edison schools, put in place the same rigidly structured back-to-basics curriculum across all their schools; a longer school day and longer school year; an emphasis on discipline and structured lessons; centralised control over what happens in the schools; performance pay for teachers and principals; and constant testing of students.

Charter school managers often assume that a major cause of problems in urban schools is lack of discipline rather than lack of funding and resources, neighbourhood and family poverty, or the feelings of hopelessness caused by high levels of unemployment in the area. Discipline is thought to be necessary to make students learn against their natural tendency to play up.[24]

Charter schools also often rely on commercially produced scripted lessons to make up for the inexperience and high turnover of teachers. For example, the reading curriculum in Edison schools, 'Success for All', leaves little scope for teacher discretion or diversion or student spontaneity and interaction.[25]

There is little reason to establish charter schools in wealthy neighbourhoods where public schools are well resourced and teachers well paid. There, the argument that the private sector can do it better has little credibility. For this reason, charter schools tend to operate in inner city areas in the US, where they are attended by a higher proportion of low-income, black and Hispanic students than the average public school.[26] However, this concentration in low-income neighbourhoods, and the fact that many charter schools cater to a particular religious or ethnic group, increases the segregation of children by class and ethnicity, which goes against a traditional aim of public education – to provide shared knowledge and educational experience to children from diverse backgrounds.

Cost-cutting at charter schools

In order for investors to make profits from charter schools that are funded on the same basis as public schools, running costs have to be cut. Proponents argue that this can be done by eliminating waste, running schools more efficiently, and innovating. The evidence suggests it is done by hiring less experienced teachers, paying teachers and non-teaching staff less, reducing equipment and book budgets, having larger classes, and avoiding high-cost special education students.[27]

Table 12.1   Charter School Teaching Staff – Some Figures

	Charter Schools	Other Public Schools
Uncertified teachers[28]	43%	9%
Teachers under 30[29]	37%	11%
Teachers leaving each year[30]	20–25%	
	40% in newer schools	11%

Charter school companies also cut costs by centralising administration costs across a number of schools, and standardising the curriculum across schools so that they can take advantage of economies of scale in their distribution of educational materials and equipment.[31] For this reason there is a tendency for franchises to develop.

Because the public funding of charter schools does not cover the cost of infrastructure such as school buildings, and many investors are unwilling to pay these large capital costs up front, charter schools are often housed in buildings that are inappropriate, such as disused factories or churches. 'Few offer a school-lunch program or bus transportation for students in outlying towns. Expensive extracurricular programs such as sports are limited. And most aren't equipped to handle students with severe special education problems, which public schools are obligated to serve.'[32]

Edison, for example, cuts costs by hiring new and inexperienced teachers, discouraging handicapped and problem students, and not paying for bussing of students. Teachers in Edison schools tend to have an average of five years' experience compared with 16 years in public schools, and turnover is high at 23 per cent per year.[33] In San Francisco, Edison was accused of 'counselling out' students with learning difficulties and behavioural problems and not providing the required bilingual and special education.[34]

The principals of charter schools have complete control over the teachers they hire and fire. In KIPP schools, for example, teachers not only have to teach much longer hours than most other teachers but are expected to be available outside class to take calls on their mobile phones from children with questions about their homework.[35] Unlike teachers in most charter schools, they get higher annual salaries than average public school teachers but many find that doesn't compensate for the long hours.[36]

Whereas once charter school owners claimed they could manage public schools for less cost, today they are complaining about inadequate funding.[37] The truth is, however, that in many states they get more funding than district-run public schools.[38] KIPP schools admit that they cost $1000–$1500 more per student to run than other publicly funded schools, because of the costs of the longer school days and field trips.[39] Edison also usually manages to negotiate more funding per student than comparable public schools.[40] When Edison's contract in Wichita, Kansas, was revoked in 2002, school board officials believed they would save half a million dollars a year by running two of Edison's schools themselves.[41] Edison's contract in Sherman, Texas, was not renewed in 1999 because the school district found that Edison had spent $2.6 million more in the first three years than would have been spent had the district been running the schools itself. [42]

Despite their extra funding, there have been several recent examples of charter schools failing on financial grounds. For example, in 2005 Charter Schools USA admitted it had lost $1.4 million on its four schools in Lee County, Florida.[43] By 2003, 31 charter schools in California had 'had their charters revoked for fiscal improprieties, substandard academic performance or other shortcomings'.[44] In 2004, the California Charter Academy, one of the nation's largest chains of charter schools, went bankrupt, forcing the closure of another 60 schools in California so that 6000 students found themselves with no school to attend and teachers found themselves unemployed. The Academy had been started by a former insurance executive, C. Steven Cox, who had no teaching experience.[45] School districts had begun 'laying the groundwork to revoke' the charters of 38 of his schools even before the bankruptcy because of management problems.[46]

There is a temptation for profit-driven companies that are having difficulty making a profit to exercise fraud in order to increase their government funding. For example, the company Opportunities for Learning was found by a Californian state audit to have overcharged the government over $57 million for its eight charter schools and 40-plus 'independent-study satellite centers' between 2002 and 2005, by falsely reporting information such as the number of credentialed teachers they employed and student–teacher ratios.[47]

Charter school performance

In general the teaching standard in charter schools varies enormously. However, studies have failed to show that, on average, charter schools perform significantly better than public schools with similar demographics. In fact some show they perform worse: 'If bonanzas are realized in some places, they are apparently offset by catastrophes in others.'[48] An Education Department analysis also found that the longer a charter school had been operating, the more test scores declined.[49] Another study by researchers at Western Michigan University found that states where charter schools are mainly run for profit have worse learning outcomes.[50]

Table 12.2   Performance of Charter Schools – Some Studies

Year	Researchers	Scope	Comparison with other Public Schools
2003	Rand Corporation for state government[51]	California	No significant difference
2003	National Assessment of Educational Progress (NAEP)[52]	fourth graders	No measurable difference
2004	Education Department[53]	fourth graders	Performance worse
2005	Economic Policy Institute[54]	eleven states and DC	No difference or performance worse
2006	Western Michigan University researchers[55]	Michigan, Ohio	Performance worse
2007	Education Policy Research Unit (EPRU), Arizona State University[56]	Six Great Lake states	Performance worse

NB: These studies compared schools and students of similar socio-economic background.

In 2006 only eleven out of the 43 privately run schools in Philadelphia met federal performance standards compared with 15 the year before (a lower percentage than district-run schools). The 20 Edison schools (a substantial proportion of Edison schools nationwide) were amongst the worst performers, although its schools received $750 more per student (or $22,000 more per classroom) than public schools.[57]

Despite the extra hours of schooling ('almost 50 percent more time in class each year than regular public school students'[58]) and higher funding, there is no evidence that Edison schools do any better than public schools at educating students. For

---

Box 12.1   Online or Virtual Schools

The private provision of online schooling has also been problematic. In early 2006 there were 147 online charter schools in 18 states catering to over 65,000 children.[59] These schools provide students with computer equipment, software and textbooks, but don't have to provide buildings, transportation, food catering, or extracurricular activities, so they can make big profits on public funding.[60]

State auditors in Colorado called for a moratorium on online schools after finding that they were not properly regulated; that their students performed worse than other students on state exams and their performance got worse over time; and that students were more likely to drop out. Five out of the 18 online schools did not employ teachers who had completed college courses in the subjects they were teaching, as required by federal regulations. Such schools generally rely on parents to provide much of the teaching. One school, for example, had only four licensed teachers for 1500 students.[61]

There has also been some controversy recently about the outsourcing of student essay marking by virtual schools to tutors in India and elsewhere.[62]

example, a 2003 American Federation of Teachers study claimed that 'averaged across all states, the typical Edison school performed below average'.[63] A 2005 Rand Corporation study, commissioned by Edison, was unable to show that Edison Schools performed any better than similar public schools.[64] Such findings do not stop Edison boasting of the achievement gains that its schools are making. Nor do they stop business leaders from citing Edison and other charter schools as the best way to educate students.

Despite the dismal record of their performance, President Barack Obama is a supporter of charter schools: 'I doubled the number of charter schools in Illinois despite some reservations from teachers unions. I think it's important to foster competition inside the public schools.'[65]

PRIVATE PROVISION IN THE UK

In the UK the total privatisation of public schools is politically unpopular and not generally considered to be a profitable enterprise by British businesses (although there are a few schools run by for-profit companies[66]). Instead education–business partnerships have been encouraged. The Blair government continued efforts, begun by conservative governments, to privatise as many aspects of public schools as possible, increasing the contracting out of educational services to private companies including school inspections and teacher training.[67] The supply of teachers is also outsourced. Private agencies like Capita Education Resourcing recruit teachers for both permanent and casual positions in the UK, and internationally.[68] UK-based companies 'are operating an unregulated global market in teachers', that was 'worth approximately 2.5 billion pounds sterling per annum' in 2000.[69]

Academies and trust schools

In 2000 the Blair government established academies, which are public schools run by private sponsors – including businesses, religious organisations, educational trusts and individuals – who contribute £2 million towards the initial capital costs of establishing the school or converting it from a normal public school. The government typically pays more than £25 million towards these schools. Yet sponsors own the school buildings and the land they are on, appoint the majority of the governing board, appoint the head teacher, dictate the curriculum and manage the school.[70] In other words sponsors own and run these publicly funded schools in return for a relatively small contribution.

The UK government envisages that 200 privately sponsored academy schools, many of them newly established schools, will be running or underway by 2010, around 60 in London boroughs, all in areas where poorer students are concentrated.[71] There were 83 academies operating by mid 2008. They mainly specialise in business/enterprise (more than half of them), sport or ICT (information and communications technology), and their sponsors tend to be either religious organisations, businesses, businesspeople or foundations.[72]

Corporate sponsors for academies are supposed to be motivated either by philanthropy, the desire to promote their corporate image, or the 'desire to promote business values' in schools.[73] Academies cannot charge fees, and if the school is labelled as 'failing' the local educational authority (LEA) will be able to intervene.

Academies have greater freedom than normal schools to set curriculum, appoint the principal, employ staff and set teacher pay and conditions.[74] They have replaced 'failing' schools on the assumption that the enthusiasm of sponsors and the freedom from government regulation – in terms of curriculum and teacher pay and conditions – will enable them to produce a better quality education. This freedom from regulation has led to several court cases against the opening of academies on the grounds that they deprive parents of the right to have a say in their children's education and to appeal if their child is excluded from the school. Some academy contracts require only one parent on the board of governors.[75]

The extra funding these schools attract, not just the sponsors' £2 million but the more substantial government funding, enables them to have new buildings, extra facilities and more staff than other public schools. This leads some to ask whether the extra funding might not have been better spent on the failing schools the academies are replacing without handing over control to wealthy sponsors. In this way they would have remained publicly accountable and under the auspices of the democratically elected local educational boards.

Despite their superior resourcing (£21,000 per student compared to £14,000 at other state schools), their ability to select 10 per cent of their students by aptitude, and their tendency to exclude and expel more students than normal, academies have seldom produced the superior results intended.[76] A Commons select committee stated in 2005: 'We fail to understand why the DfES is putting such substantial resources into academies when it has not produced the evidence on which to base the expansion of the programme.'[77] The public too has been dubious about the merits of the £5 billion academies programme, and has opposed several planned academies.[78] A majority of teachers in England are also now opposed to academies and school choice as a way of improving educational standards in deprived areas.[79]

The evidence supporting the belief that academies are successful at improving academic results is mixed, notwithstanding government claims to the contrary. In 2006, only 15.6 per cent of students in city academies received good English and mathematics grades at the end of Key Stage 4 compared with 44.9 per cent at all schools. Also academies made up about half the schools at the bottom of the performance tables.[80] This suggests that private sponsorship is not necessarily the magic solution that it is promoted to be.[81]

A 2006 study by Terry Wrigley at Edinburgh University found that the number of students getting five good General Certificate of Secondary Education (GCSE) grades (A–C) after attending academies had improved by only 0.2 per cent. Academies were encouraging less able children to take vocational subjects rather than GCSE subjects, so as to boost the average GCSE scores. Fifty-two per cent of students were taking vocational qualifications compared with 13 per cent in the schools the academies replaced.[82]

Wrigley also found that academies were ridding themselves of poorly performing students so as to do better in the school league tables.[83] Government figures confirm that academies are expelling students at four times the rate of neighbouring schools, which, teachers claim, helps them 'massage' their exam results and send troublesome students to nearby public schools that have to accept all students.[84]

Box 12.2   Academies – Some Problem Cases

The first academy school to be set up was Unity City, with business support services company Amey as sponsor. According to the *Guardian*, it 'has been dogged by problems since it opened, in September 2002', both financial and educational. It had a high staff turnover and staff absences. One in three teachers were graduate trainees or newly qualified.[85] The UK Treasury bailed the academy out of its debt of £1.5 million just before the 2005 election to prevent the school from having to close.[86]

In 2005 Unity City failed inspections by the Office for Standards in Education (Ofsted) because of poor-quality teaching, poor leadership, poor pupil progress, low attendance rates and high exclusion rates.[87] Ofsted found that the situation had not improved much one year later with eleven- and 14-year-olds getting some of the lowest English and science results in the country.[88] The academy had cost £43.6 million to set up and run (2006 estimate), more than twice the government's original estimate of £20 million.[89]

Unity City is not the only academy to fail Ofsted inspections. Some 'have received highly critical Ofsted reports and remain at the bottom of league tables with low exam results'. Others, like the Academy at Peckham, sponsored by carpet millionaire Lord Harris of Peckham, have been given overall satisfactory marks but have 'significant weaknesses'. Ofsted found that its sixth form was ineffective and the standards reached by students throughout the school were very low.[90]

Similarly Ofsted found that the sixth form of the Business Academy Bexley was inadequate. It also found that 'teaching and learning are inadequate overall' and the 'amount of unsatisfactory teaching in the secondary section is too high'.[91] Two years earlier Blair had cited this school as 'a beacon of hope and aspiration to the whole community' and suggested that 'those who fear radical change' consider the performance of the Bexley Business academy.[92] The academy cost £58 million to set up and run (2006 estimate), well over the government's original estimate of £20 million.[93]

Also, although academies were set up to cater to poor students, there is some evidence that they are increasingly catering to more middle-class students and 'cherry picking' high-performing students from more affluent families. The percentage of students eligible for free school meals has dropped in the 14 academies that the *Guardian* newspaper examined. Steve Sinnott, general secretary of the National Union of Teachers, noted: 'Instead of changing the school they are changing the children.'[94]

The building of academies has tended to go over budget, on average by £3 million, so that they are more expensive than other secondary schools.[95] What is more, sponsors have been slow to pay up their £2 million share. In 2006 the *Guardian* newspaper noted that most of the sponsors had not paid their promised £2 million. There were also allegations, 'being investigated by Scotland Yard', that some sponsors had been promised peerages and honours in return for their money.[96] Because of the reluctance of businesses to pay up front, the government now allows them to make endowments later instead.[97]

Nevertheless, despite the lack of evidence that academies boost academic performance, the UK government is now establishing trust schools, which are similar to academies except that the sponsors, such as local businesses, do not have to contribute a set amount of money. Such schools would be funded by the government in the same way as normal local authority-maintained public schools but would be run by a charitable foundation or trust that appoints the board of governors, owns the school land and assets, employs school staff and sets the schools admissions policy.[98] According to the DfES: 'The Trust may bring a brand and a distinct and recognisable ethos to the school or group of schools.'[99] Companies that are interested in running trust schools in the UK include Microsoft, which already sponsors a number of specialist schools in the UK, and the transnational accountancy firm KPMG.[100]

A proposal in 2006 by the then education secretary, Ruth Kelly, to make all public schools into trust schools failed because of opposition within the ranks of Labour MPs.[101] However, failing schools may be forced by the government to become trust schools and therefore 'be taken over by external sponsors, either business or a federation of schools run by an executive "super head"'.[102]

OUTSOURCING SCHOOL ADMINISTRATION

The UK Labour government has also sought to shift local educational authorities (LEAs) 'from being a provider of education to being its local commissioner and the champion of parent choice'.[103] From 1999, LEAs running schools that were 'failing' were required by the government Ofsted to outsource some or all of their educational functions to the private sector, including school management, which covers decisions about priorities, staffing levels and equipment as well as which schools should close. Ten LEAs had privatised education services by 2005.[104] Where LEAs continue to manage educational services, they are expected to behave like private companies, seeking return on investment as a top priority.[105]

The UK government has accepted the business ideology that private companies can manage schools better than the public sector, despite the lack of educational management skills in the private sector. Private companies tend to employ the same staff as the former LEA and often poach their top management from local government senior management.[106]

Box 12.3   Education Action Zones (EAZs)

The UK government also formed Education Action Zones, and more recently Excellence in Cities (EiC) Action Zones, which enable forums including business representatives to manage low-performing schools in poor areas with the help of corporate money and extra government funding. These forums are able to determine school curricula. In this way the transnational oil company Shell helps run the London Borough of Lambeth's EAZ. It aims to 'increase understanding and experience of employer culture' as part of their 'work related learning'. Other companies involved in managing schools include British Aerospace, Tesco, ICI, Kellogg's and McDonald's.[107]

In 2002, Ofsted found that most of the LEAs that had outsourced their educational services were 'poor improvers' whereas most of them had been 'good improvers' before outsourcing.[108] 'Of the authorities which had outsourced services, five were rated as poor, three unsatisfactory and just one, Leeds, as satisfactory.'[109]

The London borough of Hackney gave Nord Anglia a contract to run some of its educational services in 1999, but it was not renewed in 2001 after Ofsted found the firm had failed to achieve any significant improvement. A non-profit trust was then created to run the services. Cambridge Education Associates, which took over all of the education services of the London borough of Islington LEA in 2000, was fined hundreds of thousands of pounds in 2002 and 2003 for failing to reach target exam results, specified in its contract. The following year the LEA lowered the exam targets but Cambridge Education Associates still failed to meet them.[110]

Other private companies have also been fined for failing to meet exam targets and in some cases exam targets have been lowered.[111] Perhaps the worst case was the London borough of Southwark, which in 2001 gave a contract to engineering consultants WS Atkins to provide its educational services. This turned out to be 'an unmitigated disaster'. Exam results fell to an all-time low and financial management was inept. Teachers were demoralised. Senior management staff quit. It owed hundreds of thousands of pounds. 'The number of Southwark schools in "special measures" – where the whole school is deemed to be failing – increased under the Atkins regime from six to eight.' Within two years, Atkins withdrew from the contract, gleaning £2.2 million from taxpayers as an exit payment.[112] Cambridge Education Associates took over.

The failure of Atkins did not, however, stop the school standards minister from awarding a £1.9 million contract, the following month, to Jarvis Educational Services to advise on how to improve British secondary schools, even though it too was an engineering conglomerate whose Educational Services division had been formed only two months earlier, and whose key personnel came from Atkins.[113]

Despite these experiences, a 2005 Confederation of British Industries (CBI) report proclaimed private outsourcing of education services to be a success and advocated the expansion of private sector involvement.[114]

Education management organisations in the US

School districts and charter schools in the US may contract out the management of schools to EMOs. In 2008 there were more than 60 for-profit EMO companies operating more than 550 schools in 28 states including the District of Columbia, attended by more than 250,000 students. Fifteen large EMOs operated over 80 per cent of them. Most EMO contracts are with charter schools, 85 per cent in 2008, including 40 virtual schools.[115]

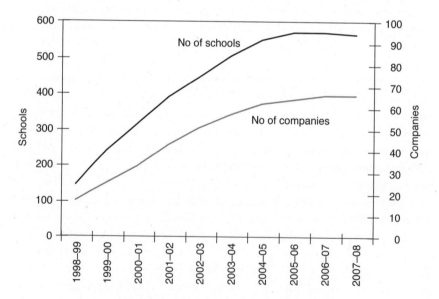

Figure 12.1   Estimated Growth and Coverage of EMOs 1998–2008

Source: A. Molnar et al. 'Profiles of for-Profit Education Management Organizations', EPIC and CERU, Arizona State University, AZ, July 2008, pp. 6–8.

Box 12.4   Education Alternatives / Tesseract

In 1986, former Xerox salesman, John Golle, set up Education Alternatives Inc. (EAI), one of the pioneers of for-profit schooling companies. Golle claimed: 'There's so much fat in the schools that even a blind man without his cane could find the way.'[121] In 1994 EAI had contracts to run 45 public schools, including nine schools in Baltimore, and all 32 Hartford public schools.[122] Its efforts to cut 300 teachers from the Hartford schools so as to increase profitability were unsuccessful. In Baltimore it had to repay money after being caught falsifying enrolment figures.

By 1997 EAI had lost all its school management contracts because of contractual disputes and because it failed to improve learning despite the extra funding it received compared with other public schools.[123] It changed its name to Tesseract, moved to Arizona and began twelve charter schools in Phoenix. Despite its inability to make a profit, its plummeting share price, and its multimillion dollar debt, Golle made millions from the company.[124] Tesseract filed for bankruptcy in 2001.[125]

The largest profitable EMO is National Heritage Academies, a private company that has 55 charter schools in six states covering 33,000 students. It was founded in 1995 by industrialist J.C. Huizenga, who invested $50 million. Edison manages 80 schools in 17 states covering 48,600 students.[116]

EMOs rapidly opened charter schools and contracted with districts to run their schools without realising the extent of costs and time involved in establishing and running a school. On top of their normal costs they had marketing costs and loan repayments and private sector executive salaries to pay. As a result, few companies have been able to make a profit from running schools.[117]

In 2002, *Fortune* magazine reported that the only profitable EMOs were Nobel Learning Communities that ran mainly private schools, and National Heritage Academies that ran 'quasi-religious schools'.[118] The difficulty that EMOs have experienced in making profits from managing schools whilst at the same time improving student test scores has led many of them to focus more on supplementary educational services such as after-school classes, summer schools and consultancy services.[119]

EMOs are not popular outside conservative policy circles. A 2002 Phi Delta Kappa–Gallup poll found that 65 per cent of those surveyed would oppose any proposal by their local school board 'contract[ed] with private profit-making corporations to run the entire operations of the public schools'.[120]

PRIVATISATION CREEP

There has been a major push for the private provision of educational services in many countries. Schooling is progressively being turned into a profit-making commercial venture. In the process the quality of education is being eroded.

An early step in this process was the introduction of business management structures into education, along with the elimination of many of the functions and professional services provided to schools for free by government education departments. This has opened the way for 'a host of private agencies, consultants and professional firms' to fill the gap on a commercial basis.[126]

Private provision has occurred at three levels: supplementary services such as catering and cleaning; private educational services provided outside of school hours, such as tutoring, educational software and after-school care; and core education services such as managing or operating schools.

Box 12.5   Outsourcing School Meals

A report by Corporate Watch in 2005 found that the outsourcing of school meals in the UK was having a detrimental impact on the health of school children because of low spending on ingredients and labour by the private companies. Despite this, school meals are actually becoming more expensive. When schools were forced to put school catering out to tender in the 1980s, the requirement that school meals meet nutritional standards was removed. In 2001, nutritional standards had to be reintroduced but they are not effectively enforced.[127]

The Soil Association found in 2003 that the average school meal failed to meet recommended nutritional guidelines. It found that school meals contained 'a low grade diet of dematerialised fish, mechanically recovered meat and poor quality produce containing pesticide residues', and were dominated by 'cheap processed and "fast" food items packed with fat, salt, or refined sugar ... and precariously low in essential nutrients'.[128] Such food not only leads to childhood obesity but can impact on the mental welfare, behaviour and academic achievement of children.

The World Trade Organisation (WTO) has become a promoter and enforcer of privatised educational services through the General Agreement on Trade in Services (GATS). Although GATS allows governments to keep control of public services, if those services are not totally provided by the public sector, they are not defined as public services. So countries which have both private and public schools cannot claim school education to be a public service. If education services are opened to international trade under GATS – and this is subject to negotiation between nations – then foreign providers of education must be treated the same way as domestic providers, with access to the same subsidies and grants, unless an exception is granted by the WTO.[129]

Degrees of privatisation

At the extreme end of the privatisation spectrum are schools that are run as businesses for profit. The extent to which for-profit schools are publicly funded varies, but in the US charter schools are almost completely funded by government.

In other countries a public abhorrence of for-profit education, combined with a scepticism on the part of the business community that profits can be made from running schools, has ruled out for-profit schools.

In Australia private schools are not for-profit, nor are they totally government funded. However they get as much as 80 per cent of their funding from government.[130] Similarly in Canada, private schools get up to half their funding from the government.[131] In the UK, schools that are almost totally funded by government are being run by private sponsors and the boards they appoint. Those sponsors may be businesses. In this way UK academies and trust schools only differ from US charter schools in that they cannot be run for profit (see Table 12.3).

Private management and administration of schools in the form of EMOs in the US and the outsourcing of LEAs in the UK are an intermediate step between public control and the full privatisation of schools. The allocation of vouchers, which will be discussed in the next chapter, is also a step on the way to privatisation. The push for privatisation by business interests (see Chapter 14) comes despite the failure of any of these experiments in privatisation to demonstrate the superiority of private provision of educational services.

Table 12.3   Some Different Types of Schools

	Funding	Management	Regulation
Public Schools	government	government or outsourced to private company	curriculum, testing regime, employment practices, admissions policies set by government
Academies (UK)	government + £2m private	private sponsors & board mainly appointed by sponsors not for-profit	can set own employment practices, admissions policy, and curriculum
Trust Schools (UK)	government + small private contribution	private trust & trust appointed board not for-profit	can set own employment practices, admissions policy, and curriculum
Charter Schools (US)	government + some private donors	private can be for-profit	can set own employment practices, admissions policy, and curriculum
Private Schools (Australia/ Canada)	government & private fees	private not for-profit	can set own employment practices, admissions policy, and curriculum

13
Turning Schools into Markets

Competition makes businesses perform. Choice can do the same for schools.
David Kearns, CEO of Xerox[1]

New Zealanders were once proud of their equalitarian education system. However a system of school choice designed to promote competition between public schools has resulted in a school system that is more inequitable than most other industrialised nations and far more segregated on the basis of race, socio-economic status and student performance.[2]

From 1991, following the recommendations of a taskforce headed by supermarket magnate, Brian Picot, NZ school children no longer had to attend their local school. Schools were expected to compete with each other for enrolments, which formed the basis of their funding.[3] Parents tended to choose schools on the basis of their ethnic mix and socio-economic status, assuming that schools with fewer Maori and Pacific Islander children, and fewer poor children, were better quality. Popular schools were able 'to choose academically motivated students from relatively affluent families'.[4] Maori children were 'significantly less likely' to be accepted into their first choice of school than other children.[5]

At the same time schools in working-class areas tended to be destabilised as upwardly mobile families moved their children to other schools in more affluent neighbourhoods causing a decline in enrolments, and therefore funding cuts and teacher cuts and, in some cases, a 'spiral of decline'.[6] These declining schools became the refuge for 'increasing concentrations of difficult-to-teach students', including those suspended from other schools.[7]

By 1998 it was clear to everyone, even government officials, that the market system did not work for poorer schools. They could not improve their enrolments no matter how much they improved their teaching quality and how well they ran their schools, because of parental prejudice. Marketing and efforts to accommodate parental needs through provision of extras such as after-school programmes did not help. They found it hard to attract qualified teachers. The causes of their downward spiral were beyond their control.[8]

In a market, it is inevitable that some businesses will fail, however, it is not acceptable for schools to fail and go bankrupt and be shut down, as it leaves the students attending them high and dry.[9] Unlike businesses

> schools in difficulty cannot use the strategies available to private business: they are unable to relocate, to shed business not regarded as core, to change suppliers of raw materials [students] in order to improve the quality of output, or to undertake radical reorganisation (because they are unable to fund the high initial costs for retraining and re-equipping).[10]

In many nations school choice has led to an increased segregation of schools based on socio-economic background or ethnicity.[11] In NSW, where public schools once had a mix of variously talented students from diverse backgrounds, school choice has resulted in 'white flight' from public schools with concentrations of Aboriginal, ethnic or Muslim students.[12] Many parents who have the choice in the US prefer to avoid schools that serve low-income, ethnically diverse neighbourhoods even if they are effective, good-quality schools. A recent US study found that parents tend to choose schools on the basis of the race and class composition of the school.[13] Various governments have made attempts to prevent schools being so selective in their enrolment, including the New Zealand government, but they cannot prevent the variability between schools that a market system inevitably produces.[14]

Education is being turned into a commodity, subject to the 'disciplines' and 'vagaries' of the market, as a consequence of business lobbying and spin. There are various ways this is being done where privatisation of schools is not an option. Firstly, schools can be funded on the basis of how many students enrol, with enrolments at each school open to all students, not just those in the immediate neighbourhood. Such an open enrolment system may be limited to public schools, as in England or New Zealand. Alternatively an open enrolment scheme may include private schools, which also receive government funding on the basis of enrolment numbers, as in some parts of Europe and Chile.[15]

Another way of encouraging markets in education is to introduce government-funded vouchers. Voucher programmes are a way to enable students to take their per-student government funding with them to the school of their choosing, including private schools. They have been promoted heavily by business interests in the US, despite public opposition to them (see Chapter 14).

Tax credits for tuition fees were designed as an alternative to vouchers that isn't so obviously dependent on government money. Corporations are able to get income tax credit for the money they give to private scholarship funds that provide vouchers or scholarships to children attending private or religious schools. Although the funds essentially come from taxes, they are completely controlled by a private fund and there is not the accountability that would normally be part of a government programme.[16]

Ideology

Think tanks and the businesses that fund them claim that if schools cannot be privatised the next best thing is to force them to operate like private for-profit companies and compete with each other in a market.[17] They have consistently argued that competition for students will reap superior outcomes in schools because, according to business management theories, it will give schools 'both the tools and the incentive to behave in more cost-effective, flexible, competitive, consumer-satisfying and innovative ways. In other words, schools would behave more like "commercial enterprises"'.[18]

Governments have been convinced by this sort of rhetoric despite the lack of evidence to support it.[19] At the international level, business-oriented education policies of competition and choice are being promoted by the World Bank, the WTO and the OECD. School choice/competition advocates claim that other factors, such as how well funded and resourced a school is and the socio-economic background of students, are not significant. They therefore oppose additional government funding of poor inner city schools but favour voucher systems and open enrolment.

In Canada the Fraser Institute has been promoting the marketisation of schools for a number of years. In 1999 it published *The Case for School Choice* and in 2006 *Why Canadian Education Isn't Improving*, which argued that government control gives special-interest groups, particularly teachers, too much say in decisions; requires too much compliance with regulations; and ensures that 'schools become excessively uniform'. In contrast, the Institute claims, a market system would provide incentives to ensure schools were performance driven.[20] The report cites think tank writers from the US.

Australian economist, Mark Harrison, typifies business ideology when it comes to schools:

> But imagine if we ran our supermarkets the way we run our schools ... we have government provided supermarkets, financed by taxes, at which shoppers can get a basket of groceries for free.
>
> Customers are forced to shop at the supermarket in their suburb, and can only change to another government supermarket with permission, and subject to room at that supermarket. ...
>
> Managers find it difficult to order supplies on time, experiment with new suppliers, fix windows, get supermarkets painted or build new facilities. All these decisions are overseen by central office and involve much bureaucracy. Most spending goes on salaries. Cuts in the equipment budget mean that shopping

trolleys are very old, most with three or four wobbly wheels. Home delivery has been abandoned as a cost-cutting measure. Many ideas introduced in the private sector, such as express checkouts, and checkout scanning devices, have not been adopted in the public sector due to union opposition.[21]

This is a ridiculous analogy that confuses the lack of government funding, necessitated by tax cuts demanded by business and their think tanks, with lack of competition and too much bureaucracy.

OPEN ENROLMENTS

In 1988 the conservative Thatcher government in the UK opened up enrolments at government schools in England to students from outside the local area and funded schools on the basis of enrolment numbers. The goal was a state-regulated, state-funded 'quasi-market' in schooling.[22] Instead of having comprehensive schools that offer an equivalent education to all students attending public schools, schools are now encouraged to specialise (see Chapter 9) in order to provide choice in an education market, with individual schools seeking market niches to attract customers.

Various Australian states have also restructured schools to introduce competition. In Victoria, where 'reforms' were the most radical, schools were de-zoned during the 1990s and their funding became dependent on enrolments. The conservative Kennett government sought 'to reconstruct the public school system as a market of competing firms'.[23]

Fifteen US states guarantee children a choice of public schools.[24] By 2001 one in four children were attending schools other than the closest one.[25] However, US politicians have been wary of opening up enrolments between districts because of the fear that voters in affluent neighbourhoods would object to paying high taxes for local schools if children from other neighbourhoods could attend them.[26]

Marketing

The consequence of making schools compete with each other is that marketing has become a major school activity upon which the school's funding, and even its survival, depend. Principals are diverting their time from efforts to deliver educational quality to managing budgets and marketing.[27] They have now become business managers seeking competitive advantage rather than professionals seeking quality, equity and non-economic value. Schools are concentrating on image management because many parents make their choice on the basis of 'superficial indicators of schooling' and outward appearances 'rather than on any knowledge or understanding of the processes and practices which lie behind them'.[28]

Around the world, newly marketised schools go out of their way to create a good impression in terms of architecture, interior layout and design, displays, publicity, open days and nights, and public performances. Appearances become all important.[29] School reception areas have been refurbished, whilst educational costs are slashed, to give the impression of a well-run, affluent business. While the cost of such marketing efforts may be justified in each school by the extra income each new student brings to the school, the total marketing bill across the school system (millions each year) is money that schools then don't have for teachers and textbooks.[30]

Schools now depend on direct advertising to attract students, a form of communication considerably at odds with education. School prospectuses are glossy, professionally produced marketing brochures, short on information and long on advertising language with colourful evocative photos aimed at attracting rather than informing.[31] Advertisements focus on presenting an image of the school that usually involves depictions of attractive, happy children, and focus on sporting and testing achievements.[32]

Because parents often value traditional educational values, such as discipline, schools tend to aim for formal teacher–student relations; neat, docile and compliant students; and an academic focus.[33] They go to great lengths to ensure that school grounds are litter free; that parent events are stage-managed and well-rehearsed; and that students are clean, tidy and well-behaved. Uniforms are especially favoured as an indicator of a well-disciplined school.

But none of this tells the parents anything about the quality of education and how well the teachers engage the students and facilitate their learning.[34] In fact, catering to parental prejudices about the need for control and discipline can interfere with the formation of closer relationships between teachers and students as well as the use of more progressive teaching methods.

Image-driven schools often take short cuts to solve problems that normally take time to rectify. For example, undesirable behaviour is dealt with quickly by expelling the students involved. Expulsions send a message to other parents that the school is tough on discipline. Expulsions can also help a school to improve its position on the league tables by ridding itself of poorly performing students. When the school does not have adequate grounds to expel a student it can pressure parents to remove the child with tactics such as the *threat* of forced expulsion and the associated social stigma.[35] In the UK, for example, school exclusion rates have been increasing over the last decade, particularly amongst lower income children.[36]

Rather than producing diversity and innovation, competition has led to homogeneity and conformity because innovation is risky.[37] When schools are trying to maximise their enrolments, given that their markets are to some extent geographically limited, it does not make sense to 'seek out niche markets'.[38]

Schools also seek to emulate the most popular schools, particularly more affluent schools and private schools.[39]

Geoff Whitty, Director of the Institute of Education at the University of London, concluded in 2002 that educational reforms had not led to substantially better use of resources or more school diversity (apart from government-funded specialisms), and the evidence with respect to improved learning outcomes was even more difficult to come by.[40]

Similarly Cathy Wylie found, in an international literature review, that competition between public schools led to more attention being paid to school image and physical presentation rather than to changes in teaching, apart from the introduction of more computers into classrooms. Most teachers and principals did not see any benefits to student learning arising from school choice.[41]

Equity and enrolments

In countries where school league tables are published, they become a major parameter used by parents to judge schools. However, the test scores these tables are based on often reveal more about the socio-economic composition of the student body than the ability of the school to enhance student achievement. Research has shown that a school's test results tend to be better if it has fewer poor disadvantaged children on its rolls.[42]

The performance of a school on standardised tests may also reflect the enrolment policy of the school rather than the quality of education they offer. Competing schools try to avoid enrolling students who do poorly in tests or who are labour intensive, that is, students with emotional problems, family problems, learning difficulties or special needs.[43] In a competitive school market, 'entrepreneurial schools positioning themselves to attract a middle-class clientele shed the poor, the troublemakers and the nonconformists as fast as they can, to the poor old "comprehensive" down the road'.[44]

Schools that are particularly good at providing for children with special needs try to avoid getting a reputation for this because they might then attract such children, and the economic returns for educating children with special needs is poor. In contrast, many schools put extra resources into educating the top performing students so as to boost their school's academic status in the eyes of parents.[45]

Competing schools are more likely to encourage weaker students to take less academically difficult subjects. In Britain the Royal Society of Chemistry has claimed that students are being discouraged from taking A-level maths because it is a difficult subject and schools want to keep their exam results as high as possible. This means universities are having to run remedial classes.[46]

Undesirable and expelled students in an open enrolment system end up in the 'undersubscribed' schools that cannot afford to pick and choose between enrolling students because they need all the students they can get to survive economically.

These schools tend to be under-staffed and under-resourced. They are then 'faced with having to support disproportionate numbers of socially and educationally vulnerable children without the resources necessary to do so properly'.[47]

A study of Boulder Valley School District in Colorado, where schools compete for students, found that parents chose schools largely on the basis of test scores, although it is mainly white middle-income parents who move their children to the high-scoring schools. This leads to even lower test scores in unpopular schools, more students moving to more popular schools, and a spiral of decline for schools with poorer student populations.[48]

In England, schools with a more affluent catchment appear to have a higher quality education and tend to be oversubscribed. In some places, where schools reach their physical limit, new enrolments are limited to children living in the neighbourhood. Those who can afford to, move to areas where such 'high performing' schools are located – the leafy suburbs with high-cost housing.[49]

Wherever there are open enrolments, the more popular schools that serve higher-income neighbourhoods are able to be selective in their enrolments and reinforce their perceived advantage by ensuring that they maintain their original social mix. In other words, some schools get to pick and choose their students, rather than the parents choosing the schools. This means that the choice offered to children from failing schools in the US, as part of No Child Left Behind (NCLB) legislation, is really a mirage. Consequently, only around 1 per cent of children who are eligible to change schools throughout the nation actually do so.[50]

In England schools are not supposed to be selective in enrolments, yet the 'gulf between the best and worst' primary schools in terms of exam performance has been widely recognised.[51] The popular schools interview parents for suitability and do their best to put off unsuitable parents in the interview and through other means.[52] In 2004/5 almost one in ten parents applying to enrol their children in secondary schools are so unhappy at being denied their choice of school that they have lodged formal appeals.[53] A study by the Institute for Public Policy Research (IPPR) found that schools in less affluent areas were covertly selecting students by ability, so that their enrolments did not reflect the social composition of the neighbourhood; particularly city academies, faith schools and foundation schools.[54]

As a result of these practices a new admissions code was introduced in September 2008 that bans schools from deciding enrolments on the basis of parental occupation, financial, marital or social status, or donations to the school. Nor are they allowed to discourage poorer families by having expensive uniforms. However, priority can be given to siblings of children who have attended the school and 10 per cent of enrolments can be based on 'aptitude'.[55]

In Australia 'some selective schools take only students in the top 1 per cent of the population, academically. Other comprehensive schools take anyone.'[56] And whilst the most popular public schools are able to pick and choose amongst potential 'customers', the weaker schools have to devote increasing resources to marketing and are struggling to survive. As a result the quality of education in those schools is actually declining.[57]

Equity and funding

It is hardly fair to expect schools to compete for students when their funding base is so inequitable, but this is what occurs. In the US there are enormous variations in government funding of schools because of the reliance on local taxes. The funding of schools varies from $3000 per student per year to $30,000.[58]

> Rich people in the United States are able to buy some of the world's finest education for their children, either in private academies or in well-financed, suburban, public-school districts. In contrast, children of the poor are often crowded into miserable rural or inner-city schools whose annual per-student support may be one-fifth or less of that in nearby, suburban public schools ... schools in slum neighbourhoods must contend with dangerous and decaying buildings, gross overcrowding, violence, and inadequate funding for even basic instruction.[59]

In Australia, successive federal governments have been increasing subsidies to private schools, 'building them as a market-based alternative to the state school system'.[60] Between 1975–76 and 1982–83 federal funding of public schools fell by 12 per cent, while it increased for private schools by 94 per cent and continued to rise in the 1980s despite a recession. The state and territory governments also increased the funding of private schools between 1988–89 and 1993–94 by 42 per cent whilst only increasing the funding of state schools by 7 per cent.[61]

These government subsidies have brought down fees in many private schools to be within reach of the middle classes and so provide competition with public schools. Catholic schools receive around 80 per cent of their operating costs from federal and state governments and are therefore able to charge relatively low fees compared with other private schools. The Anglican church has also introduced new low-fee schools to augment its high-fee elite schools.[62]

Consequently there has been a major shift in enrolments from public to private schools. 'An ideology of parental "choice" has been vigorously promoted, with the corollary that parents who care about their kids will always choose private schools.' In 2005, 67 per cent of children attended public schools compared with 77.4 per cent in 1970, and that is expected to decline further with most of those moving to private schools going to independent rather than Catholic private schools. This has fed the media-led public perception that private schools are superior and public schools are deteriorating.[63]

In Canada too, public funding has been diverted to private schools. In British Columbia private schools now receive 50 per cent of the funding per pupil that public schools receive and the proportion of students attending private schools is increasing.[64] In Québec, where private schools get 43 per cent of their income from the government (60 per cent of the cost of a public school student for each private school student), this trend is most pronounced at secondary school level where over 20 per cent of French speaking students in urban areas go to private schools; 30 per cent in Montréal.[65]

Choice versus participation

The business rhetoric behind the push for promoting competition and a market for schools is that parental choice will ensure that schools are responsive to the wishes of parents. However, the concept of giving parents choice does not extend beyond the choice between the available range of schools in their neighbourhood (often a very limited range). If they don't like the way a school is run all they can do is remove their child from it (provided there is an alternative school available). This is very different from being able to participate in school decision-making and the design of curricula or having a voice through elected parental representatives on a governing board. In practice parental choice of schools is a very weak form of participation and expression.

If there was genuine participation, parents would be able to protest, discuss, negotiate, vote and work with the school to shape the school to meet parental goals.[66] In fact, some of those promoting school choice and educational markets have spurned democratic control of schools as leading to inefficient bureaucracies and coercion by public authorities. The Fraser Institute, for example, argued that 'Political control [i.e. democratic control] of public education is preventing good people and good intentions from yielding tangible improvement.' It pointed out that government control favours collective choice over individual choice.[67] But that is not a bad thing when it comes to education.

The concept of individual parental choice in an education market encourages parents to think about how to give their own children an advantage rather than what is good for all children, or good for society. Marketisation erodes the ability of democracies to debate and deliberate on the goals of education and 'what constitutes a minimally "good" education' that should be available to all children.[68] The market, rather than an elected government, decides which schools will prosper and which go into decline through lack of enrolments and therefore lack of funds.

VOUCHERS

The idea of school vouchers is often credited to Milton Friedman who in the 1950s envisaged vouchers being offered to all parents to create a simulated market in schooling, funded by government. In this way, competition would drive underperforming schools out of business.[69] Friedman continued to promote vouchers though the Rose and Milton Friedman Foundation.

The first nation to widely implement a voucher system was Chile, which established a national voucher system in 1981 during the Pinochet dictatorship. It covered all children and all schools, private and public. The voucher system led firstly to a drop in school funding through the 1980s as the real value of vouchers dropped and parental contributions didn't keep up. Secondly one in four students moved from public municipal schools to private schools between 1979 and 1994, leaving only 57 per cent of primary students attending public schools, mainly the poorer students. Performance in standardised Spanish and maths tests for grade four students declined between 1982 and 1988 as school funding decreased. Martin Carnoy concludes in his study of Chilean schools that 'privatisation during the 1980s in Chile reduced the public effort to improve schooling since it relied on the free market to increase achievement'.[70]

Sweden introduced vouchers in 1992 as a way of improving education in the face of severe cost constraints and decreasing central government bureaucracy. Despite the vouchers most people remained committed to an equitable system of public education and few parents moved their children from neighbourhood schools – only about 10 per cent. The increase in private school enrolments was also minimal – from 0.94 to 2.16 per cent. Nevertheless the voucher system and devolution of fiscal control to schools was accompanied by cuts in school spending by the government, as in Chile. The voucher system was discarded as a failure in 1996.[71]

In the US a voucher experiment by the Nixon administration, which began in 1972 in Alum Rock, California, was abandoned in 1977 because there was no evidence that children in the programme were achieving more.[72] Nevertheless, because of a concerted campaign by business interests (see next chapter), by 2006 ten states and Washington DC offered either government-funded vouchers for students to attend private schools or tax credits/deductions for private school tuition or contributions to private scholarship programmes.[73]

Milwaukee experiment

The first state-funded voucher programme in the US was established in Milwaukee, Wisconsin in 1990, without being put to a referendum. It began with seven private schools enrolling voucher-funded children who were from low-income, mainly African-American, families and chosen by lottery.[74]

The voucher programme was expanded to include religious schools in 1997 even though an evaluation of the programme had found no gains in student achievement. The value of the voucher was increased, at the demand of the participating private schools, until it matched or even exceeded the full cost of educating a student at a public school. By 2004 the programme included 115 mainly religious private schools. Fifty of them were newly created free-market schools established to take advantage of the voucher funds. In 2006 the limit of 15,000 students in the programme was lifted to 22,500.[75]

Schools in the Milwaukee voucher programme are not required to test their students nor to publish any test results, even though they receive some $87 million of taxpayer money each year.[76] They do not have to hire certified teachers and can even hire teachers who are not college graduates. They can suspend or expel students without explanation, and do not have to 'disclose attendance, suspension, or drop out rates'. This lack of regulation is supposed to provide the schools with flexibility to innovate and compete and it is assumed by advocates that they will be kept accountable by free-market forces; if they don't deliver a high standard of education parents will move their children elsewhere.[77]

The new voucher-dependent schools tend to have inadequate facilities: 'Some were nothing more than refurbished, cramped storefronts. Some did not have any discernable curriculum and only a few books.' One 'used the back alley as a playground'.[78] In the first five years around 25 per cent of voucher schools went out of business, three during the school year, stranding their students.[79]

When the *Milwaukee Journal Sentinel* investigated the 115 schools in the voucher programme reporters were refused access to nine of them. They found 'alarming deficiencies' in another 10 per cent of the schools. They claimed that these schools did not have the 'ability, resources, knowledge or will to offer children even a mediocre education'.[80] This is not surprising given, as *Education Week* writer, Gerald Grant, pointed out: 'good schools ... are not instantaneous creations that can be thrown up like a chain of '7–11' stores'.[81]

Performance gains

Because private schools are not required to take standardised tests, it is difficult to know whether students receiving vouchers get a better education. A state mandated study of the Milwaukee programme, by Professor John Witte from the University of Wisconsin, found that although the families who received vouchers were very happy with the system, there was actually no evidence that student performance improved between 1990 and 1995 as a result of attending private schools with the help of vouchers.[82]

No subsequent evaluation was required by the state government. However, a study by Princeton economist, Cecilia Rouse, found that performance gains during the 1990s were lower for voucher students in private schools than for students in small classes in public schools.[83] This suggests that government money would be better spent on more teachers in public school.

Results in other states have been mixed with some performance gains reported for African-Americans in Washington and New York but not for Hispanic or white children receiving vouchers.[84] Researchers from the University of Indiana found that between 1998 and 2003 public school students in first to fifth grade improved more than voucher students in Cleveland, even though the public school students had a lower average family income and were more likely to be African-American.[85]

In a literature review of full-voucher programmes in the Netherlands, Belgium, France, Sweden, Chile and Vermont, undertaken for the New Zealand Council for Educational Research, Cathy Wylie concluded that:

> Research on full voucher systems covering both public and private schools shows no evidence that they provide a powerful means to overcome the gaps in achievement between low income students and others. Nor do they appear to increase overall achievement ... There is also no evidence of increased efficiencies or lower educational costs.[86]

Equity

Even if, despite the evidence to the contrary, you accept that students who receive vouchers to attend private schools are better off, those students constitute a small minority of students attending public schools. In Florida in 2002 there were 2.5 million students in public schools and kindergartens, whilst 16,000 students received vouchers costing the state taxes of around $138 million over two years, money the state could ill afford given that it was ranked near the bottom of the states in terms of public school funding.[87]

Even where voucher programmes are confined to public schools, opponents argue that vouchers result in a shift of funds away from the worst-resourced public schools and only 'concentrate underperforming and problem students in inferior schools', as has happened with open enrolment schemes.[88] They allow a few schools to improve their test scores by being selective about which students they accept. In this way 'voucher systems increase social segregation' going against a traditional aim of education which is to promote social cohesion and equity.[89]

Vouchers that fund attendance at private schools are supposedly aimed at equity and opportunities for poor children, but in practice they often fund middle-class children who are already going to or intending to go to private or religious schools. Poorer parents cannot afford the extra costs – not covered by the vouchers – of tuition, uniforms and transport to distant schools (as private schools and the better-resourced public schools tend to be sited in wealthy neighbourhoods).[90]

A report by People for the American Way Foundation found that in its first year of operation, the Washington DC programme gave vouchers to less than 75 children from public schools 'in need of improvement' out of 1300 granted. In contrast, some 200 students already attending private schools received vouchers.[91] In Pennsylvania, most of the vouchers went to children already enrolled in private or religious schools.[92] In Texas, even the children of the wealthiest families can receive vouchers to attend private schools and those schools give preference to those already enrolled.[93]

In practice voucher programmes do little more than subsidise private schools. Friedman and other free-market proponents in fact envisaged vouchers as a way of privatising schools by making vouchers available to everyone, with wealthier 'consumers' able to supplement the voucher to get into more expensive schools.[94]

Tax credits can also promote inequity. Where parents are offered tax credits, it enables wealthy parents to have private school fees subsidised. Corporate tuition tax credits, like vouchers, deprive public schools of taxpayer money and tend to be used for scholarships that go to more affluent children, despite the rhetoric about helping the poor. In Florida in the first year of operation, 2002, more than a third of recipients of the $3500 awarded by private scholarship funding organisations went to students who would have gone to private schools anyway. A company can get up to $5 million in tax credits for donations to these funding organisations amounting to up to $88 million each year.[95]

SHIFTING EDUCATIONAL PRIORITIES

Traditionally, public schools were based on a recognition that 'unequal circumstances of children's lives are not of their own making' and that all children are entitled to an equally good education, 'regardless of their parents' beliefs, capacity to pay, or personal circumstances'.[96] Business efforts to get schools to behave like businesses, competing for students in an educational marketplace, are undermining the concept that public education should provide equal opportunity to all children.

The ideal of the right of every child to a high-quality education dominated educational policy in most countries until the 1980s, but it has been replaced by the right of every parent to choose the school their child attends. This is hardly an equivalent right given the inequity that results. In some nations, private schools are being included in the competition between schools, despite their superior resources. The idea inherent in private schools – that some parents should be able to buy a better education for their children – fits well with the market ideology behind the push for competition. But it conflicts with the ideal of equal educational opportunity for all children.

The combination of devolution, accountability, competition and marketisation encourages 'schools to see themselves as free standing, entrepreneurial small businesses' and parents and students to see themselves as consumers of the product that schools offer.[97] Various publications have emerged which reaffirm the idea of 'educational consumerism', such as the *Good State Schools Guide* in the UK, and several newspaper supplements in Canada and elsewhere that provide consumer guidance to parents choosing schools.[98]

Education, once a public good, has become a private good. The market privileges those children whose parents are wealthier, or better-informed consumers of schooling.[99] Rather than public education being a community enterprise, it 'pits families and schools against each other in a battle for survival of the fittest'.[100]

As a consequence of the current business push for competition and choice in schools, combined with the reluctance of corporations and the wealthy to pay their fair share of taxes to properly fund public schools, there are now three tiers of education: private schools that cater to the elites who want to give their children social and educational advantages; other private and selective public schools that are adequately funded and able to control their enrolments; and inadequately funded public schools whose doors are open to any child, whatever their socio-economic background, religion, or ability. Students from poorer families are getting an inferior education as the school system becomes more segregated along socio-economic lines.

14

Privatisation Proponents

> I've had the experience of building a company from nothing to 4,000 stores. Why can't we do the same with schools and do it with excellence?
>
> Donald Fisher, of The Gap[1]

When Sam Walton, founder of the Wal-Mart empire, died in 1992 he left a fortune to his family – currently estimated at some $90 billion – making them the richest family in the world and putting five of them in the top ten wealthiest individuals list.[2] Wal-Mart, one of the lowest paying employers in the US, has received over a billion dollars in tax subsidies. It also campaigns for tax breaks, and against estate tax. The Waltons prefer philanthropy to taxation because it enables them to determine how their surplus money is spent and to use it for public relations and political purposes of their own choosing. According to *The Nation*, the Walton Family Foundation (WFF) 'gives a staggering number of gifts, apparently in order to buy goodwill in as many communities as possible'.[3]

Education 'reform' is a particularly favoured target for their PR spending, and between 1998 and 2003 the Waltons donated more than $700 million to educational 'reform' charities.[4] The WFF funds groups that advocate a market approach to education, including vouchers and privatisation of schools.[5] Sam's second son, John, 'reputedly the world's 11th richest man',[6] was the force behind the Waltons' donations to market-oriented education reforms before he died in the crash of a light plane he was flying in 2005. John was a great champion of charter schools.

The WFF is 'the single largest source of funding for the voucher and charter school movement'. Although it promotes competition between public schools as a way for the market to provide incentives for reform, Walton family money enables charter schools to be better resourced (per student) than neighbouring public schools, ensuring that they have an advantage in the competition. WFF gave $3 million to KIPP charter schools in 2003 alone 'and millions more to other schools using the KIPP curriculum'.[7]

Foundations and wealthy businessmen

The WFF is one of several wealthy foundations that have gained their money from large successful business enterprises. Foundations provide much of the finance for the neoconservative movement, including the push for increasing the privatisation of US schools. Although (in 2002) 'total philanthropic giving to K-12 schooling' was less than $1.5 billion, compared with some $500 billion government spending, private donors tend to make sure that their donations are leveraged to give them disproportionate influence. It enables donors to 'define effective practice, forge school–community relationships, shape policy agendas, and redirect research'.[8]

Figure 14.1 shows how a few wealthy foundations are funding a vast network of organisations in the US, which are campaigning to introduce market reforms into education, including vouchers and charter schools. These organisations and many others campaign for these reforms through local organising, mass media and political lobbying.

The Bill & Melinda Gates Foundation promotes the standard business agenda of 'rigorous' curriculum and instruction, assessments and accountability, as well as market competition between schools and the establishment of charter schools.[9] It is worth some $30 billion and gives away over a billion dollars each year, mainly in education, so it is particularly influential in education policy. It accounts for a quarter of all philanthropic donations in the school education sector. It distributes much of this money to schools but increasingly it is funding groups promoting particular types of school reform, what the Foundation calls 'advocacy work'.[10]

The Gates Foundation is a major funder of the National Centre on Education and the Economy (NCEE) which set up the New Commission on the Skills of the American Workforce.[11] It funded a report by the Commission that called for schools to be run by independent private contractors rather than school districts.[12] Tom Vander Ark, head of the education section of the Gates Foundation, 'envisions a system in which public authorities oversee schools but do not run them, and Gates Foundation money is directed towards projects that fit that vision ... Schools would receive public support only if they performed and parents chose them.'[13]

Similarly the Lynde and Harry Bradley Foundation promotes privatisation of public education via vouchers, lobbies state governments for voucher schemes, and funds private voucher programmes, including $14.4 million to Partners Advancing Values in Education (PAVE).[14]

In addition to family foundations, individual wealthy people are using their corporate wealth to promote vouchers and charter schools. Table 14.1 gives some examples.

Table 14.1   Key Individuals Funding the School Privatisation Efforts

Wealthy Individuals	Positions – past and present	Donations
Dick DeVos, President of Amway (1993–2002)	Co-chair of Kids First! Yes! Co-chair, Education Freedom Fund Board of the Children's Scholarship Fund Founder of All Children Matter (ACM) Michigan Board of Education Member Michigan Business Roundtable	Private voucher programmes Lobbying for state voucher schemes Republican Party Advocacy groups and coalitions
Betsy DeVos	Co-chair, Education Freedom Fund (EFF) Co-chair, Of the People Board of Children First America Founder of All Children Matter (ACM) Founder, chair, Great Lakes Education Project Director, James Madison Institute Chair of Michigan Republican Party	
Donald G. Fisher, founder, GAP clothing retailer	Major investor in Edison Project Board of California Business Roundtable Founder, National Alliance for Public Charter Schools Founder, Teach for America Founder, EdVoice California Board of Education	Charter school campaigns National Alliance for Public Charter Schools KIPP Foundation Investor in Edison Schools EdVoice
Ted Forstmann, venture capitalist	Co-chair, founder Children's Scholarship Fund CEO and funder, Put Parents in Charge Honorary chairman, Washington Scholarship Fund	Private voucher programmes Lobbying for state voucher schemes Voucher advertising campaigns
James Leininger	Founder, Texas Public Policy Foundation (think tank modelled on Heritage Foundation)	Private voucher programmes Lobbying for state voucher schemes Putting Children First PAC Republican Party
J. Patrick Rooney	Board, National Center for Policy Analysis (TX) Board, American Legislative Exchange Council Chair, American Education Reform Foundation Board, Washington Scholarship Fund Board, CEO America	Conservative causes Private voucher programmes Lobbying for state voucher schemes
John Walton, heir to Wal-Mart fortune	Co-chair, founder, Children's Scholarship Fund Board, CEO America Director, Tesserac T. Group Founder, Schools Research Foundation Board, AERC Past president, AERF	Private voucher programmes Lobbying for state voucher schemes Charter schools Advocacy groups and coalitions

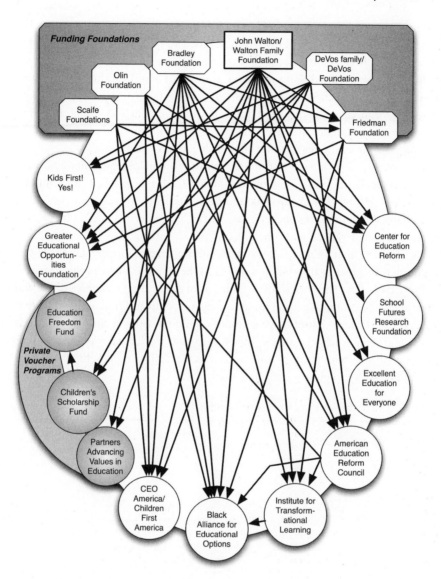

Figure 14.1   Voucher and Charter School Advocacy Groups and Some of the Foundations that Fund Them[15]

VOUCHERS CAMPAIGNS

Businessmen have spent millions of dollars trying to get voucher programmes accepted in state ballots. In Michigan the group Kids First! Yes! raised $13 million to campaign for vouchers, including large contributions from Amway Corp president Dick DeVos and his wife, Betsy; Domino's Pizza founder, Tom

Monaghan; and John Walton. The Catholic dioceses also contributed millions to the pro-voucher campaign. The opposition raised $5 million, mainly from teacher unions and school administrators.[16]

Businesspeople raised $30 million to support a ballot in California in 2000, which proposed vouchers be available to all students no matter how wealthy their parents. Silicon Valley venture capitalist, Tim Draper, donated $24 million. Draper, a 'prominent Bush fundraiser' who inherited his first fortune and made his second inventing 'viral marketing', thinks public education is 'socialistic'.[17]

Pro-voucher groups have also funded efforts to replace legislators who have opposed voucher efforts. One Political Action Committee (PAC), All Children Matter (ACM), was set up by Dick and Betsy Devos to 'recruit, train and fund candidates committed to vouchers, tax credits and other reforms'.[18] It received funds from John Walton and others.

As can be seen in Table 14.2, vouchers and tax credits for private school fees do not have a great deal of public support in the US. They have been rejected in ballot after ballot. This is despite the millions of dollars that business groups and their allies have put into getting these ballots passed. In addition, polls show that most people believe that taxpayers money would be better spent reducing class sizes, improving teacher quality or increasing teacher/principal training. Only 12 per cent of those surveyed in 2001 agreed that giving parents school vouchers was the best way to improve public schools.[19]

Table 14.2   Voucher and Tax Credits Referenda

State	Year	Vote against
MI	1970	57%
MD	1972	55%
MI	1978	74%
DC	1981	89%
UT	1988	70%
OR	1990	67%
CO	1992	67%
CA	1993	70%
WA	1996	64%
CO	1998	60%
MI	2000	69%
CA	2000	71%

Source: adapted from 'History of Failed Vouchers and Tax Credits', People for the American Way Foundation, 2002, http://www.pfaw.org/pfaw/general/default.aspx?oid=2959

Efforts to get education voucher plans approved by Congress also failed in 1983, 1985 and 1986. However Congressional support for vouchers grew in the late 1980s as a result of think tank and business campaigns. From 1989 the number of articles published on vouchers escalated dramatically. Proponents limited their proposals to public schools as a strategy to assuage concerns that vouchers would subsidise religious schools and drain funds and brighter students from the public school system. It enabled them to get vouchers 'high on the public agenda' and was therefore seen as a first step towards more universal vouchers. According to Chester Finn: 'I would rather see progress in public schools than slam my head against a brick wall.'[20]

Campaigners then began to frame vouchers as being in the interests of low-income students, particularly black and minority students.[21] A Friedman Foundation strategy paper noted that voucher programmes for low-income children were a '"beachhead" in the long march to universal school choice'.[22] This strategy enabled proponents, including the Bush administration, to reincorporate private schools into voucher schemes because this would enable poor black children to attend private schools. There were also attempts to redefine private schools as public schools. Bush senior stated in 1992 that 'any school that serves the public and is held accountable by the public authority provides public education'.[23]

The newly acquired interest in the welfare of minority students was a ruse to get vouchers more widely accepted and enrol the black community in the cause. The Black Alliance for Educational Options (BAEO), a pro-voucher organisation purporting to represent the interests of black students, is funded by neoconservative groups and wealthy right-wing foundations that critics claim had previously opposed affirmative action and promoted racist books such as *The Bell Curve* and *Hating Whitey*.[24]

Voucher proponents also tried to enrol public support through an appeal to the idea of parental choice and control over their child's education. Choice implies freedom, voluntary action, self-expression, discretion, abundance and control. Consumer choice is supposed to be one of the great benefits of an affluent capitalist society. In other sectors of the economy competition and choice are supposed to ensure lower prices and better quality. Why not in education?

Ted Forstmann, venture capitalist, founded the group Put Parents in Charge, which spent over $20 million on an advertising campaign in 2001 which included full-page advertisements in the *New York Times*, *USA Today* and the *Washington Post*, and television advertisements that featured parents of various ethnic and racial origins stating 'I want to have choices ... I want to decide where to send my kids to school.' The word voucher was avoided.[25]

In 2001, the BAEO spent $1.3 million on television and print ads for school choice in Washington city and the Friedman Foundation also spent a couple of million dollars on television ads on school choice in early 2001.[26] Attempts to introduce voucher amendments into the US House of Representatives and Senate in 2001 failed, but in 2004 Congress passed a federally sponsored voucher programme for the District of Columbia.[27]

George W. Bush used school choice as one of his presidential election themes.[28] The Bush administration has strongly supported the idea of vouchers and appointed various voucher proponents to key positions in the US Department of Education, including Nina Shokraii Rees, who had campaigned for vouchers in her former positions with various think tanks, and former deputy secretary, Eugene Hickok, who had been a fellow with the Heritage Foundation and co-founder of the Education Leaders Council, which promotes business-inspired school 'reforms'.[29]

The Bush administration has also been generous in funding pro-voucher groups like BAEO. The Department of Education gave pro-voucher/privatisation groups almost $78 million between 2001 and 2003. It allocated $50 million to a national experiment in vouchers in Washington, DC, beginning in 2004, whilst cutting overall education spending.[30]

In 2004 attempts to introduce voucher legislation failed in 26 states and only succeeded for pre-school vouchers in Florida.[31] Florida's programme was ruled unconstitutional by the Florida Supreme Court in 2006 because it violates a constitutional requirement that the state government provide a 'uniform, efficient, safe, secure, and high quality system of free public schools'.[32] This followed several other court findings in other states and at the federal level that found that funding private religious schools with government-funded vouchers was unconstitutional.

Wealthy advocates of government-funded vouchers have established their own private voucher programmes. Many private voucher programmes are also eligible for tax credits in some states so that they are, in effect, funded by the government. By 2000 there were many private voucher programmes covering 50,000 children in 80 cities, but these were still regarded as 'demonstration models' for government-funded vouchers. Fritz Steiger, president of Children First, pointed out that the privately funded vouchers were 'a drop in the bucket' and his organisation's ultimate goal was tax-supported choice.[33]

In Texas a San Antonio businessman, James Leininger, is a major financer of the school voucher campaign. In 1992 he founded the first private voucher programme in Texas in 1992, the Children's Economic Opportunity (CEO) Foundation. Leininger admits that his private funding of vouchers is part of the campaign to get government-funded vouchers.[34] Leininger is the largest donor to the state Republican party and consequently 'one of the most politically powerful men in Texas'.[35] He contributed over $1.5 million to the Republican Party in the 18 months to June 2002. He is credited with creating 'a vast web of interlocking and overlapping pressure groups to promote this agenda'.[36] He has contributed millions of dollars to candidates for state offices and has been called the 'sugar daddy of the religious right' in Texas.[37]

Box 14.1   **Some More Privately Funded Voucher Programmes**

- In 1994 Leininger persuaded his friend, newspaper publisher, Richard Collins, to start the Children's Education Fund, another private voucher programme.[38]
- In 1998 Leininger donated $50 million over ten years to the Horizon Project, 'the first privately funded voucher programme in the nation to target an entire school district'.[39]
- In 1999 John Walton partnered with 'colourful Wall Street buyout artist', Ted Forstmann, to found the Children's Scholarship Fund. Each contributed $50 million.[40]
- The Washington Scholarship Fund was created in 1983 by 'local real estate mogul', Joseph E. Robert Jr., and is funded by the WFF.[41] It administers the federal government's District of Columbia voucher programme established in 2004.

Privatisation as a long-term goal

The long-term agenda of many who promote vouchers is the eventual privatisation of school education. Vouchers are a step along the way. This goal of school privatisation has to be a long-term one in the US because of the overwhelming public support for a system of public education. 'While Americans in some communities are deeply concerned with the state of their public schools, overall support for public education remains high.'[42]

Joseph Bast, president of the Heartland Institute, is quite candid in his assertion that vouchers are the 'way to privatise schooling' which he sees as one of the last bastions of socialism. He argues: 'The complete privatisation of schooling might be desirable, but this objective is politically impossible for the time being. Vouchers are a type of reform that is possible now, and would put us on the path to further privatisation.'[43]

Box 14.2   **Steps Towards Privatisation**

1. private demonstration voucher schemes
2. government vouchers limited to public schools
3. government vouchers targeted at low income students to attend private schools
4. universal government vouchers
5. increasing private schools, decreasing public schools
6. full privatisation of education

Vouchers enable taxpayers dollars to be diverted from public schools to privately-run schools including for-profit, religious and home schools. If vouchers can be made universally available to all students, then a free market school system will be more viable and, it is hoped, the public education system will be completely undermined through lack of students and therefore lack of funds.[44]

CHARTER SCHOOL PROMOTION

Many businesspeople and the groups that support them have an ideological belief that private provision of education would necessarily be superior in terms of quality and efficiency, even though the evidence to support such beliefs is scant. For example the British think tank, the Economic Research Council, recently published a report on 'Why Our Schools Should be Privately Financed' that asserted that '[p]rivate schools work better than government schools'.[45]

In the US, privatisation proponents have lobbied school districts and state governments intensively and used their powerful political connections to persuade authorities to privatise schools and hand them over to private profit-making companies. In some cases school districts that have been battling to get adequate funding for their schools have seen privatisation as a way of shifting responsibility for poor school performance to the private sector.[46]

Wealthy businesspeople have also poured money into the charter school movement, as a way of promoting school privatisation. Doris and Donald Fisher, co-founders of The Gap clothing empire, provided a $15 million grant to set up the KIPP Foundation in 2000 to recruit and train people to run new KIPP schools nationwide, creating a schooling franchise that now includes 45 schools with 400 teachers and 9000 students, including two high schools created in 2005.[47] The Fishers have contributed more than $10 million since then. Donald Fisher, who also gave $25 million to Edison charter schools in 1998, sees 'great similarities between what the Gap did and what KIPP does ... Principals should be able to run their schools like an entrepreneur would run their own small business.'[48]

Fisher was founder of the National Alliance for Public Charter Schools.[49] He also supports vouchers as a way of encouraging and supporting charter schools. Fisher envisages national chains of brand-name charter schools like KIPP: 'I liked all the discipline and focus KIPP schools have, using techniques such as having the kids sign a contract and having their parents sign a contract. ... One way the KIPP network helps maintain quality is by functioning like a franchise operation.'[50]

The Gates Foundation gave $135 million to promote and fund charter schools between 2000 and 2004. It has provided funds for the expansion of KIPP schools to high school level.[51] It gave $1.8 million to Green Dot Public Schools in Los Angeles in 2006 for five new charter schools.[52] In 2007 the Gates Foundation promised $10 million, the Walton Family Foundation $8.7 million, and the Fishers $5.3 million, to establish 42 KIPP schools in Houston. The total raised was $65 million.[53] The California Charter Schools Association receives around $5 million per year from the WFF and the Fishers. It was set up to run field offices to help people establish and run charter schools, including recruitment and training of charter school 'leaders'.[54]

The same people have also poured money into charter school ballots such as those rejected by Washington voters in 1996, 2000 and 2004. In 2000 the pro-charter campaign was financed by $3 million from Microsoft co-founder Paul Allen.[55] In 2004 Bill Gates, John Walton and Donald Fisher each gave a million dollars to the pro-charter campaign.[56]

BUSINESS OPPORTUNITIES

As with the business support for standardised testing, there are those who view privatisation as a business opportunity despite the failures of companies such as Edison to make a profit from it (see Chapter 12). Venture capitalists and investors believe that education will offer the same opportunities that privatisation in the health industry provided, and financial experts have labelled education as 'the next growth industry'.[57] The total for-profit education sector in the US is estimated to be worth some $105 billion. 'The privateers see almost endless possibilities in the education market... They are dizzy with excitement, and never cease to remind us that education is a multi-million dollar enterprise.'[58]

During the 1990s for-profit EMOs were promoted as a hot investment.[59] 'Venture capital firms envisioned high returns and invested millions of dollars.' According to *Business Week* in 2000: 'Big-name investors are subscribing to this vision, lured by the prospect of getting on the ground floor of an entirely new industry.'[60] 'From J.P. Morgan and Fidelity Ventures to Paul Allen's Vulcan Ventures, a host of backers are sinking millions into the new school companies in the belief that for-profit education is poised for explosive growth.'[61]

The European Round Table of Industrialists (ERT) recognised in 1998: 'The provision of education is a market opportunity and should be treated as such.'[62] In the UK the 'outsourced education market' was worth £2.5 billion by 2003. For example Group 4 Falck runs a range of privatised public services and is involved in 'SfE, an online education provider that covers around 70% of secondary schools and provides online training to around 20,000 teachers'. Henry Pitman, from Falck's partner in SfE, Tribal Group, claimed that Falck's experience with young offenders gave it 'experience in dealing with difficult pupils'.[63]

Internationally, the education market is massive. 'According to UNESCO (2000), public expenditure on education worldwide is about US$1386.6 billion ... education and training stocks have seen a rise in North America of 134% since 1994'.[64] Moreover private education consultants have been promoting their services around the world.[65]

Childcare in Australia

Although schools are not privatised in Australia, the increasing privatisation of the pre-school sector gives a taste of what might be in store if it was. Corporate pre-school care centres are increasingly privately provided in Australia, with 70 per cent of the long-day care centre market run for profit. Long-day childcare centres can be very profitable because of government subsidies and high demand.[66] The market approach to pre-school care has seen prices soar because of high demand. This means many women are forced to stay home because they cannot afford childcare.[67]

Despite the high prices paid by parents, Lynne Wannan, the convener of the National Association of Community-Based Children's Services, notes: '[s]tandards have been lowered, poorly paid and inexperienced staff employed and dubious practices crept in as larger providers built bigger centres and strove to get economies of scale'. The larger childcare companies have also 'used predatory pricing to drive smaller, community-based services and even smaller private operators out of business', which has reduced supply and allowed them to subsequently put the prices up.[68]

A 2005 survey of child long-day care centre staff by The Australia Institute found that corporate chain childcare centres offered the lowest quality of childcare, compared with community-based centres, which offered the highest quality, and independent private centres which fell between the two. Aspects of quality covered in the survey included staff relationships with children, staff-to-child ratios, quality of equipment and food, and 'whether the centre's program accommodates children's individual needs and interests'.[69] The report claimed:

> The business orientation focuses on 'efficiency and production of measurable outputs' and 'considers parents to be the purchasers who are concerned with cost and affordability'. The humanist orientation, on the other hand, sees the 'care of children as personalised' rather than a product that can be standardised for all children.[70]

ABC Learning Centres dominate the Australian market, with over 900 centres in Australia and NZ. It has 23 per cent of the entire Australian market and 36 per cent of the commercial market.[71] The childcare industry has been very lucrative for founder Ed Groves, who was ranked Australia's second richest person under 40 years of age in 2005, 'with an estimated wealth of $272 million'.[72]

ABC Learning Centres gets 44 per cent of its revenue – $128 million of its $292 million revenue in 2005 – from the Australian government, mainly through tax rebates to parents. It made a half-yearly profit of $38 million in 2005.[73] Nevertheless it has been accused of underpaying employees, forcing childcare staff to clean toilets, and keeping them quiet with confidentiality agreements and the threat of law suits for defamation.[74]

ABC Learning's plans to enter the primary school market in Queensland by setting up a non-profit organisation, Independent Colleges Australia (ICA), were unsuccessful when the Queensland government changed its laws to enable it to refuse ICA permission on the grounds of its commercial ties to ABC Learning.[75] However ICA has established two private primary schools in Victoria and has two on the drawing board for NSW. It intends to extend them to cover secondary schooling over time.[76]

In 2006 ABC Learning was the largest publicly traded childcare provider in the world. It was worth $2.4 billion and aiming to be the largest provider in the US. However its expansion into the US and the UK childcare market came at a high price. In 2008 its share price collapsed when, according to the *Australian*, it was caught up in the credit crunch as a result of having too much debt. It was forced to sell off its 1000 US childcare centres and Busy Bees, which was the fifth-largest UK childcare company.[77] Towards the end of 2008 it went into receivership and the Australian government had to spend tens of millions of dollars keeping its childcare centres open until the end of the year so parents wouldn't be left in the lurch. It is unclear how this will affect ICA's schools.

THINK TANKS

A handful of foundations fund multiple think tanks and advocacy groups with matching corporate agendas and goals in order to create the impression that there is a tidal wave of support for the policies they want in place. Consequently there is a network of corporate-funded think tanks that campaign on the issue of 'education reform'.

Think tanks have become essential vehicles of business propaganda and policy marketing. Think tanks enable US corporations to more actively initiate policies and shepherd them through the policy-making process until they became government policy. This has been facilitated by an influx of corporate money into conservative think tanks. Oil industry money was invested through businesspeople like billionaire Republican, Richard Mellon Scaife, and Mobil Oil. Chemical industry money was invested through foundations such as the Olin Foundation. Lynde and Harry Bradley invested manufacturing money, Smith Richardson invested pharmaceutical money, and the Koch family invested energy money.[78]

To influence government and set the agenda in a variety of policy arenas think tanks insinuate themselves into the networks of people who are influential in particular areas of policy. They do this by organising conferences, seminars and workshops and by publishing books, briefing papers, school kits, journals and media releases for policy makers, journalists and people able to sway those policy makers. They liaise with bureaucrats, consultants, interest groups, lobbyists and others. They take advantage of informal social networks – clubs, business, family, school/university. They seek to provide advice directly to the government officials in policy networks and to government agencies and committees, through consultancies or through testimony at hearings. Ultimately think-tank employees become policy makers themselves, having established their credentials as a vital part of the relevant issue network.[79]

Some think tanks – such as the Manhattan Institute of Policy Research, the American Enterprise Institute and the Heritage Foundation – have broad neo-conservative agendas aimed at free market reforms of every aspect of life. Some, such as the Hudson Institute, have a more explicit corporate agenda. And some are specifically formed to campaign on education issues, such as the Thomas B. Fordham Institute and the Education Policy Institute. Figure 14.2 gives examples of some of the think tanks promoting school privatisation, vouchers and charter schools, and the foundations that fund them. The think tanks that are most active on the issue at any particular time change.

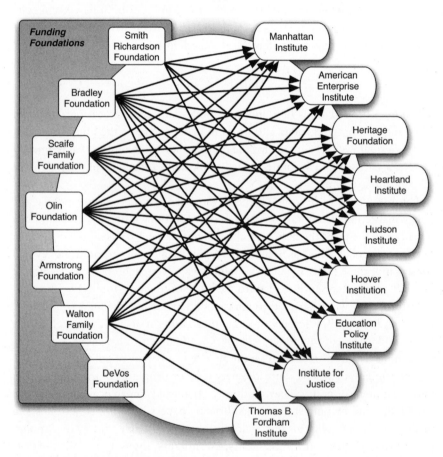

Figure 14.2   Key Think Tanks Promoting School Privatisation and Foundations that Fund Them

Source: Media Transparency, (2006), 'Media Transparency: The Money Behind Conservative Media', Cursor, Inc., http://www.mediatransparency.org

Think tanks provide the 'scholars' who write books, discussion papers and policy documents to promote charter schools, voucher and tax credits, and advocate the privatisation of public schools as the ultimate goal. They write opinion pieces that are distributed to newspapers around the country. For example, Chester E. Finn Jr., has written hundreds of articles and newspaper opinion pieces as well as eleven books. Denis Doyle has written over 150 opinion pieces for newspapers as well as co-authoring three books on education reform with key corporate CEOs (see Chapter 8).

Think-tank fellows also do media interviews, testify at government hearings, and give lectures in public forums and conferences that are often organised by these same think tanks. With all their media exposure, these think-tank 'experts' become recognised names in the public debate about school education, effectively setting its agenda and defining its terms.

Think tanks are essentially pressure groups. Nevertheless their fellows are treated by the media as independent experts. When they appear as experts on television shows or are quoted in the newspapers they have more credibility than a business executive, even though they are usually no more than paid advocates of business interests.[80]

The same group of fellows are associated with various think tanks and often have experience working in government bureaucracies (see Figure 14.3). For example, Nina Shokraii Rees 'helped to draft the blueprint' for the No Child Left Behind (NCLB) legislation whilst at the Heritage Foundation, then went to work in the Department of Education to help implement it.[81]

STIGMATISING PUBLIC SCHOOLS

School privatisation promoters such as the Milton and Rose Friedman Foundation openly welcome the publication of standardised test results as a way to 'greatly enhance and build pressure for school choice'.[82] They believe that the worse students do on the tests the more that parents will want to move their children to private schools and the more pressure there will be for vouchers and charter schools.

When one considers the requirements of the NCLB legislation in the US it seems that discrediting public education must be the primary goal. The legislation requires each state to set standards for reading, mathematics and science that, by 2014, every child should be able to achieve. Each state is then required to develop tests that students must pass to demonstrate this level of proficiency in the subject.

there is the fundamental problem that it is impossible to attain 100 percent proficiency levels for students on norm-referenced tests (when 50 percent of students by definition must score below the norm and some proportion must by definition score below any cut point selected), which are the kind of tests that have been adopted by an increasing number of states.[83]

Each state had to establish interim targets by 2003 for each year until 2014 that would allow progress to be achieved and measured annually. This is called Adequate Yearly Progress (AYP). For example, 65 per cent of students must pass the mathematics test in fourth grade at every school in the state in 2007. Such targets must be met not only by the total school population but also by each of ten specified subgroups so that 65 per cent of African-American students must pass it, as must 65 per cent of Asian, Latino, Native American, White, Low Income, Special Education, and Limited English Proficiency students. Ninety-five per cent of enrolled students in each subgroup are required to sit the test.[84] If a

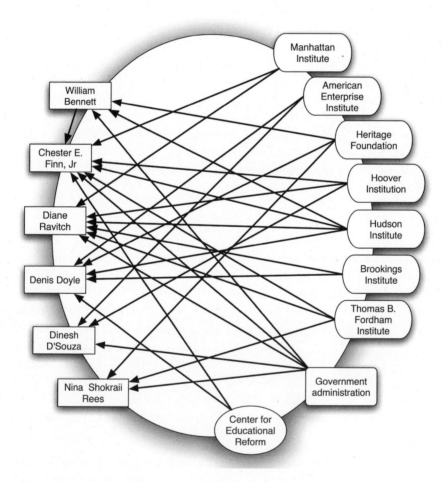

Figure 14.3   Some Key Individuals and Their Associations with Think Tanks

school fails to meet the improvement targets for just one of the ten subgroups in tests for any one subject, then the school is subject to the sanctions outlined in Chapter 7, including being converted into a charter school or giving students the option of transferring to another school.

The NCLB targets are manifestly unreasonable. 'Imagine a federal law that declared that ... all crime must be eliminated in twelve years or the local police department will face privatisation.'[85] It is particularly unreasonable to expect a high proportion of special education students to meet the subgroup targets for the very reason that they are designated as having special needs because they do badly on the tests, and if they manage to pass the tests they are generally removed from the category of special needs. Similarly, students who can pass the reading tests are transferred out of the Limited English Proficiency group.[86]

'The larger and more culturally diverse a school is, the more likely it is to be labelled as inadequate by NCLB',[87] and the fact that it is poorly resourced is not allowed to be an excuse. The poorest schools have to cope with larger classes; more disadvantaged children; more subgroups that have to meet targets; fewer teachers and counsellors; less support services; less books, materials and equipment; and substandard facilities, computers and libraries. And yet they are supposed to achieve the same targets as wealthy schools with four times the resources. And if they don't they will have to spend precious funds on tutoring children or bussing some of them to other schools.[88]

Not surprisingly the high schools that have performed best on the NCLB criteria are those that spend more per student, have more teachers per student, have fewer minority students, have very few poor or special education students, and pay teachers more.[89] Yet a survey in 2008 found that two out of three state education departments have insufficient funding and staffing to help low-performing schools.[90]

In 2006 the numbers of schools around the nation that failed to meet AYP targets grew to 29 per cent of schools (around 27,000) with 17 per cent of schools (that's over 15,000) being officially labelled in need of improvement and subject to sanctions because they have failed to meet the targets for two or more years in a row.[91] Standard & Poor's found that only 718 schools out of 16,000 schools in 18 states (4.5 per cent) were making significant progress towards NCLB goals.[92]

In some states the figures were much worse. In Washington 81 per cent of public schools did not meet the targets in 2006 (compared with 50 per cent in 2005). The 'failing' schools included some that had good reputations for providing a quality education. Tens of thousands of children now have the option of transferring to another school but there are few public schools to choose from that have met their targets. And the sanction of being converted to a charter school as a way of improving schools seems ridiculous given that only three out of 34 charter schools met AYP targets.[93]

The sanctions that NCLB imposes have no record of success as school improvement strategies, and in fact are not educational strategies at all. They are political strategies designed to bring a kind of market reform to public education. They will do little to address the pressing needs of public schools, but they will create a widespread perception of systemic failure, demoralize teachers and school communities, and erode the common ground that a universal system of public education needs to survive.[94]

Critics estimate that 'over 90% of the nation's public schools will eventually find themselves facing sanctions on the narrow basis of annual test scores and unreachable performance targets'.[95] When a majority of public schools are being labelled as 'failures', despite their educational achievements, then privatisation advocates will make sure it is trumpeted in the newspapers as a massive failure of public education. This will ensure wider public acceptance of vouchers and private charter schools, even before schools reach their six-year deadline when they will be forced to hand over management of their schools to the private sector.

Not surprisingly, teachers unions are strongly opposed to NCLB, and the largest union, the National Education Association, together with eight school districts in Michigan, Texas and Vermont, have filed suit against the legislation.[96] What is more, nearly every state has 'introduced legislation rejecting all or part of NCLB.'[97]

In other nations, the criteria for school failure is less formally set out but the tendency for poorly funded public schools to be at the bottom of standardised testing league tables adds to the impression that schools that are run by governments provide an inferior education to schools run by private interests.

15
Controlling Wayward Children

Richard Gosden

Teenage boys going to the doctor's office in the United States have
a one-in-10 chance of being prescribed a psychotropic drug.[1]

It might be expected that the routine deception and manipulation of children
and adolescents by corporate advertising, and the pressurising of children in an
increasingly competitive schooling system, might lead to some sort of reaction
amongst the more sensitive and intelligent of them. And, indeed, this is exactly
what happens.

Some children react by losing interest in school work and becoming bored
– psychiatrists label this attention deficit. Some react by showing off and being
disruptive, which is labelled hyperactivity. Some react with anger, aggression or
defiance, which is labelled conduct disorder or oppositional defiant disorder. Some
retreat into fantasy and magical thinking, or distinguish themselves by adopting
alternative fashions or habits, like nose rings or vegetarianism, which psychiatrists
increasingly treat as the early signs of schizophrenia. Some simply get unhappy,
which is called childhood depression or, if it's intermittent, bipolar disorder.

It doesn't matter what type of reaction it is: whether it involves others, or
whether it's just personal escape or misery, there is a psychiatric label and a very
profitable drug treatment waiting for those who are discovered. When children's
insecurities and anxieties are exploited by marketers, when schooling is turned
into a business and children are under enormous pressure to pass standardised
tests, when school becomes an unpleasant, competitive place where drilling and
training replace learning and exploration, then some children inevitably become
fodder for the pharmaceutical industry.

The exploitation of children and adolescents by pharmaceutical companies
selling drugs to *normalise* their thinking and behaviour is a rapidly growing
area of concern. In the new corporate-controlled culture that has erupted in
market economies many of the old child-rearing practices have been swept away.
Traditional wisdom about what is *normal* and *natural* has now largely disappeared
to be replaced by the opinions of a variety of professional advisors and corporate

spruikers. In the forefront of these are the services offered by mental health professionals. Psychiatry is now routinely used to discipline naughtiness and inattention, to modify excesses of spontaneity and creativity, to blunt anger and aggression, and to control mood variations in children.

Many people have been concerned about these developments for some time. In 2000, for instance, a report in a leading British newspaper warned about the growing reliance on psychiatric drugs to control the behaviour of children:

> More than three-quarters of a million children could be given drugs to control their behaviour – against their wishes and those of their parents. The spectre is raised by legislation planned by the government to give more powers to psychiatrists. Mental-health workers are warning that the new legislation is being drawn so widely that doctors will be given the right to drug children just because they have a difficulty with math or spelling.[2]

A more recent British newspaper article reports that the number of children said to have 'mental health disorders has more than doubled in the past 30 years, with a million experiencing problems at any one time in England'. The article was based on a report by the British Medical Association's board of science, which predicted 'one in 10 children will experience a clinically recognised mental health disorder between the ages of one and 15'.[3]

Similarly, in the US, a 2005 report by the National Institute of Mental Health claimed that at any one time about 5 per cent, 'or an estimated 2.7 million children', suffered from 'definite or severe emotional or behavioral difficulties, problems that may interfere with their family life, their ability to learn, and their formation of friendships.'[4]

With encouragement and sponsorship from drug companies psychiatrists have begun promoting the idea that early symptoms of adult mental disorders can be detected in children as young as two and that psychiatric drugs are necessary for treatment. Depression and its bipolar variation are favoured targets,[5] and there is a belief that '[d]epressed kids don't necessarily look like depressed adults: they're often irritable, rather than sad and withdrawn'.

Another psychiatric belief is that depression can be detected by assuming normal '[p]reschoolers are inherently joyful beings'. Applying this assumption, Dr Joan Luby of Washington University School of Medicine in St. Louis, for instance, conducted a study of pre-schoolers aged three to five and identified depression through their play. 'Luby had children watch two puppets discuss their emotions, then asked the kids to point to the one that sounded most like them.'[6]

In Australia, a direct result of this reduced tolerance for grumpiness has been that a 'staggering 337,553 prescriptions for antidepressants were written for children and adolescents in the past year, raising fears about whether "happy pills" are being used as a quick-fix for despondent youngsters'.[7] In the US the number of children treated for bipolar disorder increased from 20,000 in 1994 to 800,000 in 2003.[8]

Drug treatments have become the favoured tool of psychiatrists, and the prevailing conditions are creating a profit bonanza for drug companies. But the current situation is not necessarily due to either an epidemic of childhood mental disorders or developments in the efficacy of psychiatric treatments. Rather, the rapidly expanding child and adolescent market for psychiatric drugs has been skilfully crafted and directed by the drug companies themselves. Children and young people are being cynically exploited as an open-ended market due to their special vulnerability to enforced psychiatric treatment.

The mental disorders that psychiatrists identify in children and adolescents fall into two broad groupings. The first group are 'disorders usually first diagnosed in infancy, childhood, or adolescence'.[9] The second group are disorders that, until recently, were mostly only diagnosed in adults. Increasingly, mental disorders in children are being identified by reference to the boundaries of social acceptance set for adult patterns of thought, mood and behaviour.

The disorders first diagnosed in childhood, when taken as a whole, have diagnostic criteria that are so broad ranging that almost any kind of childish behaviour – only slightly troubling to parents or teachers – can be interpreted as

---

Box 15.1   Examples of Childhood Mental Disorders

Learning Disorders:
Reading Disorder; Mathematics Disorder; Disorder of Written Expression; Learning Disorder NOS – not otherwise specified. The main indications of the mental disorders associated with learning are failure to achieve academic levels that are expected for the child's age and IQ, 'as measured by individually administered standardized tests'.[10] Both common sense and tradition would suggest that what is indicated by academic failure is an educational problem rather than a medical problem.

Communication Disorders:
Expressive Language Disorder; Mixed Receptive–Expressive Language Disorder; Phonological Disorder; Stuttering; Communication Disorder NOS. Indications of these mental disorders involve weaknesses in a child's verbal expression. Failure to meet expected standards and deviations from the expected norms identify the children with these problems.[11]

Attention Deficit and Disruptive Behaviour Disorders:
Attention Deficit/Hyperactivity Disorder – three types; Attention Deficit/ Hyperactivity Disorder NOS; Conduct Disorder; Oppositional Defiant Disorder; Disruptive Behaviour Disorder NOS.[12] These are the childhood mental disorders that have become most controversial. They essentially represent a conversion of traditional problems of child discipline into problems for medical psychiatry.

symptomatic of mental disorder. Yet even with the wide scope provided by these diagnostic criteria there is an extra catch-all category for each disorder called NOS, for Not Otherwise Specified, so that diagnosing psychiatrists can find variations to meet every possible diagnostic requirement. Under the influence of pharmaceutical company research, training and sales advice, psychiatrists are now continually lowering the diagnostic thresholds for all of these disorders.

A striking feature of childhood mental disorders is the way psychiatrists use their medical authority to colonise areas that common sense would normally place well outside the scope of medical expertise.

Attention Deficit/Hyperactivity Disorder (ADHD)

Traditional methods of dealing with the indicators of attention deficit disorders usually involved combinations of rewards and punishments. These, of course, are still used, but not in the ways they used to be. The routine infliction of pain through caning, for instance, to enforce discipline and attention, is no longer permitted in schools. The withdrawal of the right of teachers to use corporal punishment has created disciplinary problems that medical psychiatry has been partly called on to deal with. This has been done by specifying diagnostic criteria that correlate with breaches of discipline by children that tend to be disruptive or irritating to adults at school or in a home setting.

The officially recognised diagnostic criteria specified for Attention Deficit/ Hyperactivity Disorder fall into two groups representing problems of (1) inattention and (2) hyperactivity-impulsivity. Each group has nine symptoms and, to label a child with ADHD, all that is required is to correlate six symptoms from either group with the child's observed behaviour.

It would be an unusual child that couldn't be portrayed as fitting these criteria, and therefore suffering from ADHD. There are no laboratory tests for supposed mental disorders such as these. A diagnosis is simply a matter of a psychiatrist interviewing and observing a child, and listening to reports of interested adults. The symptoms are merely descriptions of the way most children behave some of the time.

The question of severity, the requirement that these symptoms cause the child to be maladapted, leave scope for irritated and frustrated teachers and parents to largely decide the diagnostic outcome by what they report. In these circumstances adult irritation and frustration itself can provide prime evidence of a child being maladapted.

The stimulant drugs that are routinely prescribed to treat ADHD are a curious choice. They come from the same family of street drugs – like cocaine and amphetamines – that are used illegally by adults to relieve boredom and anxiety, and which give a sense of power and self-assuredness to the user. The prescribed

Box 15.2   Diagnostic Criteria for Attention Deficit/Hyperactivity Disorder[13]

Either (1) or (2):

(1)   six (or more) of the following symptoms of **inattention** have persisted for at least 6 months to a degree that is maladaptive and inconsistent with developmental level:

Inattention:

(a)   often fails to give close attention to details or makes careless mistakes in schoolwork, work, or other activities
(b)   often has difficulty sustaining attention in tasks or play activities
(c)   often does not seem to listen when spoken to directly
(d)   often does not follow through on instructions and fails to finish schoolwork, chores, or duties in the workplace (not due to oppositional behavior or failure to understand instructions)
(e)   often has difficulty organizing tasks and activities
(f)   often avoids, dislikes, or is reluctant to engage in tasks that require sustained mental effort (such as schoolwork or homework)
(g)   often loses things necessary for tasks or activities (e.g., toys, school assignments, pencils, books, or tools)
(h)   is often easily distracted by extraneous stimuli
(i)   is often forgetful in daily activities

(2)   *hyperactivity-impulsivity:* six (or more) of the following symptoms of hyperactivity-impulsivity have persisted for at least 6 months to a degree that is maladaptive and inconsistent with developmental level:

Hyperactivity

(a)   often fidgets with hands or feet or squirms in seat
(b)   often leaves seat in classroom or in other situations in which remaining seated is expected
(c)   often runs about or climbs excessively in situations in which it is inappropriate (in adolescents or adults, may be limited to subjective feelings of restlessness)
(d)   often has difficulty playing or engaging in leisure activities quietly
(e)   is often 'on the go' or often acts as if 'driven by a motor'
(f)   often talks excessively

Impulsivity

(g)   often blurts out answers before questions have been completed
(h)   often has difficulty awaiting turn
(i)   often interrupts or intrudes on others (e.g., butts into conversations or games)

stimulants have a similar effect on children as the street drugs do on adults, and they also have similar addictive qualities.

Serious concerns have recently been raised about the negative health effects of these drugs on children, and there were 'reports of heart attack risks last year that caused the market's lead drug, Adderall XR, to be temporarily pulled from the market in Canada'.[14] Adderall is an amphetamine and on its label Adderall XR warns that amphetamine misuse may 'cause sudden death and serious cardiovascular adverse events'. Since 2005, Strattera, another leading ADHD drug, 'has carried an FDA warning label that the drug could increase the risk of suicidal thinking in children and teens, which is the type of warning generally applied to antidepressants'.[15]

A constant flow of reports of adverse psychological reactions to ADHD drugs finally prompted the Food and Drug Administration (FDA) in the US to conduct a review. One of its panels subsequently recommended that 'labels for Concerta, Ritalin and other drugs widely used to treat attention deficit hyperactivity disorder more clearly warn of the possibility of hallucinations and suicidal tendencies in patients taking the drugs'.[16]

The possibility of sudden death, heart attack, hallucinations and suicidal tendencies seem disproportionate risks to take in dealing with the type of symptoms listed in the diagnostic criteria for ADHD. It is unlikely these risks would continue to be imposed on children were it not for the profits that have been accruing to drug companies from selling ADHD drugs. The market for ADHD drugs is worth some $2 billion a year in the US. According to one market analyst,

> [the] market growth for ADHD drugs is slowing as a result of 'increasing numbers of scary stories,' and the 5 percent market growth over the last year is weak in comparison to the previous year's 20 percent growth. Nonetheless, ... the market has a strong foundation in the United States, and will continue to be viable even with its troubled reputation.[17]

As things stand some 2 million children in the US have been diagnosed with ADHD and, according to the International Narcotics Control Board, the use of medications to treat them 'increased by more than 60% from 2001 to 2005'.[18]

The rapid expansion in the market has been largely due to drug company advertisements for stimulants, targeting parents directly. This advertising strategy began in 2001 and it has been particularly successful when directed at mothers in 'homemaker-targeted magazines, such as *Family Circle*, *Woman's Day* and *Redbook*'.[19] On top of this, to ensure the ongoing compliance of the children, drug companies have recently begun bribing ADHD children with candy-flavored drugs, and a grape-flavored, chewable tablet is now available.[20]

Other disorders

Conduct Disorder and Oppositional Defiant Disorder (ODD) are two other supposed mental illnesses in the same family as ADHD. ODD involves a 'pattern of negativistic, hostile and defiant behavior'[21] directed at adults. Arguing, annoying, or not complying with adults' requests are primary symptoms. Conduct Disorder is a children's version of Antisocial Personality Disorder and is meant to describe a child psychopath. Fifteen symptoms are specified in the *Diagnostic and Statistical Manual of Mental Disorders* (DSM IV) to outline the condition, with three needed for a diagnosis. The last three symptoms are concerned with violations of rules. A teenager can be diagnosed with this disorder if he/she 'often stays out late at night', 'has run away from home' and 'is often truant from school'.[22]

The other twelve Conduct Disorder symptoms are more serious and relate to bullying and various criminal activities. Assault, mugging and forced sexual activity are the most serious of these. Although criminal justice systems already deal with most of these problems, the application of psychiatric controls is an addition that is intended to be used for pre-emptive intervention in ways that criminal punishments cannot be applied.

Although some people, out of fear of youth crime, might think this is reasonable, it is nonetheless clear that when psychiatrists treat youth crime as a symptom of mental disease they are extending their practice beyond the boundaries of medical expertise and are undermining established systems of justice.

Psychiatrists routinely prescribe antipsychotic drugs to treat children diagnosed with Conduct Disorder. These are the same drugs used to treat schizophrenia and they have very debilitating side effects. The purpose of these drugs is that of a chemical restraint, not therapy. We will return to these drugs later in the chapter.

The prevailing medical conventions require that certain types of drug treatment be given for specific childhood disorders – stimulants for ADHD, antipsychotics for Conduct Disorder – but other disorders are treated more on an ad hoc basis, with doctors and psychiatrists sometimes experimenting with combinations of drugs.

Some of these childhood disorders – like the Learning Disorders – are rarely treated with drugs at present. However, escape from drug treatment is probably only a temporary phenomenon as the reach of drug treatment is always expanding. Drug company research is constantly striving to expand markets and to find acceptable applications for new compounds and new uses for old drugs.

EARLY INTERVENTION

One of the most useful means of expanding markets for drugs is provided by the recently developed imperative for *early intervention*. The rationale for early intervention in mental disorders – essentially meaning preventive medicine – allows doctors and psychiatrists to lower the normal thresholds required for diagnosing disorders. It also encourages them to identify and treat what they think are the early signs of adult disorders in children. At first glance this might seem like sound policy. But the problem is that, even when normal diagnostic conventions are applied to seemingly normal adults, psychiatric researchers tend to find mental illness in epidemic proportions.

A recent survey applying the standard DSM diagnostic system in the state of South Australia, for instance, found that more than one quarter of the adults studied were in need of psychiatric attention. The researchers claimed that 26.4 per cent of 1009 ordinary rural adults had mental illnesses, and that 11 per cent had two or more disorders. A similar study in Christchurch, New Zealand found that 20.6 per cent of the general population had mental illnesses, and two studies in the US found rates of 20 per cent and 29 per cent.[23]

The South Australian study found that only 4.2 per cent of the people with mental illnesses had seen a psychiatrist or psychologist in the previous twelve months, and it agreed with US researchers that 'most community residents are not treated for their psychiatric problems'. Blame for this was aimed at general practitioners who are thought to be under-diagnosing mental illness.

But the findings can be interpreted in an entirely different way. Of the 1009 people in the study there were eleven who acknowledged they had mental problems and who sought specialist treatment for them. A further 255 people were diagnosed with mental illnesses but were not receiving treatment. From the medical point of view these 255 people should receive treatment. But these same people apparently disagree and seem prepared to cope with life in their untreated state. If they were not coping without treatment they would have already come into contact with psychiatry as either voluntary or involuntary patients.

By finding more than a quarter of the population to be mentally ill, when these same people are willing to carry on with life as they are, the South Australian researchers have raised an interesting question: Are we living in a society that is quite literally part-mad, in which a quarter of the population are unaware that they have already developed mental illnesses, and where the rest of us appear unwilling to acknowledge that soon it might be our turn? Or is there something wrong with the diagnostic techniques used by the researchers?

Is there something about the way in which psychiatry is practised that predisposes psychiatrists to find mental pathology where ordinary, non-medical people might find foolishness, stupidity, aggression, laziness, boorishness, unhappiness, self-doubt and numerous other character faults that affect most people at some time or another, making us unpleasant company, but which do not really distinguish us as having diseased minds? A recent reviewer of the psychiatric bible, alarmed by the breadth of its scope, concluded that, according to the DSM IV, 'human life is a form of mental illness'.[24]

The implications for children of a tightening regime of surveillance, looking for early signs of adult forms of mental illness in their behaviour, are readily apparent. Whereas adults routinely demonstrate a high level of scepticism about psychiatric treatments for themselves, they are perhaps less cautious about its application to others, particularly children. Once decisions have been made on their behalf the children themselves have no means of resistance. In fact, any resistance is likely to be seen as a further symptom of an underlying mental illness.

At any one time tens of millions of children around the world are being routinely exploited and abused – often to the extent of suffering permanent brain damage – to provide profits for corporations selling mind-altering drugs. To understand how this situation has come about it might be useful to look at where psychiatry came from to get to this point it has now reached.

BALANCING BRAIN CHEMISTRY

Towards the end of the 1970s developments in American mental health led to the formation of a powerful coalition that has come to be known as the psycho-pharmaceutical complex. The psycho-pharmaceutical complex is a co-ordinated alliance between the psychiatric profession, organisations representing relatives of children and adults with supposed mental disorders, and drug companies. The overarching goals of the complex are to continually expand the use of drugs in treating mental disorders; and to expand the number and scope of mental disorders as a means of social control.

The arrangement within this alliance is that psychiatrists provide the professional expertise and scientific cover, the relatives' groups – representing the *consumers'* point of view – provide the moral imperative and the political momentum, while the drug companies provide the money and co-ordinate the public relations campaigns to achieve the objectives the complex sets for itself. Children are prime targets of the complex.

The developments that led to the formation of this alliance brought the three partners together at a fortuitous time for each of them. By the end of the 1970s psychiatry, as a branch of medicine, already had more than 100 years of dominance over the professional right to classify, diagnose and treat people with mental and behavioural deviance. But things were beginning to look a little grim for the future of the psychiatric profession. The alternative cultural movements that had grown through the 1960s constantly targeted mainstream psychiatry as being one of the authoritarian institutions dedicated to social control that had to be demolished. Various branches of non-medical psychotherapy, particularly those of the psychological profession, were seriously challenging the ground on which psychiatrists made their living.

On top of this, many of the treatments psychiatrists were accustomed to using had fallen into serious disrepute. The post-Second World War wonder treatments of lobotomy and electro-convulsive therapy (ECT) were no longer tolerated by a sceptical public as being suitable for routine application. Drug treatments had become the standard psychiatric tool, but already, by the 1970s, the early drugs were proving to be just as hazardous, ineffective and brain damaging as the shock and surgical treatments they replaced.

The one bright light for the psychiatric profession, at this point in time, was the development in 1965 of the brain chemistry imbalance theory to explain mental disorders.[25] This theory was set to change the fortunes of both the psychiatric profession and the pharmaceutical industry. It allowed psychiatrists to explain not only the cause of a disorder but the rationale for the drug treatment they applied to it. A drug was presented as a balancing chemical for a brain out of control due to out-of-balance chemistry. Psychiatrists in other English-speaking countries, seeing the advantages, soon adopted the American approach to mental health. All that remained from that point onwards was to win a propaganda war with the non-medical exponents of talking therapies.

A new organisation representing the relatives of people being treated for mental disorders was to become an important ally in this ensuing propaganda war. Although the National Alliance for the Mentally Ill (NAMI) purported to represent both mentally ill people and their relatives, it was from the outset essentially a support organisation for relatives.

Many of the traditional forms of talking therapy explored the past relationships of disturbed people and often honed in on childhood family life as a likely cause of any problem. Whether valid or not, the approach tended to drive a wedge between the sufferer of mental disorder and other family members who might fear being blamed for the affliction.

Following the youth culture drug binge of the 1960s and early 1970s, particularly the binge on drugs like LSD that sometimes had mind altering after-effects, many parents of mentally disordered young adults felt it was time they were no longer under suspicion of being the cause. They began to form support groups to reinforce this position and NAMI was the most important to come out of this period. Psychiatry's lurch into brain-chemistry blaming suited their needs perfectly.

Meanwhile, the pharmaceutical industry was gearing up to fully exploit the profitable opportunities it had discovered were available from selling psychotropic medications. It had found that mind-altering drugs could be blockbusters. The opportunities were especially profitable when circumstances allowed for co-operation with psychiatric and consumer allies. As the new spirit of the 1980s got underway, teams of public relations experts began to cement the complex into a more reliable, smoothly functioning machine.

By the end of the 1970s the pharmaceutical industry, and its critics, had learned a number of important lessons about psychiatric drugs: that useless drugs could be 'rediscovered' and promoted as wonder treatments for existing mental disorders; that drugs could routinely cause brain damage but this, nevertheless, could be explained as an improved mental condition; that mental disorders could be invented to fit the requirements of an otherwise unsaleable drug; and that mind-altering drugs could be blockbusters, particularly when they had addictive qualities. A drug introduced in the 1950s illustrates these lessons particularly well.

Chlorpromazine

The modern era of mind-altering medicine began with the introduction of chlorpromazine (Thorazine) in 1952 by the French company Rhone-Poulenc.[26] This synthetic chemical started its industrial life inauspiciously as a dye in the nineteenth century. It was then used as an insecticide and, after experiments on rats found it had a numbing effect, was introduced into medicine in the 1940s for use as an anaesthetic and an anti-vomiting agent. French psychiatrists then wasted little time before experimenting with it to subdue troublesome psychotic patients. They found that the new compound caused a 'vegetative syndrome'[27] that suited the needs of mental hospital staff perfectly.

It wasn't long before American psychiatrists followed their French colleagues and found chlorpromazine was useful as a chemical restraint and, although they observed it could frequently cause a Parkinson's-like effect, this was thought to be useful. William Winkelman, a researcher with Smith, Kline and French (SKF), the American licensee, first described the drug's psychiatric effect in 1953 as 'similar to frontal lobotomy'.[28]

This type of candid assessment didn't last long. When SKF realised its profit potential as a psychiatric drug, chlorpromazine was rushed through the necessary trials and given FDA approval in March 1954. A sophisticated public relations campaign was already underway to bury talk of a chemical lobotomy and radically alter its image for public consumption. In June 1954 an article in *Time* titled 'Wonder Drug of 1954' quoted a doctor employed by SKF claiming it 'relaxes patients and makes them accessible to treatment' and that 'extremely agitated and anxious types often give up compulsive behaviours'.[29]

As Robert Whitaker details in *Mad in America*, the public relations makeover of chlorpromazine was one of the truly great success stories of drug marketing. This was not a drug tailor-made to become a wonder cure for schizophrenia. Nevertheless, by June 1955 a *New York Times* article could breathlessly announce that the new psychiatric drug was actually capable of 'curing or making hitherto unreachable patients amenable to therapy'.[30]

From this point onwards SKF had a blockbuster on their hands and company 'revenues skyrocketed from $53 million in 1953 to $347 million in 1970', when chlorpromazine contributed $116 million.[31] Other pharmaceutical companies soon jumped into the antipsychotic market with similar drugs from the same family of chemical compounds.

The radical shift in psychiatric practice that followed, from talking therapies and violent somatic treatments – like ECT and lobotomy – to drug treatments, had significant consequences. The ability to restrain people outside institutional settings combined with the developing welfare state mechanisms of the 1960s and support payments for disabled people, resulted in a mass exodus from over-crowded mental hospitals. People thought to have serious mental disorders could now fend for themselves while under the control of a chemical lobotomy. The result was an epidemic of homelessness and brain damage, involving tens of millions of people over more than 40 years, that a naive public still doesn't properly comprehend.

Chlorpromazine illustrates a number of features consistent with the vast majority of psychiatric medications that have since been marketed: great profitability; in the long term they do more harm than good; unreasonable claims of efficacy; curiously unrelated original uses. These remain constant factors with most psychiatric drug treatments. But if this is true why are these conditions allowed to persist? To answer this question one has to understand the way the psycho-pharmaceutical propaganda complex works, the vast sums invested in it by drug companies, and the power of the public relations campaigns employed to pursue its strategies.

DRUG COMPANY RESOURCES

The global pharmaceutical industry is huge. Total worldwide sales for prescription drugs in 2002 were about $400 billion, with about $200 billion of this in the US alone.[32] Combined profits of the top ten drug companies on the Fortune 500 list in 2002 were $35 billion. The margins of profit of these companies – 18.5 per cent on sales, 16.3 per cent on assets and 33.2 per cent on shareholders' equity – are fairly extraordinary when compared with normal profit expectations in other industries. In the same year, for instance, 'the median net return for all other industries in the Fortune 500 was only 3.3 percent of sales ... It is difficult to conceive of how awash in money big pharma is.'[33]

The large pharmaceutical companies spend on average about 30–40 per cent of their revenues on marketing and administration, and about 12–15 per cent on research and development.[34] They have 625 paid lobbyists in Washington, DC, one per congressperson.[35] They also spend many billions of dollars every year in the US on direct-to-consumer TV and magazine advertising.

The incomes of psychiatric professional organisations in most developed countries are dependent upon drug companies. Roughly a third of the American Psychiatric Association's budget is derived from various drug sources.[36] Psychiatric conferences are usually dominated by drug company sponsored exhibits and symposia that provide attendees with a variety of enticements like music, food, drink, disc players and briefcases.

Drug companies provide substantial support to nearly all of the mental health advocacy organisations in the US, like NAMI, the National Mental Health Association (NMHA), the National Alliance for Research on Schizophrenia and Affective Disorders (NARSAD), National Depressive Disorder Screening Day and the Anxiety Disorders Association.[37]

Some of NAMI's funding sources were recently exposed in a *Mother Jones* article:

> According to internal documents obtained by *Mother Jones*, 18 drug firms gave NAMI a total of $11.72 million between 1996 and mid-1999. These include Janssen ($2.08 million), Novartis ($1.87 million), Pfizer ($1.3 million), Abbott Laboratories ($1.24 million), Wyeth-Ayerst Pharmaceuticals ($658,000), and Bristol-Myers Squibb ($613,505). NAMI's leading donor is Eli Lilly and Company, maker of Prozac, which gave $2.87 million during that period. In 1999 alone, Lilly will have delivered $1.1 million in quarterly instalments, with the lion's share going to help fund NAMI's 'Campaign to End Discrimination' against the mentally ill. In the case of Lilly, at least, 'funding' takes more than one form. Jerry Radke, a Lilly executive, is 'on loan' to NAMI, working out of the organization's headquarters.[38]

TEEN SCREENING FOR MORE DRUG CONSUMERS

The US federal government is currently spending tens of millions of dollars to expand mental health screening programmes for young people around the country.[39] In 2003 the Bush administration released the final report of the President's New Freedom Commission on Mental Health. Goal 4 of this report was to ensure that 'Early Mental Health Screening, Assessment, and Referral to Services Are Common Practice'. Goal 4.1 goes on to state a belief that 'Emerging research indicates that intervening early can interrupt the negative course of some mental illnesses.'[40] The very equivocal language should be noted here. The *research* isn't identified and it isn't said to be completed and available, but only *emerging*; it doesn't demonstrate or prove, but only *indicates*; and the unspecified intervention is only said to be effective for *some* mental illnesses. The equivocal nature of this language is important because it indicates that the authors are not prepared to take responsibility for action that might result from this report.

Nevertheless, despite its doubtful knowledge base, the report offers enthusiastic endorsement for a well-established screening programme run out of Columbia University called TeenScreen. The TeenScreen goal is described in the report as:

'To ensure all youth are offered a mental health check-up before graduating from high school. TeenScreen identifies and refers for treatment those who are at risk for suicide or suffer from untreated mental illness.'[41] The report's endorsement of this goal indicates that this is also a goal of the US government.

TeenScreen has become progressively more controversial over the last few years. Critics have come to accuse it unequivocally of being a 'Front Group for the Psycho-Pharmaceutical Industrial Complex',[42] with the primary purpose of herding unsuspecting children into expensive treatment programmes with psychiatric drugs.

The general thrust of the TeenScreen operation, according to the organisation's webpages, is to combat teenage suicide. This is the way its programmes are sold. However, reference to the details of the screening process, not to mention the goal stated by the President's New Freedom Commission report above, indicates that all young people with attitudes, thoughts, beliefs and habits that can be matched with symptoms of a mental disorder are in the TeenScreen sights.

The TeenScreen target age is nine to 18 years and it offers its screening services to all schools in the US with children in this age range. But it will also offer the service wherever it can find *partners*: 'Other communities have chosen to implement the program in doctors' offices, clinics and juvenile justice facilities – in short, anywhere that teens gather.'[43]

TeenScreen offers two different screening devices: the Columbia Health Screen, which is a '14 item, self completion pencil and paper questionnaire'; and the Diagnostic Predictive Scales which is a 52 item interview by computer in which the questions are simultaneously heard through headphones and read on the screen. The first type of screening test takes about ten minutes, the second ten to 20 minutes. Both tests are said to identify 'the likelihood that a youth has a significant mental health problem'.[44] *Significant* is a key word here, bear it in mind.

According to TeenScreen the first step in screening individual children involves parental consent, followed by the assent of the participating child. After the screening test those children who are deemed likely to have a mental problem are immediately given a short clinical interview. This is followed up with parental notification, referral for psychiatric assessment, and then on to treatment and case management.[45]

TeenScreen is quite secretive about the statistical details of their operation. They won't provide a list of the schools in which they are operating and they don't publicise the percentage of children screened who are found to have mental disorders and who are directed into drug treatments. However, on their webpages, under the title of 'Why is Screening Needed', they cite the US Surgeon General: '21% of our nation's youth suffer from a diagnosable mental disorder that causes impairment. Yet, only 20% of these youth are identified and receive mental heath services.'[46] It might be fair to assume that the screening tests would therefore be calibrated to identify mental disorders in about 21 per cent of the children screened with the goal of shepherding 100 per cent of those detected into treatment.

However, not all these children might be suffering significant impairment. An earlier 1996 study led by David Shaffer, creator and director of TeenScreen, found that while 21 per cent of children aged nine to 17 have a diagnosable mental or addictive disorder (see Table 15.1), only half of them suffer *significant* functional impairment as a result. Even so, this amounts to some 4 million children that TeenScreen are targeting for treatment, not counting the 18-year-olds.[47]

Table 15.1   Children and Adolescents Aged 9–17 Claimed to Have Disorders

Anxiety Disorders	13%
Mood Disorders	6.2%
Disruptive Disorders	10.3%
Substance-Use Disorders	2%
Any Disorder	20.9%

Source: 'Mental Health: A Report of the Surgeon General', US Department of Health and Human Services, 12 December 2007.

TeenScreen makes a point of denying that it receives any funding from drug companies. But at least two of its senior executives have longstanding links with drug companies. Shaffer, its medical director, has like most research psychiatrists received funding from several drug companies for consultancy work and as an expert witness.[48] The TeenScreen Executive Director, Laurie Flynn, moved to TeenScreen in 2001 after serving for 16 years as the Executive Director of NAMI.[49] During her long term at NAMI the organisation was progressively turned into a front group for the drug industry.[50]

Even if you accept the claim that 11 per cent of American children are suffering significant impairment due to mental disorders, and that some kind of drug treatment might do them more good than harm, there are still serious doubts about the efficacy of the screening programme. Attempting to distinguish the impaired children from other children by asking all nine- to 18-year-olds to complete a ten minute questionnaire seems somewhat bizarre, to say the least. Nine-year-old children are given the same list of questions to answer as the 18-year-olds, and their answers are evaluated against the same expectations of normality. Varying degrees of gravity, flippancy and truth-telling amongst groups of children of different locations, ages, ethnic groups and socio-economic classes are likely to dramatically influence outcomes when a computer is the only witness to the procedure.

Something that should be considered about this programme, but which seems to have been largely overlooked by critics to date, is the confidentiality aspect of the TeenScreen results. Although the TeenScreen Parent Consent Letter claims the process is confidential the details supplied aren't very reassuring:

In order to protect your child's privacy, his/her screening results and related files will be stored separately from his/her academic records. Teachers will not be involved in the screening procedure. If program staff believe that your child is in some danger or is a danger to others, they are mandated by law to take action and notify appropriate personnel and/or necessary authorities.[51]

It should be noted that records from TeenScreen will be kept. They say that: 'Only aggregate data (for example total number screened at the site) and qualitative information (for example feedback on how the program is working) are shared with Columbia.'[52] This begs a question, if the records aren't destroyed, who gets to keep them and to what use are they put? TeenScreen themselves will not be holding the files. One is left to assume that the records will continue to be held by whoever implements a TeenScreen programme at a given location.

Box 15.3 Sample Questions in TeenScreen Interviews

- Has there been a time when nothing was fun for you and you just weren't interested in anything?
- Has there been a time when you felt you couldn't do anything well or that you weren't as good-looking or as smart as other people?
- How often did your parents get annoyed or upset with you because of the way you were feeling or acting?
- Have you often felt very nervous when you've had to do things in front of people?
- Have you often worried a lot before you were going to play a sport or game or do some other activity?

Other questions relate to moods, suicidal thoughts and suicide attempts, and drug and alcohol use.

Source: 'TeenScreen: A Front Group for the Psycho-Pharmaceutical Industrial Complex', PsychSearch.net, http://www.psychsearch.net/teenscreen.html accessed 12 December 2007.

Maximum inclusiveness is certainly one of the aims of TeenScreen. Indeed, it is claimed by critics that TeenScreen has been over-zealous in maximising the return of parental approval forms. Two of the methods that critics claim are used seem ethically doubtful. One is a technique dubbed *passive consent*. Passive consent involves sending out consent forms to parents, which do not have to be returned unless the parents have an objection. A lack of response is deemed to indicate approval. This method is said to gain a 95 per cent approval rate.

The second method involves offering incentives to the children to take the consent forms home and return them quickly. The incentives said to be used involve gifts like free movie passes, food coupons and 'a $5 video store coupon to anyone who brings back a parental consent form within a two-day turnaround period'.[53]

One of the great cruelties of screening programmes is that children and adolescents who might have complaints about unfair treatment, and think that a questionnaire is an opportunity to seek support, will find that what they have actually done is provide evidence of their own inability to adapt. Admissions of anxiety, unhappiness, anger or even suicidal thoughts will not lead to any review of the situation that has given rise to these feelings. What they will lead to instead is a prescription for psychiatric drugs that will blunt the emotions and make the child less sensitive.

In the United States, one of the principal arguments supporting screening programmes is that they will identify potential school shooters and get these children on drug treatments before they have an opportunity to go berserk. One of the great ironies, however, is that most of the children who do become school shooters are taking psychiatric drugs at the time. In the face of such evidence, the psycho-pharmaceutical propaganda machine will suggest that the shooter wasn't taking his medication and call for more vigilance and coercion in the adminis- tration of psychiatric drugs. However, it is more likely that adverse reactions to psychiatric drugs – like hallucinations, aggression, agitation and suicidal feelings – play a significant role in contributing to school shootings.[54]

If some of the more spectacular incidences of youth violence are actually associated with adverse reactions to psychiatric drugs, then the finding by researchers at Brandeis University, that one in ten teenage boys going to the doctor in the US is prescribed a psychotropic drug, might give some pause for thought.[55]

16
Conclusion

In 2007 Joel Klein, chancellor of New York City schools, told an overflow meeting of parents of his plans to restructure New York schools in the form of businesses, but in the name of equity:

> In the calculus of the moment, each of the city's 1,450 schools is considered an independent franchise. Like a bank outlet or a RadioShack store, any given school is a 'key unit' in Klein's new Department of Education. Schools are headed by branch managers, or principals, whose jobs have been reconfigured as CEOs rather than as educators. Principals are expected to contract out for nearly every core service, from testing to professional development to their own support team. Quarterly returns flow out in the form of tests four times a year. Schools must compete with one another, at their peril. The lowest performers on the bell curve may be sanctioned or shut down.[1]

Such a bizarre vision might seem to be an outcome of the idiosyncratic thinking of a former businessman turned school chancellor. However, the fact that the very same 'reforms' have been sweeping the English-speaking world for the past three decades points to a broader agenda; one that goes beyond individuals, beyond regional education bureaucracies, and beyond national governments. It is an agenda pushed by transnational corporations around the world.

The corporate agenda has several goals. First, children are being targeted as potential markets for products and services. As a consequence children are learning that happiness, relationships and fulfilment can be attained through the right purchases and that others will judge them by what they have rather than who they are.

Second, corporations are seeking to ensure that school graduates will become loyal, compliant, diligent employees with basic literacy and numeracy skills, a strong work ethic, and corporate values. This is to be done at minimal cost to corporate taxpayers and without arousing a spirit of inquiry or revolutionary impulses in the process.

Third, corporations are seeking to undermine the whole notion of public schooling with its inherent notions of entitlement, equity and public good, and replace it with the idea that schooling is a commodity to be purchased by parents from a market of competing schools. Many corporations are already profiting handsomely from the increasing privatisation of educational services.

> No longer are schools, churches, and families dominant in the education of young people; corporations are. As a result, concerns for fostering and continuing a democracy, fostering certain ethics in young people, and reminding young people that a nation-state is a community based in and on the well-being of others are shuttled to the periphery while the social needs of corporations are ushered to the forefront and projected as vital goals for young people to promote.[2]

The consequence of this corporate capture of childhood is not only being felt by children, who are becoming more materialistic, overweight, stressed, depressed and self-destructive. Advertising and marketing aim to make these future citizens dissatisfied with what they have and want to consume more. Yet the health of the planet requires us to consume less. What is more, by undermining the critical-thinking faculties of future generations corporations are depriving them of the ability to solve pressing social and environmental problems; problems such as global warming, species extinction and water shortages, which are in many ways caused or exacerbated by those very corporations that are attempting to breed subservient employees and dumbed-down citizens.

Yet if nations are to deal with such problems effectively they will need to rein in and curb the activities of transnational corporations, so that their profit-making imperatives are subordinate to the public interest. The impulse to consume will have to be overcome and replaced with higher and more sophisticated motivations. More creative and innovative methods of agriculture and manufacture will be required.

In other words the qualities required of young people in today's world are the very opposite to those that corporations are seeking.

Notes

1 INTRODUCTION

1. C. Glenn Cupit, 'Valuing Children', in Stephen Frith and Barbara Biggins (eds), *Children and Advertising: A Fair Game?*, Sydney, New College Institute for Values Research, 1994, p. 72.
2. Ed Mayo, 'Shopping Generation', London, National Consumer Council (NCC), July 2005, p. 2.
3. 'Modern Life Leads to More Depression Among Children', *Daily Telegraph*, 12 September 2006.
4. UNICEF, 'Child Poverty in Perspective: An Overview of Child Well-Being in Rich Countries', Florence, UNICEF Innocenti Research Centre, 2007, pp. 2, 20, 25, 28, 30–1.
5. Michael Turtle, 'Not Enough Help for Teen Binge Drinkers: Report', *ABC News*, 25 February 2008; Julie Robotham, 'One in Three Primary Children Too Fat', *Sydney Morning Herald*, 27 October 2003, p. 3.
6. Peter Weekes, 'Children of Misfortune', *Sydney Morning Herald*, 8 September 2004, pp. 8–9 Money.
7. Joe Tucci et al., 'Children's Fears, Hopes and Heroes', Ringwood, Vic, Australian Childhood Foundation, June 2007, p. 5.
8. Jacqueline Maley, 'Childhood Depression "a Mystery"', *Sydney Morning Herald*, 10–11 September 2005, p. 5; Wendy Champagne, 'When Childhood Anxiety Becomes a Problem', *Sydney Morning Herald*, 29 January 2004, p. 3.
9. Australian Institute of Health and Welfare (AIHW), 'Making Progress: The Health, Development and Wellbeing of Australia's Children and Young People', Canberra, 2008, pp. 29–30.
10. Mission Australia, 'Youth Suicide in Australia', Mission Australia Research and Social Policy Unit, October, 2000, http://mission.com.au
11. CDC, 'Suicide Prevention', Centers for Disease Control and Prevention, 2007, http://cdc.gov/ncipc/dvp/Suicide/youthsuicide.htm
12. Henry A. Giroux, 'Youth and the Politics of Disposability: Resisting the Assault on Education and American Youth', *State of Nature*, Winter, 2007, http://www.stateofnature.org/youthAndThePolitics.html
13. John Bradshaw (ed.), *The Well Being of Children in the UK*, 2nd edn, Plymouth, UK, Save the Children, 2005.
14. Mental Health Foundation, 'Truth Hurts: Report of the National Inquiry into Self-Harm among Young People', London, Mental Health Foundation and the Camelot Foundation, 2006, p. 2.
15. 'Let Our Children Play', *Daily Telegraph*, 10 September 2007.
16. Julia Baird and Peter Gotting, 'The Verdict – They've Never Had It So Good', *Sydney Morning Herald*, 25–26 August 2001, p. 4.

2   TURNING CHILDREN INTO CONSUMERS

1. In Roy F. Fox, *Harvesting Minds: How TV Commercials Control Kids*, Westport, CT, Praeger, 1996, p. xii.
2. Langbourne Rust, 'How to Reach Children in Stores: Marketing Tactics Grounded in Observational Research', *Journal of Advertising Research* 33 (6), 1993.
3. Ibid.
4. Langbourne Rust Research, http://www.langrust.com
5. Eric Schlosser, *Fast Food Nation: The Dark Side of the All-American Meal*, New York, HarperCollins, 2002, p. 43.
6. John Geraci, 'Our Take on It', *Trends & Tudes*, August 2003, p. 2.
7. Alan Thein Durning, *How Much Is Enough? The Consumer Society and the Future of the Earth*, London, Earthscan, 1992, p. 121; Miriam H. Zoll, 'Psychologists Challenge Ethics of Marketing to Children', Mediachannel.org, 2000, http://www.mediachannel.org/originals/kidsell.shtml
8. Juliet B. Schor, *Born to Buy: The Commercialized Child and the New Consumer Culture*, New York, Scribner, 2004, p. 21.
9. Steele Tallon, 'Kids Inc', *Sunday Mail*, 17 February 2002, p. 54.
10. Anne Sutherland and Beth Thompson, *Kidfluence: The Marketer's Guide to Understanding and Reaching Generation Y – Kids, Tweens, and Teens*, New York, McGraw-Hill, 2003, pp. 105–6.
11. James U. McNeal, *Kids as Customers: A Handbook of Marketing to Children*, New York, Lexington Books, 1992, p. 160.
12. Laurie Klein, 'More Than Play Dough', *Brandweek*, 24 November 1997.
13. Quoted in 'Watch out for Children: A Mother's Statement to Advertisers', The Motherhood Project 2001. http://www.motherhoodproject.org/?cat=18
14. Benjamin R. Barber, *Consumed: How Markets Corrupt Children, Infantilize Adults, and Swallow Citizens Whole*, New York, W.W. Norton, 2007, p. 29.
15. Victoria J. Rideout et al., *Zero to Six: Electronic Media in the Lives of Infants, Toddlers and Preschoolers*, Menlo Park, CA, Henry J. Kaiser Family Foundation, Fall 2003, p. 4.
16. Newton N. Minow and Craig L. LaMay, *Abandoned in the Wasteland: Children, Television, and the First Amendment*, New York, Hill and Wang, 1995, p. 18; Richard Zoglin, 'Is TV Ruining Our Children?' *Time*, 15 October 1990.
17. Victoria Rideout et al., *Generation M: Media in the Lives of 8–18 Year-Olds, Executive Summary*, Menlo Park, CA, Henry J. Kaiser Family Foundation, March 2005, p. 6.
18. Sutherland and Thompson, *Kidfluence*, p. 58; Rideout et al., *Generation M*, p. 9; Susan Gregory Thomas, *Buy, Buy Baby: How Consumer Culture Manipulates Parents and Harms Young Minds*, Boston, Houghton Mifflin, 2007, p. 9.
19. American Academy of Pediatrics, 'Children, Adolescents, and Advertising', *Pediatrics* 118 (6), 2006, p. 2563.
20. Australian Divisions of General Practice (ADGP), 'What Are We Feeding Our Children? A Junk Food Advertising Audit', Canberra, February 2003.
21. Phil Marchionni, 'Advertising and Children: Ethical Perspectives', in Stephen Frith and Barbara Biggins (eds), *Children and Advertising: A Fair Game?*, Sydney, New College Institute for Values Research, 1994, p. 73.

22. Tallon, 'Kids Inc', p. 54; Carmel Egan, 'Crackdown on Children's Ads', *Sydney Morning Herald*, 10 June 2007.
23. Office of Communications (Ofcom), 'Childhood Obesity – Food Advertising in Context', 22 July 2004, p. 14.
24. Alissa Quart, *Branded: The Buying and Selling of Teenagers*, London, Arrow, 2003, p. xi.
25. Carlone Oates et al., 'Children and Television Advertising: When Do They Understand Persuasive Intent?', *Journal of Consumer Behaviour* 1 (3), 2001, p. 239.
26. Fox, *Harvesting Minds*, pp. 5, 6, 36.
27. Center for Media Education (CME), 'Web of Deception: Threats to Children from Online Marketing', 1996, http://www.cme.org/children/marketing/deception.pdf
28. Reproduced in 'Commercialization in Ontario Schools: A Research Report', Ontario Secondary School Teacher's Federation, September 1995, p. 19.
29. Dan Kaufman, 'Pied Piper Effect', *Icon, Sydney Morning Herald*, 1–2 June 2002, p. 3.
30. Center for Social Media (CME), 'Teensites.Com: A Field Guide to the New Digital Landscape – Executive Summary', August 2002, p. 3, http://www.centerforsocialmedia.org/resources/publications/teensitescom_a_field_guide_to_the_new_digital_landscape
31. Family Education Network, 'Kids, Tweens and Teens Sites', Pearson Education, http://www.fen.com/resources/omk/kidsteens.html
32. Elizabeth Moore and Victoria Rideout, *It's Child's Play: Advergaming and the Online Marketing of Food to Children, Executive Summary*, Menlo Park, CA, Henry J. Kaiser Family Foundation, July 2006, pp. 4, 8.
33. Campaign for a Commercial-Free Childhood (CCFC), 'The Facts About Marketing to Kids', February 2005; '"Lethal Creature" Advertising', Schmio Awards, http://www.igc.apc.org/an/schmio/mosher2.html; Susan Linn, *Consuming Kids: The Hostile Takeover of Childhood*, New York, The New Press, 2004, pp. 157–66.
34. Ibid.; Rebecca L. Collins et al., 'Early Adolescent Exposure to Alcohol and Its Relationship to Underage Drinking', *Journal of Adolescent Health*, 13 April 2007, http://www.jahonline.org/article/PIIS1054139X07000250/abstract
35. Diana Bagnall, 'What's Driving Our Kids to Drink', *Bulletin*, 9 September 2003.
36. Jill Stark, 'Revealed: Alcopops Target Teens', *Sydney Morning Herald*, 6 August 2007, pp. 1, 2.
37. http://www.kidzeyes.com
38. CME, 'Teensites.Com', p. 3.
39. Jeff Chester and Kathryn Montgomery, 'Interactive Food & Beverage Marketing: Targeting Children and Youth in the Digital Age', Berkeley Media Studies Group, May 2007, p. 34.
40. CME, 'Teensites.Com', p. 6.
41. S.G.T., 'Junior's Got Mail from Barney', *U.S. News*, 15 November 1999.
42. 'Kids in the I-World', *Selling to Kids*, 18 October 2000, http://www.findarticles.com/p/articles/mi-mOFVE/is_20_5/ai_66215820/print
43. 'Child Catchers: The Tricks Used to Push Unhealthy Food to Your Children', *Which?*, January 2006, p. 3.
44. Zoe Williams, 'Commercialisation of Childhood', Compass, December 2006, p. 8.
45. Quoted in Chester and Montgomery, 'Interactive Food & Beverage Marketing', p. 14.

46. Alex Molnar and Faith Boninger, 'Adrift: Schools in a Total Marketing Environment. The Tenth Annual Report on Schoolhouse Commercialism Trends: 2006–2007', Tempe, AZ, Commercialism in Education Research Unit (CERU), Arizona State University, October 2007, pp. 2–3.

47. 'Child Catchers', p. 3.

48. Chester and Montgomery, 'Interactive Food & Beverage Marketing', p. 32.

49. Ibid., p. 38.

50. Ibid., pp. 38–9.

51. Quoted in Ibid., p. 38.

52. Blayne Cutler, 'From Soup to Purple Dinosaur Nuts', *American Demographics* 14 (10), 1992.

53. John Geraci et al., 'Harris Interactive/Kid Power Poll of Youth Marketers', Harris Interactive 2004, p. 32, http://harrisinteractive.com/services/pubs/KidPower_Poll_Results.pdf

54. Motherhood Project, 'Watch out for Children'.

55. IQPC, 'Conference Brochure', paper presented at the Kid Power 2003, The Sydney Boulevard, 28–29 July 2003.

56. Sutherland and Thompson, *Kidfluence*, pp. x, 114.

57. Motherhood Project, 'Watch out for Children'.

58. IQPC, 'Conference Brochure', paper presented at the Kid Power, Mandalay Bay Resorts & Casino, Las Vegas, 30 November–2 December 2004.

59. James U. McNeal, *Children as Consumers: Insights and Implications*, Massachusetts, Lexington Books, 1987, pp. 76–7.

60. Dan S. Acuff, *What Kids Buy and Why: The Psychology of Marketing to Kids*, New York, The Free Press, 1997, p. 182.

61. Cited in Dale Kunkel, 'Advertising Regulation and Child Development', in Frith and Biggins (eds), *Children and Advertising*, p. 33.

62. Cited in McNeal, *Children as Consumers*, p. 78.

63. Roy F. Fox, 'Manipulated Kids: Teens Tell How Ads Influence Them', *Educational Leadership* 53 (1), 1995; Fox, *Harvesting Minds*, p. 61.

64. Erling Bjurstrom, 'Children and Television Advertising: A Critical Study of International Research Concerning the Effects of TV-Commercials on Children', Swedish Consumer Agency, October 1994, p. 28.

65. Kunkel, 'Advertising Regulation and Child Development', pp. 30, 35.

66. Linn, *Consuming Kids*, p. 2.

67. McNeal, *Children as Consumers*, p. 73.

68. Michele Simon, 'Government Abandons Children to Big Food', *Alternet*, 22 July 2005, http://www.alternet.org/story/23648

69. Kaiser Family Foundation (KFF), *The Role of Media in Childhood Obesity*, Menlo Park, CA, Henry J. Kaiser Family Foundation, February 2004, p. 5; KFF, *Food for Thought: Television Food Advertising to Children in the United States, Executive Summary*, Menlo Park, CA, Henry J. Kaiser Family Foundation, March 2007, p. 4.

70. CCFC, 'The Facts About Marketing to Kids', February 2005, p. 13.

71. KFF, *Food for Thought*, p. 3.

72. Kelly Burke, 'Heavy Guilt Trip for Working Parents', *Sydney Morning Herald*, 20 June 2006, p. 3.

73. 'Survival of the Fittest', *Sydney Morning Herald*, 12 November 2004.

74. Tallon, 'Kids Inc', p. 55.

75. Nick Galvin, 'Battle to Junk Food Ads Hots Up', *Sydney Morning Herald*, 19 January 2005, p. 13.

76. Schlosser, *Fast Food Nation*, p. 47.

77. 'Would You Like a Tank with That', *Sydney Morning Herald*, 11 August 2006.

78. Peter Gotting, 'Amazing What Spin Can Do to Chip Sales', *Sydney Morning Herald*, 15–16 February 2003.

79. Linn, *Consuming Kids*, p. 100.

80. IQPC, 'Conference Brochure', paper presented at the Teen Power Asia 2003, The Oriental, Singapore, 27–28 August 2003.

81. 'Marketing of Foods to Children', London, Food Commission, and *Which?*, October 2005, p. 21.

82. Marchionni, 'Advertising and Children: Ethical Perspectives', pp. 74–5.

83. 'Marketing of Foods to Children', p. 31.

84. Christian Catalano, 'Additive Danger Confirmed', *Age*, 7 September 2007.

85. Neville Rigby and Jeremy Preston, 'Advertising to Children: The Debate', *Ecologist*, April 2004, p. 16.

86. KFF, *The Role of Media in Childhood Obesity*, pp. 5–6.

87. McNeal, *Children as Consumers*, pp. 81–2.

88. Schor, *Born to Buy*, pp. 126, 128.

89. Cited in Julie Robotham, 'Chips, Chocolate and Cordial: The Diet That Fuels Toddlers', *Sydney Morning Herald*, 10 November 2006, p. 3.

90. Dominique Jackson, 'The Fat Trap', *Australian*, 1 September 1999, p. 11.

91. McGinnis et al., *Food Marketing to Children and Youth*, p. 2; Williams, 'Commercialisation of Childhood', p. 14; Helen Dixon, et al., 'Pester Power: Snackfoods Displayed at Supermarket Checkouts in Melbourne, Australia', *Health Promotion Journal of Australia* 17 (2), 2006, p. 120.

92. Quoted in KFF, *Food for Thought*, p. 1.

93. Cited in Williams, 'Commercialisation of Childhood', p. 15.

94. Cited in Thomas N. Robinson and Donna M. Matheson, 'Effects of Fast Food Branding on Young Children's Taste Preferences', *Archives of Pediatrics & Adolescent Medicine* 161 (8), 2007, p. 792.

95. R.J. Hancox and R. Poulton, 'Watching Television Is Associated with Childhood Obesity: But Is It Clinically Important', *International Journal of Obesity* 30, 2006.

96. Jean L. Wiecha et al., 'When Children Eat What They Watch: Impact of Television Viewing on Dietary Intake in Youth', *Archives of Pediatric & Adolescent Medicine* 160, 2006, pp. 436, 439.

97. Cited in KFF, *The Role of Media in Childhood Obesity*, p. 5.

98. J. Michael McGinnis et al. (eds), *Food Marketing to Children and Youth: Threat or Opportunity?*, Washington, DC, Institute of Medicine, National Academies Press, 2004, pp. 8–9.

99. Robinson and Matheson, 'Effects of Fast Food Branding on Young Children's Taste Preferences', pp. 792–7.

100. WHO, 'Obesity and Overweight', World Health Organization, September, 2006, http://www.who.int/mediacentre/factsheets/fs311/en/index.html

101. KFF, *The Role of Media in Childhood Obesity*, p. 1; McGinnis et al., *Food Marketing to Children and Youth*, pp. 1–2; Williams, 'Commercialisation of Childhood', p. 14.

102. Center for Science in the Public Interest (CSPI), 'Nutrition Review Questions Soda-Obesity Link', *Integrity in Science Watch*, 12 March 2007, http://www.cspinet.org/integrity/watch/200703121.html

103. Institute of Medicine, cited in A. Molnar, F. Boninger, G. Wilkinson and J. Fogarty, 'At Sea in a Marketing-Saturated World: The Eleventh Annual Report on Schoolhouse Commercialism Trends: 2007–2008', Boulder, CO, and Tempe, AZ, Education Public Interest Center and Commercialism in Education Research Unit, September 2008, p. 22.

104. Mike Stobbe, 'More Men, Children Overweight in U.S.', *U.S. News*, 5 April 2006, p. 6.

105. Angela Zimm, 'Children Sicker Now Than in Past, Harvard Report Says', Bloomberg. com, 26 June 2007, http://www.bloomberg.com/apps/news?pid=20601087&sid=a4 xmH.aERohk&refer=worldwide; McGinnis et al., *Food Marketing to Children and Youth*.

106. McGinnis et al., *Food Marketing to Children and Youth*.

107. Dhriti Jotangia et al., 'Obesity Among Children Under 11', UK Department of Health, April 2006, p. 7; Molnar et al., 'At Sea in a Marketing-Saturated World', p. 22.

108. Williams, 'Commercialisation of Childhood', p. 14.

109. NSW Health Department, 'Childhood Obesity', 16 August 2006, http://www.health. nsw.gov.au/obesity/adult/background/factsheet.html

110. Burke, 'Heavy Guilt Trip for Working Parents', p. 3.

111. Michael Bradley, 'Drink Company's Obesity Study Outrages Experts', *Sydney Morning Herald*, 4–5 September 2004, p. 6.

112. Gary Ruskin and Juliet Schor, 'Junk Food Nation: Who's to Blame for Childhood Obesity', *Nation*, 29 August/5 September 2005, p. 17.

113. Schor, *Born to Buy*, p. 128; CCFC, 'The Facts About Marketing to Kids', p. 6.

114. Carol Nader, '$330,000 Buys Maccas the Tick of Approval', *Age*, 6 February 2007.

115. Cited in CCFC, 'The Facts About Marketing to Kids', p. 14.

116. CSPI, 'Nutrition Review Questions Soda-Obesity Link'.

117. American Association of Advertisers and others, Letter to Secretary of the Department of Health & Human Services, Tommy G. Thompson, Washington DC, 3 May 2002.

118. Schor, *Born to Buy*, p. 129.

119. Ibid., p. 129.

120. McDonald's, 'Healthy Balance', McDonald's Australia Ltd, December 2001.

121. 'Child Catchers', p. 9.

122. The Coca-Cola Company, 'The Wellness Beverage Guide', *Seventeen*, April 2007, http://www.beverageinstitute.org/about_us/SeventeenFINAL.pdf

123. Ofcom, 'Childhood Obesity', p. 11.

124. Schor, *Born to Buy*, p. 130.

125. Julie Robotham, 'Tax Fast Food Like Tobacco and Ban It in Schools, Doctors Say', *Sydney Morning Herald*, 21 August 2006, p. 3.

126. Ruskin and Schor, 'Junk Food Nation', p. 17.

127. 'Child Catchers', p. 9; 'Coke's Sweet Intentions', PRWatch, 13 July 2005, http://www.prwatch.org/node/3851; The Coca-Cola Company, 'Welcome to Live It!', http://www.liveitprogram.com; Datamonitor, 'Cadbury: Eat Chocolate, Get Fit', Datamonitor, 1 April 2003, http://www.datamonitor.com; NUT, 'Briefing on School's Role in Promoting Child Health and Combating Commercialism', National Union of Teachers, 9 November 2004, p. 1; Peter Gotting, 'Capturing Hearts and Minds', *Sydney Morning Herald*, 28 February 2003, p. 14.

128. Brooks Barnes, 'Limiting Ads of Junk Food to Children', *New York Times*, 18 July 2007.

129. CCFC, 'The Facts About Marketing to Kids', p. 4; Fia Cumming, 'Doctors Spitting Chips', *Sun-Herald*, 26 May 2002, p. 5; Steele Tallon, 'Kids' Junk Food TV Ads under Fire', *Sunday Mail*, 17 February 2002, p. 13; Galvin, 'Battle to Junk Food Ads Hots Up', p. 13.

130. Kelly Burke, 'Fast Food and Gorilla Tactics', *Sydney Morning Herald*, 10 February 2007.

131. American Academy of Pediatrics, 'Children, Adolescents, and Advertising', p. 2563; André Caron, 'Children, Advertising and Television Choices in a New Media Environment', in Frith and Biggins (eds), *Children and Advertising*, p. 96; Burke, 'Fast Food and Gorilla Tactics'; 'Junk Food Ad Crackdown "Flawed"', *BBC News*, 20 December 2006.

132. Angela J. Campbell, 'US Perspectives on the Regulation of Toy TV Tie-Ins', in Stephen Frith, Barbara Biggins and Tracy Newlands (eds), *Marketing Toys: It's Child's Play*, Sydney, New College Institute for Values Research, 1995, pp. 106–8.

133. McNeal, *Children as Consumers*, pp. 63, 85.

134. Campbell, 'US Perspectives on the Regulation of Toy TV Tie-Ins', pp. 95–6; Schlosser, *Fast Food Nation*, p. 46.

135. Schor, *Born to Buy*, p. 29.

136. Williams, 'Commercialisation of Childhood'.

137. Caron, 'Children, Advertising and Television Choices', pp. 99, 103, 106–8.

138. Kunkel, 'Advertising Regulation and Child Development', p. 36; Denis Fitzgerald, 'Children and Advertising: A Fair Game or Fair Game?', in Frith and Biggins (eds), *Children and Advertising*, p. 116.

3   TURNING PLAY INTO BUSINESS

1. Benjamin R. Barber, *Consumed: How Markets Corrupt Children, Infantilize Adults, and Swallow Citizens Whole*, New York, W.W. Norton 2007, p. 231.

2. Royal Alberta Museum, 'Barbie Tidbits', 6 September 2006, http://www.royalalbertamuseum.ca/edu/infobyte/barbie.htm

3. Ellen J. Reifler, 'Babes in Toyland ... What's a Feminist Mum to do?', *Herizons* 11 (1), 1997, pp. 26–7.

4. Beth Snyder, 'Toy Fair Girds for "Phantom Mouse" Burst: Marketing to Kids', *Advertising Age*, 8 February 1999, p. 46.

5. Stuart Ewen, *Captains of Consciousness: Advertising and the Social Roots of the Consumer Culture*, New York, McGraw-Hill, 1976, p. 144.

6. Yolandi M. Simonelli, 'Advertising Dolls: Successful Selling Aids', *National Doll World* 7 (6), 1983, p. 47.

7. Gary Cross, *Kids' Stuff: Toys and the Changing World of American Childhood*, Cambridge, MA, Harvard University Press, 1977, pp. 106–7.
8. Naomi Klein, *No Logo*, London, Flamingo, 2001, p. 161.
9. Helen B. Schwartzman, *Transformations: The Anthropology of Children's Play*, New York, Plenum, 1978, p. 19.
10. Cross, *Kids' Stuff*, p. 164.
11. Knickerbocker advertisement, *Playthings*, February 1956, p. 94; Gong Bell Manufacturing advertisement, *Playthings*, February 1956, p. 189; Mattel advertisement, *Playthings*, March 1956, p. 413; ABC Paramount Character Licensing Department advertisement, *Playthings*, May 1956, p. 63.
12. Ruth Handler and Jacqueline Shannon, *Dream Doll: The Ruth Handler Story*, Stamford, CT, Longmeadow, 1994, p. 85.
13. Karen Nickel, 'Clubbing Tots', *Fortune*, 26 February 1990.
14. Eric Schlosser, *Fast Food Nation: The Dark Side of the All-American Meal*, New York, HarperCollins, 2002, p. 45.
15. James U. McNeal, *Kids as Customers: A Handbook of Marketing to Children*, New York, Lexington Books, 1992, p. 176.
16. Nickel, 'Clubbing Tots', p. 10.
17. Handler and Shannon, *Dream Doll*, pp. 84–5.
18. Undated Toys 'R' Us brochure, 'The Experts Agree', circa. 1994.
19. Michael F. Jacobson and Laurie Ann Mazur, *Marketing Madness*, Boulder, CO, Westview Press, 1995, p. 12.
20. Quoted in Mark Crispin Miller, 'Demonopolize Them! A Call for a Broad-Based Movement against the Media Trust', *Extra!*, Nov/Dec 1995, p. 9.
21. 'Kenner Features a Galaxy of Star Wars Toys', *Playthings* 83 (2), 1985, p. S-3.
22. Ron Salvatore, 'Action Figure Toys', The Star Wars Collectors Archive, http://www.toysrgus.com/images-toys/figuretoys
23. Mark Frankel, 'Penney and Pizza Hut Go Hollywood', *Adweek's Marketing Week* 29 (5), 1988, pp. 33–4.
24. Stephen Kline, 'Making Toys Communicate: Promoting Excitement and Fantasy through Marketing', in Stephen Frith, Barbara Biggins and Tracy Newlands (eds), *Marketing Toys: It's Child's Play*, Sydney, New College Institute for Values Research, 1995, p. 43.
25. William Severini Kowinski, *The Malling of America: An Inside Look at the Great Consumer Paradise*, New York, William Morrow and Co, 1985, p. 377.
26. Ibid., pp. 376–8.
27. Alex Molnar and Faith Boninger, 'Adrift: Schools in a Total Marketing Environment. The Tenth Annual Report on Schoolhouse Commercialism Trends: 2006–2007', Tempe, AZ, Commercialism in Education Research Unit (CERU), Arizona State University, October 2007, p. 4.
28. Tom Engelhardt, 'The Strawberry Shortcake Strategy', in Todd Gitlin (ed.), *Watching Television*, New York, Pantheon, 1986.
29. 'Sweet Smell of Success', *Toys International and the Retailer*, December 1981, p. 20.
30. Sydney Ladensohn Stern and Ted Schoenhaus, *Toyland: The High-Stakes Game of the Toy Industry*, Chicago, Contemporary Books, 1990, p. 153.
31. 'Care Bears', *Toys International and the Retailer*, November 1983, pp. 20–1.

32. Joani Nelson-Horchler, 'No Biz Like Toy Biz', *Industry Week*, 5 March 1984, pp. 21, 24.
33. James Forkan, 'Foods Like Toying with Tie-Ins', *Advertising Age*, 11 April 1983, p. 50. See also http://www.bobbystoys.com/adv.htm
34. Richard Steverson, 'The Selling of Toy "Concepts"', *New York Times*, 14 December 1985, p. 33.
35. Margaret B. Carlson, 'Babes in Toyland', *American Film*, January/February, 1986, pp. 57–8.
36. Steven W. Colford, 'FTC Toy-Ad Ruling Chips at Regulation', *Advertising Age*, 10 October 1984, p. 12.
37. Carlson, 'Babes in Toyland', p. 57.
38. Cynthia Alperowicz, 'Toymakers Take Over Children's TV', *Business & Society Review*, Spring 1984, pp. 47–50.
39. Jacobson and Mazur, *Marketing Madness*, p. 23.
40. Barbara Biggins, 'What's the Problem?' in Frith et al., *Marketing Toys*, p. 27.
41. Wendy Varney, 'Playing into Corporate Hands: The Hyper-Commercialisation of Toys', in Frith et al., *Marketing Toys*, p. 43.
42. Angela J. Campbell, 'US Perspectives on the Regulation of Toy TV Tie-Ins', in Frith et al., *Marketing Toys*, pp. 102–4.
43. Varney, 'Playing into Corporate Hands', p. 62.
44. 'Marketing of Foods to Children', London, Food Commission and *Which?*, October 2005, pp. 5, 7.
45. Constantine von Hoffman, 'Hey, Little Spender', *CMO Magazine*, April 2005, http://www.cmomagazine.com/read/040105/little_spender.html
46. IQPC, 'Conference Brochure', paper presented at the Kid Power Asia 2003, Grand Copthorne Waterfront, Singapore, 26–27 March 2003.
47. IQPC, 'Conference Brochure', paper presented at the Kid Power 2003, The Sydney Boulevard, 28–29 July 2003.
48. Quoted in Susan Gregory Thomas, *Buy, Buy Baby: How Consumer Culture Manipulates Parents and Harms Young Minds*, Boston, Houghton Mifflin, 2007, pp. 126–7.
49. Ibid., p. 126.
50. 'Child Catchers: The Tricks Used to Push Unhealthy Food to Your Children', *Which?*, January 2006, p. 2.
51. Cited in Schlosser, *Fast Food Nation*, p. 43.
52. Claire Scobie, 'Buy Buy Baby', *Sunday Life, Sun-Herald*, 10 December 2006, p. 22.
53. Phil Marchionni, 'Advertising and Children: Ethical Perspectives', in Stephen Frith and Barbara Biggins (eds), *Children and Advertising: A Fair Game?*, Sydney, New College Institute for Values Research, 1994, p. 75.
54. Dale Kunkel, 'Monday Memo', *Broadcasting*, 9 July 1990, p. 25.
55. 'Marketing of Foods to Children', pp. 5–9.
56. Gary Ruskin and Juliet Schor, 'Every Nook and Cranny: The Dangerous Spread of Commercialized Culture', *Multinational Monitor* 26 (1&2), 2005.
57. Cited in 'Camels for Kids', *Time*, 1991, p. 52.
58. Cited in Schlosser, *Fast Food Nation*, p. 43.

59. Paul M. Fischer et al., 'Brand Logo Recognition by Children Aged 3 to 6 Years: Mickey Mouse and Old Joe the Camel', *Journal of the American Medical Association* 266 (22), 1991.

60. Quoted in Susan Linn, *Consuming Kids: The Hostile Takeover of Childhood*, New York, The New Press, 2004, p. 169.

61. Zoe Williams, 'Commercialisation of Childhood', London, Compass, December 2006, p. 4.

62. Martin Lindstrom, *Brand Child: Remarkable Insights into the Minds of Today's Global Kids and Their Relationships with Brands*, London, Kogan Page, 2003, p. 227; 'Child Catchers', p. 6.

63. Alicia Rebensdorf, 'Has Product Placement Made Our Television Viewing Worse?' *Alternet*, 20 May 2007, http://www.alternet.org/story/52069/; Alex Molnar et al., 'At Sea in a Marketing-Saturated World: The Eleventh Annual Report on Schoolhouse Commercialism Trends: 2007–2008', Boulder, CO, and Tempe, AZ, Education Public Interest Center (EPIC) and Commercialism in Education Research Unit (CERU), September 2008, p. 10.

64. Molnar et al., 'At Sea in a Marketing-Saturated World', p. 10.

65. American Academy of Pediatrics, 'Children, Adolescents, and Advertising', *Pediatrics* 118 (6), 2006, p. 2564.

66. Study published in *The Lancet* and cited in 'Movie Smoking', *Sydney Morning Herald*, 19 June 2003; Jeffrey Kluger, 'Hollywood's Smoke Alarm', *Time*, 14 April 2007, http://www.commercialalert.org/news/archive/2007/04/hollywoods-smoke-alarm

67. American Academy of Pediatrics, 'Media Education (Re9911)', *Pediatrics* 104 (2), 1999.

68. 'International Consumer Packaged Goods Sign on to Globally Produced Digitally Animated Feature Film, Foodfight!', Threshold Digital Research Labs, 30 April 2001.

69. 'Burgers with Attitude', *Ecologist*, May 2005, p. 11.

70. Krissah Williams, 'In Hip-Hop, Making Name-Dropping Pay', *Washington Post*, 29 August 2005, p. D01.

71. 'Holy Product Placement, Batman!', PRWatch, 18 April 2006, http://www.prwatch.org/node/4736

72. Thomas, *Buy, Buy Baby*, p. 165–80.

73. Lindstrom, *Brand Child*, p. 225.

74. Molnar et al., 'At Sea in a Marketing-Saturated World', p. 18.

75. Louise Story, 'More Marketers Are Grabbing the Attention of Players During Online Games', *New York Times*, 25 January 2007.

76. IQPC, 'Conference Brochure', paper presented at the Kid Power, Mandalay Bay Resorts & Casino, Las Vegas, 30 November–2 December 2004.

77. Jeff Chester and Kathryn Montgomery, 'Interactive Food & Beverage Marketing: Targeting Children and Youth in the Digital Age', Berkeley Media Studies Group, May 2007, p. 51.

78. Matt Richtel, 'Product Placements Go Interactive in Video Games', *New York Times*, 17 September 2002.

79. Chester and Montgomery, 'Interactive Food & Beverage Marketing', p. 49.

80. Massive, 'Massive Incorporated: Video Game Advertising', 2007, http://www.massiveincorporated.com

81. Elizabeth Moore and Victoria Rideout, *It's Child's Play: Advergaming and the Online Marketing of Food to Children, Executive Summary*, Menlo Park, CA, Henry J. Kaiser Family Foundation, July 2006, p. 6.

82. Chester and Montgomery, 'Interactive Food & Beverage Marketing', p. 50.

83. Alissa Quart, *Branded: The Buying and Selling of Teenagers*, London, Arrow, 2003, pp. 127–31.

84. Richtel, 'Product Placements Go Interactive in Video Games'.

85. Cited in Chester and Montgomery, 'Interactive Food & Beverage Marketing', p. 50.

86. Michel Marriott, 'Video-Game Makers Pitch for Preschoolers', *Sydney Morning Herald*, 30–31 October 2004.

87. Matt Richtel and Brad Stone, 'Doll Web Sites Drive Girls to Stay Home and Play', *New York Times*, 6 June 2007.

88. Phillipe Aries, *Centuries of Childhood*, London, Jonathan Cape, 1962, p. 76.

89. Ibid.; Brian Sutton-Smith, 'The Child at Play', *Psychology Today*, October 1985, pp. 64–5.

90. James U. McNeal, *Children as Consumers: Insights and Implications*, Massachusetts, Lexington Books, 1987, p. 83.

91. Advertisement for 'Pink and Pretty Barbie', *Toys International and the Retailer*, February 1983, p. 21.

92. Dorothy Singer, 'Play Activities That Build Bridges across the Generations', paper presented at International Toy Research Conference, Halmstad University, Sweden, 1996, pp. 11–13.

93. Stephen Kline and Debra Pentecost, 'The Characterization of Play: Marketing Children's Toys', *Play and Culture* 3 (3), 1990, pp. 235–55.

94. Nancy Carlsson-Paige and Diane Levin, *Who's Calling the Shots? How to Respond Effectively to Children's Fascination with War Play and War Toys*, Philadelphia, New Society Publishers, 1990.

95. Lynne Bartholomew, 'Choosing Appropriate Toys for Children – Can the Concept of Piagetian Schemas Help Us There?', paper presented at International Toy Research Conference, Halmstad University, Sweden, 1996, p. 3.

96. Alex Molnar, *School Commercialism: From Democratic Ideal to Market Commodity*, New York, Routledge, 2005, p. 2.

97. Quoted in Jacobson and Mazur, *Marketing Madness*, p. 21.

98. Joe Tucci et al., 'Children's Fears, Hopes and Heroes', Ringwood, Vic, Australian Childhood Foundation, June 2007, p. 13.

99. Chester and Montgomery, 'Interactive Food & Beverage Marketing', p. 51.

4   BRANDING CHILDISH IDENTITIES

1. Quoted in 'Watch out for Children: A Mothers' Statement to Advertisers', The Motherhood Project 2001, http://www.motherhoodproject.org/?cat=18

2. Girls Intelligence Agency (GIA), 'Research & Syndicated Reports', http://www.girlsintelligencagency.com/services/default.asp

3. GIA, http://www.girlsintelligencagency.com

4. GIA, 'Research & Syndicated Reports'.

5. GIA, 'GIA Headquarters – Secret Agent Dossier', http://www.giaheadquarters.com/agentdossier.html

6. Quoted in Allen D. Kanner, 'Globalization and the Commercialization of Childhood', *Tikkun* 20 (5), 2005, p. 49.

7. Quoted in Robert Berner, 'I Sold It through the Grapevine', *Business Week*, 29 May 2006, http://www.businessweek.com/print/magazine/content/06_22/b3986060.htm

8. James U. McNeal, *Kids as Customers: A Handbook of Marketing to Children*, New York, Lexington Books, 1992, pp. 91–2.

9. Quoted in 'Commercialization in Ontario Schools: A Research Report', Ontario Secondary School Teacher's Federation, September 1995, p. 4.

10. Quoted in Michael F. Jacobson and Laurie Ann Mazur, *Marketing Madness*, Boulder, CO, Westview Press, 1995, p. 21.

11. Quoted in Anne Sutherland and Beth Thompson, *Kidfluence: The Marketer's Guide to Understanding and Reaching Generation Y – Kids, Tweens, and Teens*, New York, McGraw-Hill, 2003, pp. 134–5.

12. Quoted in Julian Lee, 'New Platform but Same Old Stuff', *Sydney Morning Herald*, 22 June 2006, p. 34.

13. McNeal, *Kids as Customers*, p. 96.

14. Susan Linn, *Consuming Kids: The Hostile Takeover of Childhood*, New York, The New Press, 2004, pp. 42–3.

15. Roy F. Fox, *Harvesting Minds: How TV Commercials Control Kids*, Westport, CT, Praeger, 1996, p. 145.

16. Claire Scobie, 'Buy Buy Baby', *Sunday Life, Sun-Herald*, 16 December 2006, p. 21.

17. Study by Patti Valkenburg and Moniek Buijzen cited in David Burke, 'Two-Year-Olds Branded by TV Advertising', *Ecologist*, September 2005, p. 10; Susan Gregory Thomas, *Buy, Buy Baby: How Consumer Culture Manipulates Parents and Harms Young Minds*, Boston, Houghton Mifflin, 2007, p. 5.

18. Joe L. Kincheloe, 'McDonald's, Power, and Children: Ronald McDonald/Ray Kroc Does It All for You', in Shirley R. Steinberg and Joe L. Kincheloe (eds), *Kinderculture: The Corporate Construction of Childhood*, 2nd edn, Boulder, CO, Westview Press, 2004, p. 132; Zoe Williams, 'Commercialisation of Childhood', London, Compass, December 2006, p. 5.

19. Thomas, *Buy, Buy Baby*, p. 3.

20. McNeal, *Kids as Customers*, pp. 97–8.

21. Eric Schlosser, *Fast Food Nation: The Dark Side of the All-American Meal*, New York, HarperCollins, 2002, pp. 48, 50.

22. Naomi Klein, *No Logo*, London, HarperCollins, 2000, p. 21.

23. Juliet B. Schor, *Born to Buy: The Commercialized Child and the New Consumer Culture*, New York, Scribner, 2004, p. 26.

24. Mark Monahan, 'The Magical Money Machines', *Sydney Morning Herald*, 13–14 October 2001, p. 53.

25. 'Child Catchers: The Tricks Used to Push Unhealthy Food to Your Children', *Which?*, January 2006, p. 7.

26. McNeal, *Kids as Customers*, pp. 98–9.

27. Ofcom, 'Childhood Obesity – Food Advertising in Context', 22 July 2004, p. 18.

28. 'Friendly Brands Make Kids Brand-Friendly', *Strategy*, 27 September 1999, p. 3, http://www.strategymag.com/articles/magazine/19990927/26762.html

29. Quoted in Schlosser, *Fast Food Nation*, p. 50.

30. Quoted in 'Watch out for Children'.
31. Jeff Chester and Kathryn Montgomery, 'Interactive Food & Beverage Marketing: Targeting Children and Youth in the Digital Age', Berkeley Media Studies Group, May 2007, p. 19.
32. DMB&B quoted in Stephen Kline, 'Limits to the Imagination: Marketing and Children's Culture', in Ian Angus and Sut Jhally (eds), *Cultural Politics in Contemporary America*, New York, Routledge, 1989, p. 304.
33. Quoted in Chester and Montgomery, 'Interactive Food & Beverage Marketing', p. 26.
34. Cited in Sutherland and Thompson, *Kidfluence*, p. 136.
35. Paul M. Fischer et al., 'Brand Logo Recognition by Children Aged 3 to 6 Years: Mickey Mouse and Old Joe the Camel', *Journal of the American Medical Association* 266 (22), 1991; Schor, *Born to Buy*, p. 25.
36. Martin Lindstrom, *Brand Child: Remarkable Insights into the Minds of Today's Global Kids and Their Relationships with Brands*, London, Kogan Page, 2003, p. 59.
37. Ibid., p. 64.
38. Alissa Quart, *Branded: The Buying and Selling of Teenagers*, London, Arrow, 2003, pp. 24–5.
39. Dubit, 'Informer', http://www.dubitinformer.com
40. IQPC, 'Conference Brochure', paper presented at the Kid Power 2003, The Sydney Boulevard, 28–29 July 2003.
41. Quart, *Branded*, p. 57.
42. Peter Vilbig, 'Advertising's Sneak Attack', *New York Times Upfront*, 8 April 2002.
43. Brian Steinberg, 'Gimme an Ad! Brands Lure Cheerleaders', *Wall Street Journal*, 20 April 2007.
44. Leo Benedictus, 'Psst! Have You Heard?' *Guardian*, 30 January 2007.
45. Schor, *Born to Buy*, p. 75.
46. 'Customers for a Lifetime: Developing Brand Awareness and Affinity with Youth', *Trends & Tudes*, November 2004, p. 2.
47. Christopher Pole et al., 'New Consumers? Children, Fashion and Consumption', Cultures of Consumption Research Programme, 28 October 2006, p. 5, http://www.consume.bbk.ac.uk/pdfdocuments/KidsClothesfindings.pdf
48. Report by McCollum/Spielman Associates quoted in Kline, 'Limits to the Imagination', p. 303.
49. IQPC, 'Conference Brochure', paper presented at the Tween Power, The Grand Hyatt, Singapore, 26–29 November 2002.
50. Sutherland and Thompson, *Kidfluence*, pp. 139–41.
51. Lindstrom, *Brand Child*, p. 13.
52. Ibid., pp. 77, 111.
53. Sutherland and Thompson, *Kidfluence*, p. 90.
54. Quart, *Branded*, pp. 23–4.
55. McNeal, *Kids as Customers*, p. 55.
56. Schor, *Born to Buy*, p. 47.
57. 'Viral, Online Most Important Ways to Reach Kids', *Youth Markets Alert*, 1 March 2006, p. 1.
58. 'Child Catchers', pp. 7–8.

59. 'Marketing of Foods to Children', London, Food Commission and *Which?*, October 2005, p. 80.
60. Chester and Montgomery, 'Interactive Food & Beverage Marketing', p. 45.
61. Alex Molnar and Faith Boninger, 'Adrift: Schools in a Total Marketing Environment. The Tenth Annual Report on Schoolhouse Commercialism Trends: 2006–2007', Tempe, AZ, Commercialism in Education Research Unit (CERU), Arizona State University, October 2007, p. 5.
62. Chester and Montgomery, 'Interactive Food & Beverage Marketing', p. 45.
63. Elizabeth Moore and Victoria Rideout, *It's Child's Play: Advergaming and the Online Marketing of Food to Children, Executive Summary*, Menlo Park, CA, Henry J. Kaiser Family Foundation, July 2006, p. 10.
64. Tremor website, http://business.tremor.com
65. 'Dubit Insider', http://www.dubitinsider.com
66. Carl Bybee, 'Kids and the News', in Steinberg and Kincheloe (eds), *Kinderculture*, p. 94.
67. 'Undercover Marketing', Word Spy, 24 July 2001, http://www.wordspy.com/words/undercovermarketing.asp
68. Quoted in 'Undercover Agencies', *Australian*, 27 September 2001.
69. Quoted in Brooke E. Crescenti, 'Undercover Marketing: If Omission Is the Mission, Where Is the Federal Trade Commission?' *Journal of Law and Policy* 13, 2005, p. 702.
70. Harmon Leon, 'Secret Agents of Capitalism', *Metroactive*, 12 May 2004, http://www.metroactive.com/papers/metro/05.12.04/marketing-0420.html
71. 'Child Catchers', p. 14.
72. Lindstrom, *Brand Child*, p. 18.
73. Ibid., p. 18.
74. Chester and Montgomery, 'Interactive Food & Beverage Marketing', p. 35.
75. 'Social-Networking Sites Offer Variety of Avenues – Explicit and Otherwise – to Teens and Collegians', *Youth Markets Alert*, 1 October 2005, p. 1.
76. Chester and Montgomery, 'Interactive Food & Beverage Marketing', p. 40.
77. Ibid., p. 41.
78. Quoted in ibid., pp. 40–1.
79. Alloy Media + Marketing, http://www.alloymarketing.com
80. Ibid.
81. Chester and Montgomery, 'Interactive Food & Beverage Marketing', pp. 52–3.
82. 'Marketing of Foods to Children', p. 86.
83. Chester and Montgomery, 'Interactive Food & Beverage Marketing', pp. 54–5.
84. Alex Molnar et al., 'At Sea in a Marketing-Saturated World: The Eleventh Annual Report on Schoolhouse Commercialism Trends: 2007–2008', Boulder, CO, and Tempe, AZ, Education Public Interest Center (EPIC) and Commercialism in Education Research Unit (CERU), September 2008, pp. 16–17.
85. Quoted in Ibid., p. 55.
86. Quoted in 'Watch out for Children'.
87. Benjamin R. Barber, *Consumed: How Markets Corrupt Children, Infantilize Adults, and Swallow Citizens Whole*, New York, W.W. Norton 2007, p. 31.
88. 'Letter to APA Regarding the Use of Psychology to Exploit or Influence Children', Commercial Alert, 30 September 1999, http://www.essential.org/alert/psychology/apalet.html

89. IQPC, 'Conference Brochure', paper presented at the Kid Power Market Research 2002, Holiday Inn Victoria, London, 23–24 July 2002.
90. IQPC, 'Conference Brochure', paper presented at the Teen Insight 2002, Café Royal, London, 9–10 December 2002.
91. IQPC, 'Conference Brochure', paper presented at the Kid Power, Mandalay Bay Resorts & Casino, Las Vegas, 30 November–2 December 2004.
92. Stephen Frith, 'A Right to Advertise? Liberating the Free-Running Fox on the Free-Range Chicken Farm', in Stephen Frith, Barbara Biggins and Tracy Newlands (eds), *Marketing Toys: It's Child's Play*, Sydney, New College Institute for Values Research, 1995, p. 13.
93. Ibid., pp. 13–14; Richard Mizerski, 'The Relationship between Cartoon Trade Character Recognition and Attitude toward Product Category in Young Children', *Journal of Marketing* 59 (4), 1995.
94. Chester and Montgomery, 'Interactive Food & Beverage Marketing', p. 22.
95. Barber, *Consumed*, pp. 167, 188–9.
96. Quoted in Allen D. Kanner and Tim Kasser, 'Stuffing Our Kids: Should Psychologists Help Advertisers Manipulate Children?', Commercial Alert, 2000, http://www.essential.org/alert/psychology/stuffingourkids.html
97. Williams, 'Commercialisation of Childhood', p. 5.
98. Ed Mayo, 'Shopping Generation', National Consumer Council (NCC), July 2005, p. 3; see for example, D. Hargreaves, 'Adolescent Body Image Suffers from Media Images of the Impossibly Thin', *Flinders University Journal*, 13 (9), 2002, pp. 10–23.
99. Quart, *Branded*, pp. 146–7.
100. Ibid., pp. 165–6; CCFC, 'The Facts About Marketing to Kids', Campaign for a Commercial-Free Childhood, February 2005, pp. 21–2.
101. Molnar et al., 'At Sea in a Marketing-Saturated World', p. 3.
102. Schor, *Born to Buy*, p. 48.
103. Dan Cook, 'Lunchbox Hegemony? Kids & the Marketplace, Then & Now', *Alternet*, 21 August 2001, http://www.alternet.org/story/11370
104. Higher Education Research Institute (HERI), UCLA, 'Political Interest on the Rebound among the Nation's Freshmen, UCLA Survey Reveals', 26 January 2004.
105. Joseph L. DeVitis and John Martin Rich, *The Success Ethic, Education, and the American Dream*, Albany, NY, State University of New York Press, 1996, p. 175.
106. Schor, *Born to Buy*, pp. 12, 37.
107. Cited in Linn, *Consuming Kids*, p. 8.
108. Cited in ibid., p. 8.
109. Mayo, 'Shopping Generation', p. 2.
110. Julian Lee, 'Fads, Fame Lose Their Cool in Fragmenting Sub-Teen Market', *Sydney Morning Herald*, 15 September 2005, p. 25.
111. Quoted in Miriam H. Zoll, 'Psychologists Challenge Ethics of Marketing to Children', Mediachannel.org, 2000, http://www.mediachannel.org/originals/kidsell.shtml
112. 'Watch out for Children'.
113. Ibid.
114. Cited in Zoll, 'Psychologists Challenge Ethics of Marketing to Children'.
115. John Weaver, 'Reading Nickelodeon: Slimed by the Contradictions and Potentials of Television', in Steinberg and Kincheloe (eds), *Kinderculture*, p. 84.
116. Kanner, 'Globalization and the Commercialization of Childhood', p. 50.
117. Ibid., p. 50.

118. Center for the Study of Commercialism, quoted in Molnar and Boninger, 'Adrift', p. 2.
119. Allen Kanner quoted in Molnar et al., 'At Sea in a Marketing-Saturated World, p. 4.
120. Studies cited in Williams, 'Commercialisation of Childhood', p. 11.
121. Cited in Zoll, 'Psychologists Challenge Ethics of Marketing to Children'.
122. Schor, *Born to Buy*, p. 17.

5   TEACHING CONSUMER VALUES

1. American Academy of Pediatrics, 'Children, Adolescents, and Advertising', *Pediatrics* 118 (6), 2006, p. 2565.
2. YMI, 'Young Minds Inspired', 2007, http://www.youthmarketingint.com/why.htm
3. Ibid.
4. Ibid.
5. APK, 'Roberta Nusim', Brunico Communications, 2001, http://www.kidscreen.com/apk/2001/speakers/nusim.html
6. YMI, 'Young Minds Inspired'.
7. Ibid.
8. MBA, 'Communication with the Next Generation', http://www.mb-a.biz
9. Alex Molnar, *School Commercialism: From Democratic Ideal to Market Commodity*, New York, Routledge, 2005, p. 19.
10. David Lapp, 'Private Gain, Public Loss', *Environmental Action*, Spring 1994, p. 14.
11. Ella Drauglis, 'NUT Advice on Using Commercial Materials in Schools', National Union of Teachers (UK), August 2003, p. 1.
12. IQPC, 'Conference Brochure', paper presented at the Kid Power Market Research 2002, Holiday Inn Victoria, London, 23–24 July, 2002.
13. National Union of Teachers (NUT), 'Briefing on School's Role in Promoting Child Health and Combating Commercialism', 9 November 2004, p. 1.
14. 'What Business Does Big Business Have in our Schools?' Ontario Secondary School Teacher's Federation, 2002, http://www.media-awareness.ca/eng/med/class/edissue/cebuine2.htm
15. Edna McGill, 'Kids, Fair Game: You Betcha! No Ads in "C" Time', in Stephen Frith and Barbara Biggins (eds), *Children and Advertising: A Fair Game?*, Sydney, New College Institute for Values Research, 1994, p. 55.
16. Ibid., p. xv.
17. Rosemary Hipkins and Edith Hodgen, 'National Survey of Secondary Schools 2003', Wellington, New Zealand Council for Educational Research 2004, p. xiii.
18. Eric John Evans, *Thatcher and Thatcherism*, 2nd edn, London, Routledge, 2004, p. 71.
19. Nick Davies, 'State of Despair as Public Schools Get the Cream', *Guardian*, 8 March 2000.
20. Simon Marginson, *Markets in Education*, Sydney, Allen & Unwin, 1997, p. 5.
21. Anthony Welch, *Class, Culture and the State in Australian Education: Reform or Crisis?* Frankfurt am Main, Peter Lang, 1997, p. 7.
22. Terri Seddon et al., 'Remaking Public Education: After a Nation-Building State Changes Its Mind', in Alan Reid (ed.), *Going Public: Education Policy and Public*

Education in Australia, Canberra, Australian Curriculum Studies Association (ACSA), 1998, p. 77.

23. See for example Linda Doherty, 'Affordable Learning Top of Wish List', *Sydney Morning Herald*, 31 July 2004, p. 10.

24. Ann Morrow et al., 'Public Education: From Public Domain to Private Enterprise?' in Reid (ed.), *Going Public*, p. 9; Marginson, *Markets in Education*, p. 64; Vicky Ziegelaar, 'Public Education: Prince or Pauper', 16 February 2001, http://www.aeufederal.org.au/Publications/Brisgraphs/index.htm, slide 3.

25. Kathy Newnam, 'State Schools Crumbling, Report Reveals', *Green Left Weekly*, 29 August 2001; Anna Patty, 'Something Stinks in Our Deteriorating Schools', *Sydney Morning Herald*, 21 March 2007.

26. Julia Baird and Brigid Delaney, 'Parents Prop up Schools with Millions', *Sydney Morning Herald*, 30 July 2001, p. 1.

27. Larry Kuehn, 'The New Right Agenda and Teacher Resistance in Canadian Education', *Our Schools, Our Selves* 15 (3), 2006, p. 133.

28. Jon Young and Ben Levin, 'The Origins of Educational Reform: A Comparative Perspective', *Canadian Journal of Educational Administration and Policy* 12, 1999.

29. Véronique Brouillette, 'The Centrale Des Syndicats Du Québec and the Struggle against Neo-Liberal Schooling', *Our Schools, Our Selves* 15 (3), 2006, p. 117.

30. Grazia Scoppio, 'Common Trends of Standardisation, Accountability, Devolution and Choice in Educational Policies in England, U.K., California, U.S.A., and Ontario, Canada', *Current Issues in Comparative Education* 2 (2), 2002, p. 137.

31. Ibid., p. 131.

32. Kath Emery and Susan Ohanian, *Why Is Corporate America Bashing Our Public Schools?*, Portsmouth, NH, Heinemann, 2004, p. 32.

33. National Access Network, 'Overview', Teachers College, Columbia University, 2006, http://www.schoolfunding.info/litigation/litigation.php3

34. Ibid.

35. Linda Doherty, 'The New Class Struggle', *Sydney Morning Herald*, 5 October 2004, p. 9.

36. Stephen Smith, John L. Myers and Julie Underwood, 'Blowing in the Wind', *American School Board Journal*, 190 (5), 2003.

37. Steve Smith and Josiah Pettersen, 'Putting the Financial Squeeze on Schools', *State Legislatures* 29 (8), 2003, p. 23.

38. David M. Herszenhorn, 'New York Court Cuts Aid Sought by City Schools', *New York Times*, 21 November 2006.

39. Baird and Delaney, 'Parents Prop up Schools with Millions', p. 1.

40. Australian Senate, 'Not a Level Playing Field: Private and Commercial Funding in Government Schools', Chapter 1; Morrow et al., 'Public Education', p. 15.

41. Marginson, *Markets in Education*, pp. 196–8.

42. Jill Blackmore, '"Privatising the Public": The Shifts in Priorities of Self-Managing Schools Away from Public Education and Social Justice', *Curriculum Perspectives* 19 (1), 1999, p. 70.

43. Hipkins and Hodgen, 'National Survey of Secondary Schools 2003', p. xiii.

44. Kuehn, 'The New Right Agenda', p. 131.

45. 'What Business Does Big Business Have in our Schools?'

46. Steven Manning, 'The Littlest Coke Addicts', *Nation*, 25 June 2001, http://www. thenation.com/doc/20010625/manning; Campaign for a Commercial-Free Childhood (CCFC), 'The Facts About Marketing to Kids', February 2005.

47. Cited in Alex Molnar, 'The Ninth Annual Report on Schoolhouse Commercialism Trends: 2005–2006', Tempe, AZ, Commercialism in Education Research Unit (CERU), Arizona State University, November 2006, p. 33.

48. Mike West, 'Coca-Cola High', *Progressive*, November 1997, p. 26; CCFC, 'The Facts About Marketing to Kids'; Zoe Weil, 'The Business of Brainwashing', *Animals Agenda* 20 (1), 2000, p. 30.

49. American Academy of Pediatrics, 'Children, Adolescents, and Advertising', p. 2565.

50. Molnar, 'The Ninth Annual Report on Schoolhouse Commercialism Trends', p. 43.

51. Eve Lazarus, 'Cafeteria Blues', *Marketing Magazine*, 19 January 2004, http://www. marketingmag.ca/shared/print.jsp?content=2004119_60038_60038

52. NUT, 'Briefing on School's Role in Promoting Child Health and Combating Commercialism', p. 1.

53. Su Clark, 'Advertising in Schools', *Times Education Supplement*, 25 June 2004, http://www.tes.co.uk/search/story/?story_id=396901

54. Steven Manning, 'Students for Sale', *Nation*, 27 September 1999, http://www. thenation.com/doc/19990927/manning

55. Geof Rayner, 'Today's Lesson: Get Munching!' *Health Matters* 44, 2001.

56. Quoted in Eric Schlosser, *Fast Food Nation: The Dark Side of the All-American Meal*, New York, HarperCollins, 2002, pp. 53–4.

57. AAP, 'Ohio AAP Statement on Soft Drink Contracts in Schools', Ohio Chapter, American Academy of Pediatrics, 2001, http://www.ohioaap.org/softdrinks.htm

58. 'Coke Protects School Vending Machines', *O'Dwyers PR Daily*, 24 September 2001, http://www.odwyerpr.com/0924coke.htm

59. Caroline E. Mayer, 'PTA Turning to Corporate Sponsors for Funds', *Washington Post*, 21 June 2003, p. E01.

60. Michelle Simon, 'Big Soda's Publicity Stunt', *Alternet*, 29 August 2005, http://www. alternet.org/module/printversion/24647

61. Molnar, 'The Ninth Annual Report on Schoolhouse Commercialism Trends', pp. 32, 34.

62. Marion Burros and Melanie Warner, 'Bottlers Agree to a School Ban on Sweet Drinks', *New York Times*, 4 May 2006.

63. Lazarus, 'Cafeteria Blues'; Malcolm Brown, 'Coke Quits Primary Schools – the Real Think or Just Sweet Talk?' *Sydney Morning Herald*, 17–18 July, 2004, p. 5.

64. Molnar, 'The Ninth Annual Report on Schoolhouse Commercialism Trends', p. 34.

65. Annys Shin, 'Removing Schools' Soda Is Sticky Point', *Washington Post*, 22 March 2007, p. D03.

66. Stewart Lansley, *After the Gold Rush: The Trouble with Affluence: 'Consumer Capitalism' and the Way Forward*, London, Century Business Books, 1994, p. 97.

67. Stephanie Dunnewind, '"And Now, Class, a Word from Our Sponsors"', *Seattle Times*, 24 September 2005.

68. Jane Coulter, 'Who Profits from Public Education? An Internal Audit of Private Provision of Services to Public Education', Sydney, Public Sector Research Centre,

University of NSW, 1995, p. 14; Jennifer Connell, 'Parents and Teachers Slice Schools' Pizza Cash Scheme', *Sydney Morning Herald*, 16 November 1994; Wendy Busfield, 'Fast-Food Schooling', *Herald-Sun*, 11 June 1998.

69. Rick Smith, 'Is Tide Starting to Turn on Advertising in School?' *International Herald Tribune*, 18 February 2003.

70. 'Ronald McDonald Gets the Big Red Boot', *CBC News*, 20 November 2006.

71. George R. Kaplan, 'Profits R Us: Notes on the Commercialization of America's Schools', *Phi Delta Kappan* 78 (3), 1996.

72. Molnar, *School Commercialism*, p. 52.

73. 'Box Tops for Books', Nestlé, http://www.boxtops4books.co.uk/home.aspx

74. Business in the Community (BITC), 'Walkers Snacks Ltd – Free Books for Schools', 2006, http://www.bitc.org.uk/resources/case_studies/crmwalkers.html

75. CRM, 'Tesco Computers for Schools', Business in the Community, 2000, http://www.crm.org.uk/step1/step2/case_studies/tcfs.htm

76. Joanna Waller, 'Free Books for Schools: An Inquiry into the Commercial Sponsorship of School Resource Materials', thesis, University of Sheffield, 1999, p. 57.

77. Sue Lowe, 'Schools' Dud Giveaways Eat Computer Budgets', *Sydney Morning Herald*, 5 December 2002, p. 9.

78. 'What Better Marketing Could a Store Ask For?', *Ecologist*, September 2004, p. 54.

79. 'School Lunch Program Finds Opportunities', *Youth Markets Alert*, 1 December 2006, p. 5.

80. Manning, 'Students for Sale'.

81. US Government Accountability Office (GAO), 'Commercial Activities in Schools', September 2000, p. 22.

82. CCFC, 'The Facts About Marketing to Kids'; Tamar Lewin, 'In Public Schools, the Name Game as a Donor Lure', *New York Times*, 26 January 2006; Lazarus, 'Cafeteria Blues'; Molnar, *School Commercialism*, p. 27; see also http://www.bairdsmainfreight.school.nz/page/11

83. GMV Conseil, 'Marketing in Schools', Brussels, European Commission, October 1998.

84. 'A Better Way to Communicate', JazzyMedia, http://www.jazzybooks.com

85. Ruth Callaghan, 'No Business Like Kid Business', *West Australian*, 10 June 2001.

86. GAO, 'Commercial Activities in Schools', p. 22.

87. Cover Concepts, 'Cover Concepts Programs', 2007, http://www.coverconcepts.com

88. Quoted in David France, 'This Lesson Is Brought to You By...', *Good Housekeeping*, February 1996.

89. Marianne Manilov, 'Whittling Away Student's Education', *Environmental Action*, Spring 1994, p. 17.

90. Claire Atkinson, 'Kicked out of Class: Primedia Sheds in-School Net Channel One', *Advertising Age*, 23 April 2007, http://www.commercialfreechildhood.org/news/primediashedschannelone.htm

91. Alloy Media + Marketing, 2007, http://www.alloymarketing.com; 'Alloy Education', http://www.alloymarketing.com/education/index.html

92. Jonothan Kozol, 'The Sharks Move In', *New Internationalist*, October 1993, p. 8; Jeffrey E. Brand and Bradley S. Greenberg, 'Commercials in the Classroom: The Impact of Channel One Advertising', *Journal of Advertising Research* 34 (1),

1994; Amy Aidman, 'Advertising in Schools', University of Illinois, Illinois, ERIC Clearinghouse on Elementary and Early Childhood Education, December 1995; Roy F. Fox, 'Manipulated Kids: Teens Tell How Ads Influence Them', *Educational Leadership* 53 (1), 1995.

93. Michael J. Sandel, 'Ad Nauseaum', *New Republic*, 1 September 1997, p. 23.

94. Jeffrey E. Brand, 'Teaching Students to Want: TV Advertising in American Schools and Lessons for Australia', in Tracy Newlands and Stephen Frith (eds), *Innocent Advertising? Corporate Sponsorship in Australian Schools*, Sydney, New College Institute for Values Research, University of NSW, 1996, pp. 30–2.

95. Ibid., p. 30.

96. Aidman, 'Advertising in Schools'; Manilov, 'Whittling Away Student's Education', p. 18; Erica Weintraub Austin et al., 'Benefits and Costs of Channel One in a Middle School Setting and the Role of Media-Literacy Training', *Pediatrics* 117 (3), 2006, p. e424.

97. Brand and Greenberg, 'Commercials in the Classroom'; Brand, 'Teaching Students to Want', pp. 36, 39.

98. Fox, 'Manipulated Kids'.

99. Michael F. Jacobson and Laurie Ann Mazur, *Marketing Madness*, Boulder, CO, Westview Press, 1995, p. 30.

100. Austin et al., 'Benefits and Costs of Channel One', pp. e429–30.

101. Smith, 'Is Tide Starting to Turn on Advertising in School?'

102. BusRadio, 'About Us', http://www.busradio.net; quoted in Caroline E. Mayer, 'The Next Niche: School Bus Ads', *Washington Post*, 4 June 2006.

103. Jill Tucker, 'Schools' Efforts Fail to Keep Marketers out of the Classroom', *San Francisco Chronicle*, 8 December 2006.

104. Caroline E. Mayer, 'A Growing Marketing Strategy: Get 'Em While They're Young', *Washington Post*, 3 June 2003, p. A01; Martin Lindstrom, *Brand Child: Remarkable Insights into the Minds of Today's Global Kids and Their Relationships with Brands*, London, Kogan Page, 2003, p. 220; Juliet B. Schor, *Born to Buy: The Commercialized Child and the New Consumer Culture*, New York, Scribner, 2004, p. 94.

105. Rachel Cloues, 'My Year with Nike', *Rethinking Schools Online* 19 (2), 2004/5.

106. 'What Better Marketing Could a Store Ask For?', p. 54.

107. Kate Cole-Adams, 'Soft Sell Goes to School', *Time Australia* 8 (46), 1993, p. 55.

108. Molnar, 'The Ninth Annual Report on Schoolhouse Commercialism Trends', p. 10.

109. Quoted in Caroline E. Mayer, 'Today's Lesson, Sponsored By...', *Washington Post*, 15 June 2003, p. A01.

110. Samuels & Associates, 'Food and Beverage Marketing on California High School Campuses Survey: Findings and Recommendations', Public Health Institute, March 2006.

111. Mayer, 'Today's Lesson, Sponsored By...' , p. A01.

112. Ibid.

113. Molnar, 'The Ninth Annual Report on Schoolhouse Commercialism Trends', p. 9.

114. GMV Conseil, 'Marketing in Schools'.

115. Ibid.

116. RES, 'Real Event Solutions', 2007, http://www.real-event.ie/services.htm

117. Mayer, 'Today's Lesson, Sponsored By...' , p. A01; Lazarus, 'Cafeteria Blues'; Molnar, *School Commercialism*, p. 51; Solomon Hughes, 'McLabour Exposed', *Ecologist*,

March 2004, p. 31; Lisa Roner, 'McDonald's – Reading, Writing and Junk Food Advertising', *Ethical Corporation*, 18 February 2008, http://www.ethicalcorp.com/content_print.asp?ContentID=5719

118. Pizza Hut, 'About Book It!', http://www.bookitprogram.com/general/generaloverview.asp

119. Jane Levine, 'Junk-Food Marketing Goes Elementary', *Education Digest* 65 (5), 2000, p. 33; Julia Baird, 'McSchool: How Good Burghers Raise Funds', *Sydney Morning Herald*, 1 August 2001.

120. Quoted in 'Inviting the McWolf into the Fold', *Corporate Watch*, Spring 1999, http://www.corporatewatch.org/magazine/issue8/cw8rep.html

121. Quoted in Ibid.

122. 'McDonald's Check It Out Summer Reading Program', PRCentral, 2000, http://www.prcentral.com/protected/knowledge/cipra00/mcdonalds3.htm

123. Susan Carney, 'Books, Pizza Hut and Bratz Dolls: Does in-School Marketing Push Unhealthy Products on Our Kids?', Youth Development Suite, 2 March 2007, http://youthdevelopment.suite101.com/article.cfm/books_pizza_hut_and_bratz_dolls

124. GMV Conseil, 'Marketing in Schools'.

125. Lazarus, 'Cafeteria Blues'.

126. Bernie Froese-Germain, 'National Survey of School Commercialism in Canada', *Perspectives* 5 (3), 2005, p. 7.

127. Jonathan Woodward, 'School Board Set to Expel Corporate Logos', *Toronto Globe and Mail*, 5 November 2005.

128. Deborah Ely-Lawrence, 'Writing Classroom Materials That Make the Grade', *Public Relations Journal*, April 1994; Susan Schaefer Vandervoot, 'Big "Green Brother" Is Watching: New Directions in Environmental Public Affairs Challenge Business', *Public Relations Journal*, April 1991, p. 18; 'Commercial Pressures on Kids at Schools', *Education Digest* 61 (1), 1995.

129. David Shenk, 'Ethics, Inc.', *SPY Magazine*, July/August, 1994.

130. Quoted in Drauglis, 'NUT Advice on Using Commercial Materials in Schools', p. 2.

131. DfES et al., 'Commercial Activities in Schools: Best Practice Principles', EdComs 2004, http://www.edcoms.com/images_main/ISBA_CA_Schools_principles.pdf

132. GMV Conseil, 'Marketing in Schools'.

133. Kaplan, 'Profits R Us'.

134. Manning, 'Students for Sale'.

135. Andrew Hornery, 'Logo Literacy Kit Branded an Outrage', *Sydney Morning Herald*, 12 September 1998.

136. Kenneth Saltman, *Collateral Damage: Corporatizing Public Schools – a Threat to Democracy*, Lanham, MD, Rowman & Littlefield, 2000, p. xi.

137. Ibid., p. x.

138. Phyllis Schlafly, 'Commercialism is Rampant in the Schools', *EagleForum.org*, 15 November 2000, http://www.eagleforum.org/column/2000/nov00/00-11-15.shtml

139. CCFC, 'The Facts About Marketing to Kids'.

140. Schor, *Born to Buy*, p. 93.

141. Calvin Reid, 'Disney Comics Goes to School', *Publishers Weekly*, 7 May 2007, http://www.publishersweekly.com/index.asp?layout=articlePrint&articleID=CA6439438

142. Marek Fuchs, 'Sex Ed, Provided by Old Spice', *New York Times*, 29 May 2005.

143. Jack Neff, 'Clearasil Marches into Middle-School Classes', *Advertising Age*, 13 November, 2006, http://www.commercialalert.org/issues/education/k12-schools/clearasil-marches-into-middle-school-classes

144. Constance L. Hays, 'Math Book Salted with Brand Names Raises New Alarm', *New York Times*, 21 March 1999, p. 1.

145. James Norman, 'Net Marketers Target Kids', *Age*, 18 June 2000.

146. Breakthrough to Literacy, 'Take-Me-Home Book Ideas', Breakthrough to Literacy, 2007, http://www.breakthroughtoliteracy.com/index.html?PHPSESSID=&page=cm_te_takehome

147. France, 'This Lesson Is Brought to You By...'.

148. Holley Knaus, 'The Commercialized Classroom', *Multinational Monitor*, March 1992, p. 16; Lapp, 'Private Gain, Public Loss', p. 17; Shenk, 'Ethics, Inc.'.

149. Jacobson and Mazur, *Marketing Madness*, p. 37.

150. George Gerbner, 'Foreword', in Roy F. Fox, *Harvesting Minds: How TV Commercials Control Kids*, Westport, CT, Praeger, 1996, p. xiii.

151. Sandel, 'Ad Nauseaum', p. 23.

152. Jon Berry, 'A Nation Still Academically at Risk', *Brandweek*, 13 July 1992, p. 12.

6 TURNING SCHOOLS INTO BUSINESSES

1. Press report quoted in Jane Kenway and Elizabeth Bullen, *Consuming Children: Education–Entertainment–Advertising*, Maidenhead, Philadelphia, Open University Press, 2001, p. 123.

2. Lynell Hancock, 'School's Out', *Nation*, 9 July 2007.

3. Ibid., p. 20.

4. Jia Lynn Yang, 'He's at the Head of the Class', *Fortune*, 19 February 2007.

5. Hancock, 'School's Out'.

6. 'Visit NYC Chancellor of Education', Media Statement, Australian Labor Party, Canberra, 7 October 2008.

7. Richard Garner, 'Testing Blamed for Rise in Primary School Truancy', *Independent*, 22 September 2006; Katherine Sellgren, 'Tests "Reduce Pupils to Widgets"', *BBC News*, 4 May 2007.

8. David C. Berliner and Bruce J. Biddle, *The Manufactured Crisis: Myths, Fraud, and the Attack on America's Public Schools*, Cambridge, MA, Perseus Books, 1995, p. 151.

9. Peter Brimelow, 'What to Do About America's Schools', *Fortune*, 19 September 1983.

10. Deron Boyles, *American Education and Corporations: The Free Market Goes to School*, New York, Garland Publishing, 1998, p. 49.

11. Ellen Graham, 'A Head Start – Bottom-Line Education: A Business-Run School in Chicago Seeks to Improve Learning without a Big Rise in Costs', *Wall Street Journal*, 9 February 1990.

12. Erika Shaker, 'Customers in the Classroom', *Education Forum*, Fall 1995, p. 28.

13. Jenny Ozga, 'Education Governance in the United Kingdom: The Modernisation Project', *European Educational Research Journal* 1 (2), 2002, pp. 337–8.

14. Richard Hatcher and Bill Anderson, 'Labour's Transformation of the School System in England', *Our Schools, Our Selves* 15 (3), 2006, p. 169.

15. Sharon Gewirtz et al., *Markets, Choice and Equity in Education*, Buckingham, Open University Press, 1995, p. 94.

16. Susan L. Robertson and Roger R. Woock, 'The Political Economy of Educational "Reform" in Australia', in Mark Ginsburg (ed.), *Understanding Educational Reform in Global Context*, New York, Garland Publishing, 1991, p. 100.

17. Simon Marginson, *Markets in Education*, Sydney, Allen & Unwin, 1997, p. 192.

18. Alan Reid, 'Regulating the Educational Market: The Effects on Public Education Workers', in Alan Reid (ed.), *Going Public: Education Policy and Public Education in Australia*, Canberra, Australian Curriculum Studies Association (ACSA), 1998, p. 62.

19. Ibid., p. 60.

20. Marginson, *Markets in Education*, p. 119.

21. Alfie Kohn, 'Students Don't "Work" – They Learn', in Alfie Kohn and Patrick Shannon (eds), *Education, Inc. Turning Learning into a Business*, revised edn, Portsmouth, NH, Heinemann, 2002, p. 65.

22. Quoted in Nancy J. Perry, 'Where We Go from Here', *Fortune*, 21 October 1991.

23. Anthony Welch, *Class, Culture and the State in Australian Education: Reform or Crisis?*, Frankfurt am Main, Peter Lang, 1997, p. 5; Michael Engel, *The Struggle for Control of Public Education: Market Ideology vs Democratic Values*, Philadelphia, Temple University Press, 2000, pp. 3, 6.

24. Marginson, *Markets in Education*, pp. 3–4.

25. Ibid., pp. 92–3.

26. Australian Council of Deans of Education (ACDE), 'New Learning: A Charter for Australian Education', Canberra, October 2001, p. 1.

27. Kenneth Saltman, *Collateral Damage: Corporatising Public Schools – a Threat to Democracy*, Lanham, MD, Rowman & Littlefield, 2000, p. xii.

28. Dexter Whitfield, *Making It Public: Evidence and Action against Privatisation*, London, Pluto Press, 1983, p. 44; Barry Spicer et al., *Transforming Government Enterprises: Managing Radical Organisational Change in Deregulated Environments*, St Leonards, NSW, Centre for Independent Studies, 1996, p. 10.

29. Welch, *Class, Culture and the State in Australian Education*, p. 87.

30. Geoff Whitty et al., *Devolution and Choice in Education: The School, the State and the Market*, Melbourne, Australian Council for Educational Research, 1998, p. 51.

31. Heather-Jane Robertson, 'Traders and Travellers: Public Education in a Corporate-Dominated Culture', Ottawa, Canadian Teachers' Federation, May 1995.

32. 'Corporate Responsibility: The Facts', *New Internationalist*, December 2007.

33. David R. Francis, 'As Corporate Taxes Shrink, Who Pays?' *Christian Science Monitor*, 14 March 2005, http://www.csmonitor.com/2005/0314/p17s02-cogn.html

34. Michael Scherer, 'Make Your Taxes Disappear', *Mother Jones*, March/April 2005, p. 75.

35. David Brancaccio, 'Corporate Tax Rates and Yours', Now, PBS, 9 April 2004, http://www.pbs.org/now/politics/corptax2.html

36. Jonathan Weisman, 'Corporate Taxes: Going, Going...', *Washington Post*, 26 December 2004, p. F04.

37. Robert S. McIntyre and T.D. Coo Nguyen, 'State Corporate Income Taxes 2001–2003', Citizens for Tax Justice and the Institute on Taxation and Economic Policy, February 2005, p. 3.

38. Ibid., p. 1.
39. Roderick Kiewiet, 'Californians Can't Blame Everything on Proposition 13', *Public Affairs Report* 40 (6), 1999.
40. Robert A. Lawson, 'Could Derolph Lead to an Ohio Tax Revolt?', Buckeye Institute for Public Policy Solutions, 1 December 1997, http://www.buckeyeinstitute.org/printe.php?id=356
41. Arthur O'Sullivan and Terri A. Sexton, *Property Taxes & Tax Revolts: The Legacy of Proposition 13*, Cambridge, Cambridge University Press, 1995, p. 2.
42. Jim Shultz, 'How Big Corporations Became Proposition 13's Biggest Winners', *Democracy in Action*, Fall 1997, http://www.democracyctr.org/demaction/proposition13.html
43. O'Sullivan and Sexton, *Property Taxes & Tax Revolts*, p. 3.
44. Shultz, 'How Big Corporations Became Proposition 13's Biggest Winners'.
45. Sherry Posnick-Goodwin, 'Kirst Explains Historical Downfall of Ca Schools', *California Educator*, 28 February 2005, http://ed.stanford.edu/suse/faculty/display-FacultyNews.php?tablename=notify1&id=359
46. Peter Schrag, 'The Silver Anniversary of Proposition 13', California State University, Sacramento, 2003, http://webpages.csus.edu/~sac15356/Proposition%2013.htm
47. Posnick-Goodwin, 'Kirst Explains Historical Downfall of Ca Schools'.
48. Linda Darling-Hammond, 'From "Separate but Equal" to "No Child Left Behind"', in Deborah Meier and George Wood (eds), *Many Children Left Behind: How the No Child Left Behind Act Is Damaging Our Children and Our Schools*, Boston, MA, Beacon Press, 2004, p. 8.
49. Shultz, 'How Big Corporations Became Proposition 13's Biggest Winners'.
50. Dan Morain, 'Firm's Prop13 Savings Are Coveted', *Los Angeles Times*, 30 June 2003.
51. Shultz, 'How Big Corporations Became Proposition 13's Biggest Winners'; Morain, 'Firm's Prop13 Savings Are Coveted'.
52. O'Sullivan and Sexton, *Property Taxes & Tax Revolts*, p. 1.
53. Editors, 'Financing Better Schools', *Education Week*, 6 January 2005, http://www.edweek.org/ew/articles/2005/01/06/17exec.h24.html
54. Berliner and Biddle, *The Manufactured Crisis*, p. 85.
55. Cited in Russell Mokhiber and Robert Weissman, 'Stealing Money from Kids', *Focus on the Corporation*, 28 January 2003, http://lists.essential.org/pipermail/corp-focus/2003/000142.html
56. Berliner and Biddle, *The Manufactured Crisis*, pp. 84–5.
57. Robert Reich quoted in Joel Spring, *Political Agendas for Education: From the Religious Right to the Green Party*, Mahwah, NJ, Lawrence Erlbaum, 2002, p. 88.
58. Ira Shor, *Culture Wars: School and Society in the Conservative Restoration 1969–1984*, Boston, Routledge & Kegan Paul, 1986, pp. 20–1.
59. Welch, *Class, Culture and the State in Australian Education*, p. 6.
60. Marginson, *Markets in Education*, pp. 123–4.
61. Ibid., pp. 125–6.
62. Quoted in Berliner and Biddle, *The Manufactured Crisis*, p. 70.
63. Marginson, *Markets in Education*, p. 127.
64. Ibid., pp. 128–30.

65. The Business Roundtable (BRT), 'Continuing the Commitment: Essential Components of a Successful Education System', Washington, DC, May 1995, p. 9.

66. Mark B. Ginsburg and Susan F. Cooper, 'Conceptual Issues in "Educational Reform": Ideology, the State, and the World Economic System', in Val D. Rust (ed.), *International Perspectives on Education and Society: Education Reform in International Perspective*, Greenwich, CT, JAI Press, 1994, p. 58.

67. Marginson, *Markets in Education*, p. 127.

68. Pat Thomson, 'Thoroughly Modern Management and a Cruel Accounting', in Reid (ed.), *Going Public*, p. 40.

69. Chester E. Finn, 'Making School Reform Work', *Public Interest*, 1 July 2002.

70. Ramin Frahmandpur, review of Jonathan Kozol, *The Shame of the Nation* (2005), *Education Review*, 15 February 2006, http://edrev.asu.edu/reviews/rev468.htm

71. Jonathan Kozol, *The Shame of the Nation: The Restoration of Apartheid Schooling in America*, New York, Crown Publishers, 2005, pp. 169–71.

72. David Goodman, 'Class Dismissed', *Mother Jones*, May/June 2004, p. 43; Carey Gillam, 'US States Face Lawsuits on Funding Cash-Poor Schools', *Reuters News*, 18 August 2004; John Milburn, 'House Panel Dismantles Senate's $161 Million School Package', *Associated Press Newswires*, 24 June 2005.

73. Ruth E. Sternberg, 'Can You Save My Job?' *American School Board Journal* 191 (6), 2004.

74. Goodman, 'Class Dismissed', pp. 42–6.

75. Stan Karp, 'Money, Schools and Justice', *Rethinking Schools Online* 18 (1), 2003.

76. Steve Smith and Josiah Pettersen, 'Putting the Financial Squeeze on Schools', *State Legislatures* 29 (8), 2003, p. 23; Sternberg, 'Can You Save My Job?'; Stephen Smith et al., 'Blowing in the Wind', *American School Board Journal* 190 (5), 2003; Sam Dillon, 'School Is Out in Oregon, but Not Everyone Is Rejoicing', *New York Times*, 24 May 2003.

77. Editorial, 'Tough Start to the School Year', *New York Times*, 31 August 2003.

78. Cited in Berliner and Biddle, *The Manufactured Crisis*, pp. 74–8.

79. John M. Beam, 'The Blackboard Jungle: Tamer Than You Think', *New York Times*, 20 January 2004.

80. Reid, 'Regulating the Educational Market', p. 60.

81. Welch, *Class, Culture and the State in Australian Education*, p. 16.

82. Reid, 'Regulating the Educational Market', p. 63.

83. Blackmore et al. quoted in Whitty et al., *Devolution and Choice in Education*, p. 56.

84. Henry D.R. Miller and Mark B. Ginsburg, 'Restructuring Education and the State in England', in Ginsburg, *Understanding Educational Reform in Global Context*, p. 50; Hatcher and Anderson, 'Labour's Transformation of the School System in England', pp. 163–4.

85. Engel, *The Struggle for Control of Public Education*, pp. 122–3.

86. New Commission on the Skills of the American Workforce, 'Tough Choices or Tough Times', National Center on Education and the Economy, December 2006, p. 15.

87. Marginson, *Markets in Education*, pp. 192–3.

88. John Barrington, 'Educational Reform in New Zealand', in Ginsburg, *Understanding Educational Reform in Global Context*, pp. 286, 299–301, 304; Marginson, *Markets in Education*, pp. 190–1; Edward B. Fiske and Helen F. Ladd, 'A Distant Laboratory',

Education Week, 17 May 2000, http://www.edweek.org/ew/articles/2000/05/17/36fiske.h19.html

89. Ibid., pp. 56, 62.
90. 'Non-Teachers "Could Lead Schools"', *BBC News*, 18 January 2007.
91. Marginson, *Markets in Education*, pp. 196–7.
92. Anna Patty, 'Low-Income Families Turn to Private Schools', *Sydney Morning Herald*, 24 July 2006, p. 5.
93. Australian Senate, 'Not a Level Playing Field: Private and Commercial Funding in Government Schools', Canberra, Senate Employment, Workplace Relations, Small Business and Education Committee, June 1997, Chapters 1 and 3.
94. Kath Emery and Susan Ohanian, *Why Is Corporate America Bashing Our Public Schools?* Portsmouth, NH, Heinemann, 2004, p. 27.
95. Thomson, 'Thoroughly Modern Management and a Cruel Accounting', p. 44.
96. Kozol, *The Shame of the Nation*, pp. 46–8.
97. Emery and Ohanian, *Why Is Corporate America Bashing Our Public Schools?*, p. 27.
98. Welch, *Class, Culture and the State in Australian Education*, pp. 3–4.
99. Winnie Hu and Ford Fessenden, 'Data Show Wide Differences in New Jersey School Spending', *New York Times*, 24 March 2007.
100. Alison Cowan, 'School's Deep-Pocketed Partners', *New York Times*, 3 June 2007.
101. Kozol, *The Shame of the Nation*, pp. 45–6.
102. Ibid., p. 125.
103. Julia Baird and Brigid Delaney, 'Parents Prop up Schools with Millions', *Sydney Morning Herald*, 30 July 2001, p. 1.
104. Australian Senate, 'Not a Level Playing Field: Private and Commercial Funding in Government Schools', Canberra, Senate Employment, Workplace Relations, Small Business and Education Committee, June 1997, http://www.aph.gov.au/senate/committee/eet_ctte/completed_inquiries/1996-99/pcf/report/index.htm, Chapter 3.
105. Campaign for State Education (CASE), 'Sponsorship and Advertising in Schools – a Captive Audience?', 2006, http://www.casenet.org.uk/edubusiness/index.html
106. Hedley Beare, '"Enterprise": The New Metaphor for Schooling in a Post-Industrial Society', in Tony Townsend (ed.), *The Primary School in Changing Times: The Australian Experience*, London, Routledge, 1998, p. 14.
107. Eva Cox, 'Foreword: Growing Social Capital', in Reid (ed.), *Going Public*, p. ix; Bob Connell, 'A Moment of Danger', *Education Links*, Spring 1998, p. 10.
108. Engel, *The Struggle for Control of Public Education*, p. 33.

7   MAKING SCHOOLS ACCOUNTABLE

1. Robert B. Reich, 'The Real Supply Side', *American Prospect*, October, 2003, p. 40.
2. Peter Whoriskey, 'Political Backlash Builds over High Stakes Testing', *Washington Post*, 23 October 2006, p. A03.
3. Scott J. Cech, 'Academic Pressure on Rise for Teens, Poll Finds', *Education Week* 27 (45), 2008.
4. Penelope H. Bevan, 'Let Children Be Children', *San Francisco Chronicle*, 2007, p. E-2.

5. George Wood, 'Introduction', in Deborah Meier and George Wood (eds), *Many Children Left Behind: How the No Child Left Behind Act Is Damaging Our Children and Our Schools*, Boston, MA, Beacon Press, 2004, p. xii.

6. George Wood, 'A View from the Field: NCLB's Effects on Classrooms and Schools', in Meier and Wood (eds), *Many Children Left Behind*, p. 42; Carla Rivera, 'Tutors Prepare Them – for Preschool and Kindergarten', Los Angeles Times, 24 September 2006.

7. William McKeith, 'Even for Seven-Year-Olds, Exams Are Taking the Fun Out of Being a Kid', *Sydney Morning Herald*, 2003, p. 15.

8. 'Tests "Stopping Children Playing"', *BBC News*, 5 April 2007.

9. Richard Garner, 'Testing Blamed for Rise in Primary School Truancy', *Independent*, 22 September 2006; Katherine Sellgren, 'Tests "Reduce Pupils to Widgets"', *BBC News*, 4 May 2007.

10. Quoted in McKeith, 'Even for Seven-Year-Olds, Exams Are Taking the Fun Out of Being a Kid', p. 15.

11. David M. Herszenhorn, 'Many in City Summer School Won't Go on to Next Grade', *New York Times*, 1 September 2006.

12. Valerie Strauss, 'The Rise of the Testing Culture', *Washington Post*, 10 October 2006, p. A09.

13. Jonathan Kozol, *The Shame of the Nation: The Restoration of Apartheid Schooling in America*, New York, Crown Publishers, 2005, pp. 113–15.

14. Strauss, 'The Rise of the Testing Culture', p. A09.

15. Sharna Olfman, 'All Work and No Play', *Rethinking Schools Online* 19 (2), 2004/5.

16. Bob Peterson, 'Dangers of Early Childhood Testing', *Rethinking Schools Online* 14 (4), 2000; Richard Rothstein, 'No Child Left Untested', *Rethinking Schools Online* 19 (2), 2004/5.

17. Edward B. Rust, 'Business Issues in Elementary and Secondary Education', paper presented at the Committee on Education and the Workforce, US House of Representatives, 1 July 1999.

18. Edward B. Rust, 'Statement to Hearing On "Business Views of Assessments and Accountability in Education"', Committee on Education and the Workforce, US House of Representatives, 8 March 2001, http://www.house.gov/ed_workforce/hearings/107th/edr/account3801/rust.htm

19. 'National Alliance of Business Honors Intel CEO for Contributions to Public Education', *Business Wire*, 7 November 2001.

20. Edward B. Rust, 'No Turning Back: A Progress Report on the Business Roundtable Education Initiative', Washington, DC, Business Roundtable, August 1999, p. 3.

21. Alfie Kohn, 'Introduction: The 500-Pound Gorilla', in Alfie Kohn and Patrick Shannon (eds), *Education, Inc. Turning Learning into a Business*, revised edn, Portsmouth, NH, Heinemann, 2002, p. 4.

22. Kozol, *The Shame of the Nation*, p. 115.

23. Department for Education in 1992, cited in Geoff Whitty, *Making Sense of Education Policy: Studies in the Sociology and Politics of Education*, London, Sage, 2002, p. 81.

24. Henry D.R. Miller and Mark B. Ginsburg, 'Restructuring Education and the State in England', in Mark B. Ginsburg (ed.), *Understanding Educational Reform in Global Context*, New York, Garland Publishing, 1991, p. 67.

25. Tony Blair, 'Speech Given at Ruskin College, Oxford', Education-Line, 16 December 1996, http://www.leeds.ac.uk/educol/documents/000000084.htm

26. Editorial, 'Exams That Have Been Put to the Test and Found Wanting', *Independent*, 11 June 2007.

27. 'Tests Scrapped for 14-Year-Olds', *BBC News*, 14 October 2008, http://news.bbc.co.uk/go/pr/fr

28. Geoff Whitty, Sally Power, and David Halpin, *Devolution and Choice in Education: The School, the State and the Market*, Melbourne, Australian Council for Educational Research, 1998, p. 25.

29. Jon Young and Ben Levin, 'The Origins of Educational Reform: A Comparative Perspective', *Canadian Journal of Educational Administration and Policy* 12, 1999.

30. Clara Morgan, 'A Retrospective Look at Educational Reforms in Ontario', *Our Schools, Our Selves* 15 (2), 2006, pp. 130, 132–3; Grazia Scoppio, 'Common Trends of Standardisation, Accountability, Devolution and Choice in Educational Policies in England, U.K., California, U.S.A., and Ontario, Canada', *Current Issues in Comparative Education* 2 (2), 2002, p. 136.

31. Alfie Kohn, *The Case against Standardized Testing: Raising the Scores, Ruining the Schools*, Portsmouth, NH, Heinemann, 2000, p. 2.

32. Lynell Hancock, 'School's Out', *The Nation*, 9 July 2007.

33. Janet Giles, 'Resisting Basic Skills Testing', *South Australian Educational Leader* 6 (5), 1995, p. 2.

34. Kevin Donnelly, *Why Our Schools Are Failing*, Sydney, Duffy & Snellgrove, 2004, pp. 28–9.

35. Lucy Ward, 'What Did You Learn Today?' *Guardian*, 31 October 2003, p. 15.

36. Teachers Network, 'Results from a Survey of Teachers on No Child Left Behind', New York, Teachers Network, March 2007, pp. 5–6, 9.

37. *New York Post* cited in Kozol, *The Shame of the Nation*, p. 122.

38. Barbara Comber et al., 'Literacy Debates and Public Education: A Question of "Crisis"?', in Alan Reid (ed.), *Going Public: Education Policy and Public Education in Australia*, Canberra, Australian Curriculum Studies Association (ACSA), 1998, p. 27.

39. Linda Darling-Hammond, 'From "Separate but Equal" to "No Child Left Behind"', in Meier and Wood (eds), *Many Children Left Behind*, p. 22.

40. Richard Hatcher and Bill Anderson, 'Labour's Transformation of the School System in England', *Our Schools, Our Selves* 15 (3), 2006, p. 169.

41. Dave Toke, *Green Politics and Neo-Liberalism*, London, Macmillan, 2000, p. 118.

42. Kohn, *The Case against Standardized Testing*, p. 20.

43. Karen Brandon, 'Test-Prep Pressure Hits Grade Schools', in Kohn and Shannon (eds), *Education, Inc.*, p. 59.

44. J. Kozol quoted in Henry A. Giroux, 'Schools for Sale: Public Education, Corporate Culture, and the Citizen-Consumer', in Kohn and Shannon (eds), *Education, Inc.*, p. 108.

45. David C. Berliner and Bruce J. Biddle, *The Manufactured Crisis: Myths, Fraud, and the Attack on America's Public Schools*, Cambridge, MA, Perseus Books, 1995, p. 199.

46. California Business for Education Excellence (CBEE), 'Closing Achievement Gaps at All Grade Levels: The Next Phase in Improving California's Public Schools', 2005, p. 10.

47. Wood, 'A View from the Field', p. 37.

48. Ibid.

49. Frederick M. Hess, 'The Case for Being Mean', *AEI Online*, 1 December 2003, http://www.aei.org/publications/pubID.19614/pub_detail.asp

50. 'The ABCs Of "AYP": Raising Achievement for All Students', The Education Trust, Spring 2003, p. 4, http://www2.edtrust.org/NR/rdonlyres/37B8652D-84F4-4FA1-AA8D-319EAD5A6D89/0/ABCAYP.PDF

51. Sam Dillon, 'For Children Being Left Behind, Private Tutors Face Rocky Start', *New York Times*, 16 April 2004, p. 1.

52. Alan Reid, 'Regulating the Educational Market: The Effects on Public Education Workers', in Reid (ed.), *Going Public*, p. 65.

53. Michele Smart, 'Computers Cold Comfort for Students with Little Else', *Sydney Morning Herald*, 28 July 2008, p. 11.

54. Whitty et al., *Devolution and Choice in Education*, p. 67.

55. Vaishali Honawar, 'Schools Have No Handle on $7 Billion Cost of Teacher Turnover, Study Finds', *Education Week*, 20 June 2007, http://www.edweek.org/ew/articles/2007/06/20/43teachercost_web.h26.html

56. Jill Tucker, 'Teachers Not Staying in the Profession, Report Finds', *San Francisco Chronicle*, 20 June 2007.

57. Teachers Network, 'Results from a Survey', p. 9.

58. 'More Teachers Are Retiring Early', *BBC News*, 18 January 2007.

59. Bill Anderson and Richard Hatcher, 'The Blairite Vision: School in England under New Labour', *Our Schools, Our Selves* 14 (3), 2005, p. 89.

60. Gary Eason, 'Stressed Teachers "Taking Drugs"', *BBC News*, 9 April 2007.

61. Barbara Miner, 'Testing: Full Speed Ahead', *Rethinking Schools Online* 14 (2), 1999.

62. Ross Gittins, 'Teachers Know Money Isn't Everything', *Sydney Morning Herald*, 6 September 2006, p. 11.

63. Children Schools and Families Committee, 'Testing and Assessment: Third Report of Session 2007–08', House of Commons, 13 May 2008, p. 21.

64. Teachers Network, 'Results from a Survey', p. 7.

65. Kohn, *The Case against Standardized Testing*, p. 26.

66. Karen Brandon, 'Test-Prep Pressure Hits Grade Schools', in Kohn and Shannon (eds), *Education, Inc.*, p. 61.

67. Joe Smydo, 'No Child Left Behind Has Altered the Face of Education', *Pittsburgh Post-Gazette*, 28 August 2006.

68. Teachers Network, 'Results from a Survey', pp. 8–9.

69. Anthony P. Carnevale, 'No Child Gets Ahead', *Education Week* 27 (5), 2007.

70. Anderson and Hatcher, 'The Blairite Vision: School in England under New Labour', p. 90; Children Schools and Families Committee, 'Testing and Assessment', p. 3.

71. Anthony Welch, *Class, Culture and the State in Australian Education: Reform or Crisis?*, Frankfurt am Main, Peter Lang, 1997, pp. 122, 123–4.

72. Children Schools and Families Committee, 'Testing and Assessment', p. 51.

73. Brent Staples, 'Schools Fail Children, Not the Other Way Around', *New York Times*, 6 April 2004.
74. Alfie Kohn, 'NCLB and the Effort to Privatize Public Education', in Meier and Wood (eds), *Many Children Left Behind*, p. 81.
75. Berliner and Biddle, *The Manufactured Crisis*, p. 31.
76. Wood, 'A View from the Field', p. 37.
77. Staples, 'Schools Fail Children, Not the Other Way Around'.
78. Kohn, 'NCLB and the Effort to Privatize Public Education', p. 94.
79. Darling-Hammond, 'From "Separate but Equal"...' , p. 21.
80. Kozol, *The Shame of the Nation*, pp. 208–9.
81. Tamar Lewin and Jennifer Medina, 'To Cut Failure Rate, Schools Shed Students', *New York Times*, 31 July 2003.
82. Kozol, *The Shame of the Nation*, pp. 280–2.
83. Ibid., p. 207.
84. Nanette Asimov and Todd Wallack, 'The Teachers Who Cheat', *San Francisco Chronicle*, 13 May 2007.
85. Greg Toppo, 'What Makes a Teacher "Effective"?' *USA Today*, 14 February 2007, p. 2D.
86. David Marley, 'Ethical Code for Exams', *Times Educational Supplement*, 2 May 2008, p. 1.
87. Kohn, *The Case against Standardized Testing*, p. 3.
88. Olfman, 'All Work and No Play'.
89. Quoted in Wood, 'A View from the Field', p. 41.
90. Kozol, *The Shame of the Nation*, p. 131.
91. Australian Council of Deans of Education (ACDE), 'New Learning: A Charter for Australian Education', Canberra, October, 2001, p. 93.
92. Kohn, *The Case against Standardized Testing*, pp. 8, 10, 13.
93. Ibid., p. 4.
94. Ibid., pp. 8, 12.
95. Bill Ayers quoted in ibid., p. 17.
96. Ibid., p. 18.
97. ACDE, 'New Learning', pp. 85, 88.
98. 'Measuring Standards in English Primary Schools', Statistics Commission, February 2005, p. 4.
99. Peter Tymms et al., 'Standards in English Schools: Changes Since 1997 and the Impact of Government Policies and Initiatives', CEM Centre, University of Durham, April 2005, p. 21; 'Education: Standards', Reform, 2006, http://www.reform.co.uk/website/education/schoolssystemperformance/standards.aspx
100. Wood, 'A View from the Field', p. 35.
101. Children Schools and Families Committee, 'Testing and Assessment', pp. 43, 45.
102. Kozol, *The Shame of the Nation*, p. 281.
103. Susan Kinzie, 'No Tests? College's Students Must Relearn How to Learn', *Washington Post*, 25 December 2006.
104. Children Schools and Families Committee, 'Testing and Assessment', p. 49.
105. Olfman, 'All Work and No Play'.
106. Amit R. Paley, 'Test Scores at Odds with Rising High School Grades', *Washington Post*, 23 February 2007.

8   BUSINESS CAMPAIGNS

1. Alex Molnar, *Giving Kids the Bu$iness: The Commercialization of America's Schools*, Boulder, CO, Westview, 1996, p. 2.
2. Ed Dinger, 'Edward B. Rust, Jr.', International Directory of Business Biographies, http://www.referenceforbusiness.com/biography/M-R/Rust-Edward-B-Jr-1950.html
3. Edward B. Rust, 'No Turning Back: A Progress Report on the Business Roundtable Education Initiative', Washington, DC, Business Roundtable, August 1999, p. 6.
4. Mike France, 'State Farm: What's Happening to the Good Neighbor?' *Business Week*, 8 November 1999, http://www.businessweek.com/1999/99_45/b3654189.htm
5. Ibid.
6. Ibid.
7. Janet L. Holt, 'Utah High Court Reinstates Punitive Award for State Farm's "Egregious" Misconduct', *Trial*, February 2002.
8. Nancy J. Perry, 'How to Help America's Schools', *Fortune*, 4 December 1989.
9. Ibid.
10. Nancy J. Perry, 'Where We Go from Here', *Fortune*, 21 October 1991.
11. Keith H. Hammonds, 'The Mission: David Kearns's Crusade to Fix America's Schools', *Business Week*, 22 March 1999, http://www.businessweek.com/1999/99_12/b3621153.htm
12. Jaclyn Fierman, 'Giving Parents a Choice of Schools', *Fortune*, 4 December 1989.
13. Hammonds, 'The Mission'.
14. New American Schools, 'New American Schools: Driven by Results', http://www.naschools.org
15. Doug Garr, *IBM Redux: Lou Gerstner and the Business Turnaround of the Decade*, revised edn, New York, HarperCollins, 2000.
16. IBM, 'Louis V. Gerstner, Jr.', http://www-03.ibm.com/press/us/en/biography/10153.wss
17. 'About Us', The Teaching Commission, 2006, http://www.theteachingcommission.org/about
18. Daniel Pryzbyla, 'Spellings: In God We Trust; All Others Bring Data', *Education News*, 21 June 2005, http://www.educationnews.org/wriers/daniel/spellings-in-god-we-trust-all-ot.htm
19. IBM, 'Louis V. Gerstner, Jr.'; 'Reinventing Education', Department of Education and Training, Victoria, http://www.sofweb.vic.edu.au/ict/pd/reinvent.htm
20. 'Poor Basic Skills "Costing Firms"', *BBC News*, 20 February 2007.
21. Business Coalition for Student Achievement (BCSA), 'Key Talking Points', http://www.biz4achievement.org
22. Heather-Jane Robertson, 'Traders and Travellers: Public Education in a Corporate-Dominated Culture', Ottawa, Canadian Teachers' Federation, May 1995.
23. The Business Roundtable (BRT), 'Continuing the Commitment: Essential Components of a Successful Education System', Washington, DC, May 1995, p. 1.
24. BRT, 'A Business Leader's Guide to Setting Academic Standards', Washington, DC, June 1996, p. 2.
25. BRT, 'Building Support for Tests That Count', Washington, DC, November 1998, p. 4.

26. Edward B. Rust, 'Business Issues in Elementary and Secondary Education', paper presented at the Committee on Education and the Workforce, US House of Representatives, 1 July 1999.

27. Jeffrey R. Henig, *Rethinking School Choice: Limits of the Market Metaphor*, Princeton, NJ, Princeton University Press, 1994, p. 3; Hammonds, 'The Mission'; David C. Berliner and Bruce J. Biddle, *The Manufactured Crisis: Myths, Fraud, and the Attack on America's Public Schools*, Cambridge, MA, Perseus Books, 1995, p. 212; Edward H. Berman, 'The Politics of American Education and the Struggle for Cultural Dominance, 1996–', *Melbourne Studies in Education* 37 (1), 1996, p. 28; Barbara Miner, 'Testing: Full Speed Ahead', *Rethinking Schools Online* 14 (2), 1999.

28. BRT, 'Building Support for Tests That Count', p. 6.; BRT, 'A Business Leader's Guide to Setting Academic Standards', pp. 4–8.

29. Molnar, *Giving Kids the Bu$iness*, p. 8.

30. Quoted in ibid., p. 7.

31. Rust, 'No Turning Back', p. 4; BRT, 'Issue Ads: Keep the Promise Campaign', 1 January 1998, http://www.businessroundtable.org/newsroom/document.aspx?q s=53A6BF807822B0F1AD5479167F75A70479B41

32. BRT, 'Continuing the Commitment', p. 11.

33. BRT and CVWF, 'Early Childhood Education: A Call to Action from the Business Community', Business Roundtable and Corporate Voices for Working Families, 7 May 2003, p. 3.

34. BRT, 'Building Support for Tests That Count', pp. 5–6.

35. Rust, 'No Turning Back', p. 2.

36. Rust, 'Business Issues in Elementary and Secondary Education'.

37. Catherine Gewertz, 'Business Group Merges with Education Center', *Education Week* 22 (11), 2002, p. 5.

38. 'Brochure', paper presented at the 2002 Business and Education Conference: The New Era of Education Reform, New York, 5–6 November 2002.

39. Rust, 'No Turning Back', p. 4.

40. NAB, 'National Alliance of Business Releases Math and Science Achievement Business Guide', *PR Newswire*, 20 May 1998.

41. BRT, 'Building Support for Tests That Count', pp. 10–13.

42. Ibid., p. 8.

43. BRT, 'Transforming Education Policy: Assessing 10 Years of Progress in the States', June 1999.

44. BRT, 'Using the "No Child Left Behind Act" to Improve Schools in Your State: A Tool Kit for Business Leaders', March 2005, p. 24.

45. David J. Hoff, 'Big Business Goes to Bat for NCLB', *Education Week*, 18 October 2006, http://www.edweek.org//ew/articles/2006/10/18/08biz.h26.html

46. BRT, 'Using the "No Child Left Behind Act"'.

47. Richard S. Dunham, 'Business Gets Behind "No Child"', *Business Week*, 7 May 2007.

48. BCSA, 'Business Coalition for Student Achievement', 2007, http://www.biz4achievement.org

49. Hoff, 'Big Business Goes to Bat for NCLB'.

50. Erik W. Robelen, 'Gates, Broad to Push Education in Presidential Campaign', *Education Week*, 2 May 2007.

51. Jeff Archer, 'U.S. Chamber Adds Business Viewpoint on School's Quality', *Education Week* 26 (11), 2007.
52. Lynn Olson, 'U.S. Urged to Reinvent It's Schools', *Education Week*, 20 December 2006, http://www.edweek.org//ew/articles/2006/12/20/16skills.h26.html
53. New Commission on the Skills of the American Workforce, 'Tough Choices or Tough Times', National Center on Education and the Economy, December 2006, pp. 12–14.
54. Brochure for The 2006 Business and Education Conference: Global Public-Private Partnerships in Education, Washington DC, 11–12 September 2006.
55. G. William Domhoff, *Who Rules America Now? A View for the '80s*, Englewood Cliffs, NJ, Prentice-Hall, 1983, p. 89.
56. Alfie Kohn, 'Introduction: The 500-Pound Gorilla', in Alfie Kohn and Patrick Shannon (eds), *Education, Inc. Turning Learning into a Business*, revised edn, Portsmouth, NH, Heinemann, 2002, p. 7.
57. Kath Emery and Susan Ohanian, *Why Is Corporate America Bashing Our Public Schools?*, Portsmouth, NH, Heinemann, 2004; http://www.achieve.org/achieve.nsf/AboutAchieve?OpenForm
58. http://www.dataqualitycampaign.org/partners/managing_partners.cfm
59. http://www.achieve.org/achieve.nsf/AboutAchieve?OpenForm
60. 'The ABCs Of "AYP": Raising Achievement for All Students', The Education Trust, Spring 2003, http://www2.edtrust.org/NR/rdonlyres/37B8652D-84F4-4FA1-AA8D-319EAD5A6D89/0/ABCAYP.PDF
61. Berman, 'The Politics of American Education', p. 21.
62. National Commission on Excellence in Education (NCEE), 'A Nation at Risk', April 1983
63. Ibid., Introduction.
64. Molnar, *Giving Kids the Bu$iness*, Chapter 1.
65. Ira Shor, *Culture Wars: School and Society in the Conservative Restoration 1969–1984*, Boston, Routledge & Kegan Paul, 1986, p. 110.
66. Berliner and Biddle, *The Manufactured Crisis*, pp. 92–3.
67. Shor, *Culture Wars*, p. 126.
68. Ibid., p. 110.
69. BRT, 'A Business Leader's Guide to Setting Academic Standards', pp. 2–3.
70. Hoff, 'Big Business Goes to Bat for NCLB'.
71. Charles Kolb, 'A Continuum of Necessary Investments for Learning', *Education Week*, 4 January 2007, http://www.edweek.org//ew/articles/2007/01/04/17kolb.h26.html
72. Robertson, 'Traders and Travellers'.
73. Hoff, 'Big Business Goes to Bat for NCLB'.
74. New Commission on the Skills of the American Workforce, 'Tough Choices or Tough Times', p. 8.
75. Cited in John Barrington, 'Educational Reform in New Zealand', in Mark B. Ginsburg (ed.), *Understanding Educational Reform in Global Context*, New York, Garland Publishing, 1991, p. 297.
76. Anthony Welch, *Class, Culture and the State in Australian Education: Reform or Crisis?*, Frankfurt am Main, Peter Lang, 1997, p. 114.

77. Pat Thomson, 'Thoroughly Modern Management and a Cruel Accounting', in A. Reid (ed.), *Going Public: Education Policy and Public Education in Australia*, Canberra, Australian Curriculum Studies Association (ACSA), 1998, p. 39.

78. Ken Jones and Nathalie Duceux, 'Neo-Liberalism in the Schools of Western Europe', *Our Schools, Our Selves* 15 (3), 2006, p. 94.

79. 'Brown Sets out His Education Goal', *BBC News*, 25 September 2006.

80. Mike Baker, 'Why Skills Are the New Education', *BBC News*, 9 December 2006.

81. Susan L. Robertson and Roger R. Woock, 'The Political Economy of Educational "Reform" in Australia', in Ginsburg (ed.), *Understanding Educational Reform in Global Context*, p. 93.

82. Cited in ibid., p. 93.

83. Shor, *Culture Wars*, p. 88; Welch, *Class, Culture and the State in Australian Education*, p. 84.

84. Jim Dempsey, 'Current Literacy Crisis Just the Latest', *Telegram & Gazette*, 17 February 1992, p. D1.

85. Ford Foundation Project on Social Welfare and the American Future, 'The Common Good: Social Welfare and the American Future', New York, NY, The Ford Foundation, May 1989, pp. 30–1.

86. Ben Clarke, 'Exam Privatization Threatens Public Schools', CorpWatch, 23 September 2004, http://www.corpwatch.org/article.php?id=11543; Kathleen Kennedy Manzo, 'Reading Law Fails to Bring Innovations', *Education Week*, 13 December 2006, http://www.edweek.org/ew/articles/2006/12/13/15read.h26.html

87. Bruce Hunter, American Association of School Administrators, quoted in Barbara Miner, 'Keeping Public Schools Public: Testing Companies Mine for Gold', *Rethinking Schools Online* 19 (2), 2004/5.

88. Karen Brandon, 'Test-Prep Pressure Hits Grade Schools', in Kohn and Shannon (eds), *Education, Inc.*, p. 59.

89. Eleanor Chute, 'Back to School: Education Booms into a $850 Billion Enterprise', *Pittsburgh Post-Gazette*, 30 August 2006.

90. June Kronholz, 'Education Companies See Dollars in Bush School-Boost Law', *Wall Street Journal*, 24 December 2003, p. B1.

91. David Bacon, 'Testing Companies Go for the Gold', *Rethinking Schools Online* 16 (3), 2002.

92. Kronholz, 'Education Companies See Dollars in Bush School-Boost Law', p. B1.

93. Ibid.; Jeremy Quittner, 'Trends: Not Left Behind', *Business Week*, Fall 2006, http://www.businessweek.com/print/magazine/conent//06_38/b4001829.htm?chan=gl

94. Miner, 'Keeping Public Schools Public'.

95. Warwick Mansell, 'Markers Quit over "Fiasco"', *Times Education Supplement*, 16 May 2008, p. 1.

96. Clarke, 'Exam Privatization Threatens Public Schools'.

97. Mary Ann Zehr, 'U.S. Test Developers Cashing in on Markets Abroad', *Education Week*, 30 August 2006, http://www.edweek/org/ew/articles/2006/08/30/01test.h26.htm

98. 'McGraw-Hill Education From McGraw-Hill School Solutions Group', The McGraw-Hill Companies, 22 August 2006, http://www.mcgraw-hill.com/releases/education/20060822.shtml

99. Miner, 'Keeping Public Schools Public'.

100. Stephen Metcalf, 'Reading between the Lines', in Kohn and Shannon (eds), *Education, Inc.*, p. 52.
101. Ibid.
102. Clarke, 'Exam Privatization Threatens Public Schools'.
103. Ibid.
104. Quoted in Bacon, 'Testing Companies Go for the Gold'.
105. Chute, 'Back to School'.
106. 'Pearson Education', Pearson, http://www.pearson.com/index.cfm?pageid=18
107. Walter F. Roche, 'Bush's Family Profits from "No Child" Act', *Los Angeles Times*, 22 October 2006.
108. Brandon, 'Test-Prep Pressure Hits Grade Schools', p. 58.
109. Carla Rivera, 'Tutors Prepare Them – for Preschool and Kindergarten', *Los Angeles Times*, 24 September 2006.
110. Tamar Lewin, 'As Math Scores Lag, a New Push for Basics', *New York Times*, 14 November 2006.
111. Brandon, 'Test-Prep Pressure Hits Grade Schools', p. 59; Alfie Kohn, 'The 500-Pound Gorilla: The Corporate Role in the High-Stakes Testing Obsession & Other Methods of Turning Education into a Business', ReclaimDemocracy.org, October 2002, http://www.reclaimdemocracy.org/weekly_article/corporate_influence_education_kohn.html
112. Clarke, 'Exam Privatization Threatens Public Schools'.
113. Sam Dillon, 'For Children Being Left Behind, Private Tutors Face Rocky Start', *New York Times*, 16 April 2004, p. 1.

9   MADE TO ORDER

1. David Grann, 'Back to Basics', *New Republic*, 7 May 1999, http://www.cs.unm.edu/~sto/maunders/educate/grann.html
2. Ibid.
3. Susan Headden, 'Two Guys ... And a Dream', *US News and World Report*, 20 February 2006.
4. Joan Capuzzi Giresi, 'Earning Their Wings', *Penn Arts & Sciences Magazine*, Spring 2006, p. 16, http://www.sas.upenn.edu/sasalum/newsltr/spring04/earning_wings.html
5. Jeanne Russell, 'Charter Schools Sets Kids' Sights on College', *San Antonio Express News*, 9 January 2005.
6. Jodi Wilgoren, 'Seeking to Clone Schools of Success for Poor', *New York Times*, 16 August 2000.
7. 'KIPP: Knowledge Is Power Program', http://www.kippschools.org
8. Russell, 'Charter Schools Sets Kids' Sights on College'.
9. Tyler Currie, 'Braving Disney', *Washington Post*, 9 November 2003.
10. For example, Roger B. Hill and Gregory C. Petty, 'A New Look at Selected Employability Skills: A Factor Analysis of the Occupational Work Ethic', *Journal of Vocational Education Research* 20 (4), 1995; Gillian Flynn, 'Attitude More Valued Than Ability', *Personnel Journal* 73 (9), 1994, p. 16; Peter Cappelli, 'Is the "Skills Gap" Really About Attitudes?' *California Management Review* 37 (4), 1995; 'Work Ethic Top Job Skill', in *CPA Journal*, 1994; House of Representatives Standing Committee on Employment, Education and Training, 'Youth Employment:

A Working Solution', Canberra, Parliament of the Commonwealth of Australia, September 1997.

11. John Kenneth Galbraith, *The Anatomy of Power*, London, Hamish Hamilton, 1984, pp. 32–3.

12. W. Neff quoted in Adrian Furnham, *The Protestant Work Ethic: The Psychology of Work-Related Beliefs and Behaviours*, London, Routledge, 1990, pp. 146–7.

13. Cited in Deron Boyles, *American Education and Corporations: The Free Market Goes to School*, New York, Garland Publishing, 1998, p. 4.

14. The Business Roundtable (BRT), 'Continuing the Commitment: Essential Components of a Successful Education System', Washington, DC, May 1995, p. 5.

15. Justin Norris, 'National Exam May Spell End for HSC', *Sydney Morning Herald*, 26 May 2005, p. 1.

16. Ann Morrow et al., 'Public Education: From Public Domain to Private Enterprise?', in Alan Reid (ed.), *Going Public: Education Policy and Public Education in Australia*, Canberra, Australian Curriculum Studies Association (ACSA), 1998, p. 10.

17. Council of Australian Governments (COAG), 'National Reform Agenda: Victoria's Plan to Improve Literacy and Numeracy Outcomes', April 2007, p. 7.

18. New Commission on the Skills of the American Workforce, 'Tough Choices or Tough Times', National Center on Education and the Economy, December 2006, p. 9.

19. Samuel Bowles, 'The Integration of Higher Education into the Wage-Labor System', in Michael B. Katz (ed.), *Education in American History: Readings on the Social Issues*, New York, Praeger, 1973, p. 143.

20. Ross Laver, 'Giving Kids a Head Start: What Canada Can Learn from Other Countries', *Maclean's*, 9 November 1992.

21. Robert D. Kennedy, 'Let Candles Be Brought: The Case for Business Involvement in Education', *Vital Speeches* 60 (8), 1994.

22. Chester E. Finn, 'Making School Reform Work', *Public Interest*, 1 July 2002.

23. Jodi Wilgoren, 'Calls for Change in Scheduling of the School Day', *New York Times*, 10 January 2001, p. 1; Diana Jean Schemo, 'Failing Schools See a Solution in Longer Day', *New York Times*, 26 March 2007.

24. 'Johnson Plans Classes on Saturday', *BBC News*, 25 September 2006.

25. Jonathan Kozol, *The Shame of the Nation: The Restoration of Apartheid Schooling in America*, New York, Crown Publishers, 2005, p. 121.

26. Margaret Simons, 'Home Invasion', *Age*, 4 February 2005.

27. 'Duke Study: Homework Helps Students Succeed in School, as Long as There Isn't Too Much', Duke University, 7 March 2006, http://www.dukenews.duke.edu/2006/03/homework.html

28. David K. Cohen and Marvin Lazerson, 'Education and the Corporate Order', in Katz (ed.), *Education in American History*, p. 330.

29. Nadya Labi, 'Burning out at Nine?', *Time*, 23 November 1998, p. 86.

30. Kozol, *The Shame of the Nation*, pp. 120–1; Debra Nussbaum, 'Before Children Ask, "What's Recess?"', *New York Times*, 10 December 2006.

31. George Wood, 'A View from the Field: NCLB's Effects on Classrooms and Schools', in Deborah Meier and George Wood (eds), *Many Children Left Behind: How the No Child Left Behind Act Is Damaging Our Children and Our Schools*, Boston, MA, Beacon Press, 2004, p. 42; Carla Rivera, 'Tutors Prepare Them – for Preschool and Kindergarten', *Los Angeles Times*, 24 September 2006.

32. 'No Playground for "Super School"', *BBC News*, 6 May 2007.

33. Cohen and Lazerson, 'Education and the Corporate Order', p. 325.

34. Valerie Strauss, 'Jumping in to the Rigors of Learning', *Washington Post*, 26 October 2004.

35. Ralph Gardner, 'Poppet on a String', *Good Weekend*, 11 September 2004, p. 51.

36. 'Public Schools Inc.: Inside Edison's Schools', *Frontline*, PBS, 3 July 2003, http://www.pbs.org/wgbh/pages/frontline/shows/edison/; Kenneth Saltman, *The Edison Schools: Corporate Schooling and the Assault on Public Education*, New York, Routledge, 2005, pp. 67, 83–4, 122.

37. Grann, 'Back to Basics'.

38. Kozol, *The Shame of the Nation*, p. 65.

39. Sam Dillon, 'Cameras Watching Students, Especially in Biloxi', *New York Times*, 24 September 2003.

40. Ann Therese Palmer, 'Spit and Polish Comes to Chicago Schools', *Business Week*, 25 June 2001, p. 4EU2, http://www.businessweek.com/magazine/content/01_26/b3738134.htm

41. Ibid.

42. Ibid.

43. Rebecca Smithers, 'City Academy Raises Exam Grades by Paying Pupils Cash Bonuses', *Guardian*, 17 November 2005.

44. Sara B. Miller, 'How to Keep Those Kids in Class? Pay Them', *Christian Science Monitor*, 29 July 2005.

45. Kozol, *The Shame of the Nation*, pp. 96–7.

46. David C. Berliner and Bruce J. Biddle, *The Manufactured Crisis: Myths, Fraud, and the Attack on America's Public Schools*, Cambridge, MA, Perseus Books, 1995, p. 194.

47. Alfie Kohn, 'Introduction: The 500-Pound Gorilla', in Alfie Kohn and Patrick Shannon (eds), *Education, Inc. Turning Learning into a Business*, revised edn, Portsmouth, NH, Heinemann, 2002, p. 3.

48. Alfie Kohn, 'Students Don't "Work" – They Learn', in Kohn and Shannon (eds), *Education, Inc.*, p. 64.

49. Samuel Bowles and Herbert Gintis, 'Schooling in Capitalist America', in Kohn and Shannon (eds), *Education, Inc.*, p. 95.

50. Currie, 'Braving Disney'; Headden, 'Two Guys ... And a Dream'; Wilgoren, 'Seeking to Clone Schools of Success for Poor'.

51. David M. Herszenhorn, 'When the Bank Teller Is Still in High School', *New York Times*, 9 August 2006.

52. Glen Evans and Milicent Poole, 'Experiencing Work: Bridges to Adulthood', in Milicent Poole (ed.), *Education and Work*, Hawthorn, Victoria, Australian Council for Educational Research, 1992, pp. 117–8.

53. Grann, 'Back to Basics'.

54. Kozol, *The Shame of the Nation*, pp. 90–2.

55. Robert Sherman, 'Vocational Education and Democracy', in David Corson (ed.), *Education for Work: Background to Policy and Curriculum*, New Zealand, Dunmore Press, 1988, pp. 67–8.

56. Stephen Dolainski, 'Partnering with the (School) Board', *Workforce*, May 1997; Leo Giglio and Lawrence Bauer, 'School-to-Work Programmes and Partnerships', *Educational Horizons* 76 (2), 1998.

57. Colin Wringe, 'Education, Schooling and the World of Work', in Corson (ed.), *Education for Work*, p. 33; Gary McCulloch, 'Technical and Vocational Schooling: Education or Work', in ibid., p. 115.

58. Gary Eason, 'Schools Fail to Hit Basics Target', *BBC News*, 11 January 2007.

59. Department for Education and Skills (DfES), 'Five Year Strategy for Children and Learners', July 2004, p. 73, http://www.standards.dfes.gov.uk/primary/features/literacy/952369

60. DfES, 'The Standards Site: Specialist Schools Welcome', 2006, http://www.standards.dfes.gov.uk/specialistschools; Alexandra Smith, 'Q&A: Specialist Schools', *Guardian*, 9 February 2007, http://education.guardian.co.uk/newschools/story/0,,2009763,00.html

61. DfES, '14–19 Education and Skills', February 2005, p. 6, http://publications.dcsf.gov.uk/default.aspx?PageFunction=productdetails&PageMode=publications&ProductId=CM%25206476&pdfs/14-19WhitePaper.pdf; DfES, 'Five Year Strategy for Children and Learners', pp. 7–8; Richard Hatcher and Bill Anderson, 'Labour's Transformation of the School System in England', *Our Schools, Our Selves* 15 (3), 2006, pp. 168, 176.

62. Press Association, 'City Academy Criticised for "Exceptionally Low" Standards', *Guardian*, 22 February 2006.

63. Government discussion paper quoted in Matthew Thompson, 'More Vocational Courses for High School Students', *Sydney Morning Herald*, 14 January 2005, p. 5.

64. Ibid.

65. Ministerial Council on Education, Employment, Training and Youth Affairs (MCEETYA), 'The Adelaide Declaration on National Goals for Schooling in the Twenty-First Century', 28 July 1999, http://www.mceetya.edu.au/mceetya/nationalgoals/natgoals.htm

66. Board of Studies, Victoria, 'VET in Schools Retail Operations', December 1997; Jane Kenway and Lindsay Fitzclarence, 'Consuming Children? Public Education as a Market Commodity', in Reid (ed.), *Going Public*, p. 47.

67. Board of Studies, Victoria, 'VET in Schools', 1996, http://ww.bos.vic.edu.au/vce/vet

68. Justin Norrie, 'Nice Little Earner for Pupil Who Had Loathed School', *Sydney Morning Herald*, 18 August 2005, p. 13.

69. 'High School Students to Get the Toyota T3 Feeling', *Campus Review*, 18–24 July 2001, p. 7.

70. Patrick Lawnham, 'Drive to Clinch Jobs in Industry', *Australian*, 15 December 1999.

71. Peter Gotting, 'File It and Step Nearer Your Place at Uni', *Sydney Morning Herald*, 9 November 2001.

72. Brian Robins, 'HSC Vocational Courses Soar in Popularity', *Sydney Morning Herald*, 15 October 2007, p. 3.

73. Standing Committee on Education and Training, 'Learning to Work: Report on the Inquiry into Vocational Education in Schools', House of Representatives, March 2004, pp. xv–xvi.

74. Norrie, 'Nice Little Earner for Pupil Who Had Loathed School', p. 13.

75. House of Representatives Standing Committee on Employment, Education and Training, 'Youth Employment', pp. xvii, 39.

76. Ibid., p. 16.
77. Helen Pidd, 'Burger Bar A-Level for Staff at McDonald's', *Guardian*, 28 January 2008.
78. See for example Ulla Hytti and Colm O'Gorman, 'What Is "Enterprise Education"? An Analysis of the Objective and Methods of Enterprise Education Programmes in Four European Countries', *Education + Training* 46 (1), 2004, p. 12; Kate Lewis and Claire Massey, 'Delivering Enterprise Education in New Zealand', *Education + Training* 45 (4), 2003, p. 198; Howard Davies, 'A Review of Enterprise and the Economy in Education', Department for Children, Schools and Families, February 2002, Annex D.
79. Hytti and O'Gorman, 'What Is "Enterprise Education"?', p. 14.
80. Ofsted, 'Learning to Be Enterprising', August 2004, p. 7.
81. DfES, 'The Standards Site: Specialist Schools Welcome', http://www.standards.dfes. gov.uk/specialistschools
82. Ofsted, 'Developing Enterprising Young People', November 2005, p. 1.
83. HM Treasury, 'Creating an Enterprise Culture: Discussion Paper', Enterprise Insight, Small Business Service, 26 January 2004, p. 3.
84. Enterprise Insight, 'Make Your Mark: Start Talking Ideas', 2005, http://www.start-talkingideas.org; HM Treasury, 'Creating an Enterprise Culture: Discussion Paper', p. 6.
85. Enterprise Insight, 'Make Your Mark: Start Talking Ideas'.
86. 'PDC WRL & Enterprise', Personal Development Curriculum, http://www.workingo-nenterprise.com
87. 'What Youngbiz Is About!', http://www.youngbizuk.co.uk/Business/aboutus.html
88. Junior Achievement, http://www.ja.org
89. Young Achievement Australia, http://www.yaa.org.au
90. Young Enterprise, http://www.young-enterprise.org.uk
91. Enterprise New Zealand Trust, 'What Enterprise New Zealand Trust Does', 2004, http://www.enzt.co.nz/~enztWeb/enzt.asp
92. 'NFTE – Teaching Entrepreneurship to Youth', National Foundation for Teaching Entrepreneurship, http://www.nfte.com
93. DtS, 'Determined to Succeed', InfoScotland.com, http://www.determinedtosucceed. co.uk
94. Jim Cumming, 'National Education Agenda 1997–8', Australian Principals' Associations Professional Development Council, August, 1997, http://ww3.beecoswe-bengine.org/servlet/Web?s=157573&p=RE_nateduag97; Curriculum Corporation, *Enterprise Education*, March, http://www.curriculum.edu.au/enterprise/eenwsltr/ eenws7.htm
95. Department of Education, Science and Training (DEST), 'Enterprise Education', http:// www.dest.gov.au/sectors/career_development/programmes_funding/programme_ categories/key_career_priorities/Enterprise_education
96. DEST, 'Enterprise Education for the 21st Century Initiative', http://www.dest. gov.au/sectors/career_development/programmes_funding/programme_categories/ key_career_priorities/Enterprise_education/enterprise_learning_for_the_21st_ century_initiative.htm
97. Cumming, 'National Education Agenda 1997–8'; John Smyth, 'Schooling and Enterprise Culture: Pause for a Critical Policy Analysis', *Journal of Education Policy* 14 (4), 1999, p. 439.

98. Clinton E. Boutwell, *Shell Game: Corporate America's Agenda for Schools*, Bloomington, Indiana, Phi Delta Kappa Educational Foundation, 1997, p. 1.
99. Wringe, 'Education, Schooling and the World of Work', p. 44.
100. Linda Darling-Hammond quoted in Alfie Kohn, 'Introduction: The 500-Pound Gorilla', in Kohn and Shannon (eds), *Education, Inc.*, 2002, p. 6.
101. Patrick Shannon, 'We Can Work It Out', in Kohn and Shannon (eds), *Education, Inc.*, p. 69.
102. Ibid., p. 41.
103. Corson (ed.), *Education for Work*, p. 52.
104. Cath Blakers, 'School to Work: Transition and Policy', in Poole, *Education and Work*, p. 65.
105. Cohen and Lazerson, 'Education and the Corporate Order', p. 51.

10   DUMBING DOWN FUTURE CITIZENS

1. Alfie Kohn, 'Students Don't "Work" – They Learn', *Education Week*, 3 September 1997, http://www.alfiekohn.org/teaching/edweek/sdwtl.htm
2. Jeffrey R. Henig, *Rethinking School Choice: Limits of the Market Metaphor*, Princeton, NJ, Princeton University Press, 1994, p. 50.
3. Merill Sheils, 'Why Johnny Can't Write', *Newsweek*, 8 December 1975, p. 58.
4. Ira Shor, *Culture Wars: School and Society in the Conservative Restoration 1969–1984*, Boston, Routledge & Kegan Paul, 1986, p. 93.
5. Henry D.R. Miller and Mark B. Ginsburg, 'Restructuring Education and the State in England', in Mark B. Ginsburg (ed.), *Understanding Educational Reform in Global Context*, New York, Garland Publishing, 1991, p. 57.
6. Geoff Whitty et al., *Devolution and Choice in Education: The School, the State and the Market*, Melbourne, Australian Council for Educational Research, 1998, pp. 17–18.
7. Miller and Ginsburg, 'Restructuring Education and the State in England', p. 60.
8. Henig, *Rethinking School Choice*, p. 42.
9. Ibid., pp. 27–8; Shor, *Culture Wars*, p. 74.
10. David C. Berliner and Bruce J. Biddle, *The Manufactured Crisis: Myths, Fraud, and the Attack on America's Public Schools*, Cambridge, MA, Perseus Books, 1995, pp. 20–2, 26; Shor, *Culture Wars*, p. 64.
11. Henig, *Rethinking School Choice*, pp. 33, 38–9.
12. Berliner and Biddle, *The Manufactured Crisis*, pp. 58–9.
13. National Commission on Excellence in Education (NCEE), 'A Nation at Risk', April 1983, http://www.ed.gov/pubs/NatAtRisk/index.html
14. Berliner and Biddle, *The Manufactured Crisis*, p. 169.
15. Shor, *Culture Wars*, p. 105.
16. Quoted in Berliner and Biddle, *The Manufactured Crisis*, p. 143.
17. Walter Shapiro, 'Tough Choice', *Time*, 16 September 1991, p. 54.
18. Dennis Baron, 'Will Anyone Accept the Good News on Literacy?', *The Chronicle of Higher Education* 48 (21), 2002, p. B10.
19. Kenneth Saltman, *Collateral Damage: Corporatizing Public Schools – a Threat to Democracy*, Lanham, MD, Rowman & Littlefield, 2000, p. 20.
20. Barbara Comber et al., 'Literacy Debates and Public Education: A Question of "Crisis"?' in Alan Reid (ed.), *Going Public: Education Policy and Public Education*

in Australia, Canberra, Australian Curriculum Studies Association (ACSA), 1998, pp. 19–20; John Smyth, 'Schooling and Enterprise Culture: Pause for a Critical Policy Analysis', *Journal of Education Policy* 14 (4), 1999, p. 435.

21. Comber et al., 'Literacy Debates and Public Education', pp. 18–19.
22. Anthony Welch, *Class, Culture and the State in Australian Education: Reform or Crisis?*, Frankfurt am Main, Peter Lang, 1997, p. 127.
23. Harriet Alexander, 'Teens in Top Five out of 41 Countries', *Sydney Morning Herald*, 7–8 October 2006, p. 7.
24. Whitty et al., *Devolution and Choice in Education*, p. 43.
25. Clara Morgan, 'A Retrospective Look at Educational Reforms in Ontario', *Our Schools, Our Selves* 15 (2), 2006, p. 129.
26. Sol Cohen, 'Language and History: A Perspective on School Reform Movements', in Val D. Rust (ed.), *International Perspectives on Education and Society: Education Reform in International Perspective*, Greenwich, CT, JAI Press, 1994, p. 25.
27. R. Usher and R. Edwards, cited in Sally Power and Geoff Whitty, 'Teaching New Subjects? The Hidden Curriculum of Marketised Education Systems', *Melbourne Studies in Education* 37 (2), 1996, p. 2.
28. 'Elementary and Secondary Education Act Reauthorization', US Senate Committee on Health, Education, Labor, and Pensions, 29 April 1999.
29. Cited in Heather-Jane Robertson, 'Traders and Travellers: Public Education in a Corporate-Dominated Culture', Ottawa, Canadian Teachers' Federation, May 1995.
30. J.A. Savage, 'Is California Handing over Its Schools to Business?', *Business and Society Review*, Summer 1994, p. 14.
31. Miller and Ginsburg, 'Restructuring Education and the State in England', p. 61; John Barrington, 'Educational Reform in New Zealand', in Ginsburg (ed.), *Understanding Educational Reform in Global Context*, p. 298; Raewyn Connell, 'The New Right Triumphant: The Privatization Agenda and Public Education in Australia', *Our Schools, Our Selves* 15 (3), 2006, p. 144; Edward H. Berman, 'The Politics of American Education and the Struggle for Cultural Dominance, 1996–', *Melbourne Studies in Education* 37 (1), 1996, p. 37.
32. Welch, *Class, Culture and the State in Australian Education*, p. 84.
33. Shor, *Culture Wars*, p. 18.
34. Welch, *Class, Culture and the State in Australian Education*, p. 85.
35. Shor, *Culture Wars*, pp. 89, 14.
36. Linda Doherty, 'Government Staffer Says New-Age Warriors Waging Culture Wars in Class', *Sydney Morning Herald*, 3 May 2004, p. 3.
37. Farrah Tomazin, 'Back to Basics: Studies Scrapped in Curriculum Revamp', *Age*, 24 April 2007.
38. Mark Davis, 'Fads, Sludge Eroding Education, PM Says', *Sydney Morning Herald*, 9 February 2007.
39. Frederick M. Hess, 'The Case for Being Mean', *AEI ONline*, 1 December 2003, http://www.aei.org/include/pub_print.asp?pubID=19614
40. Connell, 'The New Right Triumphant', p. 151; Berliner and Biddle, *The Manufactured Crisis*, p. 184; Jonathan Kozol, *The Shame of the Nation: The Restoration of Apartheid Schooling in America*, New York, Crown Publishers, 2005, p. 118.
41. Joe Smydo, 'No Child Left Behind Has Altered the Face of Education', *Pittsburgh Post-Gazette*, 28 August 2006.

42. AP, 'Students Getting Double Dose of the Three R's', *CNN*, 4 August 2006.
43. David Hursh, 'Neoliberalism and the Control of Teachers, Students and Learning: The Rise of Standards, Standardization, and Accountability', *Cultural Logic* 4 (1), 2000.
44. Heather Hollingsworth, 'Students Double up on English, Math', Associated Press, 5 August 2006, http://www.azstarnet.com/allheadlines/140886
45. Bill Boyle and Joanna Bragg, 'A Curriculum without Foundation', *British Educational Research Journal* 32 (4), 2006.
46. Richard Hatcher and Bill Anderson, 'Labour's Transformation of the School System in England', *Our Schools, Our Selves* 15 (3), 2006, p. 165.
47. Children, Schools and Families Committee, 'Testing and Assessment: Third Report of Session 2007–08', House of Commons, 13 May 2008, pp. 3, 43, 50.
48. Alfie Kohn, 'Save Our Schools ... From Business', *School Administrator*, October 1995, p. 36.
49. Heather MacDonald, 'Why John Can't Write: Teaching Grammar and Logic to College Students', *Public Interest*, 22 June 1995.
50. Simon Marginson, *Markets in Education*, Sydney, Allen & Unwin, 1997, p. 89.
51. Kevin Donnelly, *Why Our Schools Are Failing*, Sydney, Duffy & Snellgrove, 2004, pp. 19–20.
52. Cohen, 'Language and History'.
53. William Torrey Harris quoted in ibid., p. 31.
54. Alan Reid, 'Regulating the Educational Market: The Effects on Public Education Workers', in Reid (ed.), *Going Public*, p. 59.
55. Dave Hill, '"Education, Education, Education", or "Business, Business, Business"?', paper presented at the European Educational Research Association Annual Conference, Lahti, Finland, 22–25 September 1999, p. 16.
56. Australian Council of Deans of Education (ACDE), 'New Learning: A Charter for Australian Education', Canberra, October 2001, pp. 2–3.
57. Cited in Kozol, *The Shame of the Nation*, p. 194; US Department of Education (USDE), *What Works: Research About Teaching and Learning*, 2nd edn, 1987, p. 57.
58. USDE, *What Works*, p. 47.
59. Brodinsky paraphrased in Shor, *Culture Wars*, pp. 78–9.
60. Cited in Kenneth Saltman, *The Edison Schools: Corporate Schooling and the Assault on Public Education*, New York, Routledge, 2005, pp. 107–9.
61. Tamar Lewin, 'As Math Scores Lag, a New Push for Basics', *New York Times*, 14 November 2006.
62. Ken Jones and Nathalie Duceux, 'Neo-Liberalism in the Schools of Western Europe', *Our Schools, Our Selves* 15 (3), 2006, pp. 103–4.
63. ACDE, 'New Learning', pp. 85, 88.
64. Bill Anderson and Richard Hatcher, 'The Blairite Vision: School in England under New Labour', *Our Schools, Our Selves* 14 (3), 2005, p. 90; Miller and Ginsburg, 'Restructuring Education and the State in England', p. 54.
65. Hatcher and Anderson, 'Labour's Transformation of the School System in England', p. 164.
66. '"Free up Curriculum" Teachers Say', *BBC News*, 26 September 2006.
67. Children, Schools and Families Committee, 'Testing and Assessment', pp. 12, 25.
68. Kozol, *The Shame of the Nation*, pp. 111–12.

69. George Wood, 'A View from the Field: NCLB's Effects on Classrooms and Schools', in Deborah Meier and George Wood (eds), *Many Children Left Behind: How the No Child Left Behind Act Is Damaging Our Children and Our Schools*, Boston, MA, Beacon Press, 2004, p. 39.

70. Kozol, *The Shame of the Nation*, pp. 112–13, 268.

71. Ibid., p. 133.

72. Elizabeth Jaeger, 'Silencing Teachers in an Era of Scripted Reading', *Rethinking Schools Online* 20 (3), 2006.

73. Kozol, *The Shame of the Nation*, pp. 71–2.

74. Ibid., p. 106.

75. Jones and Duceux, 'Neo-Liberalism in the Schools of Western Europe', pp. 103–4.

76. Cited in Berman, 'The Politics of American Education', p. 34.

77. Kathleen Vail, 'Core Comes to Crooksville', *American School Board Journal*, March 1997, http://asbj.com/199703/asbj0397.html

78. Power and Whitty, 'Teaching New Subjects?', p. 15.

79. The Qualifications and Curriculum Authority (QCA), 'About Us', 2006, http://www.qca.org.uk/7.html

80. Shor, *Culture Wars*, pp. 13, 23, 92; Stan Karp, 'Leaving Public Education Behind: The Bush Agenda in American Education', *Our Schools, Our Selves* 15 (3), 2006, p. 184.

81. Welch, *Class, Culture and the State in Australian Education*, p. 119.

82. Ibid., pp. 120–1.

83. Lynn Bell, 'Education Minister Calls for National Curriculum', *ABC Online*, 6 October 2006; AAP, 'Federal Takeover of Curriculum', *SBS World News Australia*, 6 October 2006.

84. Jewel Topsfield and David Rood, 'Lib Calls for National Curriculum', *Age*, 6 October 2006.

85. Shor, *Culture Wars*, p. 65.

86. Ibid., p. 11.

87. Sheils, 'Why Johnny Can't Write'.

88. Carmel Tebbutt, 'A Broad View Is the Key to the Best Education', *Sydney Morning Herald*, 13 October 2006, p. 13.

89. Justine Ferrari, 'Blainey to Lead History Review', *Australian*, 26 June 2007.

90. Joel Spring, *Political Agendas for Education: From the Religious Right to the Green Party*, Mahwah, NJ, Lawrence Erlbaum, 2002, pp. 69–71.

91. Barbara Miner, 'Testing: Full Speed Ahead', *Rethinking Schools Online* 14 (2), 1999.

92. M. Middleton quoted in Welch, *Class, Culture and the State in Australian Education*, p. 124.

93. The Business Roundtable (BRT), 'A Business Leader's Guide to Setting Academic Standards', Washington, DC, June 1996, p. 9.

94. Foundation for Teaching Economics et al., 'National Voluntary Content Standards for Pre-College Economics Education', 12 June 1998, http://www.fte.org/standard.html

95. Canadian Foundation for Economic Education (CFEE), 'EconomicsCanada: Introduction and Overview', 2004, http://www.cfee.org/economicscanada/intro2.html

96. National Council on Economic Education, 'About NCEE: Campaign for Economic Literacy', http://www.ncee.net/cel; NCEE, 'National Council on Economic Education', http://www.nationalcouncil.org; Mark Maier, 'Teaching About Stocks – for Fun and Propaganda', *Dollars & Sense*, March, 2001.

97. Foundation for Economic Education (FEE), 2004, http://www.fee.org

98. Ibid.

99. John J. Siegfried and Bonnie T. Meszaros, 'Voluntary Economics Content and Standards for America's Schools: Rationale and Development', *Journal of Economic Education* 29 (2), 1998.

100. Ibid.

101. NCEE, 'Survey of the States: Economic and Personal Finance Education in Our Nation's Schools in 2002', April 2003, p. 4, http://www.ncee.net/about/survey2002

102. Sam Dillon, 'Good Scores on National Economics Test', *New York Times*, 8 August 2007.

103. Mark Maier, 'Corporate Curriculum', *Rethinking Schools Online*, Summer 2002, http://www.rethinkingschools.org/archive/16_04/Corp164.shtml

11   TEACHING CORPORATE VALUES

1. Consumers Union Education Services (CUES), 'Captive Kids: Commercial Pressures on Kids at School', New York, 1995, p. 2.

2. D. Michael Fry, 'How Exxon's "Video for Students" Deals in Distortions', *Textbook Letter*, January–February 1993, http://www.textbookleague.org/36exx.htm

3. Ibid.

4. Sheila Harty, *Hucksters in the Classroom: A Review of Industry Propaganda in Schools*, Washington, DC, Center for Study of Responsive Law, 1979, p. 15.

5. John J. Fried, 'Ongoing Corporate Polluters Flood Schools with Environmental Lesson Aids', *Knight-Ridder/Tribune Business News*, 28 March 1994.

6. CUES, 'Captive Kids', pp. 1, 12–13.

7. Harty, *Hucksters in the Classroom*, p. 8.

8. Ibid.

9. Paola Totaro, 'Metherell's Rewrite Order Sparks Revolt', *Sydney Morning Herald*, 9 May 1990, p. 1.

10. Jacqueline Isles, 'Corporations in the Classroom', *Consuming Interest* 42, October 1989, p. 8.

11. David Shenk, 'The Pedagogy of Pasta Sauce; Pretending to Help Teachers, Campbell's Teaches Consumerism', *Harper's Magazine* 291, September 1995; Rhoda H. Karpatkin and Anita Holmes, 'Making Schools Ad-Free Zones', *Educational Leadership* 53 (1), 1995; Michael F. Jacobson and Laurie Ann Mazur, *Marketing Madness*, Boulder, CO, Westview Press, 1995, p. 31.

12. Weekly Reader Corporation (WRC), 'Welcome to Weekly Reader Publishing Group', 2007, http://www.weeklyreader.com/corporate/about.asp

13. Edith D. Balbach and Stanton A. Glantz, 'Tobacco Information in Two Grade School Newsweeklies: A Content Analysis', *American Journal of Public Health* 85 (12), 1995, p. 1652.

14. Weekly Reader Publishing (WRC), 'Teen Magazine Network', 2006, http://www.weeklyreader.com

15. Video Placement Worldwide (VPW), 'Opportunities for Sponsors', 2007, http://www. vpw.com/opportunities; Alex Molnar, 'The Ninth Annual Report on Schoolhouse Commercialism Trends: 2005–2006', Tempe, AZ, Commercialism in Education Research Unit (CERU), Arizona State University, November 2006, p. 18.

16. EdComs, 'What Is Edcoms?', 2007, http://www.edcoms.com/what_is_edcoms. html

17. Alex Molnar, *Giving Kids the Bu$iness: The Commercialization of America's Schools*, Boulder, CO, Westview, 1996, p. 36.

18. Scholastic, 'InSchool Marketing/Solutions', http://www.scholastic.com/ aboutscholastic/divisions/inschool_marketing.htm

19. Molnar, *Giving Kids the Bu$iness*, p. 31; Stephanie Dunnewind, 'Scholastic Wins Numbers Game in the Schools', *Seattle Times*, 24 September 2005.

20. Scholastic, 'Scholastic 6 & under Custom Marketing', http://www.scholastic.com/ aboutscholastic/divisions/six_and_under.htm

21. Quoted in Molnar, *Giving Kids the Bu$iness*, p. 30.

22. Jane Levine, 'Junk-Food Marketing Goes Elementary', *Education Digest* 65 (5), 2000, p. 33.

23. Martin Lindstrom, *Brand Child: Remarkable Insights into the Minds of Today's Global Kids and Their Relationships with Brands*, London, Kogan Page, 2003, p. 220.

24. Zoe Weil, 'The Business of Brainwashing', *Animals' Agenda* 20 (1), 2000, p. 30.

25. Levine, 'Junk-Food Marketing Goes Elementary', p. 33.

26. Juliet B. Schor, *Born to Buy: The Commercialized Child and the New Consumer Culture*, New York, Scribner, 2004, p. 93.

27. Kellogg's Australia, 'Occasional Snacks and Physical Activity', 2007, http://www. kidshealthand fitness.com.au

28. Ella Drauglis, 'NUT Advice on Using Commercial Materials in Schools', UK, National Union of Teachers, August 2003, p. 2.

29. Cited in National Union of Teachers, 'Education Not Exploitation', 9 November 2004, http://www.teachers.org.uk/resources/pdf/EXPLOITATION05.pdf

30. Katharine Ainger, 'Schools in a Spin', *New Internationalist*, July 2001, p. 6.

31. Nestlé, 'Russian Federation', http://www.community.nestle.com/Europe/ Russian+Federation/Nutrition+Education

32. Nestlé, 'Jamaica', http://www.community.nestle.com/Americas/Jamaica/ Nutrition+Education

33. Nestlé Australia, 'About AIS Classroom', http://www.nestle.com.au/Fun/AIS/About/ Default.htm

34. Molnar, 'The Ninth Annual Report on Schoolhouse Commercialism Trends', p. 36.

35. Quoted in David Lapp, 'Private Gain, Public Loss', *Environmental Action*, Spring 1994, p. 16.

36. Alex Molnar et al., 'At Sea in a Marketing-Saturated World: The Eleventh Annual Report on Schoolhouse Commercialism Trends: 2007–2008', Boulder, CO, and Tempe, AZ, Education Public Interest Center (EPIC) and Commercialism in Education Research Unit (CERU), September 2008, p. 28.

37. 'A Well Managed Forest Keeps Giving and Giving', Riegelwood, NC, International Paper, 2002, http://www.internationalpaper.com/PDF/PDFs_for_Forest/wellmanaged. pdf

38. 'Forestry Overview', Forest Way, WA, Weyerhaeuser Company, April 2007, http://www.weyerhaeuser.com/aboutus/facts/7.2_WYForestryOverview.pdf

39. American Forest & Paper Association, 'Forest Protection: Growing Tomorrow's Forests Today', Washington, DC, 2006, http://www.paperrecylces.org/issues/forest_protection.pdf

40. 'Forests for Generations: Managing Forests to Meet People's Needs and to Protect the Environment', Forest Way, WA, Weyerhaeuser Company, May 2004, http://www.weyerhaeuser.com/ourbusinesses/forestry/timberlands/sustainableforestry/pdfs/rgb.pdf

41. Jutta Kill and Ben Pearson, 'Forest Fraud: Say No to Fake Carbon Credits', Gloucestershire, UK, Fern and Sinks Watch, November 2003, p. 3, http://www.cdmwatch.org/files/forestfraud.pdf; Larry Lohmann, 'The Dyson Effect: Carbon "Offset" Forestry and the Privatization of the Atmosphere', *Corner House Briefing* 15, 1999.

42. Project Learning Tree, 'About PLT', http://www.plt.org/cms/pages/21_19_1.html

43. John Borowski, 'Please Read About Project Learning Tree', Audubon discussion list, 18 October 2001, http://list.audubon.org/wa.exe?A2=ind0110&L=audubon-chat&T=0&P=2568

44. Project Learning Tree, 'The PLT Education Operating Committee', http://www.plt.org/cms/pages/23_27_21.html

45. Canadian Forestry Association (CFA), 'Recover Me!', December 2006, p. 21.

46. CFA, 'Shrinking Habitat – Share the Space', December 2006, http://www.canadianforestry.com/pdfs/vol5_e.pdf/08_recover_me_e.pdf

47. National Association of Forest Industries (NAFI), 'Timbertrek Online: Quick Facts', http://www.timbertrek.com.au/quickfacts.asp?cDoc=qfstateharv

48. The Tasmanian Conservation Trust cited in The Wilderness Society (TWS), 'Submission to the Review of the RFA (Failures of the RFA)', Hobart, Tasmania, 29 June 2002.

49. 'A Well Managed Forest Keeps Giving and Giving'.

50. 'Harvest and Regeneration Methods', Forest Way, WA, Weyerhaeuser Company, April 2007, http://www.weyerhaeuser.com/aboutus/facts/7.4_HarvestRegeneration.pdf

51. NAFI, 'Timbertrek Online'.

52. Australian Academy of Science (AAS), 'Interviews with Australian Scientists – Dr Hugh Tyndale-Biscoe', http://www.science.org.au/scientists/noteshtb.htm

53. TWS, 'Submission to the Review of the RFA'.

54. NAFI, 'Timbertrek Online'.

55. ACF, 'Woodchipping the Facts', http://www.green.net.au/boycott/archive/woodchip.htm

56. CLEAR, 'Get 'Em While They're Young: Oil and Gas Industry to Target School Kids in Re-Focus of PR Campaign', *CLEAR View*, 2 March 1999.

57. Ratte quoted in ibid.

58. American Petroleum Institute, 'Classroom Energy!', http://www.classroom-energy.org/energy_101/aaas_module/index.html

59. Kenneth Saltman, *Collateral Damage: Corporatizing Public Schools – a Threat to Democracy*, Lanham, MD, Rowman & Littlefield, 2000, p. x.

60. Anne Hammond, *The Big Book of Oil and Gas*, Canberra and Melbourne, Australian Institute of Petroleum, Australian Petroleum Production & Exploration Association Ltd, The Australian Gas Association, undated, p. 2.

61. Sian Powell and Bernard Zuel, 'Marketers' Influence over Young Challenged', *Sydney Morning Herald*, 3 September 1993.

62. 'Australia's Petroleum Industry Goes Back to School', *Petroleum Gazette* 30 (1), 1995, p. 18.

63. Quoted in The Center for Commercial-Free Public Education (CCPE), 'Consumers or Citizens: An Unplug Report', 1996, p. 3.

64. American Coal Foundation (ACF), 'Coal and the Environment: Land and Air', 2007, http://www.teachcoal.org/aboutcoal/articles/coalenv.html

65. Hammond, *The Big Book of Oil and Gas*, p. 14.

66. Australian Institute of Petroleum (AIP), *Why Keep Lead in Petrol? A Question That Concerns Your Car, Your Pocket, Your Environment, Your Country's Energy Supplies*, Melbourne, 1981.

67. Laurie David, 'Science a La Joe Camel', *Washington Post*, 26 November 2006.

68. Saltman, *Collateral Damage*, p. xi.

69. ExxonMobil, 'Energy and the Environment', http://www.energychest.net/energy_and_the_environment/index.html

70. Project Learning Tree, 'Energy & Me: A Successful Partnership', http://www.plt.org/cms/pages/21_44_19.html

71. American Chemistry Council (ACC), 'Hands on Plastics Jr.: Elementary Science Education Activities & Games', 2007, http://www.americanchemistry.com/s_plastics/hop_jr/activities/index.html

72. Plastics and Chemicals Industry Association of Australia (PACIA), 'Education', http://www.pacia.org.au/index.cfm?mmid=004

73. ACC, 'Facts About Plastic', 2007, http://www.plasticsresource.com/s_plasticsresource/sec.asp?TRACKID=&CID=127&DID=229

74. Karen Pearce, 'No Bag, Thanks!', Australian Broadcasting Corporation (ABC), http://www.abc.net.au/science/features/bags

75. Plastics and Chemicals Industry Association of Australia (PACIA), 'Plastics – Materials for Our Future', http://www.pacia.org.au/index.cfm?menuaction=mem&mmid=004&mid=004.015

76. Richard Lindsay Stover et al., 'Report of the Berkeley Plastics Task Force', Berkeley, CA, The Ecology Center, 8 April 1996, p. 11; 'Fall 1998 Greenwash Award', Corporate Watch, 1998, http://www.corpwatch.org/greenwash/education.html

77. Sue Bennett, 'PVC: Shaping Your World', Melbourne, ICI Australia, undated.

78. Chemical Industry Education Centre (CIEC), 'What Is PVC?', http://www.sustainability-ed.org/pages/pvc1-1.htm

79. ACC, 'Plastic Disposal', 2007, http://www.plasticsresource.com/s_plasticsresource/sec.asp?TRACKID=&CID=88&DID=129

80. Society of the Plastics Industry (SPI), 'Don't Let a Good Thing Go to Waste', 2005, http://www.plasticsindustry.org/outreach/school/DontLetaGoodThing.pdf

81. ACC, 'Background on Plastics and Resource Conservation', 1999, http://www.plasticsresource.com/s_plasticsresource/sec.asp?TRACKID=&CID=131&DID=233

82. Sustain Ability International, 'Ollies World', 2007, http://www.olliesworld.com

83. Marianne Manilov quoted in CCPE, 'Consumers or Citizens'.

84. Sharon Beder, *Free Market Missionaries: The Corporate Manipulation of Community Values*, London, Earthscan, 2006.

85. National Council on Economic Education, 'About NCEE: Campaign for Economic Literacy', http://www.ncee.net/cel; NCEE, 'Affiliated Councils & Centers', http://www.ncee.net/network/network.php; 'Economics America', http://www.economicsamerica.org/schools.html

86. NCEE, 'EconomicsInternational', http://www.ncee.net/ei; NCEE, 'National Council on Economic Education', http://www.nationalcouncil.org

87. The Foundation for Teaching Economics (FTE), 'Annual Review', 2002, http://www.fte.org

88. FTE, 'Big Business and Regulation', 1999, http://fte.org/teachers/programs/history/lessons/lesson04.htm

89. FTE, 'The Great Depression and the New Deal', 1999, http://fte.org/teachers/programs/history/lessons/lesson09.htm

90. John Templeton Foundation, 2004, http://www.templeton.org; FTE, 'Annual Review'.

91. Canadian Foundation for Economic Education, 'About CFEE', http://www.cfee.org/en/about.shtml

92. Centre for Economic Education (CEE), http://www.cee.org.au

93. CEE, 'International Trade', http://www.cee.org.au/globalisation/trade.htm

94. Securities Industry Foundation for Economic Education (SIFEE), 'Teachers Only', http://www.smgww.org/frm_teachers.html

95. SIFEE, 'The Stock Market Game', 2003, http://www.smgww.org.

96. Mark Maier, 'Teaching About Stocks – for Fun and Propaganda', *Dollars & Sense*, March 2001.

97. Australian Securities Exchange (ASX), 'All About the ASX Schools Sharemarket Game', https://www9.asx.com.au/Smg/SchoolInfo; James Cockington, 'Schoolkids Beat the Market', *Sydney Morning Herald, Money*, 6 December 2006, p. 3.

98. Pro Share, 'The Proshare Portfolio Challenge', http://www.proshare.org/comps/portfolio.asp

99. Pro Share, 'At School', http://www.proshare.org/about/ar01-02/school.asp; 'Your Money, Be Wise', http://yourmoneybewise.org

100. National Union of Teachers, 'Academies', January 2005, http://www.teachers.org.uk/story.php?id=2704

101. Maier, 'Teaching About Stocks'.

102. Ibid.

103. SIFEE, 'Teachers Only'.

104. Isles, 'Corporations in the Classroom', p. 8.

105. NSW Department of Education and Training, 'Online Resources', http://www.dse.nsw.edu.au/staff/F1.0/F1.3/online/onlinesearch.cgi

106. See, for example, Carolyn Glascodine, *Essentially Oil and Gas: An Australian Petroleum Industry Resource for Secondary Schools*, Melbourne and Canberra, Australian Institute of Petroleum, Australian Petroleum Production & Exploration Association Ltd, 1998, and Anne Hammond, *Our World: A Schools' Project for Upper Primary Schools*, Melbourne and Canberra, Australian Institute of Petroleum, Australian Petroleum Production & Exploration Association Ltd, undated.

107. The Association for Science Education (ASE), 'Welcome to Schoolscience.Co.Uk', 2007, http://www.schoolscience.co.uk

108. National Science Teachers Association (NSTA), 'The Power of Partnerships: 2001–2002 Annual Report', August 2002, http://www.nsta.org/pdfs/PowerOfPartnerships02. pdf

109. John Borowski, 'World's Largest Science Teachers' Organization Awash in Denials', *Truthout*, 13 December 2006, http://www.truthout.org/cgi-bin/artman/exec/view. cgi/67/24453

110. David, 'Science a La Joe Camel'.

111. John Borowski, 'Largest Science Teachers Organization Rejects Gore Video ... Why?', *Truthout*, 28 November 2006, http://www.truthout.org/cgi-bin/artman/exec/view. cgi/66/24120

112. David, 'Science a La Joe Camel'.

113. Quoted in NSTA, 'The Power of Partnerships', p. 11.

114. David, 'Science a La Joe Camel'.

12   PRIVATISING SCHOOLS

1. David Moberg, 'How Edison Survived', *Nation*, 15 March 2004, p. 22.

2. Ibid., p. 22.

3. Nelson D. Schwartz, 'The Nine Lives of Chris Whittle', *Fortune*, 27 October 2003.

4. Brian O'Reilly, 'Why Edison Doesn't Work', *Fortune*, 9 December 2002.

5. Chuck Sudetic, 'Reading, Writing, and Revenue', *Mother Jones*, May/June, 2001, http://www.motherjones.com/news/feature/2001/05/edison.html

6. *New York Times* quoted in Kenneth Saltman, *The Edison Schools: Corporate Schooling and the Assault on Public Education*, New York, NY, Routledge, 2005, p. 50.

7. Barbara Miner, 'For-Profits Target Education', in Alfie Kohn and Patrick Shannon (eds), *Education, Inc. Turning Learning into a Business*, revised edn, Portsmouth, NH, Heinemann, 2002, p. 136.

8. Paul Socolar, 'Edison Takes Aim at Philly', *Rethinking Schools*, Winter 2001/2, http://www.rethinkingschools.org/archive/16_02/edis162.shtml; Philadelphia Social Workers Club, 'A Philadelphia Story', *Political Affairs Magazine*, December 2002, http://www.politicalaffairs.net/article/articlevew/13/1/16

9. Alex Molnar, *School Commercialism: From Democratic Ideal to Market Commodity*, New York, Routledge, 2005, p. 99.

10. Saltman, *The Edison Schools*, p. 54.

11. Molnar, *School Commercialism*, p. 106.

12. Saltman, *The Edison Schools*, p. 55; Moberg, 'How Edison Survived', p. 22; Sudetic, 'Reading, Writing, and Revenue'; Tali Woodward, 'Edison's Failing Grade', CorpWatch, 20 June 2002, http://www.corpwatch.org/article.php?id=2688

13. Quoted in Saltman, *The Edison Schools*, p. 74.

14. Quoted in ibid., p. 29.

15. Ibid., pp. 2, 40; Parents Advocating School Accountability (PASA), 'Edison Schools' False Numbers Obscure Contract Losses', San Francisco, 20 June 2005, http://www. pasasf.org/edison/pdfs/pr063005.pdf

16. Edison Schools, 'Edison Schools', 2007, http://www.edisonschools.com; Alex Molnar et al., 'Profiles of for-Profit Education Management Organizations: Eighth Annual

Report 2005–2006', Tempe, AZ, Education Policy Studies Laboratory, Arizona State University, May 2006, pp. 7, 29.

17. O'Reilly, 'Why Edison Doesn't Work'.

18. Alex Molnar et al., 'Profiles of for-Profit Education Management Organizations: Ninth Annual Report 2006–2007', Tempe, AZ, Education Policy Studies Laboratory, Arizona State University, May 2007, p. 13.

19. Edison Schools, 'Edison Schools'.

20. Ibid.

21. 'US Firm to Manage UK State School', *BBC News*, 23 April 2007.

22. Molnar et al., 'Profiles of for-Profit Education Management Organizations: Eighth Annual Report 2005–2006', pp. 8, 12; 'Charter Schools', *Education Week* 27 (5), 2007; National Assessment of Educational Progress (NAEP), 'America's Charter Schools: Results from the NAEP 2003 Pilot Study', US Department of Education 2003, p. 3.

23. 'Charter Schools', *EPE Research Center*, 10 September 2004, http://www.edweek. org/rc/issues/charter-schools

24. Saltman, *The Edison Schools*, pp. 123–6.

25. 'Public Schools Inc.: Inside Edison's Schools', *Frontline*, PBS, 3 July 2003, http://www. pbs.org/wgbh/pages/frontline/shows/edison/; Saltman, *The Edison Schools*, p. 67.

26. NAEP, 'America's Charter Schools', p. 1.

27. Saltman, *The Edison Schools*, pp. 2, 168.

28. Lisa Swinehart, 'Charter Schools Don't Solve Real Problems', *Humanist* 65 (5), 2005; Chris Moran, 'Push Is on for Charter Schools', *San Diego Union-Tribune*, 22 October 2003.

29. Gary Miron and Brooks Applegate, 'Teacher Attrition in Charter Schools', Education Policy Research Unit (EPRU), Arizona State University and Education and the Public Interest Center (EPIC), University of Colorado at Boulder, May 2007.

30. Ibid.

31. Saltman, *The Edison Schools*, p. 15.

32. W.C. Symonds, A.T. Palmer, D. Lindorf, J. McCann, 'For-Profit Schools: They're Spreading Fast', *Business Week*, 7 February 2000.

33. Moberg, 'How Edison Survived', p. 22; Saltman, *The Edison Schools*, p. 124.

34. Woodward, 'Edison's Failing Grade'.

35. Knowledge is Power Program, 'KIPP: Knowledge Is Power Program', http://www. kippschools.org

36. Jeanne Russell, 'Charter Schools Sets Kids' Sights on College', *San Antonio Express News*, 9 January 2005.

37. Molnar et al., 'Profiles of for-Profit Education Management Organizations: Eighth Annual Report', p. 10.

38. Ed Muir, 'Are Charter Schools a Threat?' *American Teacher* 91 (4), 2007, p. 22.

39. Jay Mathews, 'Charter School Effort Gets $65 Million Lift', *Washington Post*, 20 March 2007, p. A01.

40. Moberg, 'How Edison Survived', p. 22.

41. 'Public Schools Inc.', *Frontline*, PBS.

42. Quoted in Sudetic, 'Reading, Writing, and Revenue'.

43. Molnar et al., 'Profiles of for-Profit Education Management Organizations: Eighth Annual Report', p. 10.

44. Moran, 'Push Is on for Charter Schools'.

45. Sam Dillon, 'Collapse of 60 Charter Schools Leaves Californians Scrambling', *New York Times*, 17 September 2006, p. 1.
46. Joetta L. Sack, 'Calif. Charter Failure Affects 10,000 Students', *Education Week*, 1 September 2004, http://www.edweek.org/ew/articles/2004/09/01/01cca.h24.html
47. 'California Charter Schools Accused of Corruption', CNN.com, 10 August 2006.
48. Martin Carnoy et al., 'The Charter School Dust-Up: Examining the Evidence on Enrollment and Achievement', Washington, DC, Economic Policy Institute 2005, p. 3.
49. Diana Jean Schemo, 'A Second Report Shows Charter School Students Not Performing as Well as Other Students', *New York Times*, 16 December 2004.
50. Editorial, 'Reining in Charter Schools', *New York Times*, 10 May 2006.
51. Cited in 'Charter Schools', *EPE Research Center*.
52. NAEP, 'America's Charter Schools', p. 1.
53. Schemo, 'A Second Report...'.
54. Carnoy et al., 'The Charter School Dust-Up', p. 2.
55. Editorial, 'Reining in Charter Schools'.
56. Gary Miron et al., 'Evaluating the Impact of Charter Schools on Student Achievement: A Longitudinal Look at the Great Lakes States', Education Policy Research Unit (EPRU), Arizona State University and Education and the Public Interest Center (EPIC), University of Colorado at Boulder, June 2007.
57. Susan Snyder, 'Private Managers in District Face Cuts', *Philadelphia Inquirer*, 15 November 2006.
58. Barbara Miner, 'Business Goes to School: The for-Profit Corporate Drive to Run Public Schools', *Multinational Monitor*, January/February 2002, p. 15.
59. Andrew J. Rotherham, 'Virtual Schools, Real Innovation', *New York Times*, 7 April 2006; Molnar et al., 'Profiles of for-Profit Education Management Organizations: Eighth Annual Report', p. 11.
60. Glenn Cook, 'The Cyber Charter Challenge', *American School Board Journal*, September 2002, http://www.asbj.com/specialreports/0902Special%20Reports/S2.html
61. Nancy Mitchell, 'Online Schools Slammed', *Rocky Mountain News*, 12 December 2006.
62. Andrew Trotter, 'K12 Inc. Scraps India Outsourcing', *Education Week*, 10 September 2008.
63. Quoted in Saltman, *The Edison Schools*, p. 72.
64. Molnar et al., 'Profiles of for-Profit Education Management Organizations: Eighth Annual Report', p. 10.
65. 'Barack Obama on Education', *On the Issues*, 2008, http://www.ontheissues.org/2008/Barack_Obama_Education.htm
66. Geoff Whitty, *Making Sense of Education Policy: Studies in the Sociology and Politics of Education*, London, Sage, 2002, p. 51.
67. Richard Hatcher and Bill Anderson, 'Labour's Transformation of the School System in England', *Our Schools, Our Selves* 15 (3), 2006, p. 167.
68. Capita Education Resourcing, 'Education Recruitment Agency for UK Teaching Jobs and Teacher Recruitment', 2006, http://www.capitaers.co.uk
69. Jenny Ozga, 'Education Governance in the United Kingdom: The Modernisation Project', *European Educational Research Journal* 1 (2), 2002, p. 337.

70. Rebecca Smithers, 'Failed Academy Has Not Got Any Better, Says Ofsted', *Guardian*, 20 March 2006; Francis Beckett, 'Why the Academies' Programme Is Unfair', *Independent*, 22 April 2007.

71. Department for Education and Skills, 'Five Year Strategy for Children and Learners', July 2004, p. 51; DfES, 'Higher Standards, Better Schools for All: More Choice for Parents and Pupils', October 2005, p. 3.

72. DfES, 'The Standards Site', http://www.standards.dfes.gov.uk/academies

73. Hatcher and Anderson, 'Labour's Transformation of the School System in England', p. 168.

74. Ibid., p. 168; DfES, 'The Standards Site'.

75. Rebecca Smithers and Matthew Taylor, 'The People Versus Academies', *Guardian*, 13 June 2006.

76. Roy Hattersley, 'And Now, over to Our Sponsors', *Guardian*, 6 June 2005; Alex Molnar et al., 'At Sea in a Marketing-Saturated World: The Eleventh Annual Report on Schoolhouse Commercialism Trends: 2007–2008', Boulder, CO, and Tempe, AZ, Education Public Interest Center (EPIC) and Commercialism in Education Research Unit (CERU), September 2008, p. 32.

77. Quoted in Rebecca Smithers, 'Researchers Raise More Doubts on City Academies', *Guardian*, 30 June 2005.

78. Beckett, 'Why the Academies' Programme Is Unfair'.

79. Matthew Taylor, 'Teachers' Views Harden on Parent Choice and Academy Schools', *Guardian*, 6 January 2006.

80. Gary Eason, 'School Results Tables under Fire', *BBC News*, 19 January 2006.

81. Alexandra Smith, 'Audit Office Criticises Spiralling Cost of Academies', *Guardian*, 23 February 2007.

82. Matthew Taylor, 'Academies Fail to Improve Results, Study Says', *Guardian*, 22 May 2006.

83. Ibid.

84. Alexandra Smith, 'Concern over High Academy Exclusion Rates', *Guardian*, 29 January 2007.

85. Liz Ford, 'Ofsted Fails Academy School', *Guardian*, 27 May 2005.

86. 'Treasury Paid £1.5m to Rescue Failing Academy 10 Days before Election', *Times*, 30 April 2006.

87. Ford, 'Ofsted Fails Academy School'.

88. Smithers, 'Failed Academy Has Not Got Any Better'.

89. David Hencke and Matthew Taylor, 'MPs Reveal £101m Cost of Two Academies', *Guardian*, 17 October 2006.

90. Press Association, 'City Academy Criticised for "Exceptionally Low" Standards', *Guardian*, 22 February 2006.

91. Ofsted, 'The Business Academy Bexley: Inspection Report', London, Office for Standards in Education, 2005.

92. Tony Blair, 'PM speech at the Business Academy in Bexley, Kent', 18 September 2003, http://www.number10.gov.uk/Page4492

93. Hencke and Taylor, 'MPs Reveal £101m Cost of Two Academies'.

94. Matthew Taylor, 'City Academies Accused of Deserting Poor', *Guardian*, 31 October 2005.

95. Smith, 'Audit Office Criticises Spiralling Cost of Academies'.

96. Matthew Taylor and Rob Evans, 'Sponsors Fail to Hand over Academy Cash', *Guardian*, 3 May 2006.
97. Molnar et al., 'At Sea in a Marketing-Saturated World', p. 32.
98. Alexandra Smith, 'What Are Trust Schools?' *Guardian*, 9 February 2007, http://education.guardian.co.uk/print/0,,329711261-113799,00.html
99. DfES, 'What Trust Schools Offer', February 2006, p. 2.
100. Mike Baker, 'Who Will Run "Trust" Schools?', *BBC News*, 10 March 2006, http://news.bbc.co.uk/go/pr/fr/-/2/hi/uk_news/education/4794646.stm
101. Taylor, 'Teachers' Views Harden on Parent Choice and Academy Schools'.
102. Hatcher and Anderson, 'Labour's Transformation of the School System in England', p. 176.
103. Tony Blair in DfES, 'Higher Standards, Better Schools for All', p. 1.
104. DfES, 'Five Year Strategy for Children and Learners', pp. 7–8; Kevin Farnsworth, 'Business in Education: A Reassessment of the Contribution of Outsourcing to LEA Performance', *Journal of Education Policy* 21 (4), 2006; Francis Beckett, 'How the Private Sector Failed to Deliver', *New Statesman*, 14 April 2003, p. 29; National Union of Teachers (NUT), 'Outsourcing', January 2005, www.teachers.org.uk/resources/pdf/priv3-updatejan05.doc
105. Ulf Fredriksson, 'Studying the Supra-National in Education: GATS, Education and Teacher Union Policies', *European Educational Research Journal* 3 (2), 2004, p. 423.
106. Beckett, 'How the Private Sector Failed to Deliver', p. 28.
107. George Monbiot, *Captive State: The Corporate Takeover of Britain*, London, Pan Books, 2000, pp. 335–6; Bernard Regan, 'Education for Sale', 2002, http://www.ett.org.uk/art50_3_br.html
108. Farnsworth, 'Business in Education', p. 486.
109. NUT, 'The Privatisation of Education – an Overview', 8 July 2004, p. 2.
110. Beckett, 'How the Private Sector Failed to Deliver', p. 28; NUT, 'Outsourcing'.
111. NUT, 'Outsourcing'.
112. Kevin Toolis, 'Will They Ever Learn?' *Guardian*, 22 November 2003.
113. Ibid.
114. Farnsworth, 'Business in Education'.
115. Alex Molnar, Gary Miron and Jessica Urschel, 'Profiles of for-Profit Education Management Organizations', EPIC and CERU, Arizona State University, AZ, July 2008, pp. 1–2, 6–8.
116. Ibid., p. 14; Miner, 'For-profits target education', p. 134.
117. Ibid.
118. O'Reilly, 'Why Edison Doesn't Work'.
119. Molnar et al., 'Profiles of for-Profit Education Management Organizations', pp. 1–4.
120. People for the American Way Foundation (PFAW), 'The Voucher Veneer: The Deeper Agenda to Privatize Public Education', Washington, DC, July 2003, p. 23.
121. Quoted in 'The Great Education Scandal', *New Internationalist*, August 1999, http://www.newint.org/issue315/keynote.htm
122. Patricia Cazares, 'The Private Management of Public Schools: The Hartford, Connecticut, Experience', paper presented at the Annual Meeting of the American Research Association, Chicago, IL, 25–28 March 1997, p. 5.

123. National Education Association, 'For-Profit Management of Schools', CorpWatch, 8 July 1998; 'The Great Education Scandal'.

124. Barbara Miner, 'For-Profit Firm on the Ropes', *Rethinking Schools Online* 14 (3), 2000.

125. Woodward, 'Edison's Failing Grade'.

126. Hedley Beare, '"Enterprise": The New Metaphor for Schooling in a Post-Industrial Society', in Tony Townsend (ed.), *The Primary School in Changing Times: The Australian Experience*, London, Routledge, 1998, p. 15.

127. Corporate Watch UK, 'School Meals', September 2005, http://www.corporatewatch.org/?lid=2045

128. Quoted in ibid.

129. Fredriksson, 'Studying the Supra-National in Education', p. 428.

130. Ann Morrow et al., 'Public Education: From Public Domain to Private Enterprise?', in Alan Reid (ed.), *Going Public: Education Policy and Public Education in Australia*, Canberra, Australian Curriculum Studies Association (ACSA), 1998, pp. 9–10.

131. Larry Kuehn, 'The New Right Agenda and Teacher Resistance in Canadian Education', *Our Schools, Our Selves* 15(3), 2006, pp. 130–1.

13   TURNING SCHOOLS INTO MARKETS

1. Jaclyn Fierman, 'Giving Parents a Choice of Schools', *Fortune*, 4 December 1989.

2. Kirsti Melville, 'Schools of the Third Millennium', *Background Briefing, ABC Radio National*, 19 July 1998, http://www.abc.net.au/rn/talks/bbing/stories/s11343.htm

3. John Barrington, 'Educational Reform in New Zealand', in Mark B. Ginsburg (ed.), *Understanding Educational Reform in Global Context*, New York, Garland Publishing, 1991, p. 304.

4. Edward B. Fiske and Helen F. Ladd, 'A Distant Laboratory', *Education Week*, 17 May 2000, http://www.edweek.org/ew/articles/2000/05/17/36fiske.h19.html; Cathy Wylie, 'Ten Years On: How Schools View Educational Reform', Wellington, New Zealand Council for Educational Research, 1999, p. xix.

5. Geoff Whitty, *Making Sense of Education Policy: Studies in the Sociology and Politics of Education*, London, Sage, 2002, p. 56.

6. Simon Marginson, *Markets in Education*, Sydney, Allen & Unwin, 1997, p. 178.

7. Fiske and Ladd, 'A Distant Laboratory'.

8. Ibid.; Wylie, 'Ten Years On', pp. xv–xx.

9. Fiske and Ladd, 'A Distant Laboratory'.

10. Cathy Wylie, 'Can Vouchers Deliver Better Education? A Review of the Literature: With Special Reference to New Zealand', Wellington, New Zealand Council for Educational Research, 1998, pp. 14–15.

11. Whitty, *Making Sense of Education Policy*, p. 57.

12. Gerard Noonan, 'Not So Great a Jump from Dem Ol' Days', *Sydney Morning Herald*, 10 March 2008, p. 5.

13. Natalie Lacireno-Paquet and Charleen Brantley, 'Who Chooses Schools, and Why?', Education Policy Research Unit, Arizona State University and Education and Public Interest Center, University of Colorado, January 2008, p. 5.

14. Fiske and Ladd, 'A Distant Laboratory'; David Hill, 'Global Neo-Liberalism and the Perversion of Education', Reclaim Our Education Conference, University of East London, 2000, p. 5, http://www.ieps.org.uk/PDFs/hill2002.pdf

15. Wylie, 'Can Vouchers Deliver Better Education?', p. 9.
16. People for the American Way Foundation (PFAW), 'Unaccountable by Design: Corporate Tuition Tax Credit Schemes Drain Millions from States', Washington, DC, September 2003, p. 1.
17. Whitty, *Making Sense of Education Policy*, p. 47.
18. Sharon Gewirtz, Stephen J. Ball and Richard Bowe, *Markets, Choice and Equity in Education*, Buckingham, Open University Press, 1995, p. 90.
19. Australian Senate, 'Not a Level Playing Field: Private and Commercial Funding in Government Schools', Canberra, Senate Employment, Workplace Relations, Small Business and Education Committee, June 1997, chapter 1.
20. John Merrifield et al., 'Why Canadian Education Isn't Improving', Fraser Institute, September 2006, http://www.fraserinstitute.org/researchandpublications/publications/3152.aspx
21. Mark Harrison, 'What If Supermarkets Were Run Like Schools?' School Choices 1998, http://www.schoolchoices.org/roo/harris1.htm
22. Whitty, *Making Sense of Education Policy*, p. 46.
23. Raewyn Connell, 'The New Right Triumphant: The Privatization Agenda and Public Education in Australia', *Our Schools, Our Selves* 15 (3), 2006, p. 145.
24. Dan Lips and Evan Feinberg, 'School Choice: A Progress Report', *USA Today*, January 2007.
25. Jodi Wilgoren, 'Schools Are Now Markets Where Choice Is Taking Hold', *New York Times*, 20 April 2000.
26. Fierman, 'Giving Parents a Choice of Schools'.
27. Cited in Whitty, *Making Sense of Education Policy*, p. 52.
28. Gewirtz et al., *Markets, Choice and Equity in Education*, pp. 91–4, 134; Wilgoren, 'Schools Are Now Markets Where Choice Is Taking Hold'.
29. Jane Kenway and Lindsay Fitzclarence, 'Consuming Children? Public Education as a Market Commodity', in Alan Reid (ed.), *Going Public: Education Policy and Public Education in Australia*, Deakin West, ACT, Australian Curriculum Studies Association and Centre for the Study of Public Education, University of South Australia, 1998, p. 50.
30. Gewirtz et al., *Markets, Choice and Equity in Education*, pp. 127, 131–2.
31. Ibid., p. 130.
32. Kenway and Fitzclarence, 'Consuming Children? Public Education as a Market Commodity', p. 49.
33. Ibid., p. 50.
34. Gewirtz et al., *Markets, Choice and Equity in Education*, pp. 135–6.
35. Ibid., pp. 158–9.
36. John Bradshaw (ed.), *The Well Being of Children in the UK*, 2nd edn, Plymouth, UK, Save the Children, 2005.
37. Connell, 'The New Right Triumphant', p. 150.
38. Fiske and Ladd, 'A Distant Laboratory'.
39. Kenway and Fitzclarence, 'Consuming Children? Public Education as a Market Commodity', p. 54.
40. Whitty, *Making Sense of Education Policy*, pp. 52–4.
41. Cited in ibid., pp. 55–6.
42. Ibid., p. 54.
43. Connell, 'The New Right Triumphant', p. 151.

44. Bob Connell, 'A Moment of Danger', *Education Links*, Spring 1998, p. 11.
45. Gewirtz et al., *Markets, Choice and Equity in Education*, pp. 139–41, 168–72.
46. 'Pupils "Are Urged to Drop Maths"', *BBC News*, 24 April 2007.
47. Gewirtz et al., *Markets, Choice and Equity in Education*, p. 160.
48. Kenneth Howe et al., 'School Choice Crucible: A Case Study of Boulder Valley', in Alfie Kohn and Patrick Shannon (eds), *Education, Inc. Turning Learning into a Business*, revised edn, Portsmouth, NH, Heinemann, 2002.
49. Dave Toke, *Green Politics and Neo-Liberalism*, London, Macmillan, 2000, pp. 124–5.
50. Jonathan Kozol, *The Shame of the Nation: The Restoration of Apartheid Schooling in America*, New York, Crown Publishers, 2005, pp. 137, 203.
51. 'Primary Teaching "Varies Widely"', *BBC News*, 3 January 2007.
52. Gewirtz et al., *Markets, Choice and Equity in Education*, p. 163.
53. 'The Problem with School "Choice"', *BBC News*, 3 March 2007.
54. 'Schools "Selecting by Back Door"', *BBC News*, 31 May 2007.
55. 'School Admissions Rules Finalised', *BBC News*, 10 January 2007.
56. Suzanne Keen, 'Passing the Funding Test', *Australian Educator*, Spring 2005, p. 4.
57. Simon Marginson, 'Putting the "Public" Back into Public Education', in Reid (ed.), *Going Public*, p. 75.
58. Linda Darling-Hammond, 'From "Separate but Equal" to "No Child Left Behind"', in Deborah Meier and George Wood (eds), *Many Children Left Behind: How the No Child Left Behind Act Is Damaging Our Children and Our Schools*, Boston, MA, Beacon Press, 2004, p. 6.
59. David C. Berliner and Bruce J. Biddle, *The Manufactured Crisis: Myths, Fraud, and the Attack on America's Public Schools*, Cambridge, MA, Perseus Books, 1995, p. 58.
60. Connell, 'The New Right Triumphant', p. 146.
61. Ann Morrow et al., 'Public Education: From Public Domain to Private Enterprise?', in Reid (ed.), *Going Public*, pp. 9, 12; Anthony Welch, *Class, Culture and the State in Australian Education: Reform or Crisis?*, Frankfurt am Main, Peter Lang, p. 210.
62. Morrow et al., 'Public Education', pp. 9–10, 12.
63. Connell, 'The New Right Triumphant', pp. 146, 149; Morrow et al., 'Public Education', p. 12; Anna Patty, 'Low-Income Families Turn to Private Schools', *Sydney Morning Herald*, 24 July 2006, p. 5; AAP, 'Low Birth Rate to Hit Schools', *Sydney Morning Herald*, 20 July 2006, p. 3; Linda Doherty, 'Push for Values Drives Public School Exodus', *Sydney Morning Herald*, 9 August 2004, p. 1.
64. Larry Kuehn, 'The New Right Agenda and Teacher Resistance in Canadian Education', *Our Schools, Our Selves* 15 (3), 2006, pp. 130–1.
65. Véronique Brouillette, 'The Centrale Des Syndicats Du Québec and the Struggle against Neo-Liberal Schooling', *Our Schools, Our Selves* 15 (3), 2006, pp. 120–1.
66. Henry Levin cited in Marginson, *Markets in Education*, p. 180.
67. Merrifield et al., 'Why Canadian Education Isn't Improving'.
68. Erik C. Owens, 'Taking the "Public" out of Our Schools: The Political, Constitutional and Civic Implications of Private School Vouchers', *Journal of Church & State* 44 (4), 2002.
69. Marginson, *Markets in Education*; Owens, 'Taking the "Public" out of Our Schools', p. 89.

70. Martin Carnoy, 'National Voucher Plans in Chile and Sweden: Did Privatization Reforms Make for Better Education?' *Comparative Education Review* 42 (3), 1998; Wylie, 'Can Vouchers Deliver Better Education?', pp. 71–2.

71. Ibid.

72. PFAW, 'A Brief History of Vouchers', Washington, DC, 21 August 2003, p. 4.

73. Lips and Feinberg, 'School Choice: A Progress Report'.

74. Miner, 'A Brief History of Milwaukee's Voucher Program', *Rethinking Schools Online* 20 (3), 2006; PFAW, 'History of Failed Vouchers and Tax Credits' 2002, pp. 2, 5 http://www.pfaw.org/pfaw/general/default.aspx?oid=2959; Martin Carnoy, 'Do School Vouchers Improve Student Performance?', *American Prospect*, 1–15 January 2001, p. 43.

75. Ibid.

76. American Federation of Teachers, 'School Vouchers: The Research Track Record', Washington, DC, 2005, p. 3.

77. Barbara Miner, 'Keeping Public Schools Public: Free-Market Education', *Rethinking Schools Online* 20 (1), 2005; Miner, 'A Brief History of Milwaukee's Voucher Program'.

78. Miner, 'Keeping Public Schools Public'.

79. PFAW, 'The Voucher Veneer: The Deeper Agenda to Privatize Public Education', Washington, DC, July 2003, p. 16.

80. Quoted in Miner, 'Keeping Public Schools Public'.

81. Quoted in PFAW, 'The Voucher Veneer', p. 16.

82. Cited in Carnoy, 'Do School Vouchers Improve Student Performance?', p. 43.

83. Cited in ibid., p. 43.

84. Ibid.

85. American Federation of Teachers, 'School Vouchers', p. 4.

86. Wylie, 'Can Vouchers Deliver Better Education?', p. 73.

87. PFAW, 'Unaccountable by Design', pp. 9–10.

88. Owens, 'Taking the "Public" out of Our Schools'.

89. Wylie, 'Can Vouchers Deliver Better Education?', pp. 7, 12.

90. Berliner and Biddle, *The Manufactured Crisis*, p. 175.

91. PFAW, 'Flaws and Failings', Washington, DC, February 2005, pp. 2–3.

92. PFAW, 'Unaccountable by Design', p. 4.

93. PFAW, 'The Voucher Veneer', p. 22.

94. Jeffrey R. Henig, *Rethinking School Choice: Limits of the Market Metaphor*, Princeton, NJ, Princeton University Press, 1994, p. 65.

95. PFAW, 'Unaccountable by Design', pp. 2–3.

96. Lyndsay Connors, 'There's a Class Act in Education but It Must Be Defended', *Sydney Morning Herald*, 5 July 2004, p. 11.

97. Kenway and Fitzclarence, 'Consuming Children? Public Education as a Market Commodity', p. 48.

98. Sharon Gewirtz et al., *Markets, Choice and Equity in Education*, Buckingham, Open University Press, 1995, p. 21; Clara Morgan, 'A Retrospective Look at Educational Reforms in Ontario', *Our Schools, Our Selves* 15 (2), 2006, p. 134; Kuehn, 'The New Right Agenda', pp. 137–8.

99. Pat Thomson, 'Thoroughly Modern Management and a Cruel Accounting', in Reid (ed.), *Going Public*, p. 44.

100. Michael Engel, *The Struggle for Control of Public Education: Market Ideology Vs Democratic Values*, Philadelphia, Temple University Press, 2000, p. 69.

14   PRIVATISATION PROPONENTS

1. 'Mass-Producing Excellence', *Philanthropy*, July/August, 2005, http://www.philanthropyroundtable.org/magazines/2005/julaug/printable/interview.htm
2. Liza Featherstone, 'On the Wal-Mart Money Trail', *Nation*, 21 November 2005, http://www.thenation.com/doc/20051121/featherstone
3. Ibid.
4. Jim Hopkins, 'Wal-Mart Heirs Pour Riches into Reforming Education', *USA Today*, 11 March 2004.
5. Featherstone, 'On the Wal-Mart Money Trail'.
6. 'John Walton: Hugely Wealthy Wal-Mart Family Member Who Used His Billions to Promote Rightwing US Causes', *Guardian*, 29 June 2005.
7. Featherstone, 'On the Wal-Mart Money Trail'; Andy Serwer, 'The Waltons', *Fortune*, 15 November 2004.
8. Frederick M. Hess, 'The Challenge of Giving: How New Donors Are Changing the Philanthropic Equation', *Education Week*, 18 January 2006, http://www.aei.org/include/pub_print.asp?pubID=23711
9. Erik W. Robelen, 'Gates Learns to Think Big', *Education Week*, 11 October 2006, http://www.edweek.org/ew/articles/2006/10/11/07gates.h26.html; June Kronholz, 'Education Battle Brews in Washington State', *Wall Street Journal*, 4 October 2004; 'Gates Gives $1 Million to Pro-Charter Effort', *Seattle Post-Intelligencer*, 14 October 2004; Paul T. Hill, 'Bill and Melinda Gates Shift from Computers in Libraries to Reform in High Schools', *Education Next*, Winter 2006, p. 49, http://www.educationnext.org
10. Hill, 'Bill and Melinda Gates'; Robelen, 'Gates Learns to Think Big'.
11. Lynn Olson, 'U.S. Urged to Reinvent Its Schools', *Education Week*, 20 December 2006, http://www.edweek.org/ew/articles/2006/12/20/16skills.h26.html
12. New Commission on the Skills of the American Workforce, 'Tough Choices or Tough Times', National Center on Education and the Economy, December 2006, p. 16.
13. Hill, 'Bill and Melinda Gates', p. 50.
14. Neas, 'Following the Money: Funding and Support for Voucher Programs', p. 3.
15. R.G. Neas, 'Following the Money: Funding and Support for Voucher Programs', Washington, DC, People for the American Way Foundation, 2003; Media Transparency, 'Media Transparency: The Money Behind Conservative Media', Cursor, Inc, http://www.mediatransparency.org; American Association of School Administrators (AASA), 'Vouchers: Who's Behind It All?', 21 October 2005, http://www.aasa.org/edissues/content.cfm?ItemNumber=964
16. Amy Franklin, 'Devos Family Gives $4.5 Million to Voucher Campaign', *Associated Press Newswires*, 31 October 2000.
17. Jennifer Kerr, 'Fund Raising for Three 2000 School Initiatives Tops $116 Million', *Associated Press Newswires*, 7 February 2001; 'V-Day for Vouchers?' *Economist*, 15 July 2000; Margot Hornblower, 'Look out, It's Voucher Man', *Time Magazine*, 17 July 2000, p. 47.
18. Quoted in Paul Rolly, 'Stakes Raised in the Fight over Tuition Vouchers', *Salt Lake Tribune*, 19 February 2006.

19. NSBA, 'School Vouchers: What the Public Thinks and Why', NSBA/Zogby International Poll, 25 September 2001.

20. Jeffrey R. Henig, *Rethinking School Choice: Limits of the Market Metaphor*, Princeton, NJ, Princeton University Press, 1994, pp. 72–9, 86; Jaclyn Fierman, 'Giving Parents a Choice of Schools', *Fortune*, 4 December 1989.

21. People for the American Way Foundation (PFAW), 'History of Failed Vouchers and Tax Credits', 2002, http://www.pfaw.org/pfaw/general/default.aspx?oid=2959, p4; Alfie Kohn, 'NCLB and the Effort to Privatize Public Education', in Deborah Meier and George Wood (eds), *Many Children Left Behind: How the No Child Left Behind Act Is Damaging Our Children and Our Schools*, Boston, MA, Beacon Press, 2004, p. 83.

22. Quoted in Barbara Miner, 'A Brief History of Milwaukee's Voucher Program', *Rethinking Schools Online* 20 (3), 2006.

23. Quoted in Henig, *Rethinking School Choice*, p. 94.

24. PFAW, 'The Voucher Veneer: The Deeper Agenda to Privatize Public Education', Washington, DC, July 2003, pp. 7–8; Megan Twohey, 'Who Vouches for the Vouchers?' *American Prospect* 13 (12), 2002, p. 14; Joel Spring, *Political Agendas for Education: From the Religious Right to the Green Party*, Mahwah, NJ, Lawrence Erlbaum, 2002, p. 33.

25. 'Edu-Options: School-Choice Movement Broadens Its Portfolio Ever Further', *Gazette*, 30 December 2000; 'Ads Promote School Choice', *NewsMax.com Wires*, 3 January 2001.

26. 'Ads Promote School Choice', *NewsMax.com Wires*.

27. AASA, 'Vouchers: Who's Behind It All?'.

28. *NewsMax.com Wires*, 'Ads Promote School Choice'.

29. PFAW, 'The Voucher Veneer', p. 12; Barbara Miner, 'Seed Money for Conservatives', *Rethinking Schools Online* 18 (4), 2004.

30. Miner, 'Seed Money for Conservatives'.

31. PFAW, 'Vouchers Hit Dead End', 2004, http://www.pfaw.org/pfaw/general/default.aspx?oid=16044

32. PFAW, 'Florida Supreme Court Rules Vouchers Unconstitutional', 5 January 2006, http://www.pfaw.org/pfaw/general/default.aspx?oid=20253

33. Stephen Hegarty, 'Voucher Program Front and Center', *St Petersburg Times*, 21 May 2000, p. 1A.

34. Scott Parks, 'Texas Businessman Puts Fortune Behind School Voucher Efforts', *Dallas Morning News*, 29 August 2002.

35. Religious Right Watch, 'Dr. James Leininger: Money Man of the Religious Right', Texas Freedom Network, 2006, http://www.tfn.org/religiousright/leininger

36. Texas Freedom Network Education Fund, 'The Anatomy of Power: Texas and the Religious Right in 2006', 2006, p. 8, http://www.tfn.org/files/fck/SORR%2006%20ReportWEB.pdf

37. Ibid.

38. Parks, 'Texas Businessman Puts Fortune Behind School Voucher Efforts'.

39. Ibid.

40. Serwer, 'The Waltons'.

41. Media Transparency, 'The Money Behind Conservative Media'.

42. PFAW, 'The Voucher Veneer', p. 23.

43. Quoted in ibid., pp. 1, 4.

44. Ibid., p. 5.
45. Professor Dennis O'Keeffe, 'The Spectre at the Economic Feast: Why Our Schools Should Be Privately Financed', London, Economic Research Council, 2007.
46. Barbara Miner, 'For-Profits Target Education', in Alfie Kohn and Patrick Shannon (eds), *Education, Inc. Turning Learning into a Business*, revised edn, Portsmouth, NH, Heinemann, 2002, p. 137.
47. KIPP, 'KIPP: Knowledge Is Power Program', 2006, http://www.kippschools.org
48. Meridith May, 'Gap Founder Big Booster of KIPP Schools', *San Francisco Chronicle*, 29 December 2004.
49. 'Gates Gives $1 Million to Pro-Charter Effort', *Seattle Post-Intelligencer*.
50. 'Mass-Producing Excellence', *Philanthropy*.
51. Robelen, 'Gates Learns to Think Big'; Kronholz, 'Education Battle Brews in Washington State'; 'Gates Gives $1 Million to Pro-Charter Effort'; Hill, 'Bill and Melinda Gates', p. 49.
52. Carla Rivera, 'Gates Foundation Gives L.A. Charter School Group $1.8 Million', *Los Angeles Times*, 20 September 2006.
53. Jay Mathews, 'Charter School Effort Gets $65 Million Lift', *Washington Post*, 20 March 2007, p. A01.
54. Chris Moran, 'Push Is on for Charter Schools', *San Diego Union-Tribune*, 22 October 2003.
55. Linda Shaw, 'Charter-School Contributions Climb', *Seattle Times*, 13 October 2004.
56. 'Gates Gives $1 Million to Pro-Charter Effort'.
57. PFAW, 'Privatization of Public Education: A Joint Venture of Charity and Power', Washington, DC, 20 April 1999, pp. 2, 15.
58. Heather-Jane Robertson, 'The Many Faces of Privatization', *Our Schools, Our Selves* 14 (4), 2005, p. 46.
59. National Education Association, 'For-Profit Management of Schools', CorpWatch, 8 July 1998.
60. Rhea R. Borja, 'Analysts Debate Long-Term Viability of EMO Model', *Education Week*, 9 August 2006, p. 10; William C. Symonds et al., 'For-Profit Schools: They're Spreading Fast', *Business Week*, 7 February 2000.
61. Symonds et al., 'For-Profit Schools'.
62. Quoted in George Monbiot, *Captive State: The Corporate Takeover of Britain*, London, Pan Books, 2000, p. 331.
63. Corporate Watch, 'Group 4 Falck: A Corporate Profile', Corporate Watch UK, July 2003, http://www.corporatewatch.org/?lid=340
64. Ulf Fredriksson, 'Studying the Supra-National in Education: GATS, Education and Teacher Union Policies', *European Educational Research Journal* 3 (2), 2004, pp. 422–3.
65. Australian Education Union (AEU), 'To Market, to Market: Privatising State Education', May 1996, http://www.aeufederal.org.au/Publications/FactSheet3Privatisation.pdf
66. Adele Horin, 'School Care Giant Poised for NSW Expansion', *Sydney Morning Herald*, 13–14 May 2006, p. 6.
67. Matt Wade, 'Shouldering the Burden', *Sydney Morning Herald*, 27–28 May, 2006, p. 34.
68. Ben Hills, 'Cradle Snatcher', *Sydney Morning Herald*, 11 March 2006.

69. Emma Rush, 'Childcare Quality in Australia', Canberra, The Australia Institute, April 2006, http://www.tai.org.au/documents/downloads/DP84.pdf
70. Ibid.
71. Malcolm Maiden, 'ABC Prepares to Extend Its Sandpit', *Sydney Morning Herald*, 1 May 2006; Wade, 'Shouldering the Burden', p. 34.
72. Hills, 'Cradle Snatcher'.
73. Natasha Johnson, 'ABC Learning Faces Court Battle', *The 7.30 Report, ABC TV*, 1 March 2006, http://www.abc.net.au/7.30/content/2006/s1581704.htm; Hills, 'Cradle Snatcher'.
74. Hills, 'Cradle Snatcher'.
75. Emma Alberici, 'Law Dampens ABC Learning's Aspirations', *The 7.30 Report, ABC TV*, 30 May 2005, http://www.abc.net.au/7.30/content/2005/s1380524.htm
76. Independent Colleges Australia (ICA), 'Welcome', http://www.icacolleges.com.au/default.htm
77. 'ABC Spends $680m around the World', *Sydney Morning Herald*, 15 December 2006; Michael Sainsbury, 'ABC Learning Axe to Fall on Part-Time Workers', *Australian*, 3 September 2008.
78. Sharon Beder, *Suiting Themselves: How Corporations Drive the Global Agenda*, London, Earthscan, 2006, p. 26.
79. Ibid.
80. Winand Gellner, 'The Politics of Policy "Political Think Tanks" and Their Markets in the U.S.-Institutional Environment', *Presidential Studies Quarterly* 25 (3), 1995, p. 162.
81. Kohn, 'NCLB and the Effort to Privatize Public Education', p. 90.
82. Quoted in ibid., p. 83.
83. Linda Darling-Hammond, 'From "Separate but Equal" to "No Child Left Behind"', in Meier and Wood (eds), *Many Children Left Behind*, pp. 9–10.
84. The Education Trust, 'The ABCs Of "AYP": Raising Achievement for All Students', Spring 2003, pp. 3–4, http://www.businessroundtable.org/pdf/TheABCsofAYP.pdf
85. Stan Karp, 'NCLB's Selective Vision of Equality: Some Gaps Count More Than Others', in Meier and Wood (eds), *Many Children Left Behind*, p. 60.
86. Darling-Hammond, 'From "Separate but Equal"', pp. 10–11.
87. Karp, 'NCLB's Selective Vision of Equality', p. 55.
88. Darling-Hammond, 'From "Separate but Equal"', pp. 6, 10.
89. George Wood, 'A View from the Field: NCLB's Effects on Classrooms and Schools', in Meier and Wood (eds), *Many Children Left Behind*, pp. 46–7.
90. Michele McNeil, 'States Cite Lack of Capacity to Meet NCLB', *Education Week* 28 (5), 2008.
91. Wood, 'A View from the Field', pp. 46–7.
92. Sam Dillon, 'Schools Slow in Closing Gaps between Races', *New York Times*, 20 November 2006.
93. V. Dion Haynes and Theola Labbé, 'Few Schools Meet Goal on New Tests', *Washington Post*, 8 September 2006, p. B01; V. Dion Haynes, 'Some Highly Touted Schools Land on Failure List', *Washington Post*, 9 September 2006, p. B04.
94. Stan Karp, 'Leaving Public Education Behind: The Bush Agenda in American Education', *Our Schools, Our Selves* 15 (3), 2006, pp. 183–4.
95. Ibid., p. 183.
96. Ibid., p. 191.
97. Stan Karp, 'Band-Aids or Bulldozers?', *Rethinking Schools Online* 20 (3), 2006.

15   CONTROLLING WAYWARD CHILDREN

1. Cited in *Multinational Monitor*, January/February 2006, p. 5.
2. Health Editor, Anthony Browne, 'Doctors Could Soon Prescribe Behaviour-Controlling Chemicals to Pre-Teens against Their Parents' Wishes', *Observer*, 27 February 2000.
3. Sarah Hall, 'Child Mental Health Disorders Have Soared, Says Report', *Guardian*, 21 June 2006.
4. National Institute of Mental Health (NIMH), 'America's Children: Parents Report Estimated 2.7 Million Children with Emotional and Behavioral Problems', http://www.nimh.nih.gov/healthinformation/childhood_indicators.cfm
5. David Healy and Joanna Le Noury, 'Pediatric Bipolar Disorder: An Object of Study in the Creation of an Illness', *International Journal of Risk and Safety in Medicine* 19 (4), 2007.
6. Claudia Kalb, 'Troubled Souls Mental Illnesses Are So Complex in Children That Health-Care Professionals Can't Always Detect Them', *Newsweek*, 23 October 2007, http://www.newsweek.com/id/60152/output/print
7. William Birnbauer, 'Fears for a Drugged Generation', *Age*, 7 January 2007.
8. M. Alexander Otto, 'Should Kids Get These Drugs?', *News Tribune*, 13 May 2008.
9. American Psychiatric Association (APA), *Diagnostic and Statistical Manual of Mental Disorders*, 4th edn, Washington, DC, 1994, p. 13.
10. Ibid., pp. 46–53.
11. Ibid., pp. 55–65.
12. Ibid., pp. 78–94.
13. Ibid., pp. 83–5.
14. Aaron Smith, 'FDA Crosshairs on ADHD Drugs: Investors Await Panel's Findings About the Psychiatric and Heart Attack Risks of Adderall XR and Other ADHD Drugs', *CNNMoney.com*, 21 March 2006, http://money.cnn.com/2006/03/21/news/companies/adhd/index.htm
15. Ibid.
16. 'FDA Panel Wants Clearer ADHD Labels: Agency Asked to Proceed with Plans for Warnings About Hallucinations, Suicide Risk', *CNNMoney.com*, 1 July 2005, http://money.cnn.com/2005/07/01/news/fortune500/fda_panel.dj/index.htm
17. Smith, 'FDA Crosshairs on ADHD Drugs'.
18. Karin Klein, 'Pencils, Pens, Meds – as Kids Head to Class, Pharmaceutical Companies Ramp up Their Drug Marketing – and It Works', *Los Angeles Times*, 20 August 2007.
19. Ibid.
20. Ibid.
21. APA, *DSM IV*, p. 93.
22. Ibid., p. 90.
23. John R. Clayer et al., 'Prevalence of Psychiatric Disorders in Rural South Australia', *Medical Journal of Australia* 163 (7), 1995, pp. 124–8.
24. L.J. Davis, 'Diagnostic and Statistical Manual of Mental Disorders, 4th Ed.', *Harper's Magazine* 294 (1761), 1997, p. 61.

25. J.J. Schildkraut, 'The Catecholamine Hypothesis of Affective Disorders: A Review of Supporting Evidence', *Journal of Neuropsychiatry and Clinical Neurosciences* 7, 1995.

26. Robert Whitaker, *Mad in America: Bad Science, Bad Medicine, and the Enduring Mistreatment of the Mentally Ill*, Cambridge, MA, Perseus, 2002, p. 142.

27. Ibid., p. 144.

28. Ibid., p. 154.

29. Ibid., p. 152.

30. Ibid., pp. 141–55.

31. Ibid., pp. 155.

32. Marcia Angell, *The Truth About Drug Companies*, New York, Random House, 2004, p. 5.

33. Ibid., p. 11.

34. M. Angell and A. Relman, 'Prescription for Profit', *Washington Post*, 20 June 2001.

35. 'The Other Drug War: Big Pharma's 625 Washington Lobbyists', *Public Citizen Congress Watch Report*, 23 July 2001.

36. *Psychiatric News*, 15 August 1997, p. 4.

37. Robert O'Harrow Jr., 'Grass Roots Seeded by Drugmaker', *Washington Post*, 9 December 2000.

38. Ken Silverstein, 'Prozac.Org: An Influential Mental Health Nonprofit Finds Its "Grassroots" Watered by Pharmaceutical Millions', *Mother Jones*, November/December, 1999, http://www.motherjones.com/news/feature/1999/11/nami.html

39. Shankar Vedantam, 'Suicide-Risk Tests for Teens Debated', *Washington Post*, 16 June 2006.

40. President's New Freedom Commission on Mental Health, 'Achieving the Promise: Transforming Mental Health Care in America', President's New Freedom Commission on Mental Health 2003, http://www.mentalhealthcommission.gov/reports/reports. htm

41. Ibid., figure 4.2.

42. PsychSearch.net, 'TeenScreen: A Front Group for the Psycho-Pharmaceutical Industrial Complex', http://www.psychsearch.net/teenscreen.html

43. TeenScreen Program, 'Program Overview', Columbia University, http://www. teenscreen.org/index.php?option=com_content&task=view&id=25&Itemid=106

44. TeenScreen Program, 'Screening Questionnaires', Columbia University, http://www. teenscreen.org/index.php?option=com_content&task=view&id=29&Itemid=111

45. TeenScreen Program, 'The Screening Process', Columbia University, http://www. teenscreen.org/index.php?option=com_content&task=view&id=27&Itemid=108

46. TeenScreen Program, 'Why Is Screening Needed', Columbia University, http://www. teenscreen.org/index.php?option=com_content&task=view&id=23&Itemid=104

47. US Department of Health and Human Services (DHHS), 'Mental Health: A Report of the Surgeon General', 12 December 2007, http://www.surgeongeneral.gov/library/ mentalhealth/chapter3/sec1.html

48. American College of Neuropsychopharmacology, 'Executive Summary, Preliminary Report of the Task Force on SSRIs and Suicidal Behavior in Youth', 21 January 2004, p. 22, http://www.acnp.org/asset.axd?id=aad01592-01b2-4672-ad28-119537460ffa

49. TeenScreen Program, 'Laura Flynn', Columbia University, http://www.teenscreen. org/index.php?option=com_content&task=view&id=56&Itemid=140

50. Silverstein, 'Prozac.Org'.

51. TeenScreen Program, 'TeenScreen Parent Consent Letter for School-Based Sites', Columbia University, http://www.teenscreen.org/index.php?option=com_content &task=view&id=28&Itemid=110

52. TeenScreen Program, 'Setting the Record Straight About TeenScreen', Columbia University, http://www.teenscreen.org/index.php?option=com_content&task=view &id=98&Itemid=206#privacy

53. PsychSearch.net, 'TeenScreen'.

54. 'Index to SSRI Stories', http://www.ssristories.com/index.php

55. Cited in *Multinational Monitor*, January/February 2006, p. 5.

16   CONCLUSION

1. Lynell Hancock, 'School's Out', *Nation*, 9 July 2007, pp. 16–17.

2. John Weaver, 'Reading Nickelodeon: Slimed by the Contradictions and Potentials of Television', in Shirley R. Steinberg and Joe L. Kincheloe (eds), *Kinderculture: The Corporate Construction of Childhood*, 2nd edn, Boulder, CO, Westview Press, 2004, p. 73.

The Authors

Professor Sharon Beder has written nine previous books as well as many articles, book chapters, conference papers, educational monographs and consultancy reports. She has also produced various teaching resources and websites. Her research has focused on how power relationships are maintained and challenged, particularly by corporations and professions. Her earlier books, some of which have been translated into other languages, include:

> *Suiting Themselves: How Corporations Drive the Global Agenda* (2006)
> *Free Market Missionaries: The Corporate Manipulation of Community Values* (2006)
> *Environmental Principles and Policies* (2006)
> *Power Play: The Fight for Control of the World's Electricity* (2003)
> *Selling the Work Ethic: From Puritan Pulpit to Corporate PR* (2000)
> *Global Spin: The Corporate Assault on Environmentalism* (1997, 2000 and 2002)
> *The New Engineer* (1998)
> *The Nature of Sustainable Development* (1993 and 1996)
> *Toxic Fish and Sewer Surfing* (1989)

Professor Beder's website is http://homepage.mac.com/herinst/sbeder/home.html

Dr Wendy Varney is an honorary fellow in the Institute for Environmental Studies at the University of NSW. She has extensive university teaching and research experience. Her doctoral thesis was on the social shaping and commodification of children's manufactured toys. She has written two books as well as numerous articles and book chapters. She is author of:

> *Fluoride in Australia: A Case to Answer* (1986)
> *Nonviolence Speaks: Communicating Against Repression* (with Brian Martin, 2003)

Dr Richard Gosden did his doctoral thesis on psychiatric controversies over the cause of the symptoms of schizophrenia. He has written a number of articles on the early treatment of schizophrenia, psychiatry and human rights, and the use of psychiatry in social control. He is the author of:

> *Punishing the Patient: How Psychiatrists Misunderstand and Mistreat Schizophrenia* (2001)

Index

Compiled by Sue Carlton